Penguin Education

Witchcraft and Sorcery

Edited by Max Marwick

Penguin Modern Sociology Readings

General Editor

Tom Burns

Advisory Board

Erving Goffman
Alvin Gouldner
Eric Hobsbawm
Edmund Leach
David Lockwood
Gianfranco Poggi
Hans Peter Widmaier
Peter Worsley
Pierre Bourdieu
Denis Wrong
Thomas Luckmann

Witchcraft and Sorcery

Selected Readings

Edited by Max Marwick

Penguin Education

Penguin Education
Penguin Books Ltd,
Harmondsworth, Middlesex, England
Penguin Books Inc, 7110 Ambassador Road,
Baltimore, Md 21207, U.S.A.
Penguin Books Australia Ltd,
Ringwood, Victoria, Australia
Penguin Books Canada Ltd,
41 Steelcase Road West,
Markham, Ontario, Canada
Penguin Books (N.Z.) Ltd, 182–190 Wairau Road,
Auckland 10, New Zealand

First published 1970
Reprinted 1972, 1975
This selection copyright © Max Marwick, 1970
Introduction and notes copyright © Max Marwick, 1970

Copyright acknowledgement for items in this volume will be
found on page 387

Made and printed in Great Britain by
C. Nicholls & Company Ltd
Set in Monotype Times

To Professor E. E. Evans-Pritchard
to whom all modern students of witchcraft and sorcery
are deeply indebted

Contents

8   Contents

Postscript
The Decline of Witch-Beliefs in Differentiated Societies 379

Introduction

Each of us in modern society becomes aware of the sinister figures of witch and sorcerer through myth and fairy-tale, and they therefore belong to our world of fantasy. This makes it difficult for us to appreciate that there are societies actually existing in which these characters have a much clearer and threatening reality. Similarly it is hard to realize how recently it was that they were part of the reality of the societies from which ours is directly descended. It is only within the past three hundred years that our emancipation from widespread belief in witchcraft has been achieved. It is true that from time to time newspaper reports appear about the esoteric practices of present-day 'witches'. These accounts sustain the belief that witchcraft has never died out in modern society, that it has continued as an underground movement since the seventeenth century when it – or rather concerted opposition to it – emitted a final flare before smoulder-ing through the intervening years, and that its flames have found new fuel in Britain since 1951 when, after more than two cen-turies, the old Witchcraft Act was repealed. But this belief is debatable, and, whether or not one accepts the view that there has been an underlying continuity of belief from the seventeenth century to the present, it is clear that modern 'witchcraft' is very different from the conceptions Europeans had of it at the time of the religious conflicts at the close of the Middle Ages and, in turn, from the traditions of an earlier period. It differs, too, from the parallel notions of present-day non-literate, so-called 'primi-tive' peoples.

Our emancipation from belief in magic is still far from com-plete, as is shown by our credulous attention to the utterances of authorities such as doctors and scientists, even when they make pronouncements outside their narrow fields of competence, and by our continued observance of superstitions.

'Witchcraft' and 'sorcery' are terms referring to closely related systems of belief of wide distribution among human societies. Common to the two systems, which often exist side by side in the same society, is the cardinal belief that certain members of the community harm their fellow men illicitly by supernatural means. In most English dictionaries 'witchcraft' and 'sorcery' are roughly synonymous. In anthropological usage they have acquired distinct meanings because an African tribe, the Azande,[1] are more precise in their categories of the supernatural than we are; and Evans-Pritchard, the anthropologist who studied them and who wrote what has become a classic in this field, found the existence in English of these two words a useful means of translating the distinction that his informants perceived.

To appreciate the Zande distinction between 'witchcraft' and 'sorcery', now adopted by most anthropologists, it is first necessary to define 'magic'. This is a morally neutral term in the sense that magic may be used with or without social approval. It refers to the activities or craft of the magician, a person who, suitably prepared, performs rituals aimed at controlling impersonal supernatural forces held responsible for the succession of events. In these rituals, material substances, often with characteristics or origins symbolically related to the objectives desired, are used to the accompaniment of verbal formulae. Although a non-literate (so-called 'primitive') society usually has its expert magicians, many forms of magic are available to its ordinary members, and the equivalents of do-it-yourself kits may be inherited, bought or borrowed.

According to the Zande distinction, the main difference between a sorcerer and a witch is that the former achieves his evil ends by magic, whereas the latter (often though not invariably conceived of as a woman) achieves hers by some mystical power inherent in her personality, a power that does not require the help of magic. There are other differences between them. As

1. The Zande people have been referred to throughout as the Azande and not the A-Zande, the rendering used in Evans-Pritchard's earlier papers. The use of a plural prefix, A-, is a Bantuism unusual in a Nilotic language. Had we adopted in this instance the now common practice among students of Bantu languages and peoples of dropping prefixes from tribal names, the appropriate form would have been Zande, not only for the adjective and the singular, as Evans-Pritchard uses it, but also for the plural. However, as Evans-Pritchard's usage pre-dates the wide adoption among Bantuists of this usage, and as his plural form, Azande, has become one of the household words of anthropology, this has been retained.

to motive, witches are considered to be slaves of aberration and addiction, and, thus conceived, are weird, sometimes tragic, figures. Sorcerers, on the other hand, are considered to be ordinary people driven by understandable, even if disapproved, urges, such as malice, envy or revenge, which are part of every-one's experience.

Propensity to witchcraft is usually considered to be hereditary or at least constitutional in the sense of having been implanted – in various ways – at an early age, whereas sorcery usually de-mands no special personal attributes and is believed to be practised by anyone who can acquire the necessary magical substances (especially in Africa) or the appropriate spells (es-pecially in Oceania).

While most anthropologists see the advantage of following the Zande distinction between witchcraft and sorcery, there are some, particularly those writing on Oceania, who use the term 'sorcery' for all forms of destructive magic regardless of whether it is socially approved – as it may be in property-protection, for in-stance – or considered illicit. Similarly the term 'witch' does not invariably have a sinister or evil connotation. There are and were societies in which she was believed on occasion to cure ailments as well as attack people, their interests or their property.

Because both witches and sorcerers incur social disapproval, generalizations about both are often made. This fact calls for a generic term that includes both. Hitherto 'witch', in addition to having the more specific meaning outlined above, has served as such a term and will be so used in this Introduction unless the context indicates the contrary. Middleton and Winter (1963, p. 3) have suggested 'wizard' and 'wizardry' as generic terms to include respectively witches and sorcerers on the one hand and their believed activities on the other. Among the Readings con-tained in this volume, only the excerpts from Crawford's book follow this recently suggested usage.

The antiquity of the belief in witches and sorcerers is indicated by its present wide distribution. While there are some human societies other than our own that lack this belief, they are ex-ceptional, and those, the majority, that have it are found in all parts of the world – 'from Africa to the South Seas and from

Asia to America', as Mayer (1954, p. 3) puts it in the lecture included in these Readings.

Whereas there must inevitably be some debate about the nature of beliefs that may be inferred from rock paintings, burials and other kinds of archaeological evidence, there is clear historical documentation in the chronicles and creative writing of classical antiquity for the existence of beliefs in witches and sorcerers. There is a close relationship, and frequently an identity, between beliefs held in these early periods of recorded history and those of later ages or those reported by modern anthropologists working among contemporary non-literate societies. In the historical societies from which ours is descended, the continuity in the conceptions of these mystical evil-doers from classical through medieval to early modern times is striking. Among human societies as a whole, it is less certain, though still highly probable, that beliefs among peoples now widely separated had a common origin in the prehistorical period. Thus Clements (1932, p. 240) has suggested that many of primitive man's widely distributed concepts of disease, including those relating to witchcraft, may be traced back to the dispersal of the Palaeolithic ancestors of modern man.

Until the close of the medieval period, European beliefs in witchcraft and sorcery had much in common with those prevailing among present-day non-literate peoples. Apart from a similarity in the content of the beliefs themselves, there also appears to be a resemblance in the relatively slight degree to which they occupied people's minds. They were a part of the pattern of life, but a relatively small part, activated in times of crisis and misfortune rather than being a source of continuous worry.

Most of the innumerable works on European witchcraft deal, not with the earlier periods when it showed a similarity to the 'witchcraft' familiar to modern anthropologists, but with the period when preoccupation with beliefs in it had reached the proportions of an epidemic. This development of an acute witch-scare on the basis of the long-standing, chronic system of beliefs was symptomatic of the rapid and fundamental changes the society of Europe was undergoing in its transition from the relatively undifferentiated feudalism of the Middle Ages to the varied, flexible and uncertain social organization that started with the Renaissance and the Reformation. During this period of institutional change, long-standing beliefs in witchcraft became entangled in the new religious and political issues of the day. Witches were identified with heretics, and this brought a new weapon to the armoury of the Church. A surviving pagan moral indignation against witches could now be directed against those who failed to conform with official Christianity. As a result of this entanglement, European witchcraft acquired some of its distinctive features, of which the most important was the notion that witches had made compacts with the Devil. Whereas in other societies witches personify evil in general, in European history they did this in a very specific way by being the earthly representatives of the Prince of Evil.

Thus it is that European witchcraft, as most of the literature portrays it, is paralleled, not by the normal, chronic belief system of a non-literate society, but rather by the cult movements that, since the second half of the nineteenth century, have been reported from virtually every part of the world where native peoples have had to adjust themselves suddenly to the advent of Western ways of life. These cult movements, according to Worsley (1957, pp. 24–5), represent 'desperate searchings for more and more effective ways of understanding and modifying' a confused environment. Similarly the witch-scares of Europe and of Old and New England seem to have been part of the general reaction to a period of rapid and uncertain change.

The ethnography of witchcraft is understandably rich. Given Western society's emancipation from it, Western travellers, missionaries, administrators and even anthropologists have often selected this, the most bizarre and exotic aspect of native life, for a disproportionate share of attention. People's witch-beliefs are as often recorded for their sheer entertainment value as for their scientific interest. They seem to reward the romantic search by both writers and readers for fantasies that come true.

Nevertheless these systems of belief are of scientific interest and importance. Though from our point of view they represent the standardized delusions of the societies concerned, the comparative analysis of such delusions is, as Monica Wilson (1951, p. 313) has expressed it, 'not merely an antiquarian exercise but one of the keys to the understanding of society'. Indeed, they have been approached from the theoretical vantage points of a number of social sciences because of the light they throw on human behaviour in general, including that of ourselves among whom they no longer command credence. Even those accounts of witchcraft that are primarily descriptive are often based on an implicit set of theoretical assumptions that serve to make them intelligible when viewed from some other society such as our own. The theories of witchcraft that have been implicitly or explicitly put forward fall into three main categories, historical or ethnological, psychological and sociological; and the last of these may be subdivided into those theories that emphasize normative aspects of social organization and those centring on tension and social change.

The first main category includes theories which, on the basis of history or conjectural history, account for the present distribution of witch-beliefs and for the developments within a particular society that have given rise to its characteristic pattern of beliefs. Here may be included theories such as Elsie Clews Parsons's relating to the diffusion of witch-beliefs in the American Southwest; Ewen's on the importation to England of ideas emanating from the Continent (1933, pp. 44–50); and Margaret Murray's well-known but no longer well-supported hypothesis that the witches of Western Europe were the lingering adherents of a cult forming part of the pagan religion displaced by Christianity. Psychological theories accounting for witchcraft are found in the writings of Kluckhohn and of Krige (specifically on witchcraft and sorcery) and of Malinowski (1954, pp. 59–60, 63, 70–72) (on magic in general, of which sorcery is a specific form). These theories stem from Freud's doctrine of the displacement of affect and derivative neo-Freudian hypotheses about the projection of urges and conflicts into culturally standardized fantasies (Dollard, 1937, pp. 442–4).

Of the two variants of the sociological theory of witchcraft, that having to do with social norms is more often encountered in the literature. In most accounts the witch is depicted as the very antithesis of the social ideal, as the one who plays the villain in the society's morality plays. So numerous and so revolting are the believed practices of witches that to accuse anyone of witchcraft is a condensed way of charging him with a long list of the foullest crimes. By graphically summing up all forms of deviance, such an accusation throws into sharper relief the positive moral precepts of the society to which the accused person belongs. The alleged witch's believed victim may also illustrate these precepts. It is a common practice for people in all societies to seek retrospectively for the causes of misfortune; and in those societies in which a belief in witchcraft exists, people who suffer misfortunes often examine their past social conduct, especially in so far as it affects people in the community who have been or who could be identified as witches. Thus, while witches are primarily negative models, they may also play positive moral roles in being the points of retrospective projection for feelings of guilt resulting from acts of foolishness and meanness that a believed victim may have committed.

The other variant of the sociological theory of witchcraft treats accusations of it as indices of social tension and as vehicles of social change. The relative frequency of accusations in various social relationships provides us with a set of social strain-gauges for detecting where the tensions and role-conflicts in a particular society lie. In keeping with the abandonment by anthropologists of a static functional model in favour of a more dynamic view of social trends and processes, this theory is undergoing modification, greater attention now being paid to the part accusations play in manipulating social situations and in involving the community as a whole in issues hitherto confined to those persons directly enmeshed in the quarrel from which the accusation stems.

All these types of theories in differing degrees raise the study of witchcraft from the level of travellers' entertaining tales and 'straight' ethnography to that of scientific analysis aimed at making generalizations about repetitive social situations and processes, and, within the range of statistical probability, at making predictions of their outcomes.

In addition to these somewhat indirect contributions that the study of witchcraft can make to behavioural science, it has more direct applications as well. Thus Evans-Pritchard's classic analysis of the part played by witch-beliefs in the total world-view of the Azande has not only clarified some of the problems relating to believed mental differences between 'primitive' and 'civilized' man, but it has even served as a model for the clearer understanding of the logic of scientific discovery (Polanyi, 1958, pp. 286–94). Similarly the analysis of past witch-scares provides principles for the better understanding of present mass movements. The parallel between the beliefs of seventeenth-century Western, or modern African, witch-finders and Joseph McCarthy's fevered dreams about red agents (Wilson, 1951) is indeed a close one, as Arthur Miller showed with subtle insight in *The Crucible* (1952).

References

CLEMENTS, F. E. (1932), 'Primitive concepts of disease', *University of California Publications in American Archaeology and Ethnology*, vol. 32, pp. 185–252.

DOLLARD, J. (1937), *Caste and Class in a Southern Town*, Yale U.P.

EWEN, C. L. (1933), *Witchcraft and Demonianism*, Heath Cranton.

MALINOWSKI, B. (1954), 'Magic, science and religion', in R. Redfield (ed.), *Magic, Science and Religion and Other Essays*, Doubleday.

MAYER, P. (1954), *Witches*, Inaugural Lecture, Rhodes University, Grahamstown.

MIDDLETON, J., and WINTER, E. H. (eds.) (1963), *Witchcraft and Sorcery in East Africa*, Routledge & Kegan Paul.

MILLER, A. (1952), *The Crucible*, Viking Press.

POLANYI, M. (1958), *Personal Knowledge*, University of Chicago Press.

WILSON, M. Hunter (1951), 'Witch beliefs and social structure', *American Journal of Sociology*, vol. 56, pp. 307–13.

WORSLEY, P. M. (1957), 'Millenarian movements in Melanesia', *Human Problems in British Central Africa*, vol. 21, pp. 18–31.

Part One **Orientation**

The first four Readings in this volume provide materials towards
defining and distinguishing the various aspects of the subject. We
assume that Evans-Pritchard's classic study of the Azande (1937)
will be consulted in the original by any serious student of
witchcraft and sorcery; no excerpts from it have been included in
this volume, though Gluckman's review-article on it will be
found in Part Four. Thus, although Evans-Pritchard brought
his influential working definitions conveniently together in his
book on the Azande (1937, pp. 8–11), we go for them in this
part to two of his earlier papers; and the second of these describes
the important process of divination by oracle. Then follows
Firth's concise discussion of terminology, which allows for
differences in usage between Africanists and Oceanianists. Since
modern anthropology necessarily gives arbitrary technical
meanings to English words of long standing, Macfarlane's
discussion of the traditional meanings of common terms
employed in this field serves as a useful corrective to a complete
surrender to professional jargon. The basic definitions considered,
we join Philip Mayer for a preliminary conducted tour.

Reference
EVANS-PRITCHARD, E. E. (1937), *Witchcraft, Oracles and Magic
among the Azande*, Clarendon Press.

1 E. E. Evans-Pritchard

Sorcery and Native Opinion

Excerpt from E. E. Evans-Pritchard, 'Sorcery and native opinion', *Africa*, vol. 4, 1931, no. 1, pp. 23–8.

The problem before us is to analyse native ideas about magic and to find out what types of magic they regard with approbation, and what types they regard with disapprobation; whether their opinions in this respect are clearly defined and held by all members of the community and backed by legal sanctions; and what are the distinguishing attributes by which we can class any type of magic as good or bad. A complete analysis of this kind has never been made either in theoretical treatises on magic nor in field-work monographs on primitive peoples. Writers of books on magic generally regard all magic which produces or protects as white magic, and those types which destroy as black magic. As we shall see later, such a classification is based entirely on European ideas and does not correspond to modes of native thought. Though much has been written about magic, the native view-point has been little studied. The monumental works of Frazer (1922) contain nothing strictly germane to our problem, since 'homeopathic' and 'contagious' magic may be either black or white (in whatever sense we use these colour-symbols); and whilst it can hardly be said that 'black' magic is ever 'public' it would be equally incorrect to suppose that 'white' magic is necessarily so. Many shortcomings in Frazer's treatment of magic were revealed in the first competent analytical study of magic by Hubert and Mauss. They were anxious to show how magic is a social fact and is not merely composed of mistaken and illogical processes of individual psychology. In demonstrating how magic is not simply an individual psychological process but is a traditional complex of ideas, beliefs and rites which are handed down from one generation to another, they laid a broader basis of approach to the problems of magic than either Frazer or their other predecessors had done (Hubert and Mauss, 1902–3). Against criticism that it would therefore appear that the traditional social facts of magic were often at war with tradition and society itself, they replied by showing that not only was sorcery, as they understood the term, beyond all doubt part and parcel of transmitted culture, but also that it was often not illicit but rather a tool of government, a fact which had emerged as clearly from Frazer's work, and it was later to be demonstrated by Malinowski's first-hand observations in the Trobriands. The problem really resolved itself into a question of how 'crime' could be said to have a useful social function. There was little data to answer this question when Hubert and Mauss wrote their paper: especially was information lacking about the concepts of 'crime' and 'law' in primitive societies. Later writers on primitive jurisprudence have assumed that in all savage communities some acts of magic are disapproved of and punished by society (e.g. Sidney Hartland, 1924). This assumption has lately been challenged by Malinowski.

Malinowski has broken away from the formal treatment of the legality of magic and has given us a more dynamic account of the actual workings of 'black' magic in a Melanesian community. The views which he presents appear, however, to spring rather from a sociological analysis of the workings of black magic than from native commentary on the same. In this community sorcery acts as a legal force upholding the norms and rules of society. Its 'criminal' aspects, if we can so term them, are restricted to an abuse of proper legal machinery in much the same way as a chief may abuse the powers with which he is invested. 'Black' magic is used by a limited number of specialists, either for personal reasons or for a fee from a chief or rich commoner, to kill those whose success in love or gardening or trading has aroused the envy of their neighbours and those who show lack of respect to their chiefs and betters. They act as a conservative agency which gets rid of the *parvenus* of native society without grave scandals and disorder. Public opinion does not appear to react strongly on moral grounds either for or against black magic. This interpretation of sorcery strikes at the roots of our problem, since Malinowski (1926a) asserts that primitive peoples do not make any clear-cut moral distinctions between the legal and criminal uses of sorcery. 'These contributions,' he says, 'show clearly how difficult it is to draw a line between the quasi-legal and quasi-criminal applications of sorcery. The "criminal" aspect of law in savage communities is perhaps even vaguer than the "civil" one, the idea of "justice" in our sense hardly applicable, and the means of restoring a disturbed tribal equilibrium slow and cumbersome.'

Dr Schapera (1927) in an able review of Malinowski's book has pointed out that the chief criticism to be levelled against it is that the author has generalized from a restricted range of data in one community in formulating a theory applicable to all savage tribes. We hope to show in this paper from data collected in an African community that whilst the dividing line between the 'criminal' and the 'legal' is often indistinct, the natives clearly mark off some types of magic as 'criminal', and that they do so according to moral principles which are vital to the whole theory of magic in this community. The problem is really to know what the natives understand by such terms as 'crime' and 'justice' in their relation to magic.

The theoretical writer on magic has been severely handicapped by lack of reliable information about savage tribes, for in field-work accounts there is seldom to be found a competent analysis of native magic, and they generally lack in particular a clear under-standing of the difference between black magic and witchcraft. If the reader will look at the better-known and easily accessible books on African tribes, such as those on the Bathonga, Baila, Akamba, Ashanti, Baganda, Shilluk, Bakongo, Lango and others, he will not find in them any detailed consideration of the legality of magic. It may be that such moral attitudes as we noted amongst the Azande are lacking amongst these other peoples, or it may be that this particular line of investigation was not followed by their observers.

Since, therefore, the particular problem which we are con-sidering has not, to our knowledge, been thoroughly inquired into, it is inadvisable to attempt to make our treatment of it a comparative one. Consequently we shall restrict our observations to a people whom we know at first hand, the Azande of the Nile–Uelle Divide. Whether the moral distinctions made by this people about their magic are common to many societies can only be answered by future field-workers, for it is essentially a field-work question and one which can only be answered at the later stages of an investigation when the observer is already well acquainted with the natives amongst whom he is working.

In the opinion of the Azande what types of magic are reputable (white) and what types are disreputable (black)? The answer to this question is that just as a good man is one who acts in accordance with the established principles of social behaviour, whereas a bad man is one who flouts the accepted laws and customs of his country, so good magic acts in favour of, and black magic acts against, justice and order. This paper will explain the Zande point of view, and will illustrate the moral grading of their magic.

Terminology of Zande Magic

First of all we must clear the ground so that we may isolate the problem and focus it clearly. Much obstruction is caused by the loose use of terms such as 'witchcraft', 'black magic', 'white magic', 'sorcery', and so on. If the reader will turn to the books by theorists and field-workers which we have mentioned above he will find that such terms are used by one writer to refer to one feature of native culture, and are used by another writer to describe a totally different feature. They are often used indiscriminately by the same writer to refer to first one thing and then another in the same book. Without expressing any opinion as to whether the terminology used in this paper is generally applicable to other cultures we find it necessary both here and in our future writings on the Azande to use terms such as 'witch', 'magician', 'sorcerer', and symbols referring to the moral and legal attributes of magic, with strict reference to what are to the Azande distinct cultural concepts. We are taking several distinct Zande ideas and are using for them a distinguishing symbol in English. To the Zande *mangu* (witchcraft) and *ngwa* (medicine or magic) are quite different things. *Mangu* is an hereditary trait which can be discovered in the stomach of a witch (*ira mangu*, possessor of *mangu*). It is a physiological fact and its functioning needs no use of the concreta of magic, the material substance of medicine, the spell, and the rite[1] *Ngwa* on the other hand is characterized by the special attributes of magic all over the world, the material element, the spell, the rite, the condition of the performer (taboo etc.) (Evans-Pritchard, 1929a; Hubert and Mauss, 1902–3, *passim*; Malinowski, 1926b). Within the complex of an act of magic particular emphasis is placed by the Azande and probably by all African peoples on the material element, generally botanical, to which we propose to restrict the term 'medicine', using the term 'magic' in a wider sense to refer to the whole complex of which medicine forms the nucleus, i.e. the spell (*simasima* in Zande), the rite, the condition of the performer, and the 'représentatives magiques' which comprise ideas and beliefs (embodied in myth or current tradition) associated with the performance. Another difference between *mangu* (witchcraft) and *ngwa* (magic) lies in the fact that it is highly improbable that an act of witchcraft ever takes place, whereas acts of magic may be witnessed daily in the life of the Azande.

We shall not discuss Zande witchcraft in this paper, as we have given a long account of it elsewhere,[2] but restrict ourselves to a consideration of magic and the people who perform magic, 'magicians' (*ira ngwa*, possessor of magic). All people who perform an act of magic are magicians, whether they are professional departmental experts or merely amateur practitioners of sporadic rites. Amongst these magicians there are some who are criminals, whose magic is illicit, and it is to identify these men that we are devoting this essay. We shall use the word 'sorcerers' to symbolize these criminals and the word 'sorcery' to represent their criminal activities. Actually the Azande have no single lexicographic expression to denote sorcery and sorcerers, but they use the same terms for all acts of magic and magicians, *ngwa* and *ira ngwa*; but the context of utterance makes it clear whether they refer to magic in general or to its legal or criminal uses respectively. If they wish to specify they will either speak of

1. Zande witchcraft, which is characterized by a special condition of the entrails, is a form of vampirism. Of the same genus are the *aira kele linde*, men whose upper teeth broke through before the lower ones, and whose influence is baneful. Other types of witchcraft, which employ no technique of magic, which we find in different African societies, are the 'evil eye', twins, monorchids, and so on (Evans-Pritchard, 1929b).

2. See next Reading – *Ed.*

magic as being good or bad (*wene* or *gbigbita*) or they will use a circumlocutory expression referring to the method or function of the magic by which the listener will know at once whether it is regarded with approval or not. We shall do the same, using the adjectives 'good' and 'bad' to denote the moral qualities of magic rather than the terms 'black' and 'white'.

For the guild or association of magicians who are found amongst the Azande in common with most African peoples we shall use the good old expression 'witch-doctors', since their main function amongst the Azande is to detect witches and to combat witchcraft. Thus in Zande society we have:

Witchcraft (*mangu*)
performed by witches (*ira mangu*)

Magic (*ngwa*)

performed by magicians (*ira ngwa*) a special association of whom are witch-doctors (*abinza* or *avule*). There are two types of *ngwa*: *wene ngwa*, good magic, and *gbigbita ngwa*, bad magic or sorcery, performed by sorcerers (*ira gbigbita ngwa*).

References

EVANS-PRITCHARD, E. E. (1929a), 'The morphology and function of magic', *American Anthropologist*, vol. 31.

EVANS-PRITCHARD, E. E. (1929b), 'Witchcraft (*mangu*) amongst the Azande', *Sudan Notes and Records*, vol. 12.

FRAZER, J. G. (1922), *The Magic Art and the Evolution of Kings*, vol. 1, Macmillan (first published 1911).

HARTLAND, E. S. (1924), *Primitive Law*, Methuen.

HUBERT, H., and MAUSS, M. (1902–3), 'Esquisse d'une théorie générale de la magie', *L'Année Sociologique*, vol. 7; reprinted in M. Mauss (1950), *Sociologie et Anthropologie*, Presses Universitaires de France.

MALINOWSKI, B. (1926a), *Crime and Custom in Savage Society*, Kegan Paul, Trench, Trubner.

MALINOWSKI, B. (1926b), 'Magic, science and religion', in J. Needham (ed.), *Science, Religion and Reality*, Macmillan; reprinted in R. Redfield (ed.), *Magic, Science and Religion and Other Essays*, The Free Press, 1948; Doubleday, 1954.

SCHAPERA, I. (1927), review of B. Malinowski's *Crime and Custom in Savage Society*, *Man*, vol. 27, July.

2 E. E. Evans-Pritchard

Witchcraft amongst the Azande

Excerpts from E. E. Evans-Pritchard, 'Witchcraft (*mangu*) amongst the Azande', *Sudan Notes and Records*, vol. 12, 1929, pp. 163–249.

Witchcraft (*mangu*) and magic (*ngwa*) have quite different connotations in Zande culture and should be clearly distinguished in an ethnological account.[1] In certain respects witchcraft and sorcery are similar. Probably neither, certainly not *mangu*, has any real existence. Both have common functions, since they are used for pernicious private ends against the lives and property of law-abiding citizens. But their technique is quite different. Zande magic comprises the common characteristics of magic the world over, rite, spell, ideas, traditions, and moral opinion associated with its use, taboo and other conditions of the magician and the rite (Evans-Pritchard, 1929; Hubert and Mauss, 1902–3; Malinowski, 1926). All these are traditional facts transmitted from one generation to another. Witchcraft operates through different channels though in similar situations to sorcery.

Let us commence our analysis of Zande witchcraft from its concrete elements, for as the nuclear equipment of sorcery is a concrete, generally botanical, medicine, so the nuclear equipment of witchcraft is an abdominal condition (*mangu*). We have never actually seen a *mangu*, but it has often been described to us as an oval, blackish swelling or sack which sometimes contains various small objects. In size about the elbow-width of a man's bent fore-arm, it is situated somewhere in the upper abdomen near the bile tract. It cannot be observed from the outside during a man's lifetime, but in the past it used often to be extracted by a post-mortem operation, and was sometimes placed hanging from a tree bordering one of the main paths leading to a chief's court. We are ignorant about the real nature of this abdominal condition, but think that it is probably the gall-

1. See previous Reading – *Ed.*

bladder or the stomach itself in certain digestive periods.[. . .]

Here we wish to state the main attributes of *mangu* in a preliminary manner before discussing the part the concept of witchcraft plays in native life and the complex and often contradictory notions associated with it in Zande mentality. The first of these attributes is its physical character. It is a physical or physiological fact, a thing, which is situated, so far as we have been able to gather, in the abdomen just below where the breast-bones meet. The second important fact which we wish to bring out about *mangu* is that it is an hereditary anatomical endowment which is transmitted in unilinear descent from parents to children. There is sex dichotomy in the biological transmission of witchcraft. Thus whilst the sons of a male witch are all witches his daughters are not, and whilst all the daughters of a female witch are also witches her sons are not.[2] Witchcraft thus regarded as an inherited biological trait transmitted along the lines of sex does not run counter to Zande ideas of kinship and descent, but is complementary to their notions about procreation and their escatalogical beliefs. We will summarize these briefly in so far as they concern our subject.

The birth of a child results from a unison of spiritual properties in the womb of a woman with spiritual properties in the sperm of a man. The foetus is derived from the union of two principles, male and female. When the spirit (*mbisimo*) of the male is stronger than that of the female a boy child is born. When the woman's spirit (*mbisimo*) is stronger, a girl child will be born. Thus, whilst a child is thought to partake of the spirits of both parents, a girl is believed to partake more of the spirit of her mother, and a boy of his father, but in certain respects a child takes after one or other parent according to its sex, in the inheritance of sexual characteristics [and] of *mangu*.[. . .]

Some nocturnal birds and animals are very definitely associat-

2. Lagae (1926, pp. 107–8), with his usual care, quotes a Zande text for the doctrine of unilateral inheritance of witchcraft: 'If a man with witchcraft in his stomach gives birth to a male child, he also is a witch because his father was one before him. It is the same with women. If a woman has witchcraft in her stomach and gives birth to a female child she also is a witch because her mother was one before her. Thus witchcraft does not worry a man who is born free from it by entering into his stomach.' (Our own free translation.)

ed with witchcraft and are thought to be the servants of human witches, and to be in league with them. Such are bats, which are universally feared for their evil attributes, and owls, which hoot forebodings of misfortune in the night. These nocturnal creatures are associated with witches because witchcraft is especially active at night, where it may sometimes be seen in motion.

For, like many primitive peoples, the Azande believe that witchcraft emits a bright light which can only be seen in the daylight by witch-doctors and by witches themselves, but which is occasionally visible at night to persons who are neither witches (all such being *amukundu*) nor witch-doctors.[3] The light of *mangu* is described as being similar to the little lights of firefly beetles, which move about like sparks kicked from a log-fire, only it is ever so much larger than they. The beetles themselves arouse no suspicion of witchcraft, but the Zande compares their phosphorescence to the emanation of *mangu*, adding that it is a poor comparison, since *mangu* has a so much greater and brighter light.[...]

We will naturally wonder what the light [is], whether it [is] the actual witch stalking his prey or whether it [is] some emanation which he [emits] to do the murder. On this point Zande theory is quite decided. The witch is asleep during the period of his activity on his bed in his hut, but he has despatched the spirit of his *mangu* (*mbisimo mangu*) to accomplish his ends. The spirit of *mangu* removes parts of the spirit of the victim's flesh (*mbisimo pasie ni* : *mbisimi* = spirit, *pasie* = flesh, *ni* = pron. suff.) and devours it. The whole act of vampirism is a spiritual one; the spirit of *mangu* removes and devours the spirit of the body. I have never been able to obtain a more precise explanation of witchcraft activities by enquiring into the meaning of *mbisimo mangu* and *mbisimo pasie*. The Zande knows that people are killed in such a way, but only a witch himself could give a circumstantial account of what exactly happens.

Witches usually combine in their destructive activities and subsequent ghoulish feasts. They assist each other in crime and

3. Lagae's textual note reads: 'Those people who see witchcraft when it goes by night to injure someone say witchcraft is on its way shining bright like fire, it shines a little and again obfuscates itself' (1926, p. 108). (Our own free translation.)

they arrange their nefarious schemes in concert. They are believed to possess a special kind of ointment (*mbiro mangu*) with which they rub their bodies and little drums which they beat to summon others to congress, where their discussions are presided over by old and experienced members of the brotherhood. For witches have their hierarchy and status and leadership in the same way as all other Zande social groupings have.[4] Experience must first be obtained under tuition of elder witches before a man is able to kill his neighbours. Growth in experience goes hand in hand with physical growth of *mangu* itself.

A child born of a witch parent of its own sex has such a small *mangu* that it can do little injury to others. It is possible that his *mangu* will remain inoperative or largely so throughout life, but generally it grows both in size and in exercise of its powers. Hence, a child is never accused of murder, and even grown boys and girls are not suspected by adults of serious offences of witchcraft, though they may be a more serious menace to their child contemporaries. Generally speaking, the older a man grows the more potent becomes his *mangu* and the more violent and unscrupulous its use. The reason for this genetic concept of witchcraft will become apparent when we explain its situations in Zande social life and its place in their system of morals.

Sooner or later, a witch will probably fall a victim to vengeance or, even if he is clever enough to avoid retribution, he will be killed by another witch or by sorcery. Is the distinction between witches (*aboro mangu*) and non-witches (*amukundu*) operative beyond the grave? We have never been given a spontaneous statement to this effect, but in answer to direct and leading questions we have been told that at death witches become . . . evil spirits . . . known as *agilisa*.[. . .]

Mangu is ubiquitous. It plays its part in every activity of Zande life, in agricultural, fishing, and hunting pursuits; in domestic life of homesteads as well as in communal life of district and court; it is the essential theme of mental life, in which it forms the background of a vast panorama of magic; its influence is plainly

4. Reference to other Readings, for instance Trevor-Roper (Reading 12, p. 124-5) and Parsons (Reading 18, p. 204) will show how widespread this kind of belief is – *Ed*.

stamped on law and morals, etiquette and religion; it is prominent in such different spheres as technology and language; [there is] no niche or corner of Zande culture into which it does not twist itself. If blight seizes the ground-nut crop it is *mangu*; if the bush is burnt vainly in pursuit of game it is *mangu*; if women laboriously ladle out water from a pool and are rewarded by but a few small fish it is *mangu*; if termites do not rise when they are due and a cold, useless, night is wasted in waiting for their flight it is *mangu*; if a wife shows herself sulky and unresponsive to her husband it is *mangu*; if a chief is cold and distant with his subject it is *mangu*; if a magical rite fails to achieve its purpose it is *mangu*; if, in fact, any failure or misfortune falls upon anyone at any time and in relation to any of the manifold activities of his life he believes that it is due to *mangu*. Those acquainted either at first hand or through reading with a normal day-to-day life of an agricultural African people will understand that there is no end to possible misfortunes arising in routine tasks and relaxations from miscalculation, incompetence, laziness, but mostly from causes over which the native has no control, since he possesses little scientific knowledge. All these are regarded as being due to *mangu* unless there is strong internal evidence and subsequent oracular confirmation that sorcery or one of those species of evil-bringing agents which we have described in the preceding section have been at work. But unless a man had previously had the misfortune of seeing *adandala*,[5] touching his wife's menstrual blood, seeing her anus, or similar experience, he would not attribute any casual misfortune to these causes.

It is strange at first to live amongst the Zande and to listen to their naïve explanation of misfortunes with the most obvious origin as products of witchcraft. A European cannot repress a smile at such crude and childish shelving of responsibility. A boy knocked his foot against a small stump of wood in the centre of a bush path, a daily occurrence in Africa, and suffered considerable pain and inconvenience in consequence. The sore, owing to its position on his toe, was continually receiving dirt and refused to heal. It was *mangu*. I pointed out that it was carelessness and advised him to look out where he was going in

5. A species of wild cat associated with witchcraft, the sight of which is believed to be fatal (Evans-Pritchard, 1937, p. 51) – *Ed*.

future, but he replied that it was quite true witchcraft had nothing to do with the stump of wood being in the path but that he had kept his eyes open, and if he had not been bewitched he would of course have seen the stump. As a conclusive argument for his view he remarked that all sores did not take days to heal, but generally close quickly, since that is the nature of sores and their usual behaviour; why, then, had not his wound closed unless there were *mangu* behind it? This I discovered before long was to be regarded as the general theory of ailments, and that there was little knowledge as to the real causes of disease. Thus, for example, when feeling unfit for several days I consulted native friends whether they thought that my consumption of bananas could have anything to do with my indisposition, but was at once informed that bananas do not cause sickness however many are eaten unless one is bewitched.[. . .]

Though a Zande will always place his misfortunes at the door of witchcraft, it must not be thought that he regards every enterprise as potentially successful so long as it is not interfered with by *mangu*. He is fully aware that people who traverse the bush will get cuts and scratches, and you will see how carefully he searches the ground in front of his bare feet whilst you, poor stranger, stumble along admiring the rich variety of the bush, but are, fortunately, provided with boots. His knowledge and absence of adequate protection make him careful. It is knowledge which each learns for himself from experience in childhood and uses throughout life. However, in spite of all precautions, cuts are sometimes unavoidable, since stumps of wood are often so close to the ground and so covered with dust or ashes that they are invisible to the most accustomed eye, or night conceals stumps and thorns from the late traveller; or a man must pursue game through sharp-edged grasses and tangled thorny undergrowth, where he can no longer keep to his beloved paths, and his attention to minor discomforts is distracted by excitement in the chase. Moreover, there are several different kinds of magic which protect him against minor injuries of this kind. I know of none which are specifically devoted to ward off bush cuts, but Zande magic is often wide-embracing and gives general protection to travellers and huntsmen away from home. If, in spite of practical caution and protective magic, he receives a nasty cut he will attribute it to the malice of his neighbours who have bewitched him. He will not, however, trouble very much about the matter unless the cut festers or refuses to close. He will then be certain that *mangu* is the cause and will begin to be resentful and possibly he will consult the oracles to find out who is causing such prolonged discomfort and inconvenience.[...]

If an illness continues in spite of the precautions taken, the relatives of the sick man will try and find out who is responsible. They will probably commence their enquiries through the *iwa*[6] oracle[7] and then check its verdict with the *benge*[8] oracle. One by one they place the names of people whom they suspect before *iwa*, and, when *iwa* has chosen one of them as the culprit, they ask it whether this is the only man responsible, or whether there are others acting in concert with him. If *iwa* says that this man is acting alone they put his name before *benge*. As we do not wish to enter here into the complicated technicalities of oracle-magic we will suppose that *iwa* chooses the name of one man and that *benge* supports the lesser oracle. The sick man and his relatives now have in their possession the name of the witch. This man was previously suspected, otherwise his name would not have been put before the oracles, and now they are certain that it is he who is bewitching their friend. As the feeling of the sick man and his relations is one of great indignation, and their first impulse is to assault the witch, it is highly important at this juncture that their actions should be well controlled by traditional procedure. There are two lines of action considered socially commendable. They may make a more or less public accusation of the witch face to face in a manner to be described shortly, or they may make a public declaration in his presence without mentioning any names, so that only they and the witch will know

6. ' ... rubbing-board oracle, which operates by means of a wooden instrument' (Evans-Pritchard, 1937, p. 11) – *Ed.*

7. The *iwa* is not so greatly relied upon as *benge* and *dakpwa*, and a man accused of witchcraft on the strength of *iwa* alone may fairly say he is being wantonly insulted. Only in the case of serious illness is it proper (though many persons do it on other occasions) to act on the verdict of *iwa* alone since, in case of severe illness, it is necessary to save time.

8. ' ... poison, oracle, which operates through the administration of strychnine to fowls, and formerly to human beings also' (Evans-Pritchard, 1937, pp. 10–11) – *Ed.*

whom is being referred to. This latter method has an advantage where the witch is a person of social standing whom they do not wish to offend, or someone enjoying the respect and esteem of his fellow citizens, whom they do not wish to humiliate. This latter method is known as *kuba*.[. . .]

Those who have listened to this dramatic declaration know the voice which has spoken, who is ill, and all the circumstances of his sickness. As the witch listens he knows that his plot is discovered and that, being a marked man, if he continues to torture his victim his name will be revealed, and that, if he kills him, the death will be avenged. Self-preservation and self-respect will make him stop before it is too late. Moreover, he will be honoured by the deference which has been paid to him by concealment of his identity from the general public, so that he may yield to flattery where he will not yield to fear.

If this effort to get the witch to cease his activities is unsuccessful, the relatives of the sick man will resort to the procedure which is generally used alone without being preceded by a *kuba*, for a *kuba* is only used if they think that it is more convenient and if the *iwa* oracle sanctions its use. The normal procedure is to put the names of all suspects before *iwa* and let it select those guilty of causing sickness. Unless the man is dangerously ill, when they will at once make known *iwa*'s selection, they will place the names chosen by *iwa* before the more reliable oracle *benge*. A red strychnic powder is given to chicken, whilst the names of the suspects are mentioned one by one, and by either killing or sparing these chicken the oracle separates the innocent from among the guilty. Maybe several will be found guilty, maybe only one, but the procedure is the same for many as for one. They cut off a wing from the hen which died to the name of the witch and thrust it on to the end of a little pointed stick, spreading its wing out in the shape of a fan, and take it home with them. One of the relatives will then go with it to a neighbouring chief's deputy, since the chief is not always accessible, and does not wish to be troubled with every little affair of this kind, and they will tell him the name of the man denounced by *benge*. Or, instead of going to him, they may again consult *iwa* about several reliable men of good social position in order to choose one of them to notify the witch of *benge*'s verdict. If they go to the chief's deputy, the wiser course, he will promise to notify the witch. He calls one of his dependants and sends him with the fowl's wing to the homestead of the witch and tells him to present him with it, to note what happens and to bring back word accordingly. The messenger goes with the wing and lays it on the ground in front of the witch, saying that his master has sent him with it because of the illness of so-and-so. Generally a witch will protest his innocence of intention and his ignorance of the harm that he is doing to his neighbour. He calls for a gourdful of water, and when his wife brings it he takes a draught, swills it round in his mouth, and blows it out in a spray over the wing. He says aloud, so that the messenger can hear his words, that if he is a witch he is unaware of his possession of *mangu*, and that he is not causing injury to others with intent. He addresses the *mangu* in his stomach beseeching it to become inactive. If he makes this appeal from his heart and not in mere pretence with his lips, then the sick man will recover. The messenger returns to his master with news of what he has seen, and the deputy tells the relatives of the sick man that his duty has been performed satisfactorily. The relatives will wait anxiously for some days to find out what effect this ceremony will have. If the sick man shows signs of recovery they will praise *benge* for having revealed so quickly and surely the name of the witch and opened up a road to recovery. If sickness continues they will again consult the oracles to find out whether the witch was only pretending repentance or whether some new aggressor had arisen to trouble their ill friend, and in this case the same formal ceremony of presentation of hen's wings will again take place.

Though chiefs appear in the past to have sometimes taken more diastic steps to ensure their safety, the procedure described above has always been the normal everyday usage of every section of society. It is an usage which maintains generally an orderly outcome to a situation fraught with considerable emotional stress on both sides for the conferring of a hen's wing upon a man often leads, on the part of the *boro mangu*,[9] to concealed

9. '*Boro* (*ira*) *mangu* witch: a person whose body contains, or is declared by oracles or diviners to contain, witchcraft-substance and who is supposed to practise witchcraft' (Evans-Pritchard, 1937, p. 9). cf. previous Reading, which gives *ira mangu* for 'witch' – *Ed.*

anger and permanent estrangement, whilst the relatives on their part feel themselves face to face with what amounts to murder of their friend and kin. The great authority of the *benge* oracle, the use of an intermediary to carry out the more offensive part of the performance, the social standing of a deputy backed up by the political power of a chief, the stereotyped mode of behaviour expected of a witch under the trying publicity which accompanies his humiliation, are factors which help to tide over this difficult impasse in human relations, whilst at the same time allowing expression of indignation along prescribed channels of conduct. For a man who were to accuse another man wantonly of witchcraft without being able to produce an oracular verdict to back up his statement would be merely laughed at for his pains if he were not beaten into the bargain. A man who went himself to deliver a hen's wing or who sent some unsuitable messenger without first consulting either the oracles or an old man of high social standing would run the risk of initiating a violent scene, and people would say that he got what an ignorant 'provincial' deserves. While, on the other hand, the man who showed temper on being presented with a hen's wing in the proper traditional manner would, as we shall show more fully in a later section, not only be considered a boor, but his behaviour would reveal blackness of heart and confirm the worst suspicions. The Zande can always tell you what is the correct behaviour in any situation, the ideal of conduct based on tradition; but people are always doing things the wrong way and troublesome consequences arise. Nevertheless, by a traditional sequence of activities from a preliminary consultation of the *iwa* oracle to a consultation of *benge*, from *benge* to *iwa* once more, from *iwa* to a dramatic declaration in the *kuba*, from the *kuba* to *iwa* again, from *iwa* to *benge*, from *benge* to a formal request to a chief's deputy and the sending of a messenger and the carrying out of a simple ceremony in the homestead of a witch, all is regulated by a well-known sequence of traditional moves and a series of behaviour-patterns which give firm social control over the unruly passions of men under severe emotional stress. [. . .]

References

EVANS-PRITCHARD, E. E. (1929), 'The morphology and function of magic', *American Anthropologist*, vol. 31.

EVANS-PRITCHARD, E. E. (1937), *Witchcraft, Oracles and Magic among the Azande*, Clarendon Press.

HUBERT, H., and MAUSS, M. (1902–3), 'Esquisse d'une théorie générale de la magie', *L'Année Sociologique*, vol. 7; reprinted in M. Mauss (1950), *Sociologie et Anthropologie*, Presses Universitaires de France.

LAGAE, C. R. (1926), 'Les Azande ou Niam–Niam', *Bibliothèque Congo*, vol. 18.

MALINOWSKI, B. (1926), 'Magic, science and religion', in J. Needham (ed.), *Science, Religion and Reality*, Macmillan; reprinted in R. Redfield (ed.), *Magic, Science and Religion and Other Essays*, The Free Press, 1948; Doubleday, 1954.

3 Raymond Firth

Reason and Unreason in Human Belief[1]

Excerpts from Raymond Firth, *Human Types: An Introduction to Social Anthropology*, Nelson, 1956, revised edition, chapter 6, pp. 155-6 163-5.

Magic, as commonly accepted, comprises a rite and verbal formula projecting man's desires into the external world on a theory of human control, to some practical end, but as far as we can see based on false premises. A broad classification of magic in terms of these practical ends, whether the promotion of human welfare, the protection of existing interests, or the destruction of individual well-being through malice or the desire for vengeance, is given in the following table:

AIM AND SPHERE	SOCIAL ASPECT
A. *Productive.* Magic of hunting. Magic of fertility, planting, and harvest in agriculture. Magic of rain-making. Magic of securing a catch in fishing. Canoe and sailing magic. Magic for trading profit. Magic of love.	Performed either by private individuals for themselves, or by specialist magicians for others or the community as a whole. Socially approved. A stimulus to effort and a factor in organisation of economic activity.
B. *Protective.* Taboos to guard property. Magic to assist collection of debts.	Performed as above, and socially approved. A stimulus to effort and a force of social control.

1. The definitions given in these two excerpts from *Human Types* are of general applicability. For a useful discussion of how they fit the beliefs and practices of the Tikopia, see Raymond Firth (1954) – *Ed.*

Magic to avert misfortune.

Magic for the cure of sickness.

Magic for safety in travelling.

Counter-magic to C.

Sorcery: performed as above, sometimes socially approved, sometimes disapproved. Often a force of social control.

C. *Destructive*.

Magic to bring storms.

Magic to destroy property.

Magic to produce sickness.

Magic to bring death.

Witchcraft: sometimes attempted, often doubtful if actually performed; and sometimes of imaginary occurrence. Classed as morally bad. Provides a native theory of failure, misfortune and death.

[...]

We may now turn to an analysis of destructive magic. Let us first compare the pattern of destructive magic in several primitive societies. Destructive magic among the Maori consists essentially in destroying some part of the victim's clothing or hair or nails or even his excreta with the recital of a powerful spell. Among the Zande of Central Africa *mangu* or witchcraft is a kind of emanation from an imaginary material substance in the bodies of some persons. It is thought to be capable of being diagnosed by oracles in the living, and is said to be discovered by autopsy on the dead. To the Zande ordinary magic and witchcraft are of quite a different order. In comparing the magic of these two societies we see that among the Maori there is no use of medicine, that destructive magic and productive magic are of the same generic kind, and that destructive magic is actually practised and relies for its success on the use of objects associated with the victim. But whereas the productive magic of the Zande is very similar to that of the Maori, Zande destructive magic has an additional category to the Maori type. Side by side with the sorcery which is actually performed and follows a special technique, is witchcraft, which does not require either formulae or exuviae of the victim, and is not actually capable of human performance. This duality in the sphere of destructive magic is commonly found in Africa as well as in Australia and parts of Melanesia. It does not, however, appear to exist in Polynesia.

Among the Daly River people of Australia two varieties of destructive magic are actually practised: the rite to bring on storms and damage one's enemies; and the burning or burying of personal exuviae to cause sickness and death. Also, there is a belief in and a great terror of *mamakpik*, the stealing of a living man's kidney fat with his resultant rapid decline and death. This presents the features of the Zande *mangu* in that it is never witnessed, and though a person may be accused of practising it he never admits to doing so, and its activity is diagnosed essentially by its supposed effects. But unlike the possessor of *mangu*, the practitioner of *mamakpik* has no supposed organic peculiarity of his body. In rare cases an attempt has actually been made to steal kidney fat in the prescribed fashion, but has naturally failed. In some parts of Melanesia there is a strong belief in a type of destructive magic, some of the cardinal features of which are physically impossible to carry out; yet there are people who actually profess to perform it. Such is the *vele* of Guadalcanal and the *vada* of south-eastern New Guinea, in which a magician is believed to daze his victim, extract vital organs, miraculously close the wound, and resuscitate him for a short time, though he cannot name his assailant and dies soon afterwards. The major difference of this from the Australian *mamakpik* is the existence of men who purport to practise this magic.

There is in all this destructive magic a set of common elements, though the emphasis upon each may vary from one community to another, and a fairly clear distinction can be drawn between one type, the practice of which is imaginary, and another type, where some ritual is actually performed. It is common to describe the first type as witchcraft and the second as sorcery, though these terms are not always uniformly so used.[. . .]

Reference

FIRTH, R. (1954), 'The sociology of "Magic"', *Sociologus*, n.s., vol. 4, pp. 97–116, reprinted as chapter 9 of R. Firth, *Tikopia Ritual and Belief*, Allen & Unwin, 1967.

4 A. D. J. Macfarlane

Definitions of Witchcraft

Excerpt from A. D. J. Macfarlane, *Witchcraft in Tudor and Stuart England,* Routledge & Kegan Paul, 1970, Appendix 2.

Recent historians of English witchcraft have had considerable difficulty in their attempts to define the basic terminology.[1] Similarly, there is no unanimity among anthropologists. The classic distinction between 'witchcraft' and 'sorcery' in Africa was first outlined by Professor Evans-Pritchard (1937, p. 21) in the following words:

Azande believe that some people are witches and can injure them in virtue of an inherent quality. A witch performs no rite, utters no spell, and possesses no medicines. An act of witchcraft is a psychic act. They believe also that sorcerers may do them ill by performing magic rites with bad medicines.

The distinction here is between different types of means: the end is similar. Both witches and sorcerers injure people. Among the Azande a person *is* a witch. Witchcraft is an inherent quality, whereas sorcerers *act* in a certain way. Sorcerers are conscious of their activities, whereas witches, whose power is internal, may not be aware that they are witches until they are accused. While the witch is the vehicle for a power greater than herself, often the unwilling agent of vast evil forces, the sorcerer controls the power inherent in certain 'medicines' or other objects. Although both are driven by antisocial feelings, the witch is permanently malicious, having inherited her power or been taught it very early in life, while the sorcerer is only dangerous at specific times and acquires the power of evil later in life by a more self-conscious transmission.

1. Briggs (1962, p. 3) discusses various definitions and suggests the effects of definitional differences among historians. Among other recent discussions, those of Ewen (1929, pp. 21–4) and Parrinder (1958, pp. 8–13) are the most helpful.

Unfortunately, these analytic distinctions have not always worked when applied to societies other than the Azande. Thus, in Ceŵa society, there are 'sorcerers' who always use outward medicines or gestures and are conscious agents, but who, like 'witches', are permanently evil and learn their evil power early in life.[2] Even the Azande themselves do not have 'witches' by all these criteria: people are not permanently motivated by witchcraft, but only on specific occasions.[3] There have been other criticisms of the whole distinction,[4] yet it has been found a useful tool in the analysis of witchcraft beliefs in Tudor and Stuart Essex. We may therefore ask to what extent people distinguished between various types of 'witchcraft' and how far there were generally accepted definitions.

Examination of historical definitions on the basis of the above distinctions immediately reveals that there was immense confusion and variation. There are a number of obvious reasons for this. Some authorities based their definitions on the works of Continental demonologists; others on the opinions of country folk. Opinions of witchcraft changed between 1560 and 1680. Attitudes differed between social and religious groups. An illustration of the way in which a number of opposing concepts were subsumed under the word 'witchcraft' occurs in the work of the Kentish squire, Reginald Scot (1584). 'Witchcraft', he said, was both good and bad in its effects, both inward and outward in its means, at least in the 'estimation of the vulgar people'. 'The effect and end' of witchcraft was 'sometimes evil, as when thereby man or beast, grasse, trees, or corne, &c., is hurt: sometimes good, as whereby sicke folkes are healed, theeves bewraied [sic], and true men come to their goods, &c.' Thus a person who cured an animal by magical means was, in common parlance, a 'witch'. Likewise, although outward rituals and medicines were used, inherent power of a personal

2. Marwick (1965, pp. 81–2) discusses the inapplicability of the 'witch-craft/sorcery' distinction in the Ceŵa setting. [Various renderings of this ethnic designation exist; Ceŵa has been adopted throughout – Ed.]

3. 'A Zande is interested in witchcraft only as an agent on definite occasions ... and not as a permanent condition of individuals' (Evans-Pritchard, 1937, p. 26).

4. One of the most forceful of the attacks on the widespread use of such a distinction was made by V. W. Turner (1964, pp. 319–24).

kind was also needed. 'The matter and instruments, wherewith it is accomplished, are words, charmes, signes, images, characters, &c.' – external qualities. But their power depended on a certain personality. 'The which words although any other creature doo pronounce, in maner and forme as they doo, leaving out no circumstance requisite or usuall for that action: yet none is said to have the grace or gift to performe the matter, except she be a witch.' A person *was* a witch and also acted as a witch.

Other writers did not agree with Scot that the 'vulgar people' did not distinguish between types of witchcraft. In fact, it was just such a tendency to make a distinction between the 'good' and the 'bad' witch that angered John Gaule. As he wrote in the middle of the seventeenth century:

According to the vulgar conceit, distinction is usually made betwixt the White and the Blacke Witch: the Good and the Bad Witch. The Bad Witch, they are wont to call him or her, that works Malefice or Mischiefe to the Bodies of Men or Beasts: The good Witch they count him or her that helps to reveale, prevent or remove the same (1646, p. 30).

The Witchcraft Statutes also distinguished between different ends. The punishments for attempting to find lost goods, for instance, were different from those for trying to kill someone by witchcraft. Yet the Statutes, by including both offences, blurred the differences. Thus a 'good witch' in popular estimation might, theoretically, be executed just like a 'bad witch'.

There seems to have been, in fact, a constant struggle between those who wished to differentiate and those who wished to amalgamate. On the one hand, there were those who wished to punish equally all who used 'magical' power, irrespective of their ends, and irrespective of the degree of their control over such power. For them all 'superstition', especially that emanating from Rome, was 'witchcraft' (cf. Perkins, 1608, pp. 150–52, 167). For them the words 'witch' and 'conjurer' were synonyms (Ady, 1656, pp. 63–4). On the other hand, there were those who wished to differentiate 'good' and 'bad' witches by their effects, and 'witches' and 'conjurers' by their degree of control over their power. The first of these distinctions we have seen in the passage by John Gaule quoted above. The second can be illustrated by the words of Sir Edward Coke (1644, p. 44):

A Conjurer is he that by the holy and powerful names of God invokes and conjures the Devill to consult with him, or to do some act. A Witch is a person, that hath a conference with the Devill, to consult with him or to do some act.

The conjurer commands; the witch obeys.[5]

Two conclusions emerge from this short discussion of definitions of terminology. The first is that, although anthropologists have provided some useful analytic distinctions, these do not really help in a number of societies. The second is that words like 'witchcraft' and 'sorcery' were used in a number of different senses in seventeenth-century England. To avoid confusion, therefore, words have been used as follows: Contrasting means and ends, 'witchcraft' is predominantly the pursuit of harmful ends by implicit/internal means. 'Sorcery' combines harmful ends with explicit means. 'White witchcraft' pursues beneficial ends by explicit means.

References

ADY, T. (1656), A Candle in the Dark: or, A Treatise Concerning the Nature of Witches and Witchcraft.

BRIGGS, K. M. (1962), Pale Hecate's Team, Routledge & Kegan Paul.

COKE, Sir E. (1644), Third Part of the Institutes of the Laws of England.

EVANS-PRITCHARD, E. E. (1937), Witchcraft, Oracles and Magic among the Azande, Clarendon Press.

EWEN, C. L. (1929), Witch Hunting and Witch Trials, Kegan Paul, Trench, Trubner.

GAULE, J. (1646), Select Cases of Conscience Touching Witches and Witchcraft.

MARWICK, M. G. (1965), Sorcery in its Social Setting, Manchester U.P.

PARRINDER, G. (1958), Witchcraft, Penguin Books.

PERKINS, W. (1608), A Discourse of the Damned Art of Witchcraft, Cambridge.

RALEIGH, Sir W. (1614), History of the World.

SCOT, R. (1584), The Discoverie of Witchcraft, p. 389 of the 1964 reprint, Preface by H. R. Williamson, Centaur Press.

TURNER, V. W. (1964), 'Witchcraft and sorcery: taxonomy versus dynamics', Africa, vol. 34, no. 4.

5. As Sir Walter Raleigh (1614, I, xi, 6, p. 209), echoing James I, put it.

5 Philip Mayer

Witches

Philip Mayer, *Witches*, Inaugural Lecture, Rhodes University, Grahamstown, South Africa, 1954.

Reality of Witchcraft in Human Experience

The idea of witchcraft, as you will know, is not confined to any one set of peoples, but is distributed through many different races, cultures, and environments. It occurs among primitive peoples from Africa to the South Seas and from Asia to America. Its record among civilized peoples is only a little shorter. Everyone knows that Joan of Arc was a convicted witch. However, it is not always recalled that witches were still being burnt in Europe down to the age of the French Revolution. The last occasion was in 1782 in Switzerland.

My object tonight is to discuss witchcraft beliefs and witch persecutions as they appear from the standpoint of modern anthropology. Our science has learnt a great deal about witches since the pioneering days of Sir James Frazer and Edward Tylor. Besides collecting much more exact knowledge we have gained a far deeper insight into the social meaning of witchcraft.

It is pleasant to be able to say that some of the most notable advances in knowledge and understanding are owed to former holders of this Chair of Anthropology at Rhodes: to Professor and Mrs Krige who studied witchcraft in the Transvaal among the Lovedu[1] (1943), and to Professor Wilson who, with her husband, studied it in Tanganyika among the Nyakyusa (Hunter, 1936; Wilson, 1951a, 1951b, 1952). My third and last predecessor, Professor Radcliffe-Brown, has been prudent enough to work only among tribes where there are no witches. But to him is due the great general illumination of principles and

1. The v in this tribal name is a bilabial fricative (β in I.P.A. script; v in that of the International African Institute); in Krige's paper (Reading 21, pp. 237–51) it is represented by a b – *Ed.*

methods without which modern Social Anthropology could not have progressed as it has. I feel that it is a special privilege and honour to have him here tonight.

In what I say tonight, I shall be drawing together some of the important points about witchcraft that have been made by various anthropologists studying particular tribes; and I shall also be outlining some general conclusions which have been suggested to me both by the literature and by my own fieldwork.

When one starts to think about witchcraft, commonsense suggests the first question how it is that ideas so absurd, fantastic and often horrible have been so widely distributed in place and time. At the same time, since witchcraft ideas are widespread without being universal, one wants to account for their absence too. Some of the most primitive peoples on earth, including Australian aboriginals and Bushmen here in South Africa, do not believe in witches.

One thing is clear: the witchcraft idea must be related to something real in human experience. Occurring at so many different times and places and cultural levels it cannot be lightly dismissed as a frill on the edge of human fantasy. Social Anthropology, then, is concerned with finding out what is the basic reality underlying witchcraft ideas. When I say reality I do not mean physical fact. Even the most optimistic fieldworker does not expect to see anyone flying on those well-known broomsticks. The kind of reality we are searching for is social and psychological. The witchcraft belief, and the persecution of witches, are a response to social and psychological strains. The more exactly we can identify those strains, the better we can hope to understand the response.

I shall first have to say what witches are. This is not a simple matter. Until Evans-Pritchard's classic work on the Azande there was little serious effort to distinguish witchcraft from sorcery or to isolate it from black magic generally. But as we have to choose a working concept, I would suggest that the essence of the witchcraft idea is simply this: People believe that the blame for some of their sufferings rests upon a peculiar evil power, embodied in certain individuals in their midst; although no material connexion can be empirically demonstrated between those individuals and the ills they are supposed to have caused.

The witch then is held to be a person in whom dwells a distinctive evilness, whereby he harms his own fellows in mysteriously secret ways. To this central mystical idea each society adds its own embellishments.

One of the fascinations of these mystical embellishments is the recurrence of identical details in astonishingly different surroundings. Shakespeare writing in seventeenth-century England about medieval Scottish witches makes them recite a list of creatures that would be just as appropriate to witches in primitive Africa. Or again: the Pueblo Indians in Mexico say that witches go round at night carrying lights that alternately flare up and die down (Parsons, 1936, p. 131); exactly the same thing was said to me in Western Kenya by the Bantu tribe among whom I worked.

One could quote many of these minute parallels. It is not my task tonight to deal with them as such nor to interpret their symbolism. But perhaps it may help us to discern order in the symbolism if we list the major elements that seem to be common to witchcraft myths nearly everywhere:

First, the myth defines a category of persons who may be witches, and states how they can be recognized by particular signs. Witches are practically always adults, very often women, and apt to spring from witch families. They may bear physical stigmata – either external, like a red eye or a Devil's mark, or internal, like a snake in the belly or a special witchcraft substance. Personally they are often reserved, stingy and quarrelsome.

Secondly, the myth tells what sorts of misfortune can be caused by witches. Often these include natural calamities such as death, sickness, drought or plague. However, the context of the misfortune is usually more significant than its intrinsic nature. Witches typically send particular and unaccountable blows that seem somehow out of the common run.

Thirdly, the myth states that witches turn against their own neighbours and kinsmen; they do not harm strangers or people from far away.

Fourthly, they work from envy, malice or spite, against individuals, rather than in pursuit of material gain as such. Sometimes they are 'just greedy', or they may have no conscious motive at all.

47

Fifthly, witches always work in secret, and especially at night.

Sixthly, witches are not entirely human. Their evil power is something *sui generis*, quite unlike ordinary ways of dealing injury such as force or poison. It may work upon its victims immediately, that is to say without the use of any instrument at all. The witch only has to wish you harm, and the harm is as good as done. A witch then is a human being who incorporates a non-human power. When a myth refers to snakes or other objects in the belly of the witch, it seems to be reflecting this notion. Other myths reflect it by saying that witches are possessed by spirits or devils, or that at night they forsake human form and turn into were-creatures.

Seventhly, witches reverse all normal standards. They particularly delight in 'unnatural' practices such as incest or bestiality; they eat their own children, they dig up corpses. They go naked instead of clothed; they excrete in the middle of the dwelling. Even when they knock on your door they stand backwards; or when they ride on baboons, as the Pondo witches do, they face towards the tail. In Christian countries witches repeat prayers or the whole Mass in reverse order.

Lastly, witchcraft is always immoral. At best it is disapproved; at worst it inspires horror like other so-called unnatural practices. Witchcraft properly so-called cannot be justified.[1]

So much for the myth of witchcraft. But though Social Anthropology is concerned with myths and beliefs, it is even more directly concerned with actions, with what men actually do and not how they live. Malinowski made popular the saying that a myth provides charter for action. We have to study the witchcraft system as a whole, the actions as well as the myths, the entire complex of beliefs, attitudes and activities. And having done this we should try to relate it to other social systems, and to find out what part it plays in the working of society as a whole.

Whether anyone ever tries to be a witch and actually perform witchcraft is a question that has to be separately determined in each society we study. In some primitive tribes the answer seems

1. Exception may be taken to stating this as a general rule in the light of instances such as the Heiban and Tira, cited by Nadel (1947, pp. 157 and 202). Personally, I would prefer to define witchcraft as something essentially immoral. See also Wilson (1951a, p. 97, note 2), about her substitution of the term 'defender' for 'defender witches'.

to be yes. More often there is no positive evidence, but even so things sometimes happen in the field that shake one's scepticism. Like Evans-Pritchard (1937) among the Azande, I have seen among the Gusii at night suggestive lights moving near my camp, lights that died down and flared up again exactly as the witchcraft myth alleges. Gusii say that witches produce this effect by raising and lowering the lids of covered fire-pots which they carry with them.

However, Social Anthropology only claims to analyse behaviour that has been properly observed, and observed with some regularity. This condition which does not as yet apply to witchcraft practices, does of course apply to the counter-action that people take against witches. Even if some individuals do try to be witches, the witchcraft power itself is surely imaginary, but the power of the idea regularly inspires people to defence or counter-attack. This therefore is the kind of action that fieldworkers have observed and analysed. We can analyse it irrespective of whether its referent is real or unreal, much as we could analyse a church service while leaving the existence of God an open question.

Let us start by distinguishing two broad categories of action against witches. These categories correspond to the two elements in the nature of the witch, who is non-human and yet human. In so far as the witchcraft power is non-human, one may try to nullify it by antidotes as mystical as itself. One may recite spells or wear amulets or put down medicines. This is a kind of duelling in the realm of fantasy, a duel between two equally imaginary forces. Judged by rational standards it cannot produce any concrete effects, as distinct from psychological ones. But because the wielder of witch-power is also a human being, one may also try to evade or control him as a human being. This is another kind of duelling, not mere fantasy but working social effects that are plain for all to see. For example, among the Gusii it is quite common for whole families to leave their homes through fear of witches; or the self-styled victims might seek reconciliation or pick quarrels, or start whispering campaigns, or complain to the elders. Or they might call in a 'smeller' which is the name they give to professional witch-detectives; in former days a witch who had been duly smelt out might be put to death, but nowadays the use of criminal sanctions against witches is not allowed by the Kenya Administration.

When we consider all the activity that is directed against supposed witches, the question must be asked when or why people start going to all this trouble: what events or situations give them the impulse to start fighting this imaginary menace. It is clear that the stimulus is a feeling of unease or anxiety; but this statement needs to be analysed further. After all, many events and many situations regularly create anxiety, but not all of them bring the witchcraft idea into operation. Death and sickness, for instance, always create anxiety, but the emotion can often be dealt with by the ordinary routine responses. The routine response to a death is a funeral, the routine response to a sickness is medical treatment. The idea of witchcraft is invoked on occasions when these routine responses alone do not give emotional satisfaction.

Events are creating a special anxiety when they are termed unnatural, or uncanny. They are seeming to run counter to the ordinary course of things. The anxiety fastens on to the question of what deeper causation can have underlain the observed event. Among ourselves, we know that some deaths arouse a special anxiety so that we feel impelled to investigate their deeper causation. It is not enough to bury the man who got drowned in the river. We may also insist on finding out why he got drowned – whether he jumped in, whether someone pushed him in, or whether it was just an accident.

The witchcraft idea is commonly invoked as a concept for explaining the deeper or indirect causation of events which seem unnatural. Evans-Pritchard has brilliantly analysed Azande witchcraft beliefs in this light. Of course, the sphere of the 'unnatural' is defined differently in every culture. The Azande explain very many deaths by witchcraft: they think it is unnatural to die unless one is very old. Other peoples explain things differently.

Within a given culture, we have also to reckon with the individual point of view. Subjective factors may largely influence the tendency to suspect witchcraft in particular cases. You may think that you have an unnatural illness; I may see nothing odd about it. And the observed facts can nearly always be given a different twist by a person with a different point of view. This was nicely illustrated for me by an old Gusii man.

Suppose there is a cattle plague [he said]. Nearly all of my cattle die, but my neighbour loses only a couple of beasts. I wonder whether he has bewitched me; it was strange that I should lose so many, and he only so few. Now that neighbour has seen that I am still able to lead out my plough with a pair of strong oxen, but the plague has killed just those two animals of his that he always used for ploughing. He says to himself how strange it is that I can still plough and not he. Perhaps *I* am the one who has bewitched *him*.

Even if only for reasons like these, the anthropologist would hardly expect to be able to predict by rule of thumb just what events will lead to the suspicion of witchcraft and what will not. But there is another limitation too. Witchcraft is usually not the *only* mystic agency that can be suspected of sending peculiar or unnatural misfortunes. Many a primitive universe is peopled with numbers of mystic agencies whose hand may be suspected behind any unusual event. Among the Gusii, for instance, strokes of bad luck may be interpreted as the work of witches, but they may also be attributed to sorcerers, or to the evil eye, or to ancestor spirits, or to broken taboos, or to perjured oaths, or to ritual uncleanliness or perhaps just to luck, 'the luck of God', as they say. A different kind of remedy or protection will be used according to which of these agencies is held responsible.

The Cosmological Setting of Witch-Beliefs

If we want to understand the functions of the witchcraft system as a response to human sufferings and anxieties, I think we have to consider how it fits into a people's entire cosmology, or view of the universe, or philosophy of life. I am especially thinking of what we ourselves call the problem of evil. For example, among those mystic agencies which I have just enumerated, the Gusii regard some as fundamentally just or good and others as fundamentally unjust or evil. Ancestor spirits belong to the first category: they are like angry fathers – always right; they do not trouble people except those who deserve to be troubled. When a Gusii thinks that his bad luck was sent by ancestor spirits, he is construing it as a moral sanction called down by some misconduct of his own. Witches belong to the second category; they are always wrong. When a Gusii thinks that his bad luck was sent by witches he is construing it as unprovoked aggression against himself. The former is a response in terms of guilt and atonement, the latter in terms of resentment and counter-attack.

Take by way of contrast the cosmology of the Andaman Islanders. They too have a cult of ancestral spirits, but unlike the Gusii they find it no blasphemy to accuse the spirits of doing wrong. As Radcliffe-Brown (1922) has shown us, when a death occurs among these people the anger is directed against the spirits and may find expression in violent railing against them. This contrast must obviously be relevant to the fact that the Andamanese do not believe in witches and the Gusii do.

Again, among the Tallensi, as Fortes (1949) has shown, the ancestor and earth cults can on the whole deal adequately with most social or psychological tensions. The idea of witchcraft, though it does exist, does not rank as equal to these in the cosmology: it appears mainly as a mixture of superstition and folklore.

The Gusii witchcraft belief helps to maintain their picture of the moral universe. By blaming witches they escape the need or temptation to blame spirits. The spirits can remain good because the witches are bad. (Incidentally, the Gusii have no answer to the question why these good and just spirits fail to protect virtuous men against evil witches. That problem is more directly tackled, among others, by the Venda in the Northern Transvaal, who say that before a witch can harm anyone the protective ancestor spirits must be caught off guard (Stayt, 1931, p. 275).

There are some cosmologies into which the concept of witchcraft does not fit at all, because they represent everything that happens as being fundamentally right, proper, or natural. Some religions, for instance, teach a Job-like submission to a divine will which brings about everything and is always just. With similar effect, Rationalism teaches that everything may be interpreted as the outcome of natural causes. In neither of these idea systems, if consistently held, is there any room for the witchcraft idea. Witches can only have place in a cosmology that admits to the possibility of things going wrong, that is, departing from the natural and the moral order. We ourselves, in spite of Christianity and Rationalism, appear to admit this possibility up to a point, as when we speak of 'uncanny' luck, meaning contrary to natural order, or of 'unfair' luck, meaning contrary to moral order.

I have been discussing how the witchcraft belief can serve to protect the picture of the moral universe, but as we know it can also protect many other ideas and beliefs. If you have cultivated your fields in the usual way, you may blame a witch for the failure of your crop, and so be saved from the thought that accepted farming techniques might be at fault. If your illness does not respond to treatment, you may blame a witch, and so be saved from doubting the worth of medical knowledge and practice. The witch system can save other belief systems from being deluged with the blame which might otherwise often deservedly fall upon them. It gives a channel into which the blame can be turned more conveniently. The power of the witch is conceived as something that can put a spoke into any wheel; this helps one to assume that, but for witchcraft, all the wheels would always be turning smoothly.

When we ourselves speak of natural disasters such as drought or epidemic, we sometimes call them 'Acts of God', meaning that no human being can be held responsible. Primitive peoples who attribute these disasters to witches are taking the opposite view; they are blaming human beings, and they may even be asserting that those human beings caused the disaster just by willing it. I think that this notion, bizarre to us at first sight, begins to look much more familiar if it is translated into slightly different wording: let us put it that the witch is debited with the moral responsibility. That is a thing distinct from the immediate physical agency. If so-and-so has been wishing for me to suffer, he seems to me morally guilty when I do suffer, no matter what the direct physical causation may be. It is but a short psychological step from attributing moral guilt in this sense to attributing clear responsibility; one is only invoking the common principle which Freud has called 'the omnipotence of thought'.

Witchcraft and Social Relationships

So far I have been discussing the witchcraft idea as a cosmological device, accounting for sufferings that people cannot or will not explain otherwise, and providing a pattern of action that the sufferer may follow when his misfortune makes him particularly uneasy. But the witchcraft idea has of course quite a different kind of social importance as well as this. It is a force in social relations; it is something that can break up a friendship or a marriage or a community; it is a banner under which people hate, denounce, and even kill one another. That is the aspect in which I now want to discuss it.

When we speak loosely of witches being tried or condemned we mean of course that individuals are being tried or condemned as witches. The witch does not exist in his own right; it is the judgement of society that creates him. Society creates the image of the witch, and pins this image down onto particular individuals. If we want to find out what individuals are chosen to fill this unenviable role, there are two ways to go about the inquiry. The first is to try to define a general category of witches. Natives define such a category when they say that all individuals with pythons in their bellies or with red rims round their eyes are witches. We might hope to substitute a more scientific formulation: we might, for instance, be able to show what personality types are most commonly associated with the role of witch in a given society.

The second way, which has been used to such excellent effect by the Kriges and the Wilsons, is to define witches in relation to those whom they bewitch. Instead of asking 'who are the witches?' *in vacuo*, one asks how witches stand related to their supposed victims or their actual accusers. A witchcraft case may end in the uprising of a whole community, but it begins as a duel between two antagonistic individuals, or even as a one-sided mistrust. Our question then is: In a given society, who is most likely to accuse whom?

Thanks to the admirable field-work that has now been done in many parts of the world, we should be able to answer this question with some confidence. Two general rules seem to emerge from the literature. The first is that witches and their accusers are nearly always people close together, belonging to one neighbourhood community or even to one household. This principle is expressed in the witchcraft myth by the notion that witches cannot harm you from far away but only from close by. The second rule is that a witchcraft accusation nearly always grows out of some personal antipathy or hostile emotion. In the myth this is expressed by saying that witches attack where they feel dislike or envy.

In the typical case, then, the alleged witch is a neighbour and perhaps a kinsman of the accuser who has not been getting on well with him or her. I think that most of the apparent exceptions to this rule, if analysed, turn out not to relate to genuine witch-craft but to other phenomena such as sorcery or the evil eye. There are a few societies where the rule does not hold, but even these exceptions may be of the sort that prove the rule, as Kluck-hohn has suggested in his studies of the Navaho (Kluckhohn, 1944; Kluckhohn and Leighton, 1946).

It is by now well established that witchcraft accusations may be significantly frequent in one or more specific relationships. For example, among many African peoples it is specially common for a woman to accuse her husband's other wife of being a witch. Among the Mesakin in the Southern Sudan, Nadel (1952, p. 24ff.) found that the accusation commonly occurred between a man and his maternal uncle. As Nadel has suggested, frequencies of this kind should be interpreted as pointers to weak spots in the social structure.

We must conclude that witches and their accusers are indivi-duals who ought to like each other but in fact do not. The two elements in the situation – the demand for a positive sentiment and the inability to provide it – are equally essential to the picture. Painful tension arises because one individual cannot feel towards another as society expects him to feel. By the standards of society one ought to get on well with one's kinsman or neigh-bour, one's co-wife or maternal uncle. If in fact one cannot get on well with him or her, the situation may become tense. When such a tension becomes insupportable, the only ways to resolve it are reconciliation on the one hand or rupture on the other. Marwick (1952, p. 126) has shown that among the Ceŵa accusations of witchcraft serve the purpose of rupturing or blasting away re-lationships that have become insupportable.

When someone starts to argue that someone else is bewitching him, this notion may serve to bring to a head the tensions and strains of their relationship. It gives a pretext for quarrelling.

There is no law under which you can denounce a person for being personally distasteful to you, but you can denounce him on grounds of witchcraft. The witch idea then is a device that enables people to dress up their animosities in an actionable guise – in the guise of an offence committed against themselves.

Although the condemnation of witches may seem arbitrary in a deeper sense, it is nevertheless carried out in due legal form. The witch's guilt is not taken on trust but is determined by some supposedly objective standard. We know of many magico-religious tests for guilt, such as ordeals, oracles, or diagnosis by magical specialists, and of judicial forms, hearings by a court or a body of elders. We know that even when a supposed witch is set upon by an angry mob and beaten or stoned to death, as used to happen in many African tribes, this is a judicial execution and not an uncontrolled lynching. The crowd is the public executioner in a non-centralized society: it is not the judge as well.

It has been observed, again by Marwick (1952, p. 129), that people accuse one another of witchcraft when they are prohibited from expressing their aggression in other ways such as physical brawling or going to law. From my experience among the Gusii, I would qualify this by adding that people who have both possibilities may still prefer to accuse each other of witchcraft, rather than to pick a legal quarrel, because the witchcraft case has a different objective. Legal cases among primitive people are usually meant to smooth out relationships by patching up quarrels over specific issues. However, among the Gusii and perhaps in most other societies the parties to a witchcraft case probably do not want to be reconciled. What they want is an excuse for rupture. In a witchcraft case the thing at stake is not a specific legal issue but the whole tone of the relationship.

It is an extremely important question what kinds of sanction are used against a witch: when will the suspect be only pursued as a private enemy by his self-styled victim, and when will he be hounded down as a public enemy by community or state? For this largely determines the degree of danger to life and liberty.

Let us consider how the matter is handled by the Gusii. Among the Gusii, for reasons I shall mention later, there was and still is a great reluctance to publicize witch cases. The first recourse is to private magic. If this does not give satisfaction, the easiest and best way to resolve the tension is to break off relations altogether. For where there is no active relationship there can be no active danger, either of being bewitched or of being suspected. If a man suspects his wife, then he will divorce her; if he suspects his sweetheart he will stop courting her; if he suspects his neighbour he may leave the neighbourhood. By these and similar personal adjustments, rupture is achieved without calling in public sanctions or even trying to enlist public opinion; in fact, secrecy is usually a great object. But there remains an alternative way of achieving rupture, and this is by an open legal challenge, which constitutes a direct appeal to public opinion. If the challenge is successful, the witch is liable to be pursued with the whole weight of public sanctions, ending in his death or banishment; at best he has become a 'known witch', a person ready to be blamed and hounded down in any future private or public calamity. If the challenge is not successful, the challenge itself has at any rate dramatically registered the quarrel as open and bitter, since witchcraft is one of the most serious accusations a Gusii can make against another.

Modern administrations and governments in Africa have tried to lessen the social perils of the witchcraft belief by refusing to recognize witchcraft as a criminal offence. In that case it is not permitted to try people for witchcraft in the public courts nor to use criminal sanctions against supposed witches. Witchcraft cases are therefore kept down to the private level. They are duels between A and B, not public issues between A and the community.

This solution has undoubtedly removed the most dramatic dangers to life and liberty. But it brings other problems in its train. The public condemnation and execution of a witch, however repugnant it was, may be considered to have served a useful function from one point of view. It was cathartic; it purged the whole community of certain anxieties for the time-being. They had found the public enemy who made things go wrong for all of them; they had destroyed him; they could all breathe more freely. But now that the anxieties cannot be purged by a few great public witch-hunts, they have to find outlet in countless little private hunts. Every sufferer has to find his own witch. It is less dangerous to be thought a witch, but there is much more likelihood of being thought one.

Since the accusation of witchcraft can be such a dangerous weapon, we have to enquire what safeguards there are against its being used too freely. We all feel that a society that gives excessive prominence to witchcraft must be a sick society, rather as a witch-ridden personality is a sick personality. This is confirmed by anthropological studies which in several cases have shown an increase of witchcraft phenomena in communities undergoing social breakdown. The native peoples of South Africa during the difficult phase of urbanization provide several cases in point.

In a normally stable society the witchcraft system is effectively controlled. It admittedly provides a vent for hatreds and anxieties that society cannot repress, but this remains after all a controlled outlet: the frequency or severity of convictions is somehow kept within bounds. It should be anthropologically valuable to compare the ways in which different societies achieve this control. Tonight, however, I shall only single out one aspect. In many societies, including the Gusii, the weapon of witchcraft accusation is given a double edge. There is good reason to think twice before you denounce your enemy as a witch, for the denunciation may very well recoil upon your own head.

The literature shows how common it is for witchcraft cases to be ambiguous in this sense. Prima facie the signs that point to a person's being a victim of witchcraft can equally well point to his being a witch himself. Let me give a few examples: I take them from the Gusii, but they would fit many other peoples too. If you have been out alone in the night you could well have been attacked by the witches whom you saw prowling in the dark. But to the person you met you looked just like a prowling witch yourself. If you have a peculiar illness, it may mean that you are being bewitched; but it may mean that someone whom you yourself have bewitched is using revenge magic against you. If you have become unusually prosperous, the witches will probably be attacking you, because they always go for people whose good fortune they envy. On the other hand, the kind of person who grows prosperous while all around him are poor is very likely to be a witch himself. If you marry into a witch family, or otherwise consort with known witches, who is more likely than you to become their next victim? On the other hand, why did you ever take up with such people if you were not yourself a witch?

If you have left your home and gone to settle in a far-away place, you may say that you fled from witches who threatened you at the old home. But other people may say that you fled as a witch fearing detection.

It may sound paradoxical to say that witches and their victims look much the same in the public eye, but it makes good sense if we remember that the matter really at stake is a sensation of distrust or hatred. There is not much essential difference between the statement 'I hate X', and the statement 'X hates me'. Even if the hatred is not actually mutual, the one who feels it will probably project it onto the other party. As Lienhardt (1951, p. 317) puts it, a man who easily hates is also one who easily believes himself to be hated.

At any rate, among the Gusii, as among many other peoples, it is almost as dangerous to accuse a witch, or to defend yourself against a witch, as it is to be a witch. The three kinds of activity merge into one another. The act of defending oneself involves a dangerous kind of black magic called *mosira*, so deadly that its use against anyone, except a witch, is considered anti-social. *Mosira*, like witchcraft itself, produces death or sickness. In view of this, the facts in a given case can always be interpreted in opposite ways. Each party can say that his own sufferings are due to his enemy's witchcraft and that his enemy's sufferings are due to his own *mosira*. A's interpretation of the evidence will thus exactly contradict B's. Besides, if a person uses *mosira* and has great success with it, people will suspect that he is probably a witch too. They will feel that if he can defeat other witches so triumphantly he must also have been well versed in their tricks himself.

To accuse a witch in public is dangerous, if only because the ordeal has to be taken by both parties; the ordeal can turn against the accuser and show that he himself was really the witch. But even if things do not get to this stage, it must be remembered that slandering a person by wantonly calling him a witch is in itself a very grave offence. The Gusii say that this kind of back-biting is just as bad as witchcraft itself; and in this they are quite logical, since both witchcraft and back-biting contain the same element of turning disloyal to one's own neighbour. Nowadays, though the government tribunals refuse to try witchcraft cases as such, they are often called upon to try cases of back-biting in this technical sense.

The Traitor within the Gates

I want to end by stating some general conclusions about the reality underlying the notion of witchcraft.

The figure of the witch, clearly enough, embodies those characteristics that society specially disapproves. The values of the witch directly negate the values of society. Typical witchcraft myths attribute to witches many kinds of vices including those that are considered unnatural or specially horrible. Lienhardt (1951, p. 317) has written of the Dinka witch as one who 'embodies those appetites and passions in every man which if ungoverned would destroy any moral law'. That is well said; and it reminds us that the witchcraft myth has after all a certain educative or normative function. In the words of Kluckhohn (Kluckhohn and Leighton, 1946, p. 179) 'Witchcraft lore affirms solidarity by dramatically defining what is bad.'

The witch myth then recognizes an opposition of moral values; an opposition of good and bad, right and wrong, proper and improper, sinful and righteous. The witch is always on the wrong side of the moral line, he is a figure of sin incarnate. However, I think that another or a more particular kind of opposition is also vitally involved. I mean the opposition between 'us' and 'them', between in-group and out-group, between allies and foes. The witch is the figure of a person who has turned traitor to his own group. He has secretly taken the wrong side in the basic social opposition between 'us' and 'them'. This is what makes him a criminal and not only a sinner.

As we have seen, the witch is conceived as a person within one's own local community, and often even within one's own household. All human societies require a basic loyalty between members of the small cooperative and defensive group. The local community, the family, the household, all in one way or another make this demand of loyalty as a categorical imperative. Persons who stand in these intimate relations must on the whole work together, not against one another, if the group is to survive as a group. In one word they have to pursue common or joint interests.

Injury to one should be felt as injury to all. But the witch is conceived as a person who withholds this elementary loyalty and secretly pursues opposed interests. He wants to spoil what his fellows most want to preserve: their life, health, strength, and fertility; their children and their livelihood. He wants to blast their crops and dry up the milk of their cattle. These fundamental interests of life, strength and subsistence are legitimately attacked by enemies in open warfare, but the witch is not fighting open war; he does not come from outside like a raider; he dwells within the group and destroys by stealth. The witch is the hidden enemy within the gate. He eats away like the maggot in the apple.

If we look upon the witch figure in this light as the arch traitor, the type of the fifth column, I think that several facts about witch beliefs are more readily understood; the main features all seem to fit readily into this pattern.

In the light of this principle we understand why the witch is regarded as not altogether human, why witchcraft is a so-called unnatural offence. The person who denies those basic loyalties to family and community outrages the sentiments, on which all social life must rest. The witch has denied the social nature of man; that is as much as to deny human nature itself. No wonder if the myth represents witches as eating their own children or consorting with hyenas and corpses. Anyone who can turn secret traitor to his nearest fellows is surely capable of all other unnatural sentiments too.

In this sense witchcraft is exactly parallel to incest. As Radcliffe-Brown (Radcliffe-Brown and Forde, 1950, pp. 70ff.) has pointed out, the great social danger of incest is that it threatens to overthrow the sentiments on which the family depends for its organized existence. It is entirely logical, on this showing, that witchcraft and incest both rank as unnatural offences, and that often both are attributed to the same individuals.

Further, we understand why witchcraft is always secret, and always associated with the night. The witch is essentially a hidden enemy but an apparent friend. If he did not appear to be one of ourselves he would not be betraying our trust. In the day he looks like anyone else: only at night does he reveal his secret inclinations. As the Lovedu say: 'You eat with him, yet it is he who eats you' (Krige and Krige, 1943, p. 263).

Above all, we understand why witchcraft is treated as a criminal offence, even in those primitive societies where criminal sanctions otherwise hardly exist. By his treason the witch has forfeited his rights as a member of the in-group; he has outlawed himself; he has pursued the interests of an enemy; then let him be treated like an enemy, killed or put to flight.

We know that some peoples punish repeated petty theft within the community in the same manner as witchcraft – in fact they make these the only two offences punishable by death. The element of disloyalty provides the link between these two offences, which to the western minds seem so different. The petty thief who steals from his own neighbours is like the witch secretly attacking the interests of his own group.

I think that the same principle helps to some extent to explain how society chooses the individuals who fill the role of witches. The disloyal person will be sought among those who have failed to give public demonstrations of their loyalty. Accordingly the witch is the woman who fails to give tokens of goodwill to her neighbours: she is reserved, uncommunicative or stingy; a withholder of gifts, or of hospitality, yet greedy for the good things that other people have.

Possibly we might also use the concept of a withheld loyalty to help to explain why witches are so often women. It would seem appropriate enough in those patrilineal societies where the new wife is brought in to join the household and community as a person from an outside group. There is a demand for the woman to merge interests and loyalties with those of her marital home, but she still keeps in her heart some private personal loyalties to her home of origin. She is thus the person who most readily fits into the image of an enemy within the gate.

What I have been saying relates to the witches of primitive society, but I think it applies equally well to certain phenomena of the civilized world. For we too are often found in situations where our basic values and basic loyalties seem threatened; and we too are apt to seek out the enemies within our gates.

In civilized societies other demands for over-riding loyalties have been added to those of the family and community. We are divided not only into groups but also into parties. We stand or fall by our ideologies, in a manner quite foreign to the primitive society with its general ideological uniformity. Civilization brings with it an opposition of sects; of orthodoxies and heresies; of rival religions and political 'isms'. Civilization still has its witches, but it is more apt to call them traitors to a cause, or an idea, or a way of life. It was consistent that for so many centuries in Christian Europe the witch was identified with the heretic or the devil worshipper, and persecuted as such by the Church. Given the idea of basic opposition between Christ and the devil, the witch would be conceived as one who had secretly left Christ and gone over to the devil. In our day we also have a feeling of fundamental cleavage, between the Communist and the Non-Communist world. When people in one of these camps start looking into corners and under beds to find hidden enemies who secretly sympathize with the other camp, we get what is very properly called a witch-hunt. The classic examples of witch-hunting in modern society are the purges of the Communist Party in Soviet Russia and other communist countries. The witch figure in the communist purge is a person who has turned traitor in this basic opposition, by harbouring secret bourgeois sympathies or secret leanings towards capitalism. He is identified and by 'confessing' at his trial he takes the blame for things he could not possibly have caused. He is purged, and the group has reaffirmed its solidarity.

It is equally proper to call McCarthyism a witch-hunt, as distinct from a simple political persecution. It is a witch-hunt because it too goes out and meets its selected victims much more than half way. It takes people who have not yet committed any crime, and tries by all means to fit them into the image of traitors to a cause, the American way of life.

Witch-hunting, then, goes together with a feeling that basic sentiments, values and interests are being endangered. A society in order to feel secure must feel that not only its material interests but also its way of life, its fundamental values, are safe. Witch-hunting may increase whenever either of these elements seems gravely threatened. Among primitive peoples, as we have seen, an increase in witch-hunting is apt to occur both when natural disasters threaten their material interests, and when culture contact threatens their way of life. If witch-hunting is a reaction to a society's feeling of insecurity, it seems unlikely to disappear from the civilized world at present, unless we can remove the radical feeling of insecurity which haunts our nations today.

References

EVANS-PRITCHARD, E. E. (1937), *Witchcraft, Oracles and Magic among the Azande*, Clarendon Press.

FORTES, M. (1949), *The Web of Kinship among the Tallensi*, Oxford U.P. for International African Institute.*

HUNTER, M. (1936), *Reaction to Conquest*, Oxford U.P. for International Institute of African Languages and Cultures*; 2nd edn, 1961.

KLUCKHOHN, C. (1944), *Navaho Witchcraft*, Papers of the Peabody Museum of American Archaeology and Ethnology, Harvard University, vol. 22, no. 2; Beacon Press, 1962.

KLUCKHOHN, C., and LEIGHTON, D. (1946), *The Navaho*, Harvard U.P.; rev. edn Doubleday, 1962.

KRIGE, E. J., and KRIGE, J. D. (1943), *The Realm of a Rain Queen*, Oxford U.P. for International Institute of African Languages and Cultures.

LIENHARDT, G. (1951), 'Some notions of withcraft among the Dinka', *Africa*, vol. 21.

MARWICK, M. G. (1952), 'The social context of Cewa witch beliefs', *Africa*, vol. 22.

NADEL, S. F. (1947), *The Nuba*, Oxford U.P. for International African Institute.

NADEL, S. F. (1952), 'Witchcraft in four African societies', *American Anthropologist*, vol. 54.

PARSONS, E. C. (1936), *Mitla: Town of the Souls, and Other Zapoteco-Speaking Pueblos of Oaxaca, Mexico*, University of Chicago Press.

RADCLIFFE-BROWN, A. R. (1922), *The Andaman Islanders*, Cambridge U.P.; The Free Press, 1964.

RADCLIFFE-BROWN, A. R., and FORDE, D. (eds.) (1950), *African Systems of Kinship and Marriage*, Oxford U.P. for International African Institute; paperback, 1967.

STAYT, H. A. (1931), *The Bavenda*, Oxford U.P. for International Institute of African Languages and Cultures.

WILSON, M. Hunter (1951a), *Good Company: A Study of Nyakyusa Age-Villages*, Oxford U.P. for International African Institute.

WILSON, M. Hunter (1951b), 'Witch-beliefs and social structure', *American Journal of Sociology*, vol. 56, January.

WILSON, M. et al. (1952), *Keiskammahoek Rural Survey*, vol. 3, *Social Structures*, Shuter & Shooter, ch. 6.

* Until the mid 1940s the International African Institute used the longer title, International Institute of African Languages and Cultures.

Part Two
From the Ethnography of Witchcraft

As Kluckhohn has remarked (1962, p. 72), 'the essentially world-wide distribution of a number of beliefs about witches . . . gives probability to Clements's intimation that a complex of certain witchcraft beliefs was part of a generalized Palaeolithic culture which, in some sense, forms the ultimate basis of all known cultures' (Clements, 1932, p. 240). Moving from the realm of archaeological and ethnological probability to that of documented historical virtual certainty, we find in respect of Europe an account of beliefs of this kind extending over at least two millenia. For the earlier periods, both in the south and in the north, the two readings from Baroja provide the documentation; and those from Apuleius, the closer, more intimate, vicarious experience. A sideways glimpse of two pre-industrial modern societies, one in Melanesia and one in Africa, reminds us of the near-universality of beliefs in witches and sorcerers before we examine the final flare-up in Europe and in New England from the dying embers of belief, a critical period, now being repeated, three centuries out of phase, in the hitherto relatively isolated societies of East Central Africa.

References
KLUCKHOHN, C. (1962), *Navaho Witchcraft*, Beacon Press (first published as Papers of the Peabody Museum of American Archaeology and Ethnology, Harvard University, 1944).
CLEMENTS, F. E. (1932), 'Primitive concepts of disease', *University of California Publications in American Archaeology and Ethnology*, vol. 32, pp. 185–252.

6 Julio Caro Baroja

Magic and Religion in the Classical World

Excerpts from Julio Caro Baroja, *The World of the Witches*, translated by Nigel Glendinning, Weidenfeld & Nicolson, 1964, pp. 18–20, 24–8, 39–40.

Let us start by studying the situation as it was in classical times (1). According to the leading authorities on magic in Greece and Rome, processes believed to be specifically magical are known to have been employed in both these societies to produce rain, prevent hail-storms, drive away clouds, calm the winds, make animals and plants prosper, increase wealth and fortune, cure sickness and so on. But magic was also used in Greece and Rome for more obviously perverted reasons: in country areas, for instance, it might be used to ruin an enemy's crops or make his cattle sicken; in the city, it was used to strike down an enemy when he was on the point of making a speech or taking an important part in some public celebration; or it was used to prevent a rival from winning a race or some other event in the public games. Death was quite frequently considered to be the result of witchery, and such beliefs were not confined to any one sector of society (2). What we might call erotic magic is a whole world in itself (3).

It is important to realize that any description or analysis of Graeco-Roman magic which fails to take into account the intention, whether good or bad, underlying specific acts, or the social stratum in which they take place, is bound to be invalid. Acts may be produced by similar processes, and yet be essentially and radically different in their ends.

Thus the practice of magic for beneficent purposes was considered legal and even necessary in Greece and Rome. It was commonly practised by a great variety of people; the priests of specific deities on the one hand, and professional people, such as doctors, on the other (4). The state itself supported those whose business it was to augur the future or make prognostications for

67

special occasions, and those who, in the public interest, discovered by divination what had happened or what was about to happen. A variety of techniques was used for this purpose, and these have been studied in detail in books on the religion and cults of the Greeks and Romans. It is not, therefore, necessary to go over the same ground here (5).

Even the austerest Roman authors included magic formulae for obtaining useful and beneficial results in their work. Treatises on agriculture and medicine and the offices used by priests for certain cults and rites, contain collections of spells and obscure writings probably of an invocational nature (6).

Occasionally it is possible to detect a kind of scepticism even there. For the same technical treatises warn farmers and country-folk not to believe foreign diviners and sorcerers (7) nor women referred to as *sagae* (8).

What of the magic and spells which were intended to cause harm? These were always held to be illegal. From the earliest times and even when there was some doubt about the spells' effectiveness, it was considered a serious criminal offence to make them. Plato made a distinction between those with a professional knowledge of maleficent practices and mere amateurs. Doctors were included among the professionals, but, speaking as a states-man rather than as a religious individual, Plato thought that pro-fessionals who tried to do evil should be condemned to death. Amateurs, on the other hand, ought to be let off more lightly (9).

But that is not all. Although almost anyone might use spells in moments of violent stress, it was generally felt that they were more usually used by a particular type of person and in very specific circumstances. And Plato attacked those who believed they could summon up the dead and even bend the gods to do their will by spells as well as by prayers (10). It is possible that the passage which contains this particular attack is a specific reference to followers of the Orphic cult. But it should be remembered that there were a number of divinities in the ancient world known to be propitious to evil actions, however odd this may seem to us today, brought up as we are, whether believers or agnostics, in an era of Christianity.

In the Christian religion, God is the very image of Good, and the Devil of Evil. But the gods of the pagans – and some pagans were shocked by this – were subject to the same forces of evil and passions as men; even to the same fleeting and capricious desires. Maleficent magic has to be seen in relation to this kind of god. And this is not easy. The simplest thing to do is to examine the concrete forms which magic took, and see whether they were the result of belief in the power of spells and invocations, or belief in the power of supplications. But the whole relationship between magic and religion in antiquity appears complex, even if we follow the views put forward by classical authors themselves.

Take Lucan for example. He was a man who liked mystery and was keen on posing questions it was difficult to answer. In the course of discussing the objects, which were capable of *forcing the gods to do something* ('vim factura deis') (11), owned by a sorcerer called Erichtho, and after enumerating the more extraordinary unnatural acts which it was possible to perform with the aid of Black Magic, Lucan asked himself how it was possible to force the gods in this way. Did the gods like obeying the spells of the sorcerer, he wondered? And did the power of these spells lie in some unknown form of piety, or were they the result of some mysterious ability to threaten (12)?

These are some of the fundamental problems of magic common to many different peoples. Lucan has expressed them very clearly. But he has not solved them. He merely presents us with three hypotheses which the student of magic and religion must constantly bear in mind.

When the magician invokes, curses or threatens the gods, he assumes that they have certain weaknesses he can exploit. This is either because the gods are capricious, or because the magician knows their secrets, which are withheld from other mortals, sometimes because of their shameful nature. Or there may be other explanations still stranger than these, such as, for instance, the existence of some strange *kinship* between the magician and the gods, or a certain affinity and sympathy with them, such as those to which Plotinus refers.

In order to understand the mentality of the magician it must first be realized that the gods of the Greeks and Romans were held to be largely subject to the same physical and spiritual laws as men. The ideas of good and evil were related to physical feelings and experiences even in the case of the gods. In other words, nature and morality, divinity and humanity could not be put in the same watertight compartments as they are today, in the philosophical and religious systems of a world ruled by science and largely secular in character. [. . .]

Maleficent Magic

Evil has its own proper setting – the night. And gods who are propitious. It also has its own qualified ministers. For evil is ultimately achieved by combining a series of techniques which have been passed down from one generation to the next. It would be out of place to mention here all the Greek and Roman texts which prove that the night was looked upon as the proper time for committing evil deeds, because of its silence and the atmosphere of secrecy that surrounds it. However, some of the more important and significant passages are perhaps worth quoting (13).

It is certainly a commonplace in classical poets for witches to appear at the most obviously secret hours. As Ovid has it:

> Nox, ait, arcanis fidissima, quaeque diurnis
> aurea cum Luna succeditis ignibus, astra . . . . (14)

In these well-known lines the Latin poet is in fact describing Medea, one of the greatest witches of classical mythology, when she is on the point of committing a particularly evil action.

Horace's witch, Canidia, invoking the powers of night, is also well worth quoting for the realistic qualities of the passage:

'Night and Diana, ye faithful witnesses of all my enterprises, who command silence when we are celebrating our most secret mysteries, come to my assistance, and turn all your power and wrath against my enemies' (15).

Here we find two of the deities who preside over magical acts mentioned in the same text. But the qualities of night are always less clearly defined than those of the moon. The moon, perhaps because it changes shape, changes its name. In Horace it is Diana: since, whatever the origin of this Roman goddess, she was held to be the equivalent of the Greek Artemis. In Theocritus, we find a similar invocation addressed to Selene (16). But there is another name which is also associated with the moon: that of Hecate, a goddess with more than one side to her nature. She was primarily looked upon as queen of the spirits of the dead, and was believed to be present both when the spirit entered the human body and when it left it; that is, at birth and at death. She lived in tombs, although she could also sit by the hearth, perhaps because that was at one time the place for family burials. And she also appeared at cross-roads on clear nights with a following of spirits and dogs who set up terrifying howls (17).

At these cross-roads offerings were placed each month to propitiate the goddess. These consisted of the remains of purifying sacrifices. Initially Caria (in Asia Minor) seems to have been the centre of the Hecate-cult, but it also existed in Thessaly. This is particularly interesting because Thessaly was always well known for its witches. Hecate is, in fact, a deity around whom secret cults and ideas of terror could easily develop (18). Her help was sought in cases of madness, since madness was believed to be caused by the souls of the departed (19).

A whole group of ideas that might be termed 'cthonic' evolved around the deities Selene, Hecate and Diana. And even today the power of the moon in relation to the mind continues to find expression in such common terms as 'lunatic', referring to someone who is thought to be under the influence of the moon, and 'moonstruck' etc. But there is more to it than that.

In my view it is clear that a particular sexual significance was attached to these deities. They are either virgin goddesses or goddesses of erotic mysteries; not mother goddesses, for whom love meant principally fertility.

Now let us turn to their ministers. The existence of two sorceresses, the celebrated sisters Medea and Circe, who are even believed to be *daughters* of Hecate, traditionally dates back to heroic times (20). Circe symbolizes seduction and is the archetype of the woman who by being 'enchanting' or 'bewitching' as well as by her skill, makes all men bow to her will. (It is interesting to notice the sexual significance which we attach to these words, regardless of their original magical connotations (21).)

Circe turns Ulysses's companions into pigs, but they still retain as animals the mental faculties they had as human beings – νοῦς (22). In Homeric times, then, people believed the reverse of what St Augustine was to believe. For the latter, metamorphosis

71

was the direct result of a mental derangement induced by the Devil, but with no physical reality. Circe ends up by falling in love with Ulysses, who turned out to be her equal in diplomacy.

Medea is perhaps less complex: she is the archetype of the tragic female and has been immortalized as such in drama. 'You have knowledge and wisdom' – she says to herself in the soliloquy in which she declares her intention of avenging herself on her unfaithful husband. 'Besides,' she adds, 'nature has made us women absolutely incapable of doing good and particularly skilful in doing evil' (23). In the same soliloquy she admits her reverence for Hecate above all other gods and speaks of her as her helper (24). In this short text, in fact, we have a woman, albeit a particular type of woman with a violently sensual and frustrated nature, who is bent on doing evil, in possession of recondite knowledge [τέχνη], and a vassal or dependent of a feminine goddess associated with terror and the night. This is the basis of a system: the 'logos' of maleficent magic or witchcraft. But Medea, like Circe, is the protagonist of events which took place in legendary times. So let us turn to texts which refer to a less obscure period.

Other texts speak of the τέχνη or *scientia* of the more ordinary witches. Even Horace, in *Epode* 17, when writing a satire on a witch he frequently attacked elsewhere, begins by speaking of the science itself. After mentioning its patrons, Proserpina and Diana, he refers to the books of incantations, *libros carminum*, and to the chief instrument used in making spells of all sorts, the *turbo* or ρόμβος (which had only to be rotated in the reverse direction to undo what had already been done). He goes on to list the various arts that are the witch's pride, such as the ability to call down the moon from the sky with her chanting, to make waxen figures move, to invoke the spirits of the dead, to make love philtres (25) – all the skills, in fact, mentioned time and again by earlier and subsequent writers.[. . .]

Conclusion

There is documentary evidence of the existence over a period of *centuries* of the belief that certain women (not necessarily always old ones) could change themselves and others at will into animals in classical times; that they could fly through the air by night and enter the most secret and hidden places by leaving their body behind; that they could make spells and potions to further their own love affairs or to inspire hatred for others; that they could bring about storms, illness both in men and animals, and strike fear into their enemies or play terrifying jokes on them. To carry out their evil designs these women met together after dark. The moon, night, Hecate and Diana were the deities who presided over them, helping them to make philtres and potions. They called on these goddesses for aid in their poetic conjurations, or threatened and constrained them in their spells when they wanted to achieve particularly difficult results.

Apart from these powers, the women who were believed to attend such meetings were supposed to be experts in the manufacture of poisons and also in cosmetic arts; sometimes they were used as go-betweens in love affairs.

In fact, a whole series of nouns can be found in the classical Greek and Latin languages which refer to the various acts, operations and materials carried out and used by the witches. And these constitute a nucleus which has its place both in the history of witchcraft and in the history of humanism. Indeed, we can put forward the theory that when Fernando de Rojas, during the Renaissance, described in his *Celestina* the kind of woman we have been discussing and what has come to be called her 'laboratory', he could do so without being thought a pedant, in spite of the fact that he based himself on Horace, Ovid and other classical writers. His literary sources provided him with material about witchcraft that was still valid in his own time, as it had been in that of the Romans.

Another important point is the condemnation of magic for evil purposes which we find in pagan laws. This was formally laid down from the very earliest Roman times (26), and continued to be the case at the period when the Roman authorities had still not accepted Christianity officially. Tacitus has painted a brilliant picture of the terror felt in Rome when the spells which were believed to have caused Germanicus's illness (some of them described as *devotiones*) were discovered (27).

Ammianus Marcellinus has also referred to prosecutions for

crimes of magic in the reigns of Constantius, Valens and Valentinian I. His writings and others on the same subject were later the basis for some of Gibbons's most eloquent pages – pages which reflect only too clearly the disbelief in magic common in Gibbons's time. But when we come to these obscure figures of the Roman Empire's declining years we are already in a new world, with a new view of the beliefs we have been discussing.

References

1. For the following pages I have drawn on my essay ' Magia en Castilla durante los siglos XVI y XVII ', in *Algunos mitos españoles y otros ensayos* (Madrid, 1944), pp. 185–213, particularly. But I have revised my views since writing this work.

2. A good deal of well-organized material can be found in the article on magic by H. Hubert, in the *Dictionnaire des antiquités grecques et romaines*, edited by Darember and Saglio (Paris, 1904), III, 2, pp. 1494–1521. Hopfner is less systematic in Pauly-Wissowa (ed.), *Real-Encyclopädie der Classischen Altertumswissenschaft*, N.B. (Stuttgart, 1930), XIV, cols. 301–93. L. F. Alfred Maury's book, *La Magie et l' Astrologie dans l' Antiquité et au Moyen Âge ou étude sur les superstitions païennes qui se sont perpétuées jusqu'à nos jours* (Paris, 1877), can still be read profitably in spite of its poor organization.

3. General histories of witchcraft contain a fair number of passages from works of the classical period. cf., for example, Soldan, *Geschichte der Hexenprozesse* (Stuttgart, 1880), I, pp. 35–51, for references to the Greeks; pp. 52–85, for the Romans.

4. A significant passage is that of Seneca, *Nat-Quaest*, IV, 6–7.

5. See Frazer, 'The magic art and the evolution of kings', *The Golden Bough*, I, chs. 3 and 4.

6. cf., for example, Cato's *De agr. cul.*, 160; cf. also 5, 4, of the same work.

7. Cato, in his *De agr. cul.*, 5, 4, writes ' Haruspicem, augurem, hariolum, Chaldaeum nequem consuluisse velit '.

8. Columela, *De re rustica*, I, 8.

9. Plato, *Leg.*, XI, 932 e, 933 d.

11. Lucan, *Bell. civ.*, VI, lines 440–41.

10. ibid., X, 909 b.

12. ibid., lines 492–6.

13. Virgil, *Aeneid*, II, line 255, '... tacita per amica silentia lunae'.

14. Ovid, *Metamorphoses*, VII, lines 192–3. 'O night,' she prayed, 'most faithful guardian of my secrets, and golden stars, who, with the moon, succeed the brightness of the day. ...'

15. Horace, *Epodes*, 5, lines 49–54:

> 'O rebus meis
> non infideles arbitrae,
> Nox et Diana, quae silentium regis
> arcana cum fiunt sacra,
> nunc, nunc adeste, nunc in hostilis domos
> iram atque numen vertite.'

16. Theocritus, *Idyl.*, II ('Pharmac.'), line 10 *et passim*.

17. cf. Heckenbach's article on 'Hekate' in Pauly-Wissowa (ed.), *Real Encyclopädie der Classischen Altertumswissenschaft*, N.B. (Stuttgart, 1912), VII, cols. 2769–82. Even more important is Erwin Rohde's invaluable book *Psyché: le culte de l'âme chez les grecs et leur croyance à l'immortalité*, ed. Auguste Reymond (Paris, 1928), pp. 328–35, 607–11.

18. Certain of Hecate's banquets can be compared to those of the witches. The Ἑκατικὰ φάσματα have much in common with witches.

19. cf. Erwin Rohde, *Psyché*, op. cit., p. 325, note 1, for references to mental illnesses.

20. Diodorus Siculus, IV, 45.

21. She also controls animals; cf. *Odyssey*, X, 240. Circe has a pleasant singing voice (X, 220–21) and can make people forget (X, 236).

22. Homer, *Odyssey*, X, 240.

23. Euripides, *Medea*, more especially lines 401–9. There are frequent references to Medea as a sorceress in Latin poets; cf., for example, Horace, *Epodes*, lines 76–81.

24. cf. Seneca's rhetorical invocation in his *Medea*, 1–55, and the more restrained speech in Euripides.

25. Horace, *Epodes*, 17, lines 16–81.

26. Seneca, *Nat. Quaest.*, IV, 7: 'et apud nos in XII tabulis cavatur, nequis alienos fructus excantassit ...'.

27. Tacitus, *Annals*, II, 69; III, 13; cf. Suetonius, *Caligula*, 3.

7 Apuleius

The Story of Thelyphron

Excerpt from Apuleius, *The Golden Ass*, translated by Robert Graves, Penguin Books, 1950, pp. 63–71.

'While I was still a University student at Miletus I came over to attend the Olympian Games. Afterwards, feeling a strong desire to visit northern Greece, I travelled through most of Thessaly. One unlucky day I arrived at Larissa, having run through nearly all the money I had brought with me, and while I was wandering up and down the streets, wondering how to refill my purse, I saw a tall old man standing on a stone block in the middle of the market place. He was making a public announcement at the top of his voice, offering a large reward to anyone who would stand guard over a corpse that night.

'I asked a bystander: "What is the meaning of this? Are the corpses of Larissa in the habit of running away?"

'"Hush, my lad," he answered. "I can see that you are very much of a stranger here, else you would realize that you are in Thessaly where witches are in the habit of gnawing bits of flesh off dead men's faces for use in their magical concoctions."

'"Oh, I see! And would you mind telling me what this guardianship of the dead involves?"

'"Not at all. It means watching attentively the whole night, one's eyes fixed on the corpse without a single sideways glance. You see, these abominable women have the power of changing their shape at pleasure: they turn into birds or dogs or mice, or even flies – disguises that would pass scrutiny even in a Court of Law, and by daylight too – and then charm the guardians asleep. I won't try to tell you all the extraordinarily ingenious tricks that they use when they want to indulge their beastly appetites; at any rate, the usual reward of from a hundred to a hundred and fifty drachmae for the night's job is hardly worth the risk. Oh – I was almost forgetting to tell you that if next morning the guardian fails to hand over the corpse to the undertakers in exactly the same condition as he found it, he is obliged by Law to have bits cut from his own face to supply whatever is missing."

'That did not frighten me. I boldly told the crier that he need not repeat the announcement. "I'm ready to undertake the job," I said. "What fee do they offer?"

'"A thousand drachmae, because this is a job that calls for more than usual alertness against those terrible harpies: the deceased was the son of one of our first citizens."

'"All this nonsense leaves me unmoved," I said. "I am a man of iron, I never trouble to go to sleep, and I have sharper eyesight than Lynceus, the *Argo*'s look-out man. In fact, I may say that I am all eyes, like the giant Argos whom Jupiter once put in charge of the nymph Io."

'I had hardly finished recommending myself for the job before the old man hurried me along to a big house with its gates locked and barred. He took me through a small side door and along corridors until I reached a bedroom with closed shutters, where a woman in deep black sat wailing loudly in the half-light.

'The crier went up to her and said: "This man undertakes to guard your husband's body tonight; and he agrees to the fee."

'She pushed back the hair that shaded her beautiful grief-stricken face, and implored me to be vigilant at my post.

'"You need have no anxiety, Madam, if you make it worth my while afterwards."

'Nodding absently, she got up and led me into an adjoining room, where she showed me the corpse lying on a slab and wrapped in a pure white linen shroud. After another fit of weeping, she called in seven mourners as witnesses, also her secretary who had his writing materials with him. Then she said: "Gentlemen, I call you to witness that the nose is undamaged, so are both ears, the eyes are still in their sockets, the lips are whole, the chin the same." She touched each feature as she mentioned it, and the secretary wrote out the inventory, which the witnesses signed and sealed.

'I asked her as she was going away: "Will you be good enough, Madam, to see that I have everything I need for my vigil tonight?"

77

'"What sort of things?"

'"A good large lamp with enough oil in it to last until day-break; pots of wine; warm water for tempering; a cup; and a plateful of cold meat and vegetables left over from your supper."

'She shook her head angrily: "What an absurd request! Cooked meat and vegetables indeed in this house of mourning, where no fire has been lighted for days! Do you imagine that you have come here for a jolly supper party? You are expected to mourn and weep like the rest of us." Then, turning to her maid: "Myrrhina, fill the lamp, bring it back at once, shut the door and leave the guardian to his task."

'All alone with the corpse, I fortified my eyes for their vigil by rubbing them hard and kept up my spirits by singing. Twilight shaded into night, and night grew deeper and deeper, blacker and blacker, until my usual bed-time had passed and it was close on midnight. I had been only a little uncomfortable at first, but now I was beginning to feel thoroughly frightened when all of a sudden a weasel squeezed in through a hole in the door, stopped close by me and fixed her eyes intently on mine. The boldness of the creature was most disconcerting, but I managed to shout out: "Get away from here, you filthy little beast, or I'll break your neck. Run off and play hide and seek with your friends the mice. Do you hear me? I mean it."

'She turned tail and skipped out of the room, but as she did so, a sudden deep sleep stole over me and dragged me down with it into bottomless gulfs of dream. I fell on the floor and lay there so dead asleep that not even Delphic Apollo could have readily decided which of us two was the corpse; the body on the slab or the body on the floor. It was almost as though I had actually died and my corpse had been left without a guardian.

'At last the darkness began to fade and

The sentries of the Crested Watch 'gan shout

– crowing so loud that I eventually awoke, picked up the lamp and ran in terror to the slab. I pulled back the shroud and examined the corpse's face closely; to my huge relief I found it unmutilated. Almost at once the poor widow came running in, still weeping, with the seven witnesses behind her. She threw herself on the corpse and after kissing it again and again had the lamp brought close to make sure that all was well. Then she turned and called: "Philodespotus, come here!"

'Her steward appeared. "Philodespotus, pay this young man his fee at once. He has kept watch very well."

'As he counted me out the money she said: "Many thanks, young man, for your loyal services; they have earned you the freedom of this house."

'Delighted with my unexpected good luck, I gently tossed the bright gold coins up and down in my hand and answered: "I am much obliged to you, Madam. I shall be only too pleased to help you out again, whenever you may need my services."

'These words were scarcely out of my mouth when the whole household rushed at me with blows and curses, in an attempt to cancel their dreadful ominousness. One punched me in the face with his fists, another dug his elbows into my shoulder, someone else kicked me, my ribs were pummelled, my hair pulled, my clothes torn and before they finally threw me out of the house I felt like Adonis mauled by the wild boar, or Orpheus torn in pieces by the Thracian women.

'When I paused in the next street to collect my senses, and realized what I had said – it had certainly been a most tactless remark – I decided that I had got off lightly enough, all considered.

'By and by, after the customary "last summons", the agonized calling of his name by the relatives in case he might be only in a coma, the dead man was brought out of the house; and since he had been a man of such importance he was honoured with a public procession. As the cortège turned into the market place, an old man came running up, the tears streaming down his face. In a frenzy of grief he tore out tufts of his fine white hair, grabbed hold of the open coffin with both hands and screamed for vengeance.

'"Gentlemen of Hypata!" he cried, his voice choking with sobs, "I appeal to your honour, I appeal to your sense of justice and public duty! Stand by your fellow-citizen, this poor nephew of mine; see that his death is avenged in full on that evil woman, his widow. She, and she alone, is the murderess. To cover up a secret love-affair and to get possession of her husband's estate she killed him – she killed him with a slow poison." He continued to sob and scream, until the crowd was stirred to indignant sympathy, thinking that he probably had good ground for his accusations. Some shouted: "Burn her! Burn her!" and some: "Stone her to death!" and a gang of young hooligans was encouraged to lynch her.

'However, she denied her guilt with oaths and tears (though these carried little conviction), and devout appeals to all the gods and goddesses in Heaven to witness that she was utterly incapable of doing anything so wicked.

'"So be it then," said the old man, "I am willing to refer the case to divine arbitration. And here is Zatchlas the Egyptian, one of the leading necromancers of his country, who has undertaken, for a large fee, to recall my nephew's soul from the Underworld and persuade it to reanimate the corpse for a few brief moments."

'The person whom he introduced to the crowd was dressed in white linen, with palm-leaf sandals on his feet and a tonsured head. The old man kissed his hands and clasped his knees in a formal act of supplication. "Your reverence," he cried, "take pity on me. I implore you by the stars of Heaven, by the gods of the Underworld, by the five elements of nature, by the silence of night, by the dams that the swallows of Isis build about the Coptic island, by the flooding of the Nile, by the mysteries of Memphis, and by the sacred rattle of Pharos – I implore you by these holy things to grant my nephew's soul a brief return to the warmth of the sun, and so re-illumine his eyes that they may open and momentarily regain the sight that he has forfeited by his descent to the Land of the Dead. I do not argue with fate, I do not deny the grave what is her due; my plea is only for a brief leave of absence, during which the dead man may assist me in avenging his own murder – the only possible consolation I can have in my overwhelming grief."

'The necromancer, yielding to his entreaties, touched the corpse's mouth three times with a certain small herb and laid another on its breast. Then he turned to the east, with a silent prayer to the sacred disk of the rising sun. The whole marketplace gasped expectantly at the sight of these solemn preparations, and stood prepared for a miracle. I pushed in among the crowd and climbed up on a stone just behind the coffin, from which I watched the whole scene with rising curiosity.

'Presently the breast of the corpse began to heave, blood began to pour again through its veins, breath returned to its nostrils. He sat up and spoke in a querulous voice: "Why do you call me back to the troubles of this transitory life, when I have already drunk of the stream of Lethe and floated on the marshy waters of the Styx? Leave me alone, I say, leave me alone! Let me sleep undisturbed."

'The necromancer raised his voice excitedly: "What? You refuse to address your fellow-citizens here and clear up the mystery of your death? Don't you realize that if you hold back a single detail, I am prepared to call up the dreadful Furies and have your weary limbs tortured on the rack?"

'At this the dead man roused himself again and groaned out to the crowd: "The bed in which I lay only yesterday is no longer empty; my rival sleeps in it. My newly married wife has bewitched and poisoned me."

'The widow showed remarkable courage in the circumstance. She denied everything with oaths, and began contradicting and arguing with her late husband as though there were no such thing as respect for the dead. The crowd took different sides. Some were for burying the wicked woman alive in the same grave as her victim: but others refused to admit the evidence of a senseless corpse – it was quite untrustworthy, they said.

'The corpse soon settled the dispute. With another hollow groan it said: "I will give you incontrovertible proof that what I say is true, by disclosing something that is known to nobody but myself." Then he pointed up at me and said: "While that learned young student was keeping careful watch over my corpse, the ghoulish witches who were hovering near, waiting for a chance to rob it, did their best to deceive him by changing shape, but he saw through all their tricks. Though the bedroom doors were carefully bolted, they had slipped in through a knot-hole disguised as weasels and mice. But they threw a fog of sleep over him, so that he fell insensible, and then they called me by name, over and over again, trying to make me obey their magical commands. My weakened joints and cold limbs, despite convulsive struggles, could not respond immediately, but this student who had been cast into a trance that was a sort of death, happened to have the same name as I. So when they called: 'Thelyphron, Thelyphron, come!' he answered mechanically. Rising up like a senseless ghost he offered his face for the mutilation that they intended for mine; and they nibbled off first his nose and then his ears. But to divert attention from what they had done, they cleverly fitted him with a wax nose exactly like his own, and a pair of wax ears. The poor fellow remains under the illusion that he has been well rewarded for his vigilance, not meanly compensated for a frightful injury."

'Terrified by this story, I clapped my hand to my face to see if there were any truth in it, and my nose fell off; then I touched my ears, and they fell off too. A hundred fingers pointed at me from the crowd and a great roar of laughter went up. I burst into a cold sweat, leaped down from the stone, and slipped away between their legs like a frightened dog. Mutilated and ridiculous, I have never since cared to return to Miletus; and now I disguise the loss of my ears by growing my hair long and glue this canvas nose on my face for decency's sake.'

8 Apuleius

The Transformation of Lucius

Excerpt from Apuleius, *The Golden Ass*, translated by Robert Graves,
Penguin Books, 1950, pp. 88–93.

We spent the next few nights in the same delightful way, and
then one morning Fotis ran into my room, trembling with
excitement, and told me that her mistress, having made no head-
way by ordinary means in her affair with the Boeotian, intended
that night to become a bird and fly in at his bedroom window,
and that I must make careful preparations if I wished to watch
the performance.

At twilight, she led me on tip-toe, very, very quietly, up the
tower stairs to the door of the cock-loft, where she signed to me
to peep through a chink. I obeyed, and watched Pamphilë first
undress completely and then open a small cabinet containing
several little boxes, one of which she opened. It contained an
ointment which she worked about with her fingers and then
smeared all over her body from the soles of her feet to the crown
of her head. After this she muttered a long charm to her lamp,
and shook herself; and, as I watched, her limbs became gradually fledged with feathers, her arms changed into sturdy wings,
her nose grew crooked and horny, her nails turned into talons,
and soon there was no longer any doubt about it: Pamphilë
had become an owl. She gave a querulous hoot and made a few
little hopping flights until she was sure enough of her wings to
glide off, away over the roof-tops.

Not having been put under any spell myself, I was utterly
astonished and stood frozen to the spot. I rubbed my eyes to
make sure that I was really Lucius, and that this was no waking
dream. Was I perhaps going mad? I recovered my senses after a
time, took hold of Fotis's hand and laid it across my eyes. 'Dearest love,' I said, 'I beg you, by these sweet breasts of yours, to
grant me a tremendous favour – one which I can never hope to

repay – in proof of your perfect love for me. If you do this I promise to be your slave for ever more. Honey, will you try to get hold of a little of that ointment for me? I want to be able to fly. I want to hover around you like a winged Cupid in attendance on his Goddess.'

'H'm,' she said, 'so that is your game, is it, my darling? You want to play me a foxy trick: handing me an axe and persuading me to chop off my own feet? That's all very well, but it hasn't been so easy for me all this time to keep you safe from the she-wolves of Thessaly. You would have been easy meat if I hadn't protected you with my love. Now if you become a bird, how shall I be able to keep track of you? And when will I ever see you again?'

I protested: 'All the gods in Heaven forbid that I'm such a scoundrel as you make out. Listen: If I became an eagle and soared across the wide sky as Jupiter's personal courier, his thunderbolt proudly grasped in my claws, do you really suppose that even such winged glory as that would keep me from flying back every night to my love-nest in your arms? By that enchanting knot of hair on your head in which my soul lies helplessly entangled, I swear that I'm incapable by nature of loving any other woman in the whole world but my dearest Fotis. And anyhow, when I come to think of it, if that ointment really does turn me into a bird, I'll have to steer clear of the town; owls are such unlucky birds that when one blunders into a house by mistake, everyone does his best to catch it and nail it with outspread wings to the doorpost. Another thing, If I played truant from you and made love to the ladies in my owl disguise, what sort of a jolly welcome do you think they would give me? But that reminds me: once I'm an owl, what is the spell or antidote for turning me back into myself?'

'You need not worry about that,' she said. 'My mistress has taught me all the magical formulas. Not, of course, because she has a kindly feeling for me, but because when she arrives home from one of her adventures I have to prepare the necessary antidote for her to use. It really is extraordinary with what insignificant herbs one can produce a total transformation: tonight, for instance, she will need only a little anise and laurel leaves steeped in spring-water. She will drink some of the water, wash herself with the rest, and be a woman again at once. You can do the same after your flight.'

I made her reassure me on this point several times before she went, twitching with fear, up the tower stairs and brought me out one of the boxes from the casket. Hugging and kissing it I muttered a little prayer for a successful flight. Then I quickly pulled off my clothes, greedily stuck my fingers into the box and took out a large lump of ointment which I rubbed all over my body.

I stood flapping my arms, first the left and then the right, as I had seen Pamphilë do, but no little feathers appeared on them and they showed no sign of turning into wings. All that happened was that the hair on them grew coarser and coarser and the skin toughened into hide. Next, my fingers bunched together into a hard lump so that my hands became hooves, the same change came over my feet and I felt a long tail sprouting from the base of my spine. Then my face swelled, my mouth widened, my nostrils dilated, my lips hung flabbily down, and my ears shot up long and hairy. The only consoling part of this miserable transformation was the enormous increase in the size of a certain organ of mine; because I was by this time finding it increasingly difficult to meet all Fotis's demands upon it. At last, hopelessly surveying myself all over, I was obliged to face the mortifying fact that I had been transformed not into a bird, but into a plain jackass.

I wanted to curse Fotis for her stupid mistake, but found that I could no longer speak or even gesticulate; so I silently expostulated with her by sagging my lower lip and gazing sideways at her with my large, watery eyes.

When Fotis saw what had happened she beat her own face with both hands in a frenzy of self-condemnation. 'Oh, this is enough to kill me!' she wailed. 'In my flurry and fear I must have mistaken the box; two of them look exactly alike. Still, my poor creature, things are not nearly so bad as they seem, because in this case the antidote is one of the easiest to get hold of; all that you need do is to chew roses, which will at once turn you back into my Lucius. If only I had made my usual rose-garlands this evening! Then you would have been spared the inconvenience of being as ass for even a single night. At the first signs of dawn

I promise faithfully to go out and fetch what you need.' Over and over again she cursed her own stupidity and carelessness, but though I was no longer Lucius, and to all appearances a complete ass, a mere beast of burden, I still retained my mental faculties. I had a long and furious debate with myself as to whether or not I ought to bite and kick Fotis to death. She was a witch, wasn't she? And a very evil one, too. But in the end I decided that it would not only be dangerous but stupid to kill the one person who could help me to regain my own shape. Drooping my head and shaking my ears resignedly, I swallowed my rage for the time being and submitted to my cruel fate. I trotted off to the stable, where I would at least have the company of my white thoroughbred who had carried me so well while I was a man.

He was there with another ass, the property of my host – my former host – Milo, and really I did expect that, if dumb beasts have any natural feelings of loyalty, my horse would know me and take pity on my plight, welcoming me to his stable with as much courtesy as if I were a foreign ambassador on a visit to the Imperial Court at Rome. But – O Hospitable Jupiter and all the Gods of Faith and Trust! – my splendid horse and Milo's horrible ass put their heads together at once, suspecting that I had designs on their food, and formed an alliance against me. The moment I approached their manger they laid their ears back, wheeled round, and started kicking me in the face. My own horse! What gratitude! Here was I, driven right away from the very barley which only a few hours before I had measured out for him with my own hands.

As I stood in my lonely corner, banished from the society of my four-footed colleagues and deciding on a bitter revenge on them next morning as soon as I had eaten my roses and become Lucius again, I noticed a little shrine of the Mare-headed Mother, the Goddess Epona, standing in a niche of the post that supported the main beam of the stable. It was wreathed with freshly gathered roses, the very antidote that I needed. I balanced hopefully on my hindlegs, pushed my forelegs as far up the post as they would go, stretched my neck to its fullest extent and shot out my lips. But by a piece of really bad luck, before I could eat any of the roses, my slave who was acting as groom happened to catch me at work. He sprang up angrily from the heap of straw on which he was lying and shouted: 'I've had quite enough trouble from this damned cuddy. First he tries to rob his stable-mates and now he plays the same trick on the blessed gods! If I don't flog the sacrilegious brute until he's too lame to stir a hoof . . .' He groped about until he found a bundle of faggots, picked out a thick knobbly one, the biggest of the lot, and began unmercifully whacking my flanks.

A sudden loud pounding and banging on the outer gate. Distant cries of 'Thieves! Thieves!' The groom dropped his faggot and ran off in terror. The next moment, the courtyard gate burst open and armed bandits rushed in. A few neighbours hurried to Milo's assistance but the bandits beat them off easily. Their swords gleamed like the rays of the rising sun in the bright light of the torches that they carried. They had axes with them, too, which they used to break open the heavily barred door of the strong room in the central part of the house. It was stuffed with Milo's valuables, all of which they hauled out and hastily divided into a number of separate packages. However, there were more packages to carry than robbers to carry them, so they had to use their wits. They came into our stable, led the three of us out, loaded us with as many of the heavier packages as they could pile on our backs, and drove us out of the now ransacked house, threatening us with sticks. Then they hurried forward into trackless hill-country, beating us hard all the way.

9 Julio Caro Baroja

Witchcraft amongst the German and Slavonic Peoples

Excerpts from Julio Caro Baroja, *The World of the Witches*, translated by Nigel Glendinning, Weidenfeld & Nicolson, 1964, pp. 47–57.

The type of witch known in classical antiquity is not very different from the one with which we are familiar today. She continued to exist in Europe a long time after the fall of the Roman Empire and even down to our own times. The same, as we shall see, is true of the witch amongst European peoples who were not part of the classical world.

In the first place, let us consider those peoples of Germanic origin whose magical interests and activities are well documented. If we accept the evidence about them, it would appear that, among the Germanic tribes too, each individual social class had its own particular brand of magic; even the gods used magic in certain circumstances. The practice of magic in these tribes also corresponded to their logical and social order (the 'logos' and the 'ethos'), however surprising this may seem. This is also true, of course, of other communities which have recently been studied in detail; maleficent magic flourishes during certain states of tension.

In the highest levels of Germanic society the kings practised magic publicly, and their success was more or less generally admitted.

Among the Swedes, Erick 'of the windy hat' had remarkable powers as king and magician (1). In other cases, the trials and misfortunes of the community were attributed to the fact that the reigning monarch lacked the necessary magical power to deal with the adverse circumstances. But coming down in the social scale we also discover that in ancient Scandinavia every magical activity was thought to be the property of a particular family. Thus, 'all' the sooth-sayers, 'all' the witches and 'all' the magicians could be traced back to three specific forebears, just as the giants could (2).

The division of human activities according to families presupposes the handing down of knowledge from the period of myths. Witchcraft or maleficent magic has its own special terminology, and is completely defined by the word *seid* (3).

There are passages in Icelandic Sagas in which whole families are accredited with the power of witchcraft: father, mother and children (4). However, as in the classical world, women, or particular types of women, were believed to have more special powers.

The passage in Tacitus's *Germania* which relates how the men of that country believed women to be sacred and always attached great importance to their opinions, warnings and advice (5), has been the object of numerous conflicting interpretations – like other parts of that work.

But if the cases of Velleda (6) or Ganna (7), both heroines of German history, can be adduced in support of this view, there is also good reason to believe that fear as well as respect and veneration was sometimes felt for women; fear of the spells of which they were held to be capable.

Both early Germanic literature and historical works, written in Latin about the Germanic peoples at a later date, make frequent references to the ambivalent position of women in that society.

There are, for example, numerous passages in the *Edda* which allude to the skill of women in magic and the dangers run by those who allow themselves to be dominated by women:

Flee from the dangers of sleeping in the arms of a witch; let her not hold you close to her. She will make you disregard the assemblies of the people and the words of the prince; you will refuse to eat and shun the company of other men, and you will feel sad when you go to your bed.

Such were the supernatural warnings given to Lodfafner (8). These and other passages seem to support the case for the existence of a 'Circean complex' which has completely controlled men's actions at various periods.

The picture of the *old witch* is also extremely common in the *Edda*. Such a one, for example, was Angerbode, mother of the wolves who will ultimately eat the sun and the moon:

> East of Midgard, in the iron forest,
> Sat the old witch.
> She fed the fearful race
> of Fenrer ... (9).

At the same time, witchcraft, or magic for evil ends, is the constant subject of criticism as one of the most anti-social activities possible.

But it must be emphasized that in the pagan German world the gods were not only aiders and abetters of witchcraft but sorcerers themselves. Loke or Loki, the evil one, was able to say to Odin, the Father of the gods: 'They say you have practised magic in Samsoe, that you have made spells like any *Vala*: you have wandered through the country disguised as a witch. What, I say, could be viler in a man than this' (10). The same Loki could shout at Freya: 'Be silent! You are a poisoner and you work magic. Thanks to your spells the powers that were propitious to your brother have turned against him' (11).

There can be no doubt, therefore, that magic has its place in the life of gods as well as men. The question that Lucan asked himself about the gods on Olympus might well have been put by a German about those in Valhalla. A *vis magica* exists which fascinates or coerces 'them' just as it controls the strong and the meek in the world.

Several legends which have survived in more modern versions than those which have so far been quoted, prove that the Germanic peoples were dominated by fear of witches in their everyday life.

They frequently attributed the misfortunes of their kings to witches. One of the best known of these legends is the one about the death of the Danish king Frotho III. The usual source for this tale in books on magic is the German historian, A. Krantz.

The king, who is said to have lived at the same time as Christ, seems to have used magic in much the same way as other more or less legendary figures. He had a witch at his court who was famed for her magic. Her son had great faith in her powers and plotted with her on one occasion to rob the king's treasury, since the king was advanced in years. When they had carried out the robbery, they went to an isolated house they owned far from the court. The king, following the hints of a number of people, connected their flight with the robbery and decided to go in person to look for them. When the witch saw him coming she used her magical powers to change her son into a bull who went out to meet him. The king sat down to look at the animal. But the witch gave him little time for contemplation. The bull charged him violently and killed him (12).

This is roughly the story as Krantz has it, although it should be borne in mind that there are other slightly different versions (13). For present purposes, however, this will serve. The important thing in this instance is the general outline of the legend. It is also worth while pointing out that the person chiefly responsible for popularizing the story believed that old witches were perfectly capable of achieving the same or even more astonishing results in his own times (i.e. in the fifteenth and sixteenth centuries) (14).

The Germanic world was dominated by belief in witchcraft from its northern extremities to the shores of the Mediterranean where the Visigoths and Lombards lived; from the steppes of eastern Europe to the Atlantic islands. Even at the height of their power, men lived in constant fear of witches.

This fear and hatred led the Germans to accuse their enemies of practising witchcraft or of being descended from evil witches. An example of this is the traditional story about the origin of the Huns. This was first written down by a historian of the Goths called Jornandes, or Jordanes, in the sixth century, and it was later reproduced and modified by many other historians. According to the legend, King Filimer, after conducting a survey into the customs of his people at a very early period, discovered that a number of sorceresses lived among them. These he banished to the remote and deserted regions of Scythia so that they should have no ill-effect on others. However, as a result of the contact between these women and certain foul spirits who wandered about the same deserts, the Huns were born (15). Those were the sorceresses called *alrunae* or *haliurunnae* which also appear in other texts. To call someone a 'son of a witch' is a very ancient insult.

It is an equally hallowed custom to attribute black powers to one's nearest communal enemy. So far as the specific case of the Huns is concerned, it is highly probable that witchcraft was common among them (just as it later was among the Magyars and Hungarians). But their bad reputation may have been partly due to the intense fear they inspired in others; in other words, it may have been due to the feeling of comparative impotence that others felt in their presence.

More or less mythical stories about the power of specific witches are also to be found in the old Slav chronicles.

There is, for instance, a legendary episode in the earliest history of Bohemia which is worth recording. A certain chief named Krok died at the end of the seventh century, in 690, and left three daughters. The first, Kazi or Brelum, had a considerable knowledge of medicinal plants which she put to practical use. The second, called Tecka or Tekta, was a sooth-sayer and diviner; whenever there was a robbery in the country she revealed the person who was responsible and, if anything was lost, she could tell where it was. The third, Libuscha, Libussa or Lobussa, was a sybil, skilled in witchcraft and vastly better at it than any other man or woman of her times. Thanks to her magic, she was able to make the Bohemians elect Przemislaw as their leader, and then marry him. She predicted the rise of Prague and died after a long and glorious life. However, when she died, women had become so accustomed to directing affairs that they refused to submit to the rule of men again. A young maid named Wlasca, a born leader, called the women together and addressed them approximately in these words:

Our lady Libussa governed this kingdom while she was alive. Why should not I now govern with your help? I know all her secrets; the skill in spells and the art of augury which were her sister Tecka's are mine; I also know as much medicine as Brelum did; for I was not in her service for nothing. If you will join with me and help me I believe we may get complete control over the men.

Her ideas met with the approval of the women she had gathered together. So she gave them a potion to drink to make them loathe their husbands, brothers, lovers and the whole male sex immediately. Fortified by this, they slew nearly all the men and laid siege to Przemislaw in the castle of Diewin. The women are supposed to have ruled for seven years, and a series of rather comical laws are said to have been passed by them. However, in the end

Przemislaw returned to the throne, for he too was something of a magician. Later authors retold this story and added their own particular interpretations (16).

The Middle Ages was a great period for preserving traditions as well as for making them, and the magical processes described in the texts are monotonously repeated. Ones which are already to be found in the Vedic poems reappear in the darkest years of the the Middle Ages and continue to recur even today.

The story of King Duff of Scotland, for instance, supposed to have taken place at some time between A.D. 967 and 972, follows a typically well-worn pattern. According to the chronicles, an illness which he caught was attributed to witchcraft. Investigations were made and some witches were eventually found cooking a waxen image of the king over a slow fire. This explained the nature of the king's illness, since he was in a continual sweat. Once the women had been condemned the king was restored to health (17).

The Nature of Civil and Religious Laws

The laws of the barbarians, written in Latin and devised for the northern peoples who ruled for centuries over former provinces of the Roman Empire, abound in provisions against sorcerers and those who followed their advice.

In Book 6, subtitle 2, of the Spanish *Fuero Juzgo*, for example, one finds four laws of the Chindasvint period which condemn all the possible varieties of magic. The first of these applies to servants and simple folk who consult *ariolos*, *aruspices* and *vaticinatores* – diviners, fortune-tellers, and enchanters – about the health or death of the king. The second refers to those who give poisonous herbs to others. The third is about sorcerers and rain-makers who ruin the wine and the crops by their spells; those who disturb men's minds by invoking the Devil; and those who make nocturnal sacrifices to the Devil. The fourth condemns those who use verbal or written spells to harm the bodies, minds and property of others (18).

These Spanish laws and others, both civil and ecclesiastical, of the same period, condemn magic in general without any specific reference to the sex of the person in question. But similar laws in old Gaul, and other countries which were also under the rule of christianised barbarians, make frequent references to the sex of the sorcerers and also make other allusions which are worth examination. Perhaps certain types of witches were more common in Gaul than in Spain under the Visigoths.

A passage in Pomponius Mela which has often been discussed seems to imply that there were women who practised magic for beneficent purposes among the ancient Gauls. Nine of them were attached to a temple, and lived under a rule of perpetual chastity (19). Whatever the truth of this may be, it does not seem to affect the general point about the place of women in witchcraft.

We know from other sources – not wholly reliable ones however – that witches abounded in Gaul in the later period of the Roman Empire. They were occasionally consulted by people of high rank, and were equated with druids (as 'druidesses' are called in texts which relate to the third century A.D.) (20). These witches continued to multiply and thrive in later periods, and they were a source of worry to more than one family of high social standing at the court of the Merovingian kings. This is revealed in the works of the best-known historians of the period, who also point out that more than one woman paid dearly for her reputation as a witch.

In 578 Queen Fredegond lost a son. Suspicious individuals suggested that his death had been caused by magic and spells. A courtier accused Mummolus, one of the prefects (who was also disliked by the Queen), of instigating the crime. But those who actually committed it were said to be certain women of Paris. The latter confessed under torture to the murder of the Queen's son, and admitted killing many other people too (21). It is not hard to imagine the fate of the prefect and the ladies in question.

This was not the only episode in the violent life of Queen Fredegond in which witches had an important role. Earlier, she accused her step-child Clovis of killing two of her sons with the aid or complicity of an old witch and her daughter. These three she also managed to kill (22). Yet this did not stop her from making spells and consulting witches herself when she felt like it (23).

Fredegond was no exception in the land over which she reigned. The repression of magic, which she herself practised and which she accused others of practising, was one of the major concerns of the civil and religious authorities at the time and at later periods.

Sometimes, however, there are noticeable variations in the ways in which repressive measures are carried out: a divergence of opinion between legal and ecclesiastical authorities.

It is a long time since a Frenchman called Garinet collected together the most famous laws passed by the Frankish kings and their successors against the practice of magic. This was ranked as one of the manifestations of paganism which had to be eradicated (as it was in the last laws made under the Roman Empire). More recently these laws have been studied in a more scholarly way. But Garinet's book is still useful (24).

Superficially there is little difference between these laws and those passed by the Christian Roman Emperors and by the Visigothic and Ostrogothic rulers in their respective kingdoms. Nor do these laws differ from others known to have been passed during the same dark ages in England, Germany and Hungary. The laws are apparently so similar that books on them are inevitably boring to read. But they are worth studying, even if not in great detail: for, suddenly, amongst the mass of virtually identical items, we find one that is quite different and extremely significant. As early as A.D. 743, Childeric III published an edict condemning pagan and magical practices as if they were much the same thing. Amongst the former are included sacrifices to the dead, and other sacrifices which were still being made at that time not to the old gods, but to Holy Martyrs and confessors in places close to the churches themselves. Among magical practices listed, we find ligatures, fortune-telling, augury, incantations and phylacteries (25).

Charlemagne, following in the footsteps of Childeric and other Merovingian kings, published several edicts urging his subjects to forsake their superstitious beliefs. When mere exhortation proved useless, he resorted to edicts which laid down sentences appropriate to these crimes. These edicts specifically condemned all kinds of witchcraft, such as the making of wax figures, summoning devils and using love philtres, disturbing the atmosphere and raising storms, putting curses on people and causing the fruits of the earth to wither away, drying up the milk of some people's domestic animals to give it to others, practising astrology and making talismans. The law laid down that, in future, those who practised the arts of the Devil would be dishonoured and treated like murderers, poisoners and thieves; those who consulted them and made use of them would be given a similar sentence, and in some cases that meant death (26).

In A.D. 873, Charles the Bald issued a decree in Quierzy-sur-Oise, declaring that he desired to fulfil his kingly duties laid down by the saints in the proper manner. He had learnt that sorcerers and witches had appeared in various parts of his kingdom, bringing illness and even death to a number of people. And his intention was to drive out the godless, and those who made philtres and poisons: 'We therefore expressly recommend the lords of the realm to seek out and apprehend with the greatest possible diligence those who are guilty of these crimes in their respective countries. If they are convicted, whether they are men or women, they must perish, for justice and the law demand it. If they are under suspicion or accused without being convicted, and if the testimony against them is not sufficient to prove their guilt, they shall be submitted to the will of God. This shall decide whether they are to be pardoned or condemned. But the associates and accomplices of those who are really guilty, both men and women, shall be put to death, so that all knowledge of such a heinous crime may vanish from our dominions' (27).

These three texts of three different periods may suffice to show how hard civil law was on those who were accused of crimes of witchcraft in the eighth and ninth centuries. Probably, these laws were often enforced in an arbitrary way, and people must frequently have been accused of such crimes in much the same violent and fanatical manner as Queen Fredegond accused her step-son. The danger of arraigning people who might be totally innocent had yet to be recognized.

This explains why the Church, which absolutely condemned paganism, let alone magic, from a theological point of view, promulgated a series of dispositions which would, on occasion, soften the harsh effects of civil law. This moderation may partially have been due to propagandistic motives, aimed to attract the great mass of people who remained unconverted to Christianity in the country areas and small towns. But perhaps the more moderate dispositions of the Church also reflect the ideas of St Augustine.

J. B. Thiers in his *Traité des superstitions* collected together a large number of references to Canon laws of Church Councils, and to other decrees which severely condemned the practice of magic, dating from the sixth, seventh and eighth centuries and later periods also (28). Some of these emphasize the dangerous spiritual effects of magic, but others insist that sorcerers themselves are often victims of the illusions and deceits of the Devil, and deny that it is necessary to believe categorically in their powers.

Even after the promulgation of the decrees of Charlemagne which have already been mentioned, the prelates who were summoned to the Council of Tours in 813 still felt the need for priests to warn the faithful that spells could not help sick or dying persons or animals; they were nothing but illusions and tricks of the Devil (29). In other instances the same ecclesiastical authorities disputed the validity of facts which civil law accepted, or qualified the conclusions that were drawn from them.

A good example of this is that of Agobard, Archbishop of Lyons (779–840), who, in spite of the general views held at the time, severely criticized those who believed that certain human beings were capable of bringing on rain and hail-storms. He also censured those who held Duke Grimald responsible for sending sorcerers to throw harmful magic powders into fields, forests and streams, when the oxen belonging to the smallholders in the diocese were striken by an epidemic (30).

The prelates who attended the sixth Council of Paris in 829 were in closer agreement with the civil laws and edicts. The eleventh canon of the Council expressed the following opinion:

There are other very dangerous evils which are certainly legacies of paganism, such as magic, astrology, incantations and spells, poisoning, divination, enchantment, and the interpretation of dreams. These evils ought to be severely punished, as the laws of God ordain. But there is no doubt, as many learned men have witnessed, that there are some people capable of so perverting the minds of others with the Devil's illusions, (by giving them philtres, drugged food and phylacteries), that they become confused and insensible to the ills they are made to suffer. It is also said that these people can disturb the air with their

97

spells, send hail-storms, predict the future, take produce and milk from one person to give to another, and do a thousand similar things. If any such be found, be they men or women, they should be severely punished, particularly since, in their malice and temerity, they fear not the Devil nor do they renounce him publicly (31).

There is undoubtedly a conflict between these views and Agobard's: one which is to be found time and again in later periods. It even occurs in certain civil laws, some of which put forward opinions which are flatly contradicted by other laws in the same code.

There is, for example, an act dated 789 amongst the laws of the Frankish kings; it refers to Saxony and condemns belief in *strigae* and their ability to eat men, expressing the view that they ought to be burnt for it. The same act prescribes capital punishment for all who believe such things (32). There is clearly a connexion between this and another law to be found in the *Leges Langobardicae*, dating probably from the reign of King Rotharius. Yet although it is conceived in much the same spirit, this law holds that, from a Christian point of view, *strigae* or *mascae* cannot be capable of the acts they are believed to perform (33).

On the other hand, the popes who were concerned with the conversion of central European and, above all, Northern peoples, gave very categorical instructions on the subject to kings and prelates of the Church. Pope Gregory II, for example, ordered Bishop Martinian and the priest called George who went with him to Bavaria, to forbid spells and enchantments, which were relics of paganism, although he makes no reference to the punishment of those involved.

On one occasion Pope Gregory VII wrote to the King of Denmark asking him to avoid, as far as possible, persecuting innocent women who were thought to have caused storms or epidemics. Earlier, Pope Leo VII had sent an instruction dated 936 to Archbishop Gerhard of Lorch, intended for the authorities of southern Germany, which again took a lenient view of those accused of witchcraft. Answering a specific enquiry he maintained that 'although, by the old law, such people were condemned to death, ecclesiastical law spared their lives so that they could repent'.

This rather ambiguous situation is typical of a period of transition like the Middle Ages. On the one hand, we have the passionate beliefs of the masses just converted to Christianity or still pagan, and on the other, the doubt and pragmatism of the ecclesiastical authorities in the face of popular beliefs and civil law.

References
1. John Magnus, *Gothorumque sueonumque historia, ex probatis antiquorum monumentis collecta* . . . (Basle, 1558), XVII, ch. 12, p. 640.
2. Mlle R. du Puget, *Les Eddas traduites de l'ancien idiome scandinave* (Paris, n.d.), p. 21 (p. 5 of Gylf's voyage) and p. 249 (p. 32 of Hyndla's poem).
3. H. Ch. Lea, *Histoire de l'Inquisition au Moyen Age*, III, pp. 486–90.
4. Fernand Mossé, *La Laxdœla Saga: Légende historique islandaise traduite du vieux norrois avec une introduction et des notes* (Paris, 1914), pp. 99, 103, 104, 105–7, 111–12.
5. Tacitus, *Germ.*, 8.
6. Tacitus, *Hist.*, IV, 61–6; VI, 22–4. Dio Casius, LXVII, 5.
7. Velleda's successor.
8. *Les Eddas*, op. cit., p. 138 (pp. 4–5 of Lodfafner's song).
9. ibid., p. 27.
10. ibid., p. 188 (p. 24 of Aeger's feast). cf. also p. 115 (p. 34 of Wola the Wise's prediction).
11. ibid., p. 190 (p. 32 of Aeger's feast). A further accusation is on p. 195 (p. 56 of Aeger's feast).
12. A. Krantz, *Regnorum Aquilonarium, Daniae, Sueciae, Noruagiae Chronica* (Frankfurt, 1583), fols. 20 v–21 1 (Book I, ch. 32).
13. See, for example, Pierre le Loyer, *Discours, et histoires des spectres, visions et apparitions des esprits* (Paris, 1605), Book II, ch. 7, p. 142.
14. A. Krantz, op. cit., fol. 16 v (Book I, ch. 23).
15. Jordanes, *De rebus gothicis*, 24. Many years afterwards, John Magnus maintained that witches had intercourse with men and not with spirits (*Gothorumque sueonumque historia*, VI, 24, pp. 258–9). The number of witches varies considerably from one edition to the next.
16. 'Chronicon Bohemiae', Book II, ch. 3-10, in *Reliquiae manuscriptorum omnis aevi diplomatum ac monumentorum ineditorum* (Halle, 1737), XI, pp. 131–45. cf. P. J. Schafarik, *Slawische Alterthümer*, II (Leipzig, 1844), p. 421.
17. H. Boethius, *Scotorum Historiae a prima gentis origine* (Paris, 1574), Book XI, fols. 220 v–221 v. Pierre le Loyer, *Discours*, op. cit., Book IV, ch. 15, pp. 369–70.
18. *Fuero juzgo en latin y castellano, cotejado con los más antiguos y preciosos códices por la Real Academia Española* (Madrid, 1815), pp. 81–2 and 104–6 (Latin with Spanish translation).

19. Pomponius Mela, III, 7.
20. *Scriptores Historiae Augustae: Alex-Sev.* (biography ascribed to Lampridius); *Numerianus* (biography ascribed to Flavius Vopiscus).
21. Gregory of Tours, *Hist. franc.*, VI, 35.
22. ibid., V, 40.
23. ibid., VII, 44.
24. Jules Garinet, *Histoire de la magie en France, depuis le commencement de la Monarchie jusqu'à nos jours* (Paris, 1818), pp. 6–7, 39–40, etc., and appendices.
25. Baluze, *Capitularia regum francorum*, I (Paris, 1677), cols. 150–52, ch. 4 of the Capitular, comprising an 'Indiculus superstitionum et paganiarum'.
26. Baluze, op. cit., I, cols. 220 (ch. 18, dated 789), 518 (ch. 40, uncertain date), 707 (ch. 21 of Book I of Ansegisus' collection), 837 (ch. 69 of Book V of the same collection), 929 (ch. 26 of Book VI), 962 (ch. 215 of Book VI), 999 (ch. 397 of Book VI), 1104 (ch. 369–70 of Book VII).
27. Baluze, op. cit., II, cols. 230–31 (§VII).
28. J. B. Thiers, *Traité des superstitions qui regardent les sacremens*, I (Paris, 1741), pp. 178, 198, and *passim*.
29. Title 3 of Canon 42. cf. Joseph Hansen, *Zauberwahn, Inquisition und Hexenprozess im Mittelalter und die Entstehung der grossen Hexenverfolgung* (München-Leipzig, 1900), pp. 66–7.
30. Agobard's work, 'Liber contra insulsam vulgi opinionem de grandinem', can be found in Migne's *Patrology*, CIV, cols. 147 ff. Nearly all writers on the subject quote it. See, for example, Hansen, op. cit., p. 73.
31. Cf. J. B. Thiers, op. cit., note 28.
32. Baluze, op. cit., I, cols. 251–2: 'VI. Si quis a diabolo deceptus crediderit, secundum morem paganorum, virum aliquem aut feminam strigam esse et homines comedere, et propter hoc ipsam incenderit, vel carnem ejus ad comedendum dederit, vel ipsam comederit, capitis sententia punietur.'
33. Hansen, op. cit., pp. 76–7, also refers to the laws promulgated by Stephen of Hungary (A.D. 997–1038). General histories like Soldan's, or the more recent one by Baissac, contain plenty of material on this period.

10 R. F. Fortune

Sorcerers of Dobu

Excerpt from R. F. Fortune, *Sorcerers of Dobu: The Social Anthropology of the Dobu Islanders of the Western Pacific*, Routledge, 1932, pp. 150–54.

Witchcraft and Sorcery

Death is caused by witchcraft, sorcery, poisoning, suicide, or by actual assault. There is no concept of accident. Falling from coconut palms or other trees is due to witchcraft; similarly of other accidents.

When the Tewara[1] men were in the Amphletts on an overseas voyage they went for the night to a small sandbank near by to obtain sea-birds' eggs. The canoe was not well beached. It floated off in the night, the supports of the outrigger boom smashed, and outrigger boom and canoe sank separately. Fortunately both were washed up on a sand-bar within swimming distance. Every man blamed the flying witches. 'They charm so that we sleep like the dead and do not guard our canoe. They lay no hand on the canoe. They say "you go to sea" and the canoe goes.' Some of the men blamed their own women of Tewara, declaring that their habits were vile. Some blamed the women of Gumasila, who were jealous, presumably, of their taking sea-birds' eggs from an island near Gumasila.

Witchcraft is the woman's prerogative, sorcery the man's. A witch does all of her work in spirit form while her body sleeps, but only at the bidding of the fully conscious and fully awake woman and as the result of her spells, it is said. Not only is all that we term accident as opposed to sickness ascribed exclusively to witchcraft, but a particular way of causing illness

1. The island on which Fortune carried out most of his research. He describes it as 'an outlying small island, with a population of forty-four in 1928, twenty-two in 1959'. It lies about twenty-three miles north-north-east of Dobu – *Ed*.

and death is the monopoly of women. This method is that of spirit abstraction from the victim.

The man, as sorcerer, has the monopoly of causing sickness and death by using spells on the personal leavings of the victim. When the diviner of the person responsible for an illness beards a witch he says: 'Restore X's spirit to him'; when he beards a man he says: 'Produce X's personal leavings that you have in your house.' Such personal leavings may be remains of food, excreta, footprints in sand, body dirt, or a bush creeper with a malevolent charm first breathed into it which the sorcerer watched his victim brush against and which he subsequently took to his house to treat further.

Moving among the men mainly I soon became aware of a convention. Death is always referred to the werebana.[2] That village is weeds and grass, that island is uninhabited now – the flying witches. Yet these same men in reality feared sorcery as much as witchcraft, all had their killing powers, and little by little I heard of what they had done with them. By convention only, death is referred to the women's activities. Underneath the convention was the knowledge that men themselves had a great hand in it – only this is not referred to by men, except in great confidence that usually betrays itself first in a panic and is pressed home from the panic by the field worker. The sorcery of other places is referred to freely – the sorcerers there, the danger of poison in the food offered one.

The women do not seem to have enough solidarity to turn the tables and to blame all death upon the barau, the male practitioner, as they might. Instead, they voice the general convention – the flying witches are responsible. The diviner takes no notice of this convention of speech. He is as likely to divine a sorcerer as a witch in any concrete case of illness.

The women, however, have a counter convention established. No woman will admit to a man that she knows a witchcraft spell. The men have the benefit of a general alibi. But a man will admit to his wife that he knows death-dealing spells, whereas she will not reciprocate. The women have the benefit of an individual alibi. The diviner, and all persons discarding courtesy of speech, take no more account of the women's alibi than of

2. Flying witches – Ed.

the men's. Courtesy of speech in direct conversation matters greatly in Dobu. If A tells B that B's greatest friend is vile, B replies: 'Yes, he is vile.' B may take secret measures to revenge himself on A, but in conversation there is never any controversy in such a matter.

The Dobuan men are quite certain that the women of the Trobiands do not practise witchcraft spells, as they are equally certain that their own women do so practise. Accordingly the men of Dobu feel safer in the Trobriands among a strange people of a strange speech than they do in their own homes – in direct and striking contrast to their greater fear in the Amphletts and in parts of Fergusson Island than in their own homes, and in contrast also to their greater fear in other Dobuan districts than in their own home districts. I saw this most clearly for myself; there was no doubt about their attitudes – considerable fear at home, sharpened greatly in all strange places, but blunted in the Trobriands. Whether this great certainty of feeling is founded on a solid fact that women in Dobu do practise witchcraft spells, or merely on acceptance of the Trobriand freedom from Dobuan-like fears, I should be loath to say. I have worked with the men intimately and I know that the diviner's discarding of the convention clearing the male sex is correct. I know the men complain about the lying they believe there is in the women's convention. But only a woman working with women could tell what the facts are – whether they are really innocent or whether they are putting up a convention counter to the men's. Personally I suspect the latter. The women certainly own *tabus*. A few men say themselves that they penetrated beneath the women's convention and actually got witchcraft spells from women by threatening them with violence. Such men are few, and may be telling the truth or not. The probability is that women do own spells, however. The witch charged as a witch by the diviner summoned to a sick person does not deny witchcraft any more often than a sorcerer in a similar position denies sorcery. Such denials are few in all, for a reason that we shall discuss later. It would be unreasonable that women should suffer so without benefit when spells may be so easily made from the natural expression of hate. Innovation in spells occurs despite native belief to the contrary. In the *kula* magic we shall meet

Tauwau, the culture hero who created galvanized iron roofs, nailed houses, bully beef in tins, and European diseases. Side by side with Tauwau in the magic are lines that are as old as any. Sometimes *kaiana*, fire vented forth from the pubes of flying witches, is seen at night. Then the village gathers together around its fires, which are kept burning all night, and none retires to the house to sleep. The entire village became more than usually dormant in the afternoon on such occasions. On other occasions a woman would wake from a nightmare convinced that the flying witches were chasing her spirit and were just outside baulked by her spirit's good luck in getting home before them. Then the night would be hideous with a ghastly yelling or alternate high and low shrieking, expressing such fear in its very sound as to be contagious enough to myself who knew its origin. Next day sometimes the woman and her husband were outwardly serene and I had to get the whole story from someone else. But sometimes the woman or her husband would be shaken and ill and drawn in appearance all day, confined to the mat – in which case I dosed the patient with salts or quinine according to taste.

Because of danger from witch or sorcerer it is not advisable to go alone. Frequently in broad daylight I was warned not to do it. 'You go alone' in surprise and in dissuasion. In strange places they looked after me well. Once in Raputat of Sanaroa I went with three natives, fresh from the canoe under the hot sun, to bathe in a cool spring ten minutes away from the shore. Two bathed and went away on an errand. One remained. I was resting in my bathing V's and not going back. My native hung about chewing a stem of grass and gazing at the distance. This lasted a long while. Finally I said: 'It's all right, Kisian, I know the track now.' 'No, I shall wait for you. New Guinea vile – witchcraft, sorcery is here.' That is typical. Even at home it is rare for anyone to be alone except on adultery or stealing bent; and often adultery and stealing are cooperative ventures, two men going together. Many means of death exist by day. Only in the night, however, bats are abroad. If a bat approaches a house, crying aloud, panic rises. They pale quite visibly, talk stops abruptly; and on several occasions it happened when natives were in my house by night, they said '*werebana*' in an undertone, sat saying nothing for five or ten minutes, and then as soon as was decent got up and slunk away. The night is a little more feared than the day because it is the time for sleep when the spirits of the sleepers go abroad in the pursuit of the black art. Most of the black art of the daytime is done in the flesh. But fear of the night work is only slightly greater than fear of the day work.

The situation created by witchcraft beliefs in marriage we have already treated. The members of village X may refer freely to their fear of certain women of village Y, until inter-marriage takes place. Then comment is forced underground, as it is a great insult to 'call witchcraft' within a husband's range of gaining report of comment upon his close relatives in law or upon his wife. All men have a nervousness of their wives' complicity, and a fear of mothers-in-law. Only the most reckless will say privily of another man: 'It would appear that last night he slept with his wife – but did he sleep with his wife? Or was she far away? With an empty skin at his side he slept.'

I may add as well as witches who are mortal women (*werebana*) there are also sea witches (*gelaboi*) who have no present human embodiment.

Methods of Divination

Divining is usually done by water-gazing or crystal-gazing. In the former case water is put into a wooden bowl and hibiscus flowers thrown on the water. The diviner charms: 'the water is water no longer'. He cuts the water-in-changed-nature open. At the bottom of the cut he sees the spirit of the witch who has abstracted the spirit of his patient and who now has it concealed, or the spirit of the sorcerer who has the *sumwana*, body leavings of the patient, and now has them concealed. Volcanic crystals may be used instead of water.

Spirit abstraction by a *gelaboi* may be indicated by the patient making delirious or semi-delirious statements about canoes at sea, canoes used by these spiritual *gelaboi*. Great attention is paid to the patient's ravings if there are any.

If the patient runs about in delirium then again his *sumwana* has been taken by a sorcerer. The sorcerer in such case has bound up the *sumwana*, winding it about in some receptable with bush creeper. This winding is compared to the way in which the tree oppossum, *Cuscus*, winds its tail around branches and darts about apparently aimlessly. The sorcerer's winding of *sumwana* has made the patient run about like the oppossum.

The diviner may bend forward the middle finger of the patient, grasping it tightly at the first joint. If the tip of the finger does not flush then spirit abstraction by a witch has occurred. If it does flush then the patient's *sumwana* has been taken by a sorcerer.

Again the diviner may tell by the body odour of the patient the sex of the person responsible. None could define how this was done.

These measures of noting the symptoms of delirium, or of trying the finger bending or the smelling tests, precede the water or crystal gazing which finally determines the exact identity of the person responsible for the illness. The attention paid to delirium narrows down the circle of people within which the diviner's judgement may operate, but the other two tests leave him free by their nebulousness. Flushing or no flushing in the finger bent is rarely so obvious as to rule out subjective appraisal of the results, a subjective factor that is even more obvious in the smelling test.

Unless the agent revealed is a *gelaboi*, a *yatala* or, as it is also called, a *bwokumatana*, follows. The diviner summons the village, a member of which he has 'seen' in his water-gazing. The person divined is charged with the deed by the diviner. Then follows a promise of cessation of enmity and of active black magic by the witch or the sorcerer charged, provided her or his just complaint against the patient is remedied by the patient immediately. The patient pays the black magician and the diviner, and recovers – unless unremedied grudges undivined as yet still exist elsewhere.

After a death the kin of the dead divine whose grudge killed their kinsman by watching the corpse as the mourners file by one by one as is the custom. When the guilty person passes the corpse it is believed to twitch in one place or another. So strong is this belief that twitches are probably often fancied. In any case common fact is often relied on rather than the pure magic of divination. If one man has sought out another's company too much and for no reason that appears customary, and the latter dies, suspicion falls on his unexplained companion. False friendship is suspected. I heard from three different sources: 'If we wish to kill a man we approach him, we eat, drink, sleep, work, and rest with him, it may be for several moons, and we wait our time; we *kawagosiana*, call him friend.' It will be recalled that the black art is believed to be ineffective at a distance as it is conducted by men. Men have to work in the flesh. Even witches are believed to confine their work to within the locality to which they belong.

It is realized by the Dobuan that relationship considerations debar certain persons who might be responsible for the death from mourning, so that divination by the corpse is not perfect. As well as consideration of unreasonable companionship there is consideration of possible grudges left unhealed. Then again the possibility of poison in food eaten is canvassed. I have heard these considerations being turned over in the heat that followed the sudden death of a father and child together without marks of violence. Every meal for several days back was considered in detail. So also of companions of the pair, and old hostilities. It was all done in my presence in about ten minutes, provoked by the sudden reception of the news by two men related to the dead.

Divination in Dobu is practised by everyone without magic, and by a special class with more authority and with magic.

11 Isaac Schapera

Sorcery and Witchcraft in Bechuanaland [1]

Excerpt from Isaac Schapera, 'Sorcery and witchcraft in Bechuanaland', *African Affairs*, vol. 51, 1952, pp. 41–52.

I

In 1825 the heir to the chieftainship of the BaTlhaping, a young man named Phetlhu (son of Mothibi), died suddenly of a disease that Robert Moffat, who was present at the time, described as 'Hottentot sickness' (i.e., anthrax). His parents, however, maintained that he had been bewitched by the relatives of a girl to whom he had been formerly betrothed, but whom he had jilted for someone else. A raiding party was therefore sent to seize and kill those people, but they were forewarned and managed to escape by fleeing to a neighbouring tribe.

In 1889, a correspondent to the vernacular journal *Mahoko a Becwana* (published at Kuruman mission station) asserted that Sechele, chief of the BaKwena, had recently caused five men to be killed for witchcraft, on the accusation of a single servant maid. Sechele (who, it may be remembered, had been baptized by Livingstone in 1849) replied shortly afterwards. He admitted having killed the men, but said that there was overwhelming proof of their guilt, and that he had released many others against whom the evidence was less convincing.

Among the BaNgwaketse, during the chieftainship of Seepapitso (1910–16), records were kept of 464 cases tried at the chief's court. Of these, no fewer than twenty-six (i.e., about one in eighteen) were directly concerned with charges of witchcraft, and in another seven accusations of witchcraft figured incidentally.

In 1927 the Kwena chief Sebele II (great-grandson of Sechele) accused his paternal uncle Kebohula of having tried to bewitch him by burying a 'doctored' hoe in the royal council-place (*kgotla*). The matter was discussed for three days at a large tribal gathering, which decided that Kebohula was guilty and should be

1. Now the Republic of Botswana – *Ed.*

banished from the tribal Reserve. At this stage the Administration intervened, induced Sebele to withhold the order of banishment, and passed a Proclamation (no. 17 of 1927) which made it a penal offence, both for people to accuse others of practising witchcraft, and also for people to attempt, by the use of magic, to inflict harm upon others.

The Native Tribunals Proclamation of 1934 removed from the jurisdiction of tribal courts all statutory offences. This included cases of witchcraft. The Proclamation also provided that all cases tried before the established Native Tribunals should be recorded. An inspection that I made of 850 case records, from five different tribes for the period 1935–40, showed that despite the Proclamation thirty-one of the cases had actually been concerned with witchcraft.

In 1937 the divorced wife of the Ngwato chief Tshekedi was, under the Proclamation of 1927, tried in the Court of the District Commissioner at Serowe for attempted witchcraft against her husband. She herself maintained that the 'medicines' she had used were intended to restore his love, but the court found her and the two magicians whom she had employed guilty of the offence as charged, and sentenced them all to imprisonment. Shortly afterwards, at the request of Tshekedi, they were banished from the tribal Reserve. It was alleged at the time that she had also caused the death of Tshekedi's mother by the use of poison, but the Crown apparently did not think that there was sufficient evidence for this to justify prosecution.

II

As shown by the instances just given, the belief in sorcery was noted among the Tswana at least 130 years ago; and, although all the tribes in the Protectorate have been considerably influenced during the past eighty years by contact with Western civilization, to such an extent that the official religion of them all at the present time is Christianity, that belief still persists very strongly. It has even been given official recognition by the Administration. The (revised) Native Courts Proclamation of 1943 repeated the stipulation that tribal courts had no jurisdiction over statutory offences; but it also provided that their warrants might be specially endorsed to allow them to deal with cases of witchcraft. Since the Proclamation was passed, the right to deal with such cases has been granted to the chief's courts of three tribes (Ba-Ngwato, BaNgwaketse, and BaKgatla).

It will, of course, be remembered that during the sixteenth and seventeenth centuries belief in witchcraft also flourished in Western Europe, when many thousands of people were tortured and brutally put to death as witches. However, no matter what our predecessors may have thought, we at least maintain nowadays that these beliefs were largely superstition, with no real justification in fact. Must the beliefs of the Tswana be similarly dismissed as empty superstition, indicative merely of intellectual backwardness, or is there in fact, as suggested by the recent action of the Administration, some valid reason for their existence? To put it very simply: do people amongst the Tswana really practise sorcery, or are the accusations so often made devoid of any factual substance? The answer, if I may anticipate much of what I am going to say, is that sorcery is, in fact, practised amongst the Tswana; there are indeed people who try to inflict harm upon others by means of the various techniques locally classed together as *boloi* ('sorcery and witchcraft', or 'black magic').

In many parts of Africa, two kinds of 'black magic' are commonly distinguished. In the one, people deliberately try, with the aid of magic, to injure some specific enemy or enemies. In the other, the persons termed 'witches' are said to suffer from some hereditary pathological condition; they seek to harm others, not of their conscious volition, but because it is inherent in their nature; and in some forms of the belief it is held that they themselves are ignorant of their dreadful powers, all their activities being carried out at night by their spirits or souls while their bodies repose in sleep. Following Evans-Pritchard, it has become customary in anthropological literature to refer to the first class as 'sorcerers', and to the second as 'witches'.

The Tswana do not believe that there is any hereditary condition by virtue of which people unwittingly become witches. They maintain that all who practise *boloi* are fully aware of what they are doing, i.e. always act 'of malice aforethought'; their motive is invariably one of envy, vengeance, or greed, and any person, male or female, may become one of them. In other words, the

Tswana do not believe in 'witches', but only in 'sorcerers'.

Nevertheless, in many respects some of the Tswana beliefs about sorcerers are strongly reminiscent of what is said elsewhere about witches. They distinguish between *baloi ba bosigo*, 'night witches', and *baloi ba motshegare*, 'day sorcerers'. Of the former, many weird and wonderful beliefs are held. It is said that people of this class consist mainly of elderly women, who are not content to employ magic solely in order to injure some particular enemy, but who make a habit of bewitching. By day they go about their routine everyday activities just like other people, but at night they gather in small groups and visit one homestead after another, carrying on their nefarious practices. They wear nothing on such occasions, or very little, and their bodies are smeared with white ashes or the blood of dead people. Admission into the group is apparently open to anyone, but, before being admitted, a woman must give evidence of her zeal by causing the death of some very close relative, preferably her own firstborn child. Once initiated, she is given an ointment with which to smear her body when she goes to bed at night; this will cause her to wake instantaneously when her colleagues come to call her. Alternatively, in some tribes, it is said that a special 'medicine' is injected into her thumb, whose itching will then awake her when necessary.

Among the activities attributed to these 'night witches' is the exhumation of newly-buried corpses. This, it is said, is generally done by means of a special magic that causes the grave to open of itself and the corpse to float to the surface. The witches then take from it such parts as they wish to use with their other medicines. It is believed also that they have special medicines that will enable them to throw the inhabitants of a homestead into a deep sleep, so that they may enter at will and do what they wish. Locked doors are no barrier against their magic; and, once inside, they cut the body of their victim and insert small stones, fragments of flesh, etc., which will cause him to fall ill and ultimately die, unless he is 'doctored' in time.

Associated with these night witches are various kinds of animal familiars. Foremost among them is the owl, which acts as their spy and whose hooting warns them that someone is approaching. This bird is greatly feared by the people, who regard it as ill-omened, and if it comes near their home they try to kill it and then throw it far away. It is said also that, when the witches wish to go to a distant place, they ride on hyenas; they keep one leg on the ground, and put the other on the animal's back, and in this way are able to progress at great speed! The BaKgatla say that some witches make their own hyenas, moulding the body from porridge, which is then vitalized by means of special medicines; but the belief in robots of this kind does not appear to exist elsewhere.

It should be said at once that beliefs of the kind just mentioned, although very widely held, are not really taken seriously by most of the people. Few claim to have actually seen 'night witches' at work, and very many are openly sceptical of the practices and powers attributed to them; some even say that such persons are mere figments of the imagination.

On the other hand, there is virtually unanimous belief in the existence and activities of the *baloi ba motshegare*, 'day sorcerers'. Unlike their nocturnal counterparts, these sorcerers do not belong to bands, nor do they practise the black art habitually. They use magic solely in order to inflict harm upon some specific enemy; and the only reservations about them are in regard to some of the methods they are said to employ. All these methods involve the use of herbs or other material substances, collectively known as *ditlhare* ('medicines'), which as a rule must be obtained from professional magicians or 'doctors' (*dingaka*). Magicians themselves may be hired to inflict harm upon a person's enemies, and may do so too against their own hated rivals. In such cases they also are said to practise *boloi*, although normally their activities are regarded with great respect as being beneficial to the community.

The following are some of the more commonly described methods of bewitching. The sorcerer may sprinkle 'doctored' blood over the courtyard of his enemy, the blood being as a rule that of the latter's totem animal, or of some member of his family. Should the victim then step upon the blood, his feet become affected, and he will either die or lose the use of his limbs. Alternatively, the sorcerer may conceal a bundle of rags containing 'doctored' roots in the eaves of his victim's hut, or he may bury them in the ground at the entrance to the homestead. The mere presence of these substances about the place will bring illness or death to one of the inhabitants. Again, the sorcerer may take some dust from his victim's footprint and work upon it with medicines; or he may blow some prepared powder in the victim's direction, at the same time calling upon his name; or he may send an animal, such as a lion or leopard or snake or ox, to inflict direct bodily injury upon him. This last method, known as *go neelela*, 'to give over', is said to be very commonly used.

There is one other method, allegedly used mainly by professional magicians in disputes with their colleagues, which deserves to be mentioned. It consists in working with lightning as a destructive agent. By using the appropriate medicines, the sorcerer can direct the lightning so that it strikes his victim or the latter's hut or cattle; some magicians are even said to have the power of making themselves fly through the air and then descend upon their victim in the guise of lightning.

From our point of view, obviously none of the methods just described can really achieve the purpose for which it is intended. Were they the only ones employed by sorcerers – and, it must be noted here, at least some of them are practised in all seriousness – we would be fully justified in regarding the whole of the Tswana belief in sorcery as nothing more than fantasy or hallucination. In all fairness, however, it must be added at once that nowadays many of the Tswana themselves do not consider such methods worthy of credence. Tshekedi, for instance, has on several occasions openly stated in court, when trying cases of sorcery, that some of the practices alleged against the accused were merely 'fairy tales' (*mainane*), incapable of causing physical injury.

But there is one other method, which the Tswana almost invariably mention first when asked how people bewitch, and which they regard as by far the most efficacious and dangerous. This method, known as *go jesa*, 'to feed' or 'to give to eat', consists in putting some poisonous substance into beer or porridge or other food, which is then given to the person whom one intends to bewitch. Here, also, there is sometimes an element of fantasy. Some people, for instance, say that when the victim swallows the food, the poisonous substance changes into a miniature lion or crocodile or some similar animal, which gnaws away persistently at his entrails until he dies in excruciating pain. But the majority maintain that the substance put into the food is actually poisonous (in our sense of the term). There are several well-known herbs said to be used for the purpose, including a few whose action is very slow, so that death does not take place suddenly enough to arouse immediate suspicion of foul play. It is clear also, from the records of several cases tried in the courts, that sometimes poisons are used with which we are more familiar; for instance, caustic soda (readily purchased at the trading stores) is fairly often mentioned in this connexion.

III

It is often said by Europeans claiming to know something about tribal life that the African lives in perpetual dread of sorcery. It is true that he regards sorcery as an ever-present danger. But he is no more obsessed by fear of it than is the average inhabitant of a large city in Western Europe obsessed by fear of being involved in a traffic accident. Both are dangers that must be faced almost daily; but just as we can avoid a collision by exercising caution, so do the Tswana believe that it is possible to protect oneself against sorcery.

It is an almost universal practice amongst them that whenever a new homestead, hut, or cattle kraal, is being built, it is fortified by means of 'doctored' pegs or other objects, which are either buried in the ground or applied in some other way. The aim of the rite is to counteract any medicines that a sorcerer may bring into the place. It is believed that, as soon as he enters, his medicines will lose their power and be rendered ineffective. Some magicians claim that if the site has been properly doctored the sorcerer's medicines will turn against himself, so that the harm he intends will in fact fall upon him. It may be noted, incidentally, that one form of 'fortifying' a homestead is to bury at the entrance a long stick smeared with medicine. Then, so it is believed, if a sorcerer or any other evil-doer steps over the entrance, the stick will become a snake that bites him fatally.

However, the principal form of protection used by most people is to have their own bodies magically 'strengthened' by a doctor. In its most widespread form the doctoring consists in making small cuts on every joint of the person's body, and into each cut is smeared a little of the magical ointment specially prepared by the doctor to combat sorcery. Henceforth, not only is the client regarded as immune from the attacks of sorcerers, but if any of them try to bewitch him the attempt will rebound disastrously upon them. This ceremony of 'strengthening' the body is usually performed simultaneously on all members of a family, especially when they are building a new homestead and the doctor comes to fortify it. In such cases the father is treated first, then the mother, and then all the children in descending order of age.

Apart from this special doctoring, many people, before going to a feast or to some other place where they fear that they may be given poisoned food, take special precautions. They swallow a certain medicine with which they have been supplied by their doctor. Then, so it is believed, if they are in fact given poisoned food the medicine will cause them to vomit it out and so escape the threatened consequences. At such feasts, too, the head of the household generally gets a magician to smear protective medicines on the base of every pot in which food is to be cooked. I myself have on several occasions seen such protective magic being employed at such essentially Christian feasts as those held when a person is being baptized or married in church.

IV

In the old days, when a person had died, fallen ill, or been afflicted with some other misfortune, a doctor was invariably called to divine the cause. Occasionally the misfortune might be attributed directly to the action of God (*Modimo*), in which case nothing could be done. Far more commonly, it might be attributed to *kgaba*, i.e., punishment inflicted by the ancestral spirits because some senior member of the kinship group had been insulted or otherwise injured by a junior relative. In such cases, a sick person would usually recover after the performance of a special cleansing ceremony by the person held to have been the source of the *kgaba*. It was also fairly common, however, for the doctor to attribute the misfortune to sorcery. In such cases he would never directly mention any person by name as responsible, but would state his sex, totem, skin complexion, and the direction from which he usually came when bewitching. If the people could from the description identify the sorcerer, they would normally hold an inquiry and try to obtain further evidence of his guilt. Then, if satisfied that he was in fact the culprit, they would report him to the chief, who alone had the right to prosecute and to punish sorcerers.

The trial of a sorcerer was generally conducted along the same lines as any other case that came before the chief. If it was clear from the evidence that the accused was guilty, the chief would order him to 'undo' the patient (*go mo dirolola*), i.e., to remove the effects of his sorcery so that the patient should recover. If he refused, he would be tortured until he consented. This seems to have been the only contingency in which torture was normally employed. If the patient then recovered, the sorcerer would be let off with a severe reprimand, although sometimes he might also be removed from his home and settled somewhere else. But if the patient died, or if he was already dead when the case first came to court, the sorcerer would be killed. In several tribal capitals, there are steep precipices still pointed out today as the places where, in the old days, sorcerers and others condemned to death were executed, their bodies, after they had been clubbed or speared, being tumbled over the cliff and left to lie at the base as food for the vultures and hyenas.

Since the introduction of European rule, the chiefs no longer have the right to impose the death penalty; nor, except in the three tribes previously named, have they even the right to try any person accused of sorcery. Nevertheless, such trials are still held from time to time. It must be said at once that tribal courts are generally cautious about the type of evidence that they will accept before convicting persons accused of sorcery. For instance, judging from the records that I have consulted, they do not regard the bare findings of a divination as sufficient. They must be satisfied, beyond doubt, that the accused has in fact been discovered using one or other of the methods already described. In particular, they pay special attention to his possession of medicines. It is fairly common, for instance, for a court to order his huts to be searched, and if any medicines are found he is asked to state where he got them and what their uses are. There are always magicians present at the hearing who will be able to check the statements that he may make in this connexion. If he is able to show that his medicines are innocuous, i.e., intended for treating sickness, or for any other lawful purpose, or if none at all are found in his possession, the case against him is seldom regarded as serious.

It should also be noted here that a malicious and unfounded accusation of sorcery is itself an offence in tribal law, the accused in such cases being entitled to receive damages for 'the spoiling of his name'. Many accusations of sorcery seem to be based upon little more than the statements made by magicians when divining. Not only is such evidence, if unsupported, not accepted in the courts; but time and again chiefs have warned their people against relying too much upon the words of the magicians, and some of the latter have even been punished for falsifying the verdicts of their divining-bones.

The sentences imposed upon convicted sorcerers vary according to circumstances. Perhaps the most common nowadays is to remove the culprit from his home to some other part of the tribal territory. The reason for this will be mentioned below. Occasionally, however, if medicines are found in his possession, and he cannot satisfactorily account for them, he may be told to swallow them, the argument being that if they are not poisonous no harm will befall him, whereas if they are he deserves the fate that he will suffer. At least one instance was described to me in which the accused had died very shortly after swallowing his own medicines; but this, I hasten to add, took place in the days before the Witchcraft Proclamation of 1927 had been passed.

If the accused, although guilty, has employed methods other than the use, or attempted use, of poison, he is sometimes fined or thrashed. Or, as in the old days, he may simply be ordered to 'undo' his victim, the implication being that drastic action will be taken against him should the latter die. Sometimes, again, the court will permit the victim to have his own doctor treat him, or, if the victim is dead, his relatives will be authorized to have his grave doctored; should any misfortune then overtake the culprit, it is attributed to the 'vengeance magic' used against him. One chief, in describing to me his use of this particular type of sentence, said that he did not really believe such 'vengeance magic' could work, but at least its use gave satisfaction to the people claiming to have been harmed.

117

V

From the records of cases heard in court, and from other evidence, it is abundantly clear that sorcery is, in fact, employed amongst the Tswana. It is not a mere figment of the imagination, nor are people always accused without any foundation at all. Sorcery is a recognized method of trying to inflict harm upon one's enemies, and persons accused of the crime have at times freely admitted that they resorted to it; and although some of the techniques employed are by our standards either stupid or ridiculous, they are nevertheless employed in all seriousness, and sometimes, as when poison is used, they can be really deadly.

One very important aspect still remains to be noted. In the vast majority of instances for which I have adequate data (ninety cases in a sample of 105), the sorcerer and his victims were usually very closely related. The most common types of relationship were those of husband and wife, parent and child, brother and brother; less commonly, but also fairly frequent, the parties involved were parent-in-law and child's spouse, master and servant, or doctor and client. It is extremely rare for people to be accused of bewitching either strangers or persons living away from their own part of the tribal territory.

These facts throw a revealing light upon the nature of Tswana sorcery. It is employed predominantly in situations of domestic conflict. The immediate causes are innumerable; there may be disputes about marital fidelity, about ownership of property or succession to office, about favour shown to one member of the family at the expense of another, etc. In our own society such disputes, if they cannot be settled amicably or adjusted by process of law, generally result in the separation of the persons concerned. But in tribal law people are not free to change their residence when and as they wish; they are expected to remain living among their kinsmen, and only in exceptional circumstances will the tribal authorities permit a man to move away from his own group. Consequently, the people on terms of hostility may find themselves forced to continue living in close daily contact, and unable to avoid one another; and it is in situations of this sort that they sometimes fall back upon the traditional weapon of sorcery. It is for this reason, too, that a convicted sorcerer is generally removed from his home. Obviously, if the Tswana thought that one could harm people through sorcery at a distance, this particular remedy would be useless. But the Tswana do not have that belief; and the reason given by chiefs for ordering the removal of a sorcerer is that unless such a step is taken in time he may ultimately try more drastic methods, for instance by way of poison or the use of physical violence.

If it is asked why the Tswana continue to believe in sorcery, although so many of its techniques are (to us, at least) obviously futile, several answers can readily be given. The first, as we have seen, is that not all the techniques are in fact futile; on the contrary, the use of poison must be regarded as decidedly effective. Secondly, since sorcery is not necessarily held to achieve its purpose immediately, the chances of a victim's meeting with misfortune at some time or other are fairly considerable, no matter what technique is employed; and time and again, when one has attempted to argue on this point with the Tswana, their reply is to quote instances where people have in fact been injured by sorcery. Their evidence often rests upon little more than divination by the magicians; and it is only fair to add that at least some people accuse the magicians of deliberately fostering the belief in sorcery so as to have more employment for themselves. And it must be remembered in this connexion that there are magicians in virtually every village in Bechuanaland. Their influence is continuous and always present, and there is still very little to counteract them. Finally, it must be emphasized that belief in sorcery is still part of the cultural tradition of the Tswana. From childhood onwards, every person grows up in an environment where it not only flourishes, but is still taken for granted as a recognized method of dealing with one's enemies; and on the whole it is much easier for the average tribesman to fall into line with his fellows than to break away completely from his native beliefs.

Nevertheless, even if we characterize much of it as folk-lore or sheer fantasy, Tswana sorcery has a solid core of fact, viz., the employment of poison as a means of injuring an enemy who is at the same time a close relative or neighbour from whom one is normally unable to move away. There is nothing superstitious or fantastic about this element of the concept, nor can we dismiss it as lightly as most of the other elements. As I have already indicated, the Tswana themselves are tending more and more to be sceptical about such features as many of the beliefs relating to 'night witches', and several chiefs are nowadays stressing the absurdity of such techniques as doctoring a person's footprint; but even the most enlightened continue to believe that people can bewitch others by poisoning their food, and this belief, I submit, is well founded. People are often punished for the same offence in our own society; and the fact that the Tswana call it 'sorcery' does not justify our maintaining that it therefore cannot exist at all among them.

12 H. R. Trevor-Roper

The European Witch-Craze

Excerpts from H. R. Trevor-Roper, *Religion, Reformation and Social Change*, Macmillan, 1967, chapter 3, 'The European Witch-Craze of the Sixteenth and Seventeenth Centuries', pp. 90–192.[1]

Rise of the Craze

The belief in witches in the sixteenth and seventeenth centuries was not, as the prophets of progress might suppose, a lingering ancient superstition, only waiting to dissolve. It was a new explosive force, constantly and fearfully expanding with the passage of time. In those years of apparent illumination there was at least one-quarter of the sky in which darkness was positively gaining at the expense of light.

Yes, gaining. Whatever allowance we may make for the mere multiplication of the evidence after the discovery of printing, there can be no doubt that the witch-craze grew, and grew terribly, after the Renaissance. Credulity in high places increased, its engines of expression were made more terrible, more victims were sacrified to it. The years 1550–1600 were worse than the years 1500–1550, and the years 1600–1650 were worse still. Nor was the craze entirely separable from the intellectual and spiritual life of those years. It was forwarded by the cultivated popes of the Renaissance, by the great Protestant reformers, by the saints of the Counter-Reformation, by the scholars, lawyers and churchmen of the age of Scaliger and Lipsius, Bacon and Grotius, Bérulle and Pascal. If those two centuries were an age of light, we have to admit that, in one respect at least, the Dark Age was more civilized.

For in the Dark Age there was at least no witch-craze. There were witch-beliefs, of course – a scattered folk-lore of peasant superstitions: the casting of spells, the making of storms, con-

1. An earlier version of this chapter appeared as 'Witches and witch-craft: an historical essay', *Encounter*, vol. 28 (1967), no. 5, pp. 3–25 and no. 6, pp. 13–34 – *Ed*.

verse with spirits, sympathetic magic. Such beliefs are universal, in time and place, and in this essay I am not concerned with them. I am concerned with the organized, systematic 'demonology' which the medieval Church constructed out of those beliefs and which, in the sixteenth and seventeenth centuries, acquired a terrible momentum of its own. And when we make this necessary distinction between the organized witch-craze and the miscellaneous witch-beliefs out of which it was constructed, we have to admit that the Church of the Dark Age did its best to disperse these relics of paganism which the Church of the Middle Ages would afterwards exploit. Of course it was not entirely successful. Some of the pagan myths, like pagan gods and pagan rites, had crept into the Christian synthesis at an early date and had found lodgment in its outer crannies. St Augustine in particular, with his baroque mind and African credulity, did much to preserve them: they form an incidental bizarre decoration of the huge doctrinal construction which his authority launched into western Christendom. But in general, the Church, as the civilizer of nations, disdained these old wives' tales. They were the fragmentary rubbish of paganism which the light of the Gospel had dispelled.

So, in the eighth century, we find St Boniface, the English apostle of Germany, declaring roundly that to believe in witches and werewolves is unchristian (1, p. 178–82). In the same century Charlemagne decreed the death penalty for anyone who, in newly converted Saxony, burnt supposed witches. Such burning, he said, was 'a pagan custom' (2). In the next century St Agobard, Bishop of Lyon (3), repudiated the belief that witches could make bad weather, and another unknown Church dignitary declared that night-flying and metamorphosis were hallucinations and that whoever believed in them 'is beyond doubt an infidel and a pagan'. This statement was accepted into the canon law and became known as the *canon Episcopi* or *capitulum Episcopi* (1, pp. 178–82). It remained the official doctrine of the Church. In the eleventh century the laws of King Coloman of Hungary declined to notice witches 'since they do not exist' (1, p. 1252), and the twelfth-century John of Salisbury dismissed the idea of a witches' sabbat as a fabulous dream (1, p. 172). In the succeeding centuries, when the craze was being built up, all this salutary doctrine would have to be reversed. The laws of Charlemagne and Coloman would be forgotten; to deny the reality of night-flying and metamorphosis would be officially declared heretical; the witches' sabbat would become an objective fact, disbelieved only (as a doctor of the Sorbonne would write in 1609 (4)) by those of unsound mind; and the ingenuity of churchmen and lawyers would be taxed to explain away that inconvenient text of canon law, the *canon Episcopi*.

By the end of the Middle Ages this reversal would be complete. By 1490, after two centuries of research, the new, positive doctrine of witchcraft would be established in its final form. From then on it would be simply a question of applying this doctrine: of seeking, finding and destroying the witches whose organization has been defined.

The monks of the late Middle Ages sowed: the lawyers of the sixteenth century reaped; and what a harvest of witches they gathered in! All Christendom, it seems, is at the mercy of these horrifying creatures. Countries in which they had previously been unknown are now suddenly found to be swarming with them, and the closer we look, the more of them we find. All contemporary observers agree that they are multiplying at an incredible rate. They have acquired powers hitherto unknown, a complex international organization and social habits of indecent sophistication. Some of the most powerful minds of the time turn from the human sciences to explore this newly discovered continent, this America of the spiritual world. And the details which they discover, and which are continually being confirmed by teams of parallel researchers – field researchers in torture-chamber or confessional, academic researchers in library or cloister – leave the facts more certainly established and the prospect more alarming than ever.

Consider the situation as shown at any time in the half-century from 1580 to 1630; that half-century which corresponds with the mature life of Bacon and brings together Montaigne and Descartes. The merest glance at any report by the acknowledged experts of the time reveals an alarming state of affairs. By their own confession, thousands of old women – and not only old women – had made secret pacts with the Devil, who had now emerged as a great spiritual potentate, the Prince of Darkness, bent on recovering his lost empire. Every night these ill-advised ladies were anointing themselves with 'devil's grease', made out of the fat of murdered infants, and, thus lubricated, were slipping through cracks and keyholes and up chimneys, mounting on broomsticks or spindles or airborne goats, and flying off on a long and inexpressibly wearisome aerial journey to a diabolical rendezvous, the witches' sabbat. In every country there were hundreds of such sabbats, more numerous and more crowded than race-meetings or fairs. There were no less than 800 known meeting-places in Lorraine alone. Some countries had national, some international centres. Such were the Blocksberg or Brocken in the Harz Mountains of Germany, the 'delicate large meadow' called Blåkulla in Sweden and the great resort of La Hendaye in south-west France where no less than 12,000 witches would assemble for the gathering known as the *Aquelarre*. The meetings too were remarkably frequent. At first the interrogators in Lorraine thought that they occurred only once a week, on Thursday; but, as always, the more the evidence was pressed, the worse the conclusions that it yielded. Sabbats were found to take place on Monday, Wednesday, Friday and Sunday, and soon Tuesday was found to be booked as a by-day. It was all very alarming and proved the need of ever greater vigilance by the spiritual police.

And what happened when the witch had reached the sabbat? The unedifying details, alas, were only too well authenticated. First, she was surprised to observe nearly all her friends and neighbours, whom she had not previously suspected to be witches. With them there were scores of demons, their paramours, to whom they had bound themselves by the infernal pact; and above all, dominating them all, was the imperious master of ceremonies, the god of their worship, the Devil himself, who appeared sometimes as a big, black, bearded man, more often as a stinking goat, occasionally as a great toad. Those present recognized their master. They all joined to worship the Devil and danced around him to the sound of macabre music made with curious instruments – horses' skulls, oak-logs, human bones, etc. Then they kissed him in homage, under the tail if he were a goat, on the lips if he were a toad. After which, at the word of command from him, they threw themselves into promiscuous sexual orgies or settled down to a feast of such viands as tempted their national imagination. In Germany these were sliced turnips, parodies of the Host; in Savoy, roast or boiled children; in Spain, exhumed corpses, preferably of kinsfolk; in Alsace, fricassees of bats; in England, more sensibly, roast beef and beer. But these nice distinctions of diet made little difference: the food, all agreed, was cold and quite tasteless, and one necessary ingredient, salt, for some arcane demonological reason, was never admitted.

Such was the witches' sabbat, the collective orgy and communal religious worship of the new diabolical religion. In the intervals between these acts of public devotion, the old ladies had, of course, good works to do in the home. They occupied themselves by suckling familiar spirits in the form of weasels, moles, bats, toads or other convenient creatures; by compassing the death of their neighbours or their neighbours' pigs; by raising tempests, causing blights or procuring impotence in bridegrooms; and as a pledge of their servitude they were constantly having sexual intercourse with the Devil, who appeared (since even he abhors unnatural vice, 5) to she-witches as an *incubus*, to he-witches as a *succubus*.

What Gibbon called 'the chaste severity of the Fathers' was much exercised by this last subject, and no detail escaped their learned scrutiny. As a lover, they established, the Devil was of 'freezing coldness' to the touch; his embrace gave no pleasure – on the contrary, only pain; and certain items were lacking in his equipment. But there was no frigidity in the technical sense: his attentions were of formidable, even oppressive solidity. That he could generate on witches was agreed by some doctors (how else, asked the Catholic theologians, could the birth of Luther be explained?); but some denied this, and others insisted that only certain worm-like creatures, known in Germany as *Elben*, could issue from such unions. Moreover, there was considerable doubt whether the Devil's generative power was his own, as a Franciscan specialist maintained ('under correction from our Holy Mother Church'), or whether he, being neuter, operated with borrowed matter. A nice point of theology was here involved and much interested erudition was expended on it in cloistered solitudes. Some important theologians conjectured that the Devil equipped himself by squeezing the organs of the dead. This view was adopted (among others) by our King James (6). Other experts advanced other theories, more profound than decent. But on the whole, Holy Mother Church followed the magisterial ruling of the Angelic Doctor, St Thomas Aquinas, who, after St Augustine, must be regarded as the second founder of demonological science. According to him, the Devil could discharge as *incubus* only what he had previously absorbed as *succubus*. He therefore nimbly alternated between these postures ... There are times when the intellectual fantasies of the clergy seem more bizarre than the psychopathic delusions of the madhouse out of which they have, too often, been excogitated.

Such were the human witches, the fifth column of Satan on earth, his front-line agents in the struggle for control of the spiritual world. All through the sixteenth century, and for much of the seventeenth, men believed in the reality of this struggle. Laymen might not accept all the esoteric details supplied by the experts, but they accepted the general truth of the theory, and because they accepted its general truth, they were unable to argue against its more learned interpreters. So the experts effectively commanded the field. For two centuries the clergy preached against witches and the lawyers sentenced them. Year after year inflammatory books and sermons warned the Christian public of the danger, urged the Christian magistrate to greater vigilance, greater persecution. Confessors and judges were supplied with manuals incorporating all the latest information, village hatreds were exploited in order to ensure exposure, torture was used to extract and expand confessions, and lenient judges were denounced as enemies of the people of God, drowsy guardians of the beleaguered citadel. Perhaps these 'patrons of witches' were witches themselves. In the hour of danger, when it almost seemed that Satan was about to take over the world, his agents were found to be everywhere, even in judges' seats, in university chairs and on royal thrones.

But did this campaign against the witches in fact reduce their number? Not at all. The more fiercely they were persecuted, the more numerous they seemed to become. By the beginning of the seventeenth century the witch-doctors have become hysterical. Their manuals have become encyclopedic in bulk, lunatic in pedantry. They demand, and sometimes achieve, wholesale purges. By 1630 the slaughter has broken all previous records. It has become a holocaust in which lawyers, judges, clergy themselves join old women at the stake. That at least, if nothing else, must have enforced an agonizing reappraisal.

And indeed, it was in the wake of the greatest of all purges – perhaps in revulsion after it – that the solidity of the witch-hunters began to give way. In the middle of the seventeenth century – in the 1650s – scepticism, unavailing hitherto, begins at last to break through. Imperceptibly, the whole basis of the craze begins to dissolve, in Catholic and Protestant countries alike. By the 1680s the battle is effectively won, at least in the West. The old habits of mind may linger on; there will be pockets of resistance here and there, recurrence of persecution now and then, but somehow the vital force behind it is spent. Though the argument may go on, the witch-trials and witch-burnings have become once again mere sporadic episodes, as they had been before the Renaissance. The rubbish of the human mind which for two centuries, by some process of intellectual alchemy and social pressure, had become fused together in a coherent, explosive system, has disintegrated. It is rubbish again. [. . .]

Emergence of Systematized Beliefs

The mythology of the witch-craze [. . .] was the articulation of social pressure. In a religious society such articulation generally takes the form of heresy. But before examining any heresy it is useful to ask who in fact articulated it. Was it the heretics themselves, or was it the inquisitors who articulated it for them? This is an important question, applicable to many historic heresies. It applies, among others, to the Albigensians and to the Vaudois. So, when the inquisitors discovered a new 'heresy' beneath the ruins of Albigensianism, we naturally ask the same question. Did they really discover this new heresy, or did they invent it?

It has been argued by some speculative writers that the demonology of the sixteenth century was, in essence, a real religious system, the old pre-Christian religion of rural Europe which the new Asiatic religion of Christ had driven underground but never wholly destroyed. But this is to confuse the scattered fragments of paganism with the grotesque system into which they are only long afterwards arranged. The primitive peoples of Europe, as of other continents, knew of charms and sorcery, and the concept of night-riding 'with Diana or Herodias' survived into the early Christian centuries; but the essential substance of the new demonology – the pact with Satan, the witches' sabbat, the carnal intercourse with demons, etc., etc. – and the hierarchical, systematic structure of the kingdom of the Devil, are an independent product of the later Middle Ages (7). All the evidence makes it clear that the new mythology owes its system entirely to the inquisitors themselves. Just as anti-semites build up, out of disconnected titbits of scandal, their systematic mythology of ritual murder, poisoned wells and the world-wide conspiracy of the Elders of Zion, so the Hammerers of Witches built up their systematic mythology of Satan's kingdom and Satan's accomplices out of the mental rubbish of peasant credulity and feminine hysteria; and the one mythology, like the other, once launched, acquired a momentum of its own. It became an established folk-lore, generating its own evidence, and applicable far outside its original home.

How that folk-lore was established is clear enough to anyone who reads the successive manuals of the inquisitors. Fighting against the enemies of the Faith, they had easily divided the world into light and darkness, and having systematized the kingdom of God in a *Summa Theologiae*, what was more natural than to systematize the kingdom of the Devil in a *Summa Daemonologiae*? The method was the same: the only difference lay in the nature of the material. The basic evidence of the kingdom of God had been supplied by Revelation. But the Father of Lies had not revealed himself so openly. To penetrate the secrets of his kingdom, it was therefore necessary to rely on indirect sources. These sources could only be captured members of the enemy intelligence service: in other words, confessing witches. [. . .]

But if the theory of Satan's kingdom, with its hierarchy of demons and witches, rested ultimately on the confessions of witches, how were those confessions obtained? This question is crucial. If the confessions were freely given, we have to admit at least the 'subjective reality' of the experiences confessed, and then the remarkable identity of those confessions, which converted many a sixteenth-century sceptic, becomes a real problem. On the other hand, if the confessions were obtained by torture, that problem hardly exists. The similarity of answers can be explained by a combination of identical questions and intolerable pain. [. . .]

It is easy to see that torture lay, directly or indirectly, behind most of the witch-trials of Europe, creating witches where none were and multiplying both victims and evidence. Without torture, the great witch-panics of the 1590s and the late 1620s are inconceivable. But can we ascribe the whole craze, in effect, to torture, as some liberal writers seem to do? Can we suppose that witchcraft had no other basis than the fanaticism and prurience of the inquisitors, spellbound by their own inventions? I must confess that I find this difficult to believe. The problem seems to me more complex than that. If the confessions were merely a response to torture we should have to explain why even in England, where there was no judicial torture, witches confessed to absurd crimes (8); why the people were so docile in the face of such a mania; and above all, why some of the most original and cultivated men of the time not only accepted the theory of witchcraft, but positively devoted their genius to its propagation. [. . .]

That external suggestion alone does not account for witches' confessions is clear when we descend to detail. Again and again, when we read the case histories, we find witches freely confessing to esoteric details without any evidence of torture, and it was this spontaneity, rather than the confessions themselves, which convinced rational men that the details were true. [. . .]

The Dominican inquisitors [and] [. . .] their successors [. . .] did not, of course, discover a concealed world of demons, objectively there (as they supposed). They did not even discover a systematic illusion, a false religion of paganism behind the true religion of Christ. Doubtless there were some pagan survivals in witchcraft just as there were some pagan survivals in Christianity. In Lorraine, for instance, the sabbat was ascribed, incidentally, to the old 'high places' of pre-Christian worship (9). But what was taken over was mere fragments, not a system: it was the inquisitors who supplied the system. Nor did those inquisitors invent a purely imaginary system, in the ordinary sense of that verb: they may have used their ingenuity to create the system, but they did not create the basic evidence on which it rested. They found it in the confessions of supposed witches; and as those confessions seemed genuine to the witches who made them, we can hardly blame the inquisitors for supposing them to be genuine too. What was 'subjective reality' to the penitent was 'objective reality' to the confessor. Out of those fragments of truth, spontaneously given if also amplified by suggestion and torture, a total picture of Satan's kingdom could, by logic, by the 'rationalism' of the time, be built up. [. . .]

Link with Religious Conflict

If the Catholic evangelists had launched the craze, the Protestant evangelists would soon revive and extend it. Already, in the 1540s, there had been warning signs. In 1540, in Luther's Wittenberg, four witches were burnt. On this subject Luther himself was as credulous as any Dominican, and as he grew older, he contrived to believe more: *succubi*, *incubi*, night-flight and all. Witches, he declared, should be burnt even if they did no harm, merely for making a pact with the Devil (10). In Zürich, Zwingli's successors did not imitate his restraint (11). In Geneva, Calvin held the same language as Luther. 'The Bible', he declared, preaching to the Elect on the Witch of Endor, 'teaches us that there are witches and that they must be slain . . . God expressly commands that all witches and enchantresses shall be put to death; and this law of God is an universal law.' The law of God was stated most explicitly in Exodus xxii. 18: 'thou shalt not suffer a witch to live'. On this savoury text the Protestant clergy – Lutheran, Calvinist, Zwinglian – were to preach, with grim relish, for the next century; and they did not fail to point out that the law of God, unlike the law of the Emperor, made no exception in favour of 'the good witch' (12).

Wherever they went, they carried the craze with them. It was Lutheran preachers who first brought it to Denmark (13), Calvinist missionaries who implanted it in Transylvania (14). Like the Dominicans before them, the Protestant evangelists introduced the systematic mythology of the Inquisition into countries which hitherto had known only the disconnected superstitions of the countryside. It was Lutheran preachers who brought the witch-craze in the 1560s into Brandenburg, Württemberg, Baden, Bavaria, Mecklenburg. It was the Calvinist revolution which brought the first witch-law to Scotland in 1563 and thus inaugurated a century of terror. In the previous year the first general witch-law had been passed by the English Parliament. In both Scotland and England the pressure came from the 'Marian exiles' – the Protestant clergy who, in the days of persecution, had sat at the feet of Calvin or other Reformers, in Switzerland and Germany (15).

The responsibility of the Protestant clergy for the revival of the witch-craze in the mid-sixteenth century is undeniable. It has led some commentators to argue that Protestantism has a special responsibility for such beliefs. But this is absurd: it is to judge on far too narrow a basis. To dispose of such a conclusion, we need only look back to the Dominicans. We may equally look forward to the Jesuits.

For if the Dominicans had been the evangelists of the medieval Counter-Reformation, the Jesuits were the evangelists of the sixteenth-century Counter-Reformation, and if Protestant evangelists carried the craze to the countries which they conquered for Reform, these Catholic evangelists carried it equally to the countries which they reconquered for Rome. Some of the most famous of Jesuit missionaries distinguished themselves in propagating the witch-craze. [. . .]

Thus, if we look at the revival of the witch-craze in the 1560s in its context, we see that it is not the product either of Protestantism or of Catholicism, but of both: or rather, of their conflict. Just as the medieval Dominican evangelists had ascribed witch-beliefs to the whole society which resisted them, so both the Protestant and Catholic evangelists of the mid-sixteenth century ascribed the same beliefs to the societies which opposed them. The recrudescence of the absurd demonology of the *Malleus* was not the logical consequence of any religious idea: it was the social consequence of renewed ideological war and the accompanying climate of fear. The parties drew on a mythology which was already there, elaborated out of a similar situation by their medieval predecessors. Perhaps, on the eve of the Reformation, that mythology was on the way out. Who can say what might have happened if Erasmus had triumphed instead of Luther and

Loyola? Then the Renaissance might have led direct to the Enlightenment and the witch-craze have been remembered as a purely medieval lunacy. But that was not to be. The frontal opposition of Catholics and Protestants, representing two forms of society incompatible with each other, sent men back to the old dualism of God and the Devil and the hideous reservoir of hatred, which seemed to be drying up, was suddenly refilled. [. . .]

That this recrudescence of the witch-craze in the 1560s was directly connected with the return of religious war is clear. It can be shown from geography: every major outbreak is in the frontier-area where religious strife is not intellectual, a dissent of opinion, but social, the dissidence of a society. When Bishop Palladius, the Reformer of Denmark, visited his diocese, he declared those who used Catholic prayers or formulas to be witches; and witches, he said, 'in these days of pure Gospel-light', must be burnt (16). When Bishop Jewel, fresh from Switzerland, told Queen Elizabeth that witches and sorcerers 'within these last few years are marvellously increased within this your Grace's realm', and demanded action against them, he was declaring Protestant war on the Catholic England of Mary Tudor (17). The persecution in England was sharpest in Essex and in Lancashire – two counties where Catholicism was strong and the Puritan evangelists particularly energetic. The Scottish Calvinists, when they obtained their witch-law, were similarly declaring war on Catholic society. Germany and Switzerland were also countries where the two religions faced each other in sharp social opposition: in Germany the persecution remained most persistent in Westphalia, the seat of medieval heresy and sixteenth-century Anabaptism (18), while in Switzerland the Calvinist cities made war on the obstinate peasantry of the country (19). In France the geographical antithesis was no less clear. The same areas which had accepted the medieval heresies became, in the sixteenth century, the solid base of the Huguenots: in the Wars of Religion the Protestant south opposed the Catholic north and the last redoubt of Protestantism was the last redoubt of Albigensianism, Languedoc. It was therefore natural that witches should be found in Protestant islands like Orleans or Normandy; that by 1609 the entire population of 'Protestant' Navarre should be declared to be witches (20); and that the capital of the witch-

burners should be the great centre of vindictive Catholic orthodoxy, Toulouse.

The same connexion can be shown from chronology. The
recrudescence in the 1560s marks the period of Protestant
evangelism. Thereafter almost every local outbreak can be
related to the aggression of one religion upon the other. The
Wars of Religion introduce the worst period of witch-persecution
in French history. The outbreak in the Basque country in 1609
heralds the Catholic reconquest of Béarn. The terrible outbreaks
in Germany, in Flanders and the Rhineland in the 1590s, and
again in 1627–9, mark the stages of Catholic reconquest. Understandably, the Catholic historians of Germany dwell with unction
on the persecutions of the 1560s and 1570s, when the witch-
burners were Protestant (21). Protestants can take their revenge by
looking back to the Dominican campaign of the later Middle
Ages, or forward to the Catholic triumphs of the early seventeenth
century.

Was there any difference between the Catholic and the Protestant craze? Theoretically, yes. The Catholics inherited the
whole medieval tradition of the later Fathers and the Schoolmen
while the Protestants rejected everything which a corrupt papacy
had added to the Bible and the primitive Fathers. Theoretically,
therefore, they should have rejected the whole demonological
science of the Inquisitors; for no one could say that *succubi* and
incubi, 'imps' or werewolves, cats or broomsticks were to be
found in the Bible. This point was constantly made by isolated
Protestant critics, but it had no effect on their official theorists.
Some Calvinist writers might be more intellectual and austere
in detail (22), but in general Catholics and Protestants vied with
each other in credulity. The authority of Luther transmitted
all the fantasies of the Dominicans to his disciples, and the
confessions of witches were regarded as an untainted supplement
to Holy Writ. So, in the end, Catholics and Protestants agreed on
the facts and drew on each other for details. The Catholic Binsfeld
cites the Protestants Erastus and Daneau; the Calvinist Voëtius
and the Lutheran Carpzov cite the Dominican *Malleus* and the
Jesuit del Rio. They all also agreed in denouncing those infamous sceptics who insisted on telling them that supposed
witches were merely deluded, 'melancholic' old ladies and that the

133

Bible, in denouncing death to 'witches', had not referred to persons like them. From either side, terrible denunciations fell upon these neuters in the holy war, these 'patrons of witches', who, together with lenient judges, were regularly declared to be witches themselves, equally deserving of the bonfire and the stake.

Scepticism Unavailing

And who were these sceptics? The most famous of them was Johann Weyer, a survivor from the civilized days of Erasmus, a pupil of the Platonist Cornelius Agrippa of Nettesheim, a doctor of medicine who had studied in the humanist France of François I and practised in Erasmian Holland. In 1550 he had been invited to Cleves by the tolerant, Erasmian Duke of Cleves-Jülich-Berg-Marck, William V (23), and it was under his protection, and with his encouragement, that he wrote, in 1563, at the age of forty-eight, his famous, or notorious work, *De Praestigiis Daemonum*. In this, while accepting the reality of witchcraft and the whole Platonic world of spirits, he argued that all the activities to which witches confessed, and for which they were now being burnt throughout Germany, were illusions created in them either by demons or by disease. Having written his work, Weyer sent copies to his friends and awaited the reaction.

The reaction was formidable. Weyer had chosen to publish his book precisely at the moment when the witch-craze, after a long lull, was beginning again. That, indeed, was what had provoked him to write. But this Erasmian Platonist – 'the father of modern psychiatry' as he has been called – was no longer heard by a generation that had repudiated Erasmus. A fellow-physician might hail him as a prophet of enlightenment, a Hercules triumphant over superstition (24), but his other readers thought differently. Weyer was told by his friends that his book must be destroyed or rewritten; by his enemies that he was a 'Vaudois', a Wycliffite, a lunatic. His work was denounced by the French Calvinist Lambert Daneau, burnt by the Lutheran University of Marburg, and put on the Index by the Catholic governor of the Netherlands, the Duke of Alba, who would ultimately secure Weyer's dismissal from the Court of Cleves. However, the book was read, and in 1577 Weyer published a sequel in which he had congratulated himself on its salutary effect. Unfortunately, he had to add, the tyrants had now resumed their murderous persecution, and so he sought, once again, to expose their errors. This second book happened to come into the hands of Jean Bodin just as Bodin was working himself into a lather of indignation at the leniency of French judges and the infamous neutrality of the French court: the 'Erasmian', 'Platonic' Court of Catherine de Médicis (25). As if he had not written rubbish enough, Bodin hastily added an appendix denouncing Weyer as an infamous patron of witches, a criminal accomplice of the Devil.

There were sceptics after Weyer, but none of them improved materially on his work. Just as the demonology of the witch-hunters, Catholic or Protestant, was laid down in final form in the *Malleus*, so the basic philosophy of the sceptics, Catholic or Protestant, was laid down by Weyer, and neither the one nor the other was modified by the argument of a century. Every champion of demonological science from Daneau and Bodin onwards took care to attack the 'vain ravings' of Weyer; no sceptic, at least in print, did more than repeat his arguments. The most famous of his successors, the Englishman Reginald Scot, if he was inspired by his own experiences, accepted the arguments of Weyer, and thereafter Weyer and Scot feature together, as an infamous couple, in the books of the orthodox. King James VI of Scotland himself wrote his treatise on *Demonologie* to refute Weyer and Scot; when he came to the English throne one of his earliest acts was to have Scot's work sent to the bonfire; and the Dutch Calvinist Voëtius, equally enraged against both sceptics, is able to dismiss their arguments by appealing to unassailable authority: Weyer was refuted by King James and Scot 'by the public burning of all copies of his book' (26).

The enemies of Weyer, Scot and other sceptics always accused them of denying the reality of witchcraft. Their defenders impatiently insisted that this was not true. Nor was it. Weyer believed implicitly in the power of Satan, but not that old women were his agents. 'Truly I deny not that there are witches', Scot had written, '... but I detest the idolatrous opinions conceived of them.' To the end of the witch-craze, although we always hear it said that there are some who disbelieve the very existence of

135

witches (27), we never actually hear the denials. To the last the most radical argument against the witch-craze was not that witches do not exist, not even that the pact with Satan is impossible, but simply that the judges err in their identification. The 'poor doting women', as Scot called them, who are haled before the law courts, and who may confess – whether through torture or delusion – to being witches, have not in fact made any pact with the Devil, or surrendered to his charms, or harmed man or beast. They are 'melancholic'. This was a very tiresome doctrine, and it drove successive orthodox commentators into tantrums of indignation. It could not be refuted. But equally it could not refute the witch-craze. Logically, it left it untouched. [. . .]

The intellectual basis of the witch-craze remained firm all through the seventeenth century. No critic had improved on the arguments of Weyer; none had attacked the substance of the myth; all that successive sceptics had done was to cast doubt on its practical interpretation: to question the value of confessions, the efficacy of torture, the identification of particular witches. The myth itself remained untouched, at least in appearance. Artificial though it was, recent though it was, it had become part of the structure of thought, and time had so entwined it with other beliefs, and indeed with social interests, that it seemed impossible to destroy it. In happy times men might forget it, at least in practice. In the early sixteenth century there had seemed a good chance that it might be forgotten – that is, dissolve again into scattered peasant superstitions. But those happy times had not lasted. The ideological struggle of Reformation and Counter-Reformation – that grim struggle which was so disastrous in European intellectual history – had revived the dying witch-craze just as it had revived so many other obsolescent habits of thought: biblical fundamentalism, theological history, scholastic Aristoteleanism. All these had seemed in retreat in the age of Erasmus and Machiavelli and Ficino; all returned a generation later to block the progress of thought for another century.

Every crucial stage in the ideological struggle of the Reformation was a stage also in the revival and perpetuation of the witch-craze. In the 1480s the Dominicans had made war, as they thought, on the relics of medieval heresy. That was the time of the Witch Bull and the *Malleus*, and the renewed persecution in those 'Alpine valleys cold' in which del Rio would afterwards see the eternal source of witchcraft and Milton the ancient cradle of Protestantism. In the 1560s the Protestant missionaries had set out to evangelize the countries of northern Europe whose rulers had accepted the new faith, and at once the witch-craze had been renewed by them. From 1580 the Catholic Counter-Reformation had begun to reconquer northern Europe and the craze became, once again, a Catholic terror, with the new Jesuits replacing the old Dominicans as evangelists. It was then that the Spaniard Francisco Peña, a canon lawyer in the Roman Curia, collected and summarized the conclusions of the Roman inquisitors: for no subject, he wrote, was now more frequently discussed by the Catholic clergy than sorcery and divination (28). Finally, the Thirty Years War, the last stage of the ideological struggle, brings with it the worst persecution of all: the 'epidémie démoniaque' which reached its climax in the year of Catholic restoration, 1629. [. . .]

Gradual Decay of the Craze

The decline and apparently final collapse of the witch-craze in the late seventeenth century, while other such social stereotypes retained their power, is a revolution which is surprisingly difficult to document. We see the controversies continue. Important names appear on both sides – but the greater names at least in England are on the side of the craze, not against it. How can the obscure and tipsy Oxford scholar John Wagstaffe or the crotchety Yorkshire surgeon-parson John Webster compete with the names of Sir Thomas Browne and Richard Baxter and the Cambridge Platonists Ralph Cudworth, Henry More and Joseph Glanville? And yet on neither side are the arguments new: they are the arguments which have always been used. On the side of orthodoxy some caution can be observed: the grosser and more preposterous details of the demonologists are silently dropped (although continental and Scottish lawyers and clergy continued to assert them) and the argument is given a more philosophic base. But on the sceptical side there is no advance. Webster is no more modern than Weyer. Nevertheless, without new argument on either side the intellectual belief quietly dissolved. The witch-trials, in spite of a few last outbursts, came to an end. The witch-laws were repealed, almost without debate.

It has been pointed out that, in this reform, Protestant countries led the way. England and Holland were regarded, in 1700, as countries long since emancipated while the Catholic prince-bishops of Germany were still burning away. Inside Germany, says a German scholar, the Protestant states abandoned persecution a full generation before the Catholic (29). In mixed societies, like Alsace, the Catholic lords had always been fiercer than the Protestant (30). And certainly Catholic manuals continued to insist on demonological doctrine when the Protestant writers had conveniently forgotten it. However, in view of the undoubted part played by the Protestant Churches in forwarding the craze after 1560, we should perhaps be chary of claiming any special virtue for Protestantism in resisting it after 1650. Calvinist and Lutheran doctrines were as uncompromising, Calvinist and Lutheran clergy as ferocious as Catholic; and where the Calvinist or Lutheran clergy had effective power – as in Scotland or Mecklenburg – the craze continued as long as in any Catholic country. To the very end, honours remained even between the two religions. If the last witch-burning in Europe was in Catholic Poland in 1793, that was an illegal act: witch-trials had been abolished in Poland in 1787. The last legal execution was in Protestant Glarus, in Switzerland, in 1782. Appropriately the craze which had been born in the Alps retreated thither to die. [. . .]

If the witch-craze were to be attacked at its centre, not merely doubted at its periphery, it was clearly necessary to challenge the whole conception of the kingdom of Satan. This neither Weyer nor Scot nor Spee had done. All through the sixteenth and seventeenth centuries it had been an axiom of faith that the Church was engaged in a life-and-death struggle with Satan. The writers of the *Malleus* had referred, in lamentable tones, to the impending end of the world whose disasters were everywhere visible (31), and the Protestant writers, reactionary in this as in all else, had used, and intensified, the same language. In the early seventeenth century millenary ideas, forgotten since the Middle Ages, were revived, and the greatest discovery of a scientific century was declared to be the calculation by a future Fellow of the Royal Society, of the hitherto elusive number of the Beast (32).

But at the very end of the century one writer did attempt to challenge the whole idea of Satan's kingdom. This was the Dutch minister Balthasar Bekker, who in 1690 published the first version of the first volume of his *de Betoverde Weereld*, 'the Enchanted World'.

Both at the time and since Bekker was regarded as the most dangerous enemy of witch-beliefs. The orthodox denounced him in unmeasured tones. Like Greve, seventy years before, he was persecuted by the Calvinist clergy of Holland and ultimately, though protected by the city of Amsterdam, driven out of the ministry. The first two volumes of his book, it is said, sold 4000 copies in two months and it was translated into French, German and English. Pamphlets were poured out against him. He was held responsible for the cessation of witch-burnings in England and Holland (33) – although witches had never been burnt in England and burnings had long ceased in Holland. Bekker, it has been regularly said, struck at the heart of the witch-craze by destroying belief in the Devil (34).

Perhaps he did in theory; but did he in fact? When we look closer, we find reasons for doubt. Bekker's foreign reputation seems largely a myth. [. . .] And anyway, he had not repudiated belief in the Devil. He merely believed that the Devil, on his fall from Heaven, had been locked up in Hell, unable further to interfere in human affairs. This purely theological point was not likely to cause a revolution in thought. In his particular arguments about witches Bekker was inspired, as he admitted, by Scot, and did not go beyond Scot.

Moreover, Bekker's radicalism was disowned by later, and perhaps more effective, opponents of the witch-craze. If any group of men destroyed the craze in Lutheran Germany it was the Pietists of the University of Halle whose leader, in this respect, was Christian Thomasius, the advocate of the vernacular language. In a series of works, beginning with a university thesis in 1701, Thomasius denounced the folly and cruelty of witch-trials. But he was careful to dissociate himself from Bekker. There is a Devil, Thomasius protests, and there are witches: this 'cannot be denied without great presumption and thoughtlessness'. But Weyer and Scot and Spee have shown that the witches who are tried in Germany are quite different from those witches whose death is prescribed in the Bible, that the demonology of the Church is a mixture of pagan and Jewish superstition, and that confessions produced by torture are false. Again and again Thomasius protests that he is falsely accused of disbelieving in the Devil. He believes in the Devil, he says, and that he still operates, externally and invisibly: he only disbelieves that the Devil has horns and a tail; and he believes in witches: he only disbelieves in their pact with the Devil, the sabbat, *incubi* and *succubi*. When we examine his arguments we find that neither he nor his friends at Halle went beyond Scot or Spee or those English writers, Wagstaffe and Webster, whose works they caused to be translated into German (35). And yet it is equally clear that the arguments which had been advanced in vain by Scot and Spee were effective when advanced by Thomasius. The witch-craze did not collapse because Bekker dislodged the Devil from his central position: the Devil decayed quietly with the witch-belief (36); and why the witch-belief decayed – why the critical arguments which were regarded as unplausible in 1563 and in 1594 and in 1631 were found plausible in 1700 – is mysterious still. [. . .]

Conclusion

I have suggested that the witch-craze of the sixteenth and seventeenth centuries must be seen, if its strength and duration are to be understood, both in its social and in its intellectual context. It cannot properly be seen, as the nineteenth-century liberal historians tended to see it, as a mere 'delusion', detached or detachable from the social and intellectual structure of the time. Had it been so – had it been no more than an artificial intellectual construction by medieval inquisitors – it is inconceivable that it should have been prolonged for two centuries after its full formulation; that this formulation should never afterwards have been changed; that criticism should have been so limited; that no criticism should have effectively undermined it; that the greatest thinkers of the time should have refrained from openly attacking it; and that some of them, like Bodin, should even have actively supported it. To conclude this essay I shall try to summarize the interpretation I have offered.

First, the witch-craze was created out of a social situation. In its expansive period, in the thirteenth century, the 'feudal' society of Christian Europe came into conflict with social groups which it could not assimilate, and whose defence of their own identity was seen, at first, as 'heresy'. Sometimes it really was heresy: heretical ideas, intellectual in origin, are often assumed by societies determined to assert their independence. So Manichaen ideas, carried – it seems – by Bulgarian missionaries, were embraced by the racially distinct society of Pyrenean France and 'Vaudois' ideas, excogitated in the cities of Lombardy or the Rhône, were adopted in the Alpine valleys where 'feudal' society could never be established. The medieval Church, as the spiritual organ of 'feudal' society, declared war on these 'heresies', and the friars, who waged that war, defined both orthodoxy and heresy in the process. [. . .]

The elaboration of the new heresy, as of the new orthodoxy, was the work of the medieval Catholic Church and, in particular, of its most active members, the Dominican friars. No argument can evade or circumvent this fact. The elements of the craze may be non-Christian, even pre-Christian. The practice of spells, the making of weather, the use of sympathetic magic may be universal. The concepts of a pact with the Devil, of night-riding to the sabbat, of *incubi* and *succubi*, may derive from the pagan folk-lore of the Germanic peoples (37). But the weaving together of these various elements into a systematic demonology which could supply a social stereotype for persecution was exclusively the work, not of Christianity, but of the Catholic Church. The Greek Orthodox Church offers no parallel. [. . .]

Such, it seems, was the origin of the system. It was perfected in the course of a local struggle and it had, at first, a local application. But the intellectual construction, once complete, was, in itself, universal. It could be applied anywhere. And in the fourteenth century, that century of increasing introversion and intolerance, among the miseries of the Black Death and the Hundred Years War in France, its application was made general. The first of the Avignon popes, themselves bishops from recalcitrant Languedoc, gave a new impulse to the craze. The weapon forged for use against nonconformist societies was taken up to destroy nonconformist individuals: while the inquisitors in the Alps and the Pyrenees continued to multiply the evidence, the warring political factions of France and Burgundy exploited it to destroy their enemies. Every spectacular episode increased the power of the myth. Like the Jew, the witch became the stereotype of the incurable nonconformist; and in the declining Middle Ages, the two were joined as scapegoats for the ills of society. The founding of the Spanish Inquisition, which empowered the 'Catholic Kings' to destroy 'judaism' in Spain, and the issue of the Witch Bull, which urged cities and princes to destroy witches in Germany, can be seen as two stages in one campaign.

Even so, the myth might have dissolved in the early sixteenth century. The new prosperity might have removed the need for a social scapegoat. The new ideas of the Renaissance might have destroyed its intellectual basis. We have seen that in the years 1500–50, outside its Alpine home, the craze died down. In those years the purified Aristoteleanism of Padua corrected the extravagance of scholastic physics; the Neoplatonism of Florence offered a more universal interpretation of Nature; the new criticism of the humanists pared down medieval absurdities. All these intellectual movements might, in themselves, be ambivalent, but they might, together, have been effective. In fact they were not. In the mid-sixteenth century, the craze was revived and extended and the years from 1560 to 1630 saw the worst episodes in its long history. It seems incontestable that the cause of this revival was the intellectual regression of Reformation and Counter-Reformation, and the renewed evangelism of the rival Churches. The former gave new life to the medieval, pseudo-Aristotelean cosmology of which demonology was now an inseparable part. The latter carried into northern Europe the same pattern of forces which the Dominicans had once carried into the Alps and Pyrenees – and evoked a similar response.

The Reformation is sometimes seen as a progressive movement. No doubt it began as such: for it began in humanism. But in the years of struggle, of ideological war, humanism was soon crushed out. The great doctors of the Reformation, as of the Counter-Reformation, and their numerous clerical myrmidons, were essentially conservative: and they conserved far more of the medieval tradition than they would willingly admit. They might reject the Roman supremacy and go back, for their Church system, to the rudimentary organization of the apostolic age. They might pare away the incrustations of doctrine, the monasticism, the 'mechanical devotions', the priestcraft of the 'corrupted' medieval Church. But these were superficial disavowals. Beneath their 'purified' Church discipline and Church doctrine, the Reformers retained the whole philosophic infrastructure of scholastic Catholicism. There was no new Protestant physics, no exclusively Protestant view of Nature. In every field of thought, Calvinism and Lutheranism, like Counter-Reformation Catholicism, marked a retreat, an obstinate defence of fixed positions. And since demonology, as developed by the Dominican inquisitors, was an extension of the pseudo-Aristotelean cosmology, it was defended no less obstinately. Luther might not quote the *Malleus*; Calvin might not own a debt to the Schoolmen; but the debt was clear, and their successors would admit it. Demonology, like the science of which it was a part, was a common inheritance which could not be denied by such conservative Reformers. It lay deeper than the superficial disputes about religious practices and the mediation of the priest. [...]

With the Catholic reconquest a generation later, the same pattern repeats itself. The Catholic missionaries too discover obstinate resistance. They too find it social as well as individual. They too find it in particular areas: in Languedoc, in the Vosges and the Jura, in the Rhineland, the German Alps. They too describe it now as Protestant heresy, now as witchcraft. The two terms are sometimes interchangeable, or at least the frontier between them is as vague as that between Albigensians and witches in the past. The Basque witches, says de l'Ancre, have been brought up in the errors of Calvinism. Nothing has spread this pest more effectively through England, Scotland, Flanders and France, declares del Rio (echoing another Jesuit, Maldonado) than *dira Calvinismi lues*. 'Witchcraft grows with heresy, heresy with witchcraft', the English Catholic Thomas Stapleton cried to the sympathetic doctors of Louvain (38). His argument – his very words – were afterwards repeated, with changed doctrinal labels, by Lutheran pastors in Germany. Whenever the missionaries of one Church are recovering a society from their rivals, 'witchcraft' is discovered beneath the thin surface of 'heresy'.

Such, it seems, is the progress of the witch-craze as a social movement. But it is not only a social movement. From its social basis it also has its individual extension. It can be extended deliberately, in times of political crisis, as a political device, to destroy powerful enemies or dangerous persons. Thus it was used in France in the fourteenth and fifteenth centuries. It can also be extended blindly, in times of panic, by its own momentum. When a 'great fear' takes hold of society, that society looks naturally to the stereotype of the enemy in its midst; and once the witch had become the stereotype, witchcraft would be the universal accusation. It was an accusation which was difficult to rebut in the lands where popular prejudice was aided by judicial torture: we have only to imagine the range of the Popish Plot in England in 1679 if every witness had been tortured. It is in such times of panic that we see the persecution extended from old women, the ordinary victims of village hatred, to educated judges and clergy whose crime is to have resisted the craze. Hence those terrible episodes in Trier and Bamberg and Würzburg. Hence also that despairing cry of the good senator de l'Ancre, that formerly witches were 'hommes vulgaires et idiots, nourris dans les bruyères et la fougière des Landes', but nowadays witches under torture confess that they have seen at the sabbat 'une infinité de gens de qualité que Satan tient voilez et à couvert pour n'estre cognus' (39). It is a sign of such a 'great fear' when the elite of society are accused of being in league with its enemies.

Finally, the stereotype, once established, creates, as it were, its own folk-lore, which becomes in itself a centralizing force. If that folk-lore had not already existed, if it had not already been created by social fear out of popular superstition within an intellectually approved cosmology, then psychopathic persons would have attached their sexual hallucinations to other, perhaps more individual figures. This, after all, is what happens today. But once the folk-lore had been created and had been impressed by the clergy upon every mind, it served as a psychological as well as a social stereotype. The Devil with his nightly visits, his *succubi* and *incubi*, his solemn pact which promised new power to gratify social and personal revenge, became 'subjective reality' to hysterical women in a harsh rural world or in artificial communities – in ill-regulated nunneries as at Marseilles, at Loudun, at Louviers, or in special regions like the Pays de Labourd, where (according to de l'Ancre) the fishermen's wives were left deserted for months. And because separate persons attached their illusions to the same imaginary pattern, they made that pattern real to others. By their separate confessions the science of the Schoolmen was empirically confirmed.

Thus on all sides the myth was built up and sustained. There were local differences of course, as well as differences of time; differences of jurisdiction as well as differences of procedure. A strong central government could control the craze while popular liberty often let it run wild. The centralized Inquisition in Spain or Italy, by monopolizing persecution, kept down its production, while north of the Alps the free competition of bishops, abbots and petty lords, each with his own jurisdiction, kept the furnaces at work. The neighbourhood of a great international university, like Basel or Heidelberg, had a salutary effect, while one fanatical preacher or one over-zealous magistrate in a backward province could infect the whole area. But all these differences merely affected the practice of the moment: the myth itself was universal and constant. Intellectually logical, socially necessary, experimentally proved, it had become a *datum* in European life, Rationalism could not attack it, for rationalism itself, as always. moved only within the intellectual context of the time. Scepticism, the distrust of reason, could provide no substitute. At best, the myth might be contained as in the early sixteenth century. But it did not evaporate: it remained at the bottom of society, like a stagnant pool, easily flooded, easily stirred. As long as the social and intellectual structure of which it was a part remained intact, any social fear was likely to flood it, any ideological struggle to stir it, and no piecemeal operation could effectively drain it away. Humanist critics, Paduan scientists, might seek to correct the philosophic base of the myth. Psychologists – medical men like Weyer and Ewich and Webster – might explain away its apparent empirical confirmation. Humane men, like Scot and Spee, by natural reason, might expose the absurdity and denounce the cruelty of the methods by which it was propagated. But to destroy the myth, to drain away the pool, such merely local operations no longer sufficed. The whole intellectual and social structure which contained it, and had solidified around it, had to be broken.

And it had to be broken not at the bottom, in the dirty sump where the witch-beliefs had collected and been systematized, but at its centre, whence they were refreshed. In the mid-seventeenth century this was done. Then the medieval synthesis, which Reformation and Counter-Reformation had artificially prolonged, was at last broken, and through the cracked crust the filthy pool drained away. Thereafter society might persecute its dissidents as Huguenots (40) or as Jews. It might discover a new stereotype, the 'Jacobin', the 'Red'. But the stereotype of the witch had gone.

References
1. H. C. Lea, *Materials toward a History of Witchcraft*, arranged and edited by A. C. Howland, Introduction by G. L. Burr (New York, 1957).
2. *Capitulatio de Partibus Saxoniae*, cap. 6. This decree, issued at Paderborn in A.D. 785, is printed in Wilhelm Boudriot, *Die alt-germanische Religion* (*Untersuchungen zur allgemeinen Religions-geschichte*, C. Clemen (ed.), Heft 2, Bonn, 1928, p. 53).
3. In his *Liber contra insulsam vulgi opinionem de grandine et tonitruis*, written *c.* A.D. 820.
4. *Joannis Filesaci Theologi Parisiensis Opera Varia*, 2nd edn (Paris, 1614), pp. 703 ff., 'De Idololatria Magica Dissertatio', Dedication.
5. Except, apparently, in Alsace. See R. Reuss, *L'Alsace au 17ᵉ siècle* (Paris, 1898), vol. 2, 106. Elsewhere 'the nobleness of his nature' repudiates it.
6. James VI, *Demonologie, in form of a Dialogue* . . . (Edinburgh, 1597), pp. 66 ff.
7. The idea that witch-beliefs were lingering relics of a systematic pre-Christian religion was first advanced by Jacob Grimm, who, in his *Deutsche Mythologie* (Göttingen, 1835), argued that the witch-cult was no other than the ancient Teutonic religion. In this form it was refuted by Soldan, who argued that, in so far as it contained pagan concepts, those concepts could be traced to Roman (and so to Greek and Oriental), not to Germanic paganism (W. G. Soldan, *Geschichte der Hexenprozesse*, Stuttgart, 1843, p. 494). The distinction may be too fine: possibly some of the coarser ingredients, though justified from literary sources, were directly derived from German paganism. But however that may be, the demonological system, as distinct from the particular details incorporated in it, is demonstrably scholastic and medieval. The fancies of the late Margaret Murray need not detain us. They were justly, if irritably, dismissed by a real scholar as 'vapid balderdash' (C. L. Ewen, *Some Witchcraft Criticisms*, 1938).
8. 'Note also', Reginald Scot wrote, 'how easily they may be brought to

confess that which they never did, nor lieth in the power of man to do.' (*Discovery of Witchcraft*, 1584, epistle to Sir Thomas Scot, J.P.)

9. See Étienne Delcambre, *Le Concept de la sorcellerie dans le duché de Lorraine au XVIe et XVIIe siècle* (Nancy, 1948–51), fasc. I, pp. 149–53.

10. Nikolaus Paulus, *Hexenwahn und Hexenprozess, vornehmlich im 16ten Jahrhundert* (Freiburg-im-Breisgau, 1910), § II, 'Luthers Stellung zur Hexenfrage', shows the growing credulity of Luther. Luther based his beliefs explicitly on the Bible and old wives' tales, but he was, of course, a renegade friar, and although he does not avow such a source, he was no doubt familiar with the more systematic demonology of the inquisitors.

11. Paulus, *Hexenwahn und Hexenprozess*, § VIII. The decline of the Zwinglian Church from the liberalism of its founder is further emphasized in the next century. See the account of Bartholomäus Anhorn, *Magiologia* (Basel, 1674), in Lea, *Materials*, p. 747.

12. Paulus, *Hexenwahn und Hexenprozess*, § IV, 'Die Bibel als Autorität für protestantische Hexenverfolgung', gives many instances of the use of this happy text. For the undeniable effect of Calvinism see the summary in G. L. Burr, 'New England's place in the history of witchcraft', in *Proceedings of the American Antiquarian Society*, 1911, reprinted in *George Lincoln Burr: His Life and Selections from His Writings* (Ithaca, N.Y., 1943), pp. 352–77.

13. The Danish oracle was Niels Hemmingsen (Hemmingius), who published his *Admonitio de Superstitionibus Magics Vitandis* at Copenhagen in 1575. He had studied at Wittenberg under Luther's successor, Melanchthon, and shows some of the good sense of his master. But he is firm on the subject of the 'good' witch; 'similis est impietas nocere et prodesse arte magica'; and he explicitly rejects the old distinction of Roman Law.

14. F. Müller, *Beiträge zur Geschichte des Hexenglaubens und des Hexenprozesses in Siebenburgen* (Brunswick, 1854), pp. 16 ff.

15. For Scotland, see G. F. Black, 'Witchcraft in Scotland 1510–1727', *Bulletin of the New York Public Library*, vol. 41, no. 2 (Nov. 1937). For England, Wallace Notestein, *History of Witchcraft in England, 1558–1718* (New York, 1909). Notestein points out that the first prosecutions under the new law were explicitly related, by the magistrate concerned, to the opinions brought by Jewel from Switzerland: 'there is a man of great cunning and knowledge come over lately unto our Queen's Majesty which hath advertised her what a company and number of witches be within England; whereupon I and other of her Justices have received commission for the apprehending of as many as are within these limits' (p. 46). It may be added that the first manual of witch-beliefs to be published in England also came from Switzerland. It was Lambert Daneau's *De Veneficis . . . Dialogus*, of which Thomas Twyne published a translation in 1575. Daneau's work had been written at Gien, near Orléans, where he was a Huguenot pastor; but it was published in Geneva, whither he had fled after the massacre of St Bartholomew

and where he had formerly learned his doctrines from Calvin himself.

16. See J. Janssen, *A History of the German People at the Close of the Middle Ages*, trans. M. A. Mitchell and A. M. Christie (1896–1925), vol. 16, p. 307.

17. Notestein, W., *History of Witchcraft, in England*, p. 116.

18. H. A. Meinders, writing in Lemgo (Westphalia) in 1716, refers to terrible abuses in witch-prosecutions in Westphalia from 1600 to 1700 in which whole towns, especially Herford and Lemgo, have been laid waste (cited in Lea, *Materials*, p. 1432; cf. also the remarks of Jacob Brunnemann, ibid., p. 429). But the persecution had begun well before 1600. It was in Lemgo, in 1583, that Scribonius had published his arguments in favour of the cold-water test, now generally used 'in hisce nostris regionibus, praesertim vero in Westphalia'. He dedicated his works to the magistrates of Lemgo and Osnabrück whom Ewich and Neuwaldt afterwards accused of 'iniquity and injustice' against witches. The Westphalian jurist Anton Praetorius, who wrote against the craze in 1598–1602, had been driven to protest by the executions he had witnessed there. (See Paulus, *Hexenwahn und Hexenprozess*, § x, 'Der calvinische Prediger Anton Praetorius, ein Bekämpfer der Hexenverfolgung'). For statistical evidence of the persecution in Osnabrück in the 1580s and 1590s, see Joseph Hansen, *Quellen und Untersuchungen zur Geschichte des Hexenwahns und der Hexenverfolgung im Mittelalter* (Bonn, 1901), p. 545, n. 1.

19. Thus, in the areas ruled by the Protestant, German-speaking city of Bern, the victims came principally from the Catholic, French-speaking Pays de Vaud: see F. Treschsel, *Das Hexenwesen im Kanton Bern* (1870) and H. Vuilleumier, *Histoire de l'Église réformée du Pays de Vaud sous le régime bernois* (Lausanne, 1927–33), vol. II, pp. 642–721.

20. This is repeatedly stated by Pierre de l'Ancre, *L'Incrédulité et mescréance du sortilège pleinement convaincue* (Paris, 1622).

21. Thus the burden of all Nikolaus Paulus' scholarly essays, printed as *Hexenwahn und Hexenprozess*, is to show (a) that before the Reformation all men, including the humanists, believed in witchcraft, so that the Catholic inquisitors deserve no special blame; (b) that in the late sixteenth century the Protestants were great burners of witches. Although Paulus carries his interest in Protestant persecution down to the end of the seventeenth century, he shows no interest in the persecutions from 1590 to 1630, which were mainly Catholic.

22. Thus William Perkins (*A Discourse on the Damned Art of Witchcraft*, Cambridge, 1608) does not mention *succubi* or *incubi* – which are absent also from English witchtrials – and rejects anything which might be regarded as popish 'conjuring'; but he accepts the pact with the Devil and the power of the Devil, by God's permission, to work whatever miracles he likes; from which all else can logically flow, even without the Dominican learning.

23. William V's father, John III, had carried out an Erasmian reform in his

duchies, and had secured, as William's tutor, Erasmus' friend Conrad von Heresbach (see A. Wolters, *Conrad von Heresbach*, Elberfeld, 1867), Carl Binz, *Doctor Johann Weyer* . . . 2nd edn (Berlin, 1896), p. 159, describes William V as 'der in den Grundsätzen des Erasmus erzogene Herzog'. Weyer's own attitude is illustrated by the fact that the whole of his chapter xviii is an extract from Erasmus' *Apologia adversus articulos aliquot per monachos quosdam in Hispaniis exhibitos* (Basel, 1529). Weyer was himself a Protestant, but his Protestantism has to be deduced: it is never stated either by him or his enemies – further evidence of his Erasmian moderation. (See Janssen, *A History of the German People*, vol. 16, pp. 320–21.) On Weyer see also Leonard Dooren, *Doctor Johannes Wier*, *Leven en Werken* (Aalten, 1940).

24. This fellow-physician was Johann Ewich, whose letter was printed by Weyer.

25. Jean Bodin attacked Charles IX as a patron of witches in his *De la démonomanie des sorciers* (Paris, 1580). Henri III was regularly attacked on the same grounds in the *Ligueur* pamphlets of 1589. See, for instance, *La Vie et faits notables de Henri de Valois*; *L'Athéisme de Henri de Valoys*; *Les Sorcelleries de Henri de Valoys*; *Charmes et caractères de sorcelleries de Henri de Valoys trouvez en la maison de Miron*, *son premier médecin*. The Erasmianism of the Court of Catherine de Médicis is well brought out by Frances Yates, *The Valois Tapestries* (*Studies of the Warburg Institute*, 1959), pp. 102–8. For Henri III as patron of Platonic 'magicians', see Frances Yates, *Giordano Bruno* (1964), p. 180.

26. *Gisberti Voetii Selectarum Disputationum Theologicarum* . . . *Pars Tertia* (Utrecht, 1649), pp. 539–632, 'de Magia'. It is amusing to note this stern Calvinist's deference to public authority: he never mentions Scot without adding 'eius liber titulo *Discoverie of Witchcraft* in Anglia combustus est', 'fuit tamen liber ille publico auctoritate combustus', or some such phrase: e.g. pp. 544, 551, 564.

27. 'Witches, if there be such creatures' is a phrase which crops up in casual records – e.g. in the remarks of an English soldier in Scotland (see *Letters and Papers Illustrating the Relations between Charles II and Scotland in 1650*, Scottish History Society, 1894, p. 136). Edward Fairfax in *A Discourse of Witchcraft* . . . (1621), refers to such as 'think that there be no witches at all', of whom he has heard that there are many, 'some of them men of worth, religious and honest'. But this absolute disbelief is not found in reasoned writing.

28. 'Nulla est fere hodie frequentior disputatio quam quae de sortilegiis et divinationibus suscipitur.' For Peña, see Hansen, *Quellen*, pp. 357–9. He concluded that *incubi* and *succubi* were real and that the night-flight to the sabbat was proved beyond doubt.

29. Sigmund Riezler, *Geschichte der Hexenprozessen in Baiern* (Cotta, 1896), p. 282.

30. Reuss, *L'Alsace au 17e siècle*, vol. 2, p. 105.

31. 'Cum inter ruentis seculi calamitates, quas (proh dolor!) non tam

legimus quam passim experimur . . . mundi vespere ad occasum declinante et malicia hominum excrescente . . .', etc. etc. *Malleus Maleficarum* (Apologia).

32. See the lyrical exclamations of the celebrated Puritan divine William Twisse in his Preface to Joseph Mede's *Key of the Revelation* (1643) and cf. Twisse's letter to Mede in Mede's *Works*, John Worthington (ed.) (1664), vol. 2, pp. 70–71.

33. Jacob Brunnemann, *Discours von betrüglichen Kennzeichen der Zauberey* (Stargard, 1708), cited in Lea, *Materials*, p. 1427.

34. This point was made by Soldan in 1843 and has been repeated ever since.

35. A German translation of Wagstaffe's *Question of Witchcraft Debated* (1669) was published at Halle, dedicated to Thomasius, in 1711. Thomasius himself wrote a preface to a German translation of Webster's *The Displaying of Supposed Witchcraft*, which was also published at Halle in 1719.

36. How little Bekker had to do with the destruction of belief among the Dutch laity is shown by the remarks of a French officer who visited Holland with Condé in 1673 – nearly twenty years before Bekker wrote. He reported that at that time most Dutchmen regarded Hell as a 'phantom' and Paradise as 'an agreeable chimera' invented by the clergy to encourage virtue. See G. B. Stoppa, *La Religion des Hollandois* . . . (Paris, 1673), p. 88.

37. This is stated by Weiser-Aall in Bächtold-Stäubli, *Handwörterbuch des deutschen Aberglauben III* (Berlin and Leipzig, 1930–31), pp. 1828 ff., s.v. 'Hexe'.

38. 'Crescit cum magia haeresis, cum haeresi magia.' Thomas Stapleton's dissertation on the question 'Cur magia pariter cum haeresi hodie creverit', delivered on 30 August 1594, is printed in *Thomae Stapleton Angli S.T.D. Opera Omnia* (Paris, 1620), vol. 2, pp. 502–7.

39. P. de l'Ancre, *Tableau de l'inconstance des mauvais anges et démons* (Paris, 1613), dedication to Mgr de Sillery, chancelier de France.

40. Thus in 1685 Louis XIV expelled the Huguenots from France as an unassimilable group, but as far as I know, the charges of witchcraft so furiously hurled at the Huguenots of the south in 1609 were not repeated. The Huguenot became again, *per se*, the stereotype of social hatred, and so remained long afterwards, as shown by the Calas affair in 1762. The social significance of that affair is well brought out in D. D. Bien, *The Calas Affair: Persecution, Toleration and Heresy in Eighteenth-Century Toulouse* (Princeton U.P., 1960).

13 Joyce Bednarski

The Salem Witch-Scare Viewed Sociologically

Abridged version of Joyce Bednarski, *The Salem Witch-Scare Viewed Sociologically*, 1968, original MS.

The Salem witch-scare has become a classic part of American history, if for no other reason than because it is unique on the American continent. Historians have been enthralled with its brutality and hysteria since its occurrence almost three hundred years ago. Immediately following the incident, several books were published, the most notable being: Cotton Mather's *Wonders of the Invisible World* and Robert Calef's *More Wonders of the Invisible World*, (see Burr, 1914) the latter author making the former one appear to be a somewhat foolish and superstitious man blinded toward the facts (Starkey, 1961, p. 246). This clash of opinions about the witch-scare was the first in a long line of disagreement which was to follow. Even the men who witnessed the trials could not agree on their meaning and relevance. This, one might suggest, is not unusual; people involved in an event are often led by their emotional attachment to the situation to interpret it according to their bias.

However, this uncertainty about Salem did not end with the generation who lived through it. Interestingly enough, it has continued to our own day, and the fanatical goings-on of that year are still surrounded by an aura of mystery and superstition which even the scientific age of the twentieth century has not successfully dispelled. In the nineteenth century, more literature was written on Salem in an attempt to explain the seemingly inconsistent outbreak of passion in the severe Puritan Community. Charles W. Upham's *Salem Witchcraft* (1867) is an extensive study of, not only the witch trials, but also the way of life which existed in the Bay Colony and provides sketches of the personalities involved in the trials. For all his work, however, Upham seems to come up with few answers. Indeed, in his more than 500 pages, he does little more than relate the history of those few years; admittedly he sets forth some causal hypotheses, but all of these he concludes are not valid after investigation of the facts. Many other documents could be cited: there is Brooks Adams's *The Emancipation of Massachusetts* (1887), one section of which deals with witchcraft, Winfield S. Nevin's *Witchcraft in Salem Village in 1692*, (1892) somewhat a repetition of Upham, but not chronologically organized and therefore confusing to the student who is not already familiar with the story. This list is hardly exhaustive, but it serves to illustrate my point that the Salem witch hunt has been a subject of continuous interest ever since it occurred and continues to the present day to haunt the minds of American historians of this early era with its seeming incongruity and ill defined effects on our culture.

The aim of this paper is to re-examine the major events of the trials and analyse them sociologically. My account is based on Marion Starkey's *The Devil in Massachusetts* (1961) as well as extensive reading in the earlier accounts of Cotton Mather, Robert Calef and others, tempered with some general background reading on the life and times, the *mores* and customs, of these early Puritans (see, Miller (1952), Taylor (1908), Winthrop (1853)). In the absence of any sociological evaluation of the events of 1692, much of my paper will be speculative.

A brief account of what took place in Salem Village (now the Boston suburb of Danvers) towards the close of the seventeenth century is a necessary preliminary to sociological analysis and should provide a deeper understanding of the social and emotional climate which nurtured the witch-scare.

The Salem witch-scare began quietly and gradually in the home of the Reverend Samuel Parris, minister in the local church. Several of the young girls of the village had taken a liking to listening to Parris's colored domestic servant, Tituba, tell stories of the supernatural which she had learned in the Barbados. They were enthralled by the excitement of her tales of witches, curses and spells, and began to spend more and more time at her feet listening to these accounts. She, too, was probably encouraged by their admiration and attention to rack her memory for the most fantastic and hair-raising of her repertoire. At what point this harmless pastime turned into the tragic action which was to sweep the community, no one knows. At any rate, some of the children were so taken by these stories that they began to feel supernatural powers working upon them.

By the end of the winter, several of the children began to suffer from a strange malady. They would, for no apparent reason, fall into convulsions, scream inhumanly, and engage in other extraordinary behavior. As their malady became public knowledge, more and more of the village children succumbed to it. While some adults were sceptical about their antics, most were horrified and puzzled by the onslaught and could do little but stand in helpless awe of the situation.

And so Dr Griggs, the town physician, was called in. He tried all his remedies; he reread all of his medical books, but to no avail. Finally he admitted that the affliction of these children was outside the realm of medicine; his considered opinion was that they were bewitched. Given the stage of medical knowledge at that time, this was not an unreasonable assumption.

The problem was passed on to the spiritual mentors of the community. Parris took the situation in hand and called together ministers from the neighboring area to decide what should be done. After witnessing the girls' contortions, the clergy agreed that Satan had come to Salem; and the only recourse was immediate action; the children would have to identify the witches who were harassing them. All this talk of witchcraft, coupled with Tituba's hair-raising tales, certainly helped to convince the girls that they were bewitched. In addition, the continuous pleading from the clergy that they reveal the identity of their tormentors must have induced them to accuse their first three 'witches'.

The character and background of those they named are significant. The first was Tituba, an obvious choice because of her vast knowledge of the 'art' and her cultural alienation from the community. The second, Sarah Good, was the town hag; a pipe-smoking tramp who wandered over the countryside begging from everyone and cursing those who refused her. Hated and disdained by all the upright Salemites, she was a prime target. The third, Sarah Osbourne, was of high social status, but her reputation was tainted by the scandal that she had lived with a man nearly a year before marrying him. To the Puritan mind, this was among the worst of sins. Besides, she had not attended church in fourteen months, and that was judged as a further sign of her degeneracy and involvement with the forces of evil.

If the coaxing of the girls can be said to have elicited the first accusations, it was the hearings at which the three accused women were examined that produced the snowballing effect which was to follow in which no one, no matter how virtuous, could feel secure from the barrage of name-calling. The children were in attendance at the hearings, where they made their presence known by crying out and rolling on the floor in agony. Everyone assumed that the women on trial were responsible for their suffering. Furthermore, when Tituba was put on the stand, she did not deny the accusations as had Sarah Good and Sarah Osbourne, but rather gave her audience an exuberant confession. She warned the onlookers that, besides herself and her two fellow accused, Satan had many more conspirators in the village.

The hearing, then which was supposed to bring a quick end to the scare, had exactly the opposite effect. The people began to look around for the additional witches to whom Tituba had made reference; the girls' status was elevated – no longer were they merely afflicted children, but oracles or diviners who could help to weed out the evil elements in the community. All the attention they received must have encouraged them to continue their antics so that they would not fall from favor. Indeed, once one had become one of the 'diviners', there was virtually no way out. This fact is exemplified by the case of Mary Warren who tried to renounce her accusations when her master, John Proctor, was cried out upon. Not only would no one listen to her, but several of the girls intimated that Mary had finally succumbed to the power of the Devil and was trying to undermine the forces of good working against him. So, within a short time, Mary 're-pented' and returned to the fold.

After the initial hearings, accusations fell like raindrops. Most of the village would have been happy if the scandal had ended with the indictment of the first three 'witches', but anyone with insight might have guessed that this was not to happen. Barely a week had passed when another accusation was made, this time not of a ne'er-do-well, but of an upstanding and pious member of the community – Martha Cory. Hers was followed by those of Dorcas Good, the five-year-old daughter of Sarah Good, and of

Rebecca Nurse and her two sisters, Mary Esty and Sarah Cloyce, three of the most saintly and respected members of the Church. And so it went – John Proctor, Giles Cory, Abigail Hobbes, Bridget Bishop, Sarah Wild, Susannah Martin, Dorcas Hoar and the Reverend George Burroughs – most of whom had previously been considered fine, God-fearing members of the community. The county jail was bursting at its seams, and the list of upcoming trials grew to an unprecedented length.

The hysteria had run wild. By spring, it no longer confined itself to Salem, but spread to Andover and other surrounding towns. At this point, the colonial officials intervened. They decided to set up a Court of Oyer and Terminer to try the cases of the suspected witches. Even this move was not sufficient to stem the growing tide of mass mania. The judges who were appointed were as easily convinced of the girls' sincerity and the accuseds' dishonesty as the Salem magistrates had been before them. Those who confessed were spared (but kept in prison), while those who refused to admit that they were agents of the Devil were hanged.

William Phips, the new governor of the Colony, admitted that he had no solution to the problem, and busied himself with the Indian wars which had been causing some trouble on the northern frontier. Meanwhile, the girls continued to cry out against an extraordinary number of people. At one point, even Lady Phips was named. When Samuel Willard, president of Harvard College and pastor of the First Church of Boston, was accused, the magistrates flatly told the girls that they were mistaken. This act marked the beginning of the end. As more and more persons of irreproachable character were cried out upon, more and more of the judges and men in authority questioned the justice of the whole procedure. The validity of spectral evidence had always been a bone of contention, and now seemed even more in doubt in view of the worsening situation. It was brought to the attention of the authorities that in the Bible the Devil had appeared in the form of Samuel, a highly regarded saint. This raised the question of whether Satan might indeed be able to impersonate an innocent person. If this were so, the spectres haunting the girls could very well be 'freelance' apparitions; and thus the prosecution would have no case at all.

In the face of growing doubts, Governor Phips dismissed the

Court of Oyer and Terminer in October, and released several persons from Prison. However, more than one hundred and fifty remained in custody, and an additional two hundred had been accused. In December, Phips instituted the Superior Court of Judicature to try those cases still on the calendar. The magistrates agreed to admit spectral evidence only in marginal cases. Of fifty-two persons tried, only three were found guilty – an amazing reversal, considering that, up to that time, there had not been a single acquittal. Phips responded by signing reprieves for the three accused as well as for five others who had been condemned previously. Finally the governor issued a general pardon for those still under suspicion, and discharged all who remained in jail. This marked the end of the Salem witch-hunt. It was over less than a year after it began, but in the course of that time nineteen persons had been hanged, two had died in prison, and Giles Cory, who had adopted the course of standing mute at his trial, had been crushed under a pile of rocks (a persuasive procedure used by the magistrates to induce confession) – a grand total of twenty-two lives sacrificed to the hysterical screechings of a pack of adolescent girls.

This is the story. Many things have been left out. Only a detailed reading of the annals of 1692 can communicate the full horror of what went on. But from this sketchy account the trend is clear; it is the story of a society gone mad – a society blind to rationality and reason, driven by fear and distrust. The question remains as to the reasons for this outburst and the effects it had on the development of events after its conclusion.

An answer to this question must be qualified by the recognition that human interaction is subject to many influences, and single causes of events can seldom be determined. Another qualification needs to be made. George Kittredge has said: 'It is easy to be wise after the fact – especially when the fact is two hundred years old' (1929, p. 373). This he sets forth as an admonition to those who would judge seventeenth-century actions by twentieth-century standards. Many ascribe the tenets of the New Englanders in the matter of witchcraft to their Puritan theology. This, he feels, is a serious error. He argues that: 'Our forefathers believed in witchcraft, not because they were Puritans, not because they were Colonials, not because they were New Englanders, but because they were men of their own time and not of ours' (1929, p. 357). He then goes on to substantiate his statement with copious evidence of a universal belief in witchcraft in the seventeenth century. This point is not ill taken. There is always the chance that the analyst will try to superimpose his cultural values and judgements on a situation in which they do not pertain and will subsequently come up with conclusions which are equally unbased. Our ideas and values have changed considerably since 1692, and therefore I am perhaps unjustified when I speak of Salem as a society gone mad – blind to all rationality and reason – for indeed this kind of rationality and reason did not come into its own until about the time of the French Revolution, almost a century after the Salem incident. However, if kept within the context of what Salem appears to be to our contemporaries, I think it is a valid statement: such hysteria is madness in any age. So long as the reason for its existence, i.e. the belief in witches, is not viewed as foolish and insane, there seems to be no injustice done.

What were the conditions which caused the Salem witch-scare? Broadly speaking, most writers will agree that scares and crazes arise during a time of struggle, upheaval and change. In an era of uncertainty men will act and react in extraordinary ways. Sometimes they will make amazing strides and on other occasions they will revert to anti-social behavior. It is a simple sociological hypothesis that when conventional avenues of conduct in a society are blocked or cut off, men will be forced to establish new ones. In this process, several structures may be tried before an acceptable one is found, and in the interim anomie may prevail.

The Bay Colony was experiencing a metamorphosis of this sort in both her political and religious-moral realms at the end of the seventeenth century. Because of the overemphasis on the Puritan ethic as the driving force behind the colonists, the political dilemma is not commonly understood. At best, the political situation in 1690 could be described as uncertain. The problems had begun more than 30 years earlier during the Quaker persecutions. King Charles's decrees had brought about only minor changes in the political outlines of the Colony; however, they had made the people uneasy about their future. The King's dispatching of four commissioners to the Commonwealth of Massachusetts to see that his orders were being carried out made the colonists even more apprehensive. In 1676, Charles II began to review property claims; in 1679, he ordered Massachusetts to allow the establishment of an Anglican Church (hitherto outlawed by the colonists). One event led to another and in 1686 James revoked the Charter and sent a Royal Governor named Andros (both an Anglican and a disdainer of colonial self-assertion) to govern the Colony. In 1689, Bostonians revolted and imprisoned Andros. Luckily for them, William of Orange had succeeded in overthrowing James, in the Glorious Revolution, and they were not reprimanded by William for their revolt against James's lackey (Erikson, 1966, p. 138).

Meanwhile, Increase Mather had gone to England in 1688 to negotiate for the reinstitution of the Charter (Kittredge, 1929, p. 371). He returned home in 1692 with a new charter instead, some of the provisions of which would make the colonists very unhappy. Indeed they had already gotten wind of the bad news, for two of Mather's fellow delegates had refused to accept the new charter and had sailed home early to warn the populace and denounce Mather. The change which incensed them stated that the electorate was no longer to be limited to members of the Covenant, but broadened to include propertied members of every Christian sect except Catholics. This provision was a considerable blow to the Puritan political theocracy: previously, law had ensured that the elect, i.e., members of the Covenant, would remain in power, regardless of their numbers. With the new ruling, there was a strong possibility that the damned would rule (those outside the Covenant heavily outnumbered those within it). Furthermore, William insisted that he name the governors of the Commonwealth, a bitter pill for the colonists to swallow, since they had been electing their own governors since the founding of the Colony more than fifty years before (Starkey, 1961, p. 131).

From this, it is apparent that the political structure of the Commonwealth had collapsed. Not only had the machinery broken down, but the theocratic philosophy which upheld it had been abandoned as well. The whole system was ready for the scrap-heap – and there were no alternatives to replace it. This fact is most significant. That the Colony was left without a measuring stick of its actions, a standard for evaluating its past and directing its future, is the very fact which generated a climate receptive to an outburst like the witchcraft mania of 1692.

The crisis in the political sphere was paralleled by one in the religious-moral realm. This was inevitable in a theocratic society such as that of the Puritans. The 'Puritan ethic' was undergoing a metamorphosis, too. But its upheaval was not the action of an outside force, as was the political change; its destruction came from within. The Puritan movement, when founded in England had been international in scope. After fifty years in the New World, the Colonial Puritans had lost most of their meaningful contacts with the outside world, and no longer looked forward to a worldwide communion of the elect (Erikson, 1966, p. 156). The sense of mission which had sustained the sect in its infancy was gone.

Furthermore, the Puritan God was omnipotent. Believers had learned to accept tragedy and failure as God's will. However, by the 1690s, they saw all around them nothing but progress (Erikson, 1966, p. 156). Man had worked, and what he had produced was good. Where effort was put forth, progress had been made. There was no evidence of a God Who, by the wave of His mysterious hand, brought tragedy or plenty. And so the people began to move from a reliance on fate to a confidence in man's ability. This idea was not congruent with the original Puritan belief in predestination and was thus another rent in the fabric of the Puritan ethic.

Still another factor which undermined the stability of the society and laid it open for the witchcraft episode was the deterioration of the strong sense of community within the Colony. When the settlers landed in America, they were a body united against the evil world. Their very existence was threatened by the wilderness, full of dangerous wild beasts and hostile Indians. Only as a unit could they hope to stand up to these adversaries which they believed to be a manifestation of Satan. Now these adversaries had been overcome. The Indians and the wild beasts had retreated with the frontier – and Massachusetts was no longer the frontier (Erikson, 1966, p. 158). Even their righteous opposition to those who did not profess the 'True Faith' was taken away from them when the decree of 1679 ordered religious toleration (at least for Anglicans) in the Bay Colony (Erikson, 1966, p. 138). It is a simple sociological fact that a strong sense of community cannot exist without a purpose. and there seemed to be no purpose for unity among the Puritans by 1690. And so the people grew away from their neighbors. Feelings of distrust and suspicion built up within the community because there was no effective avenue for channeling them toward an outside enemy.

The foregoing reasons, I feel, are causes of the Salem incident which stem from the breaking down of the system. The men of the Bay had lost their purpose and, in so doing, had lost their way. In the process of redirecting themselves, there ensued a brief period of anomie, the primary manifestation of which was the witch-scare.

On the other hand, I feel that there are factors within the workings of Puritanism which also contributed to the witch-scare. Admittedly, they may be secondary, but I still feel they are worth mentioning. In many ways, the Puritan ethic is not unlike Lockean philosophy, both subjectively and structurally. Both are highly idealistic, and yet both are racked by confusion and latent contradictions. The subjective parallel carries through on the political level, where both attempt to reconcile authority and freedom. In the Puritan treatise, man is told on the one hand that he should cling to authority, dogma and revelation while on the other hand he is permitted to appeal to nature, reason and logic. The juxtaposition of these two propositions is paradoxical, because they are polemically removed from each other and have never been successfully reconciled. These inconsistencies exist within the spiritual realm of Puritan theology as well – in the fruitless attempts meaningfully to reconcile piety with intellect and spirit with reason (Miller, 1939, p. 430). These inconsistencies loom large in the trial procedures, which serve as classic illustration of how these opposing qualities cannot exist together. It is apparent that all reason and logic had given way to dogma and revelation at the height of the hysteria and that no reason existed until the validity of dogma and revelation was dispelled.

The Puritan spirit is often looked upon as being tragic; a point with which Perry Miller strongly disagrees. Conversely, he feels that there is no sense of tragedy in Puritanism, that there is no provision in the philosophy for failure, and, therefore, no capability for its perception (1939, p. 38). Furthermore, Puritanism is unique in its absolutism and its refusal to make allowance for weakness (1939, p. 57). Coupling these two factors, one can see how the Puritan ethic encouraged a belief in witchcraft, i.e. if human failure is impossible, then any human flaw must be the work of the Devil.

There is also the possibility that the Salem witch-scare served as nothing more than a valve by which the community let off steam. They adopted the desperate piety and sense of impending doom from late medieval religion, but rejected the festivities and color which softened the harshness of that theology. Consequently, they were left without an emotional outlet. As the pressure built up, the society looked for a release, and it pounced on the first opportunity – the witch trials. That this is a major causal factor seems doubtful, but it may have had a secondary effect.

Another aspect of Puritanism is its lack of intermediaries between God and man. The pre-Calvin God was a personal God, easily accessible through saints and symbols. Reformation God, however, became elevated and aloof – outside of man's reach and understanding. Denied of this relationship, man looked for signs of God elsewhere – and the only place for him to turn was the world. If man could discern the faces of good and evil in material form, he felt more secure in his faith. From this it might be hypothesized that the aloofness of the Puritan God drove man to seek the struggle between good and evil within men in the persons of the bewitched and the witch. A further corollary to this point is that, once man no longer could find the faces of evil (the Devil) working from outside the community, he would be forced to look inward and accuse his fellows.

In summary, then, I would contend that the causes of the Salem witch-scare were both external and internal. In one respect the system was too weak to withstand the test of unity; in another it was too rigid to make allowances for the needs of its adherents not specifically provided for by the system. In the 1690s, then, Puritanism was like a rusty bridge girder: it was too brittle to stand up under the weight of controversy and not flexible enough to bend and make allowances for the changing tide of the times. In a word, it was antiquated.

What, then, were the ramifications of the Salem witch trials? Their most apparent effect was that they hastened the end of the Puritan era, and ushered in the age of reason. However, there is a more subtle proposition which I wish to set forth: that the Salem witch trials in some way affected and influenced the growth of New England as a major intellectual community. This hypothesis rests on Turner's analysis of the social drama which he sums up as follows:

Implicit in the notion of reintegration is the concept of social equilibrium. This concept involves the view that a social system is made up of interrelated units, of persons and groups, whose interests are somehow maintained in balance; and further, that when disturbance occurs, readjustments are made which have the effect of restoring the balance. But it is necessary to remember that after disturbance has occurred and readjustments have been made, there may have taken place profound modifications in the internal relations of the group. The new equilibrium is seldom a replica of the old. The interests of certain persons and groups may have gained at the expense of those of others. Certain relations between persons and groups may have increased in intensity while others may have diminished. Others again may have been completely ruptured while new relationships have come into being. A social system is in dynamic movement through space and time, in some way analogous to an organic system in that it exhibits growth and decay, in fact, the process of metabolism (1957, p. 161).

In essence, he is saying that a disturbance such as a witch hunt can act as a dynamic of social change. It can rearrange social units on the preference ladder by the very nature of its phases: breach, crisis, operation of redressive mechanisms, and either reintegration of the social groups or social recognition of irreparable schisms (1957, p. 161). A simple analogy could be made between a pyramid of children's blocks and a social system. The weak spot in both is the breach. The crisis occurs when the blocks fall down and when the basic values of the society are evaluated (indirectly by the witch hunt). The last phase entails the rebuilding of the pyramid on the one hand and the reshaping of the society on the other. Neither is likely to have all the same parts in the same places. To continue the analogy, some blocks will be higher on the pyramid than before, others lower.

This is what I contend happened in Salem in 1692. Although

the intellectual heritage was a definite part of the Puritan ethic, it ranked pretty low on the pyramid. Above it were authoritarianism, pietism, revelation, dogma, and moralism, to mention only the major ones. The crisis (the trials) proved that the most elevated values left something to be desired, and therefore when the system was rebuilt, another arrangement was tried. This rearrangement of values was taking place in the beginning of the eighteenth century when the scientific method and the concept of reason were coming into their own. These were the new and exciting ideas of the time. New England had some basis for accepting them in her intellectual heritage and high opinion of education left over from the Puritan era; and so she adopted them, and they grew and gained respect throughout the world. Consequently, by her early acceptance of these tenets, combined with their existence in an environment favorable for growth, they have developed to such a degree as to make New England an outstanding intellectual community.

References

ADAMS, B. (1887), *The Emancipation of Massachusetts*, Houghton Mifflin.

BURR, G. L. (ed.) (1914), *Narratives of the Witchcraft Cases 1648–1706*, Scribners.

ERIKSON, K. T. (1966), *Wayward Puritans*, Wiley.

KITTREDGE, G. L. (1929), *Witchcraft in Old and New England*, Harvard U.P.

MILLER, A. (1952), *The Crucible*, Viking Press.

MILLER, P. (1939), *The New England Mind*, Macmillan & Co.

NEVINS, W. S. (1892), *Witchcraft in Salem Village in 1692*, North Shore Publishing Co.

STARKEY, M. L. (1961), *The Devil in Massachusetts*, Knopf, 1950 (references are to the 1961 edn by Dolphin Books).

TAYLOR, J. M. (1908), *The Witchcraft Delusion in Colonial Connecticut*, Grafton Press.

TURNER, V. W. (1957), *Schism and Continuity in an African Society*, Manchester U.P.

UPHAM, C. W. (1867), *Salem Witchcraft*, 2 vols., Frederick Unger.

WINTHROP, J. (1853), *The History of New England*, vol. 2, Little, Brown.

14 Audrey Richards

A Modern Movement of Witch-Finders

Audrey Richards, 'A modern movement of witch-finders', *Africa*, vol. 8, 1935, no. 4, pp. 448–61.

All over present-day Africa witch-finders seem to appear, as it were from nowhere, flourish for a time, and then disappear. Either it is some individual of unusual personality in his community who announces a magic remedy for human sufferings, and so obtains a following, or else it is a more or less organized band of wonder-workers which crosses the border from some neighbouring territory with all the kudos attached to the foreign and the strange. Among these latter the celebrated *Bamucapi*, who recently swept from Nyasaland into Northern Rhodesia and later reached Southern Rhodesia and the Congo, are an interesting example. The actual origin of this movement is difficult to discover, but I watched it at its height in the Bemba country of N.E. Rhodesia in the summer of 1934, and I want in this article to describe very shortly the methods of these witch-finders, and to try to account for their success.[1]

The *Bamucapi* themselves were for the most part young and dressed in European clothing. They went about the country in ones and twos, usually paying local assistants to help them. Their leader, they said, was one Kamwende of Mlanje in Nyasaland, but he was spoken of as a person of mythical attributes rather than as an organizer in actual control. The procedure of the witch-finders was impressive. Arrived at a village, they summoned the headman, who was bidden to gather his people together and to kill and cook a chicken for the ritual meal of which all were to partake. Once assembled the men and women were lined up in separate files and passed one by one behind the back of the witch-

1. During this time Professor Malinowski, then on a tour of inspection of his pupils' fields of study, visited my area, worked himself on this problem, and generously allowed me to add his notes to my own.

finder, who caught their reflections in a small round mirror by a turn of his wrist. By his image in the glass it was claimed that a sorcerer could be immediately detected, and thus discovered, he was immediately called upon to yield up his horns (*nsengo*), a term which included all harmful magic charms. Wonderful stories were told of the perspicacity of the witch-finders. Horns wilfully concealed were apparently always unmasked. 'Look under the roof of his granary', the *Bamucapi* would cry in case of a denial by the sorcerer, and there the hidden danger would be immediately brought to light. 'We know they made no mistakes', was the significant comment of natives, 'because the men and women they spotted as sorcerers were people we had been afraid of all along!'

But with the detection of the sorcerer a cure was provided. Each man and woman drank a sip of the famous *mucapi* medicine – a fine red powder which gave a soapy solution when shaken with water in a bottle – the name of the witch-finders being said to come from the Cinyanja word *kucapa*, to rub or wash clothes. For this medicine the claim of the *Bamucapi* was staggering. It was nothing less than the complete removal of witchcraft from the territory. A man who had drunk the *mucapi* medicine, and then returned to his evil practices, was liable to instant death – a grisly death in which he was to swell to enormous proportions, his limbs crinkled with dropsy, and his body too heavy to be carried to the grave. Nor could a cunning sorcerer escape by refusing to pass in front of the magic mirror. He would merely be caught at a kind of second coming of the founder of the movement, who was to return beating a mysterious drum outside each village at night. At its sound all witches and wizards as yet undetected would be compelled to follow to the graveyard where their crimes would be finally unmasked. Some told also of the coming of a mythical woman with one breast in front and one behind. The good she would suckle in front, while the wicked would find themselves following willynilly behind. Such stories were told and retold in the villages with the myth of the original Kamwende, who, it was said, had received his revelation in the grave from which he had been resurrected after two days, with one eye, one arm, and one leg powerless, but with the secret of the *mucapi* medicine and the power to resist poisons of all kinds.

As a secondary object the *Bamucapi* sold protective charms, pinches of powder sewn up in small cloth bags. For 3d. charms could be bought against wild beasts and snakes, for 6d. powder to protect the gardens from animal pests, for 6d. a charm for luck and success and for 5s., it was rumoured, a charm for winning the favour of the local Government official. 'But you can see for yourself', my informant added, 'that very few natives have had as much money to spend as that!'

The success of the movement was from the first overwhelming. It completely captured the people's imagination, and created its myths as it spread. From hut to hut of an evening men shouted the latest exploits of the witch-finders – the number of horns found in such and such a village, or the people miraculously saved from snakes or lions. The Government, which at first allowed the movement to proceed unchecked, was universally praised. 'This is the best thing the Bwanas have ever done for us,' many natives told me. 'Now at last they are allowing us to free our country from witchcraft.' Adverse criticism of missions which refused to allow their Christians to drink the medicine was frequent. The suspicion, and often the accusations of witchcraft commonly made against unpopular Christian teachers, seemed at last to be publicly substantiated. 'If they have nothing to fear', the natives said, 'why are they afraid to put themselves to the test?' At the cross-roads outside each village was a pile of horns and other magic objects – horns which many missionaries had tried unsuccessfully for years to remove and forbid.

The cause of the success of this movement is therefore of considerable interest, the more so since it is in many ways typical of many such organizations of witch-finders which have sprung up in other parts of Africa. We have to ask ourselves first, then, why the methods of the *Bamucapi* appealed to the natives so strongly? To what fears did they seem to provide such an immediate and universal panacea? These are questions that cannot be answered by a study of the ritual and myths of the *Bamucapi* as an end in themselves. To assess the strength of the movement in any particular area we have to consider it against a background of tribal structure and belief.

In the Bemba country, for instance, it may be said that novelty was enough to account for the success of any native movement, religious or secular. The Babemba are known to be unusually credulous and unstable in temperament, the first to adopt and discard anything new. Nyasaland, the reputed home of the movement, has also a high reputation among Rhodesian natives as the land of high wages and educational facilities, and most of the clerks employed in the country are still of Nyasaland origin. Further, the Babemba are among those African peoples with whom every form of Europeanism is a positive cult. The *Bamucapi* appealed because they presented a dogma that satisfied native belief, while their ritual contained many superficial features of the white civilization. The witch-finders came as well-dressed young men, not as wrinkled old native doctors (*ŋanga*) in greasy bark-cloth. They worked in the open and lined up the natives after the manner of an official taking a census. They sold their medicine in stoppered chemist's bottles rather than in dirty old horns pulled from a skin bag. Their teaching, too, was an interesting blend of the old and the new. Their power, they said, came from Lesa, the High God on whom the *ŋanga* calls when preparing his medicine, the term being used by the missionary also to describe the Christian God. But curiously enough the efficacy of the medicine depended on the keeping of a number of taboos which are deeply embedded in native belief, such as, for instance, the taboo on a man having intercourse with a woman in the bush. Some natives said that Marya also helped the *Bamucapi*, but added quickly not the Marya of the Catholic missions, but another one; for there is no doubt the movement was anti-mission as a whole. Phrases reminiscent of Christian teaching were also used. The witch-finders addressed the villagers with a preliminary sermon, a technique quite foreign to the native *ŋanga*, and stressed such ideas as the washing of sins. Kamwende, it will be remembered, descended into the grave and rose again, and was expected to reappear at a second coming. It is interesting, too, that the *Bamucapi* followed the distinctions made by the Roman Catholic missions in the classification of native medicines. Those that contained medicine (*muti*) only were permitted, but those that contained what the Babemba call a *cifimba*, an activating principle, such as an eagle's claw or the bone of a squirrel, were to be forbidden.

But over and above the attraction of novelty there were

deeper causes behind the success of the *Bamucapi*. The witch-finders claimed as I stated, to remove the dangerous weapons of the sorcerer. We have to ask ourselves then, whether the fear of witchcraft is one which dominates native belief. Is black magic, in the sense of a definite ritual actually performed by a man in the belief that it will harm his enemy, very constantly performed among the Babemba?

An analysis of the horns collected by the *Bamucapi* throws an interesting light on this question. I took possession in one instance of the complete heap of horns and magic charms, 139 in all, which had been found in a village of some seventy huts. These lay in a tumbled heap at the cross-roads outside the village, surrounded by knots of people, mostly young men and women, murmuring under their breath at the horrors from which they had been saved. These onlookers seemed to assume to a man that the horns were dangerous objects without exception. Excited comment identified this and that small object as coming from a dead man's grave, as almost certainly part of the bone of a sorcerer's victim, or as soaked in the blood of a dead child.

The actual analysis of these horns was therefore interesting. The collection included forty-five duiker horns, admitted by most to be used as containers for charms or medicines (*muti*) usually of a harmless type such as hunting magic. Sixteen were the horns of big buck such as roan antelope, the usual containers for medicine good and bad, and even for snuff or any other substance which needs to be carried in a stoppered vessel. It would be difficult, informants admitted, to tell a container of black magic from a simple box of snuff. Of the rest of the charms, seventeen were small gourds (*misafi*) used as containers for snuff or oil with a wodden stopper fixed in the narrow end. In such tiny gourds, magic of good luck or popularity is often carried (*muti ua cisense*). Thirty-six more charms were the small cloth bags (*mikoba*) in which medicines of various sorts are sewn to be worn round the owner's neck, the *Bamucapi* themselves supplying their medicine in this form. Such medicines would be nearly always protective to the owner and not destructive to somebody else. To cut a long story short then, out of a collection of 135 horns which had drawn cries of horror and execration from the passers-by, 125 were mere containers, possibly filled with nothing more than the ordinary household remedies which the English mother keeps against coughs and digestive ailments.

Of the remainder of the horns, some were admittedly doubtful or definitely suspicious. Five were wristlets made of the skin of the water lizard or the tree iguana, which are considered ill-omened animals. Nine were bush-buck horns, and this buck (*cisongo*) has a very bad reputation among the Babemba. The animal is believed to be a *cihanda* or evil spirit, and is tabooed to chiefs, to pregnant women and others. By such a horn a sorcerer would be able to lay the spirit of his victim, sending it flying through the air by night 'glowing like a white man's torch' (*lulebanga torchi*) to the grave of the recently buried man, where it would be found sticking upright on the mound in the morning full of grave-earth and hence the injured spirit of the dead.

Some of the other objects the natives condemned in spite of all evidence of common sense, so much had they made up their minds already as to the horrors they expected to find. The parietal bone of a monkey recently shot in a garden raid was sworn to be that of a baby. The skull of a vulture with its characteristic beak was identified as an owl by natives who are good naturalists, since sorcerers are known to prowl at night with owl-like birds (*ntitimuʃi*) to steal grain from the granaries of others. A polished bit of wood was dubbed the wrist-bone of a lion by one of the best-known hunters in the district. Lastly, the two horns which raised the greatest outcry were *fimango*, or horns specially prepared by the *ŋanga* of a chief in old days to lay the spirits of sorcerers burnt after death by the *mwafi* poison ordeal; that is to say, horns which are specially made to protect people against witchcraft. These objects, filled with medicines to attract evil spirits the ends netted in and covered with red dye and black beads for the same purpose, acted, as it were, as lightning conductors, kept outside a chief's village to attract the evil spirits to the ground. *Fimango* were also used in the most important form of divination known as '*kutinta*' practised by the *ŋanga* of the chief. The main protection of the native against witchcraft in the old days was therefore cheerfully discarded on the heap at the bidding of a couple of quacks! In fact the *Bamucapi* depended a good deal for their effects on the ignorance of the young of the use of Bemba magic. Their own ignorance on the subject, and their lack of knowledge of the language, was of no account, since they defended the throwing away of a charm admittedly harmless by declaring it contained a *cifimba* unseen to the ordinary man.

Our examination of a typical heap of horns has therefore shown us that only eleven out of 135 horns were admitted by everyone to be undeniably bad destructive magic, that is to say, prepared for the injury of others. For the rest, two were actually protective magic intended to save the whole community against witchcraft, while the majority were containers of medicine, some curative and some mere charms for success, dangerous only in so far as success could be considered to be obtained at the expense of others. It would appear thus to be part of the skill of the *Bamucapi* to create the sense of danger from which they professed to save the people so miraculously. That is to say they drew out the maximum number of charms from a village by convincing each owner that detection was inevitable, either now or in a mythical future, and that even harmless charms were better out of the way. Besides, never was immunity against the charge of witchcraft secured with such ease – a penny a time and 'they give you change'! Old people who had at one time or another been accused of witchcraft, walked miles in search of the *Bamucapi* in order to drink the medicine, and so be publicly passed as free from suspicion. The pile of horns at the cross-roads naturally grew and its very height proved to the rest of the world the dangers from which it had been saved.

Are we then to believe that the sorcerer proper does not exist among the Babemba; or does he exist only, as Evans-Pritchard suggests may be the case among the Azande, not in fact, but in native opinion? (Evans-Pritchard, 1931). We know that primitive peoples are alike in their almost universal belief that death and disaster are due to supernatural agencies. They differ, on the other hand, greatly as to the proportion of human ills which they attribute to hostile fellow beings with supernatural powers and that which they believe to be inflicted by supernatural beings, angry spirits and the like, themselves.

Some communities, that is to say, are more witch-ridden than others. The Trobriand islander, Malinowski tells us, considers 'every death, without exception, as an act of sorcery (Malinowski, 1929, p. 137). Similarly, a neighbouring Melanesian people, the Dobu islanders, believe 'that all good luck is due to one's ritual being stronger than the ritual of others, which is aimed at results contràry to one's own aims (Fortune, 1932, p. 101). Of the Babemba this is emphatically not so. They believe good and bad fortune to be due to a variety of causes of which witchcraft is only one.

The place of the sorcerer in the community also varies tremendously. In some cases he practises his art, as Malinowski says, 'almost openly' (Malinowski, 1922, p. 75), the magic of healing and the magic of destruction being vested in one practitioner, who acts in the interests of the man who employs him. In such a community 'there can be no doubt that acts of sorcery are really carried out by those who believe themselves to possess black powers'. In other areas, the possession of powers of black magic is inherited in certain families and openly recognized. In other tribes, among them the Babemba, no witch-doctor will ever admit that he possesses any magic of destruction, although he may grudgingly allow that he can sometimes protect those who are attacked by the spell of a sorcerer. In this particular the natives believe that they differ from neighbouring tribes, for I heard of a man who had made a journey to the country of the Batabwa to the North-West, where he said black magic could be openly bought and sold.

This, then, is the question we shall have to ask ourselves in trying to assess the strength of the *Bamucapi*. In accounting for failing luck and disaster, what sum of human ills is debited to the sorcerers' account? It is obvious that the problem is one of practical importance to the administrator. If a native announces that his child has been killed by the evil magic of a fellow human being, he is probably punished with a legal penalty, but if the same native volunteers his bereavement to be due to the anger of his dead great-grandfather, to him an equally credible statement, he will merely be received with a tolerant smile.

Now a characteristic of Bemba belief is the number of different causes to which human ills may be attributed, and of these witchcraft is at first sight not the most important. A man may suffer harm (a) because of the anger of his ancestral spirits (*mipafi*) to whom he owes certain duties of respect, and who are ultimately responsible for punishing any infringement of tribal law. The spirit of a commoner will punish members of his own particular family, though admittedly not mortally, while the *mupafi* of a chief may inflict disaster on the whole land, either in the form of general bad luck, or some dramatic disaster such as a locust plague: (b) through the vengeance of a haunting spirit (*ciwa*), the avenging ghost of an ancestor who died neglected, injured, or wrongfully accused by his relatives: (c) through the neglect of some important ritual, such, for instance, as that protecting the purity of the household fire; or the breaking of some moral rule such as adultery committed in special circumstances: (d) through punishment sent by a chief's *mupafi* as the result of a human curse (*kulapiyfia*) when the individual concerned cannot find out who has injured or stolen from him, and calls for divine aid. In all these cases there is one common feature. Punishment is only inflicted by the supernatural power when it is deserved. The religious dogma follows strictly the tribal morality and gives it its sanction. It stresses particularly that basic sentiment of Bemba society – the attitude of a man to authority in general and in particular to his chief. *Mipafi* are injured if not given proper respect, while the whole land suffers if the chief defaults. So also in the case of the avenging *ciwa*, it is the failure to honour and stand by your relations which is punished, the typical case always given being that of the old mother who dies of starvation and neglect. Here again the *ciwa* may not even return and haunt the living without the permission of Lesa, the High-God, and only a spirit suffering under a legitimate grievance is allowed to avenge. The curse by the name of a dead chief will only light on the real offender.

To sum up, according to Bemba dogma most misfortune is believed to be due to wrong-doing, and in particular transgression of the rules of respect to authority. The cause of the disaster can be ascertained by divination, itself a mechanism socially approved and carried out by a reputable character, the *ŋanga*. The remedy can be procured by the purchase of medicine, by the performance of a laborious rite, and perhaps, most important of all, by the public admission of guilt.

In this apparently logical and orderly system there is, according to theory, only one incalculable element – the sorcerer (*muloſi*) who kills without rhyme or reason, for the sake of doing harm. The *baloſi* are enemies of society and running counter to its laws. They actually start their careers of crime by committing some outrageous act, such as father-daughter incest, or the murder of a baby of their own clan. They have various mythical attributes. They can make themselves invisible; kill at a distance; send magic birds to steal food from their enemies; and of course perform secret rites and possess and sell evil medicines. Now it is obvious that such sorcerers are actually non-existent, though their mythical attributes are readily credited to unpopular people of dour or difficult temperaments, bad mixers in the American sense, bad sharers, or persons who seem to be winning unusual success at others' expense. I would not be bold enough to say that no rites of evil magic are performed in Bemba country, or that there do not exist here and there individuals who believe themselves to possess such powers. But it is the reflection of the *buloſi* belief in the widespread use of protective magic which is, I believe, the important practical issue. In an atmosphere of suspicion and hatred, natives will believe themselves forced to buy charms from the reputable *ŋanga* of the neighbourhood, or very commonly from a witchdoctor of another tribe, to protect themselves (*kuſilika mubili*), such charms being naturally viewed with alarm by others. In such an atmosphere of mistrust, too, ordinary magic of success, hunting, and agricultural charms, or those for luck in personal relations, such as formed the bulk of the horns on our heap, assume a sinister aspect. Beauty magic bought by a young unmarried girl is not a dangerous possession, but the same charm purchased by one of two jealous co-wives would be considered a hostile act. All magic of luck and self-protection becomes dangerous, that is to say, just in so far as the success it brings is believed to hurt another. Protective magic, like protective armaments, increases the sense of insecurity it was bought to end. Herein lies the danger, especially as contact with white civilization has, in many cases, actually increased the use of such charms and counter-charms.

A little consideration will in fact show us, what is not at first sight evident, that a change in the native belief in sorcery inevitably follows changes in social structure. The strength of the fear of witchcraft in any community obviously depends on the nature of its tribal institutions.

It is clear that the strength of the belief in the power of sorcery in any community depends on the nature of its tribal institutions and, in particular, the type of authority exercised, and its legal machinery. Its incidence will vary with its system of social grouping, local or kinship, and the absence or presence of emotional tension between these groups. To explain by a contrast between two widely different cultures, the Trobriand Islander is afraid his chief may bewitch him, and hence magic acts in this community as a conservative force backing up his authority. Witchcraft has its appointed place in the whole political system. The Mubemba, living under a far more autocratic and powerful chief, says simply, 'Why should a chief bewitch a commoner since he can so easily beat him or mutilate him?' Evans-Pritchard, in fact, suggests that we shall find an interesting correlation between the morphology of magic and the type of political system in a primitive society (Evans-Pritchard, 1929).

The presence or absence of legal machinery for settling grievances obviously also affects the incidence of magic through out the society. The Melanesian often has no way of venting his grievance against his fellows except by the practice of the magic of hate. The Mubemba, in common with most other Bantu peoples, can obtain redress in a legal court. He brings a case where the former would besiege the sorcerer for more and more spells.

Again there are patterns of culture in which two social groups are legally bound together in a network of obligations mutually burdensome, and providing perpetual cause for emotional tension. Two individuals may be placed by society in a position of constant rivalry from the start. In such an atmosphere suspicion and charges of witchcraft flourish. I will instance only from the same two Melanesian societies, the relation in Trobriand matrilineal society between a man's heir, his maternal nephew, and his son; or in Dobu the hostility between the groups united in marriage (*susu*) between which the fear of witchcraft is an absolutely dominating dread. Among the Babemba differences in the marriage and kinship system do not provide groupings with interests so sharply contrasted, although the co-wives in a society where the women have never really accepted polygamy as an institution, or the rival heirs to great chieftainships, are always suspected of bewitching each other, But I believe conflicting elements in the society have lately increased.

This is, in fact, the crux of the whole matter. Missionaries all over Africa are teaching a religion which casts out fear, but economic and social changes have so shattered tribal institutions and moral codes that the result of white contact is in many cases an actual increase in the dread of witchcraft, and therefore in the whole incidence of magic throughout the group.

In Bemba society the position of the chief has materially altered. One of his functions was formerly the administration of the poison ordeal (*mwafi*) to those accused of sorcery, and this gave an ultimate sense of security to the community at large. Now he no longer performs this duty, and his subjects know, moreover, that they cannot charge a witch in a legal court, black or white. 'No one will help us now', said an informant about the *Bamucapi* movement, 'unless we help ourselves.' It must be remembered, too, that divination, itself an essential part of the native system of fixing guilt, can no longer be publicly practised. It exists, but is discredited, and in this transition stage its loss has certainly robbed the native of some of his old moral certainties.

Further, with alterations in the sanctions for the power of the chief – his wealth, military supremacy, and the belief in his supernatural powers – that attitude to authority, on which, as we saw, tribal morality so largely depended, has been rudely shaken, and with it the whole system of beliefs in supernatural punishment for wrong-doing. Some natives are abandoning tribal rules because they find them burdensome; and some are living in conditions where it is impossible to carry them out – perhaps working at a mine too far to be able to care for their kinsmen or to carry out certain religious rites. Other natives again, many of them Christians, are caught between clashing moralities. In either case the majority are suffering, I believe, from a perpetual sense of guilt, expressing itself in a constant anxiety for some kind of supernatural defence. Nowhere did I feel this more strongly than in the most civilized part of Northern Rhodesia, the copper belt. Here a Bemba woman no longer feels it necessary to keep the wearisome taboos for the protection of her household fire, but just for that reason she feels herself bound to pay as much as she can for protective charms to save the life of her child – 'just in case'. The influence of wage-earning is here again all-powerful. Money seems to the urban native his only asset in this insecure world. By it he can in effect exchange a belief in a system of ancestral spirits who demand respect, the performance of exacting ceremonial, and the keeping of tribal morality for safety bought on a hard cash basis open to all who have money, whatever their position in the society. What wonder, then, that he rushes to the seller of charms? And wherever protective magic is freely bought and sold there is an atmosphere of mutual suspicion between individuals. The fear of witchcraft increases, and witch-finders flourish.

Again, social grouping has been altered by white contact, with, as a transition stage, new causes of hostility between the individual components. In villages near European settlements, natives from other areas have intruded on original kinship units because they want to live near their work. 'We don't feel safe in this village. There are so many strangers here', an old woman said to me in a village near Kasama. In the mines it is the tribal admixture which is, I believe, at the basis of the natives' positive obsession by the fear of witchcraft. Each tribe credits the other with absolutely diabolical powers. Paralysed by the fear of the unknown, what can they do but buy more charms? Moreover, wage-earning in a large industrial undertaking provides opportunity for advance through individual initiative, and hence jealousy is rife. I know few successful clerks raised above the heads of their fellows who have not been accused at one time or another of sorcery. 'How else did he gain the bwana's favour?' is the natural question. And it is in the ranks of such men that, paradoxically enough, the most money is spent in the purchase of protective charms. I know of one ex-Government clerk in the Kasama area who had spent a Government bonus of £15 on the purchase of protective magic from a neighbouring tribe. Jealousy of the man who has adapted himself more quickly than his fellows to Europeanism is, I believe, inevitable in this transition stage.

Here, then, we must leave our study of the *Bamucapi* movement. We have seen that part of the success of these charlatans was due to their clever blend of the old and the new, and I believe that such a combination will be almost invariably found in modern witch-finder movements. Added to this we must reckon the cleverness of a technique that drew from a village its harmless as well as its dangerous horns, and by the multiplicity of charms thus produced increased the sense of the risk the whole community had run. An analysis of the horns collected led us to doubt the existence of sorcerers proper in the community, a doubt confirmed by a study of Bemba belief as to the supernatural causes of death and disaster. But native belief in witchcraft, and the widespread use of protective magic and counter-charms of all kinds, was confirmed. This latter I believe to have been actually increased by contact with the white civilization, and the resultant economic and social changes in Northern Rhodesia. Hence follows the success of modern movements of witch-finders, movements which are, I believe, inevitable as a product of violent changes in tribal organization and belief.

References

EVANS-PRITCHARD, E. E. (1929), 'The morphology and function of magic', *American Anthropologist*, vol. 31.

EVANS-PRITCHARD, E. E. (1931), 'Sorcery and native opinion', *Africa*, vol. 4, no. 1.

FORTUNE, R. F. (1932), *Sorcerers of Dobu*, Routledge.

MALINOWSKI, B. (1922), *Argonauts of the Western Pacific*, Routledge.

MALINOWSKI, B. (1929), *Sexual Life of Savages*, Routledge.

15 Max Marwick

The Bwanali-Mpulumutsi Anti-Witchcraft Movement[1]

From M. G. Marwick, 'Another modern anti-witchcraft movement in East Central Africa', *Africa*, vol. 20, 1950, pp. 100–112. Abridged by the author.

The movement to be described is the one initiated by Bwanali in Southern Nyasaland, and extended by his disciple, Mpulumutsi, alias Bonjisi, whose headquarters were near Furancungo in the district of Tete, Portuguese East Africa. Wherever possible I have quoted my own fairly literal translations of statements made in Nyanja to me or to my assistants by informants who belong to 'tribal' designations such as Ceŵa, Ntumba, Nyanja etc. who in the past were collectively known as the Malawi; a small minority, however, are Nyanja-speaking Ngoni – descendants of the Zulu-Swazi invaders who enslaved many of the Malawi peoples from about a century ago until, fifty years later, their power was broken by the Europeans.

The Nyanja witchcraft system is characterized by beliefs that witches are necrophagous, and that they attack only their matrilineal relatives. Their motives are said to be 'hunger for meat' (*nkhuli*), and/or the hatred of a kinsman, because, people say, there is no way of resolving hatred between matrikin other than the use of witchcraft. Nyanja make no clear distinction between witchcraft and sorcery. And they believe witches have familiars such as hyenas and owls.

The general opinion among Nyanja informants is that witchcraft is on the increase; and they certainly believe that it operates especially in the new situations arising from modern social changes, e.g. in quarrels between mother's brothers and sister's sons over the ownership of cattle bought with wages earned by the latter at the labour centres. The alleged increase in the incidence of witchcraft is attributed, however, to the fact that the

1. The field-work on which this paper is based was generously financed by the Colonial Social Science Research Council.

mwabvi poison ordeal, which in the old days was regularly applied as a measure of public hygiene, has been suppressed by the Europeans.

In my notes the first reference to Bwanali occurs in a text written in June 1947. Within a month or two of this time Bwanali's fame and that of his disciple, Bonjisi, alias Mpulumutsi, had quickly spread over Nyasaland and the adjoining parts of Northern Rhodesia and Portuguese East Africa. In December 1947 I was able to have a short interview with Bwanali.

When I visited him, he was living in a village on the Chikwawa side of the boundary between Neno and Chikwawa Districts, Southern Nyasaland. I found him seated on a new reed mat outside a hut. He was simply dressed in new blue shirt and shorts, and he had a white cotton robe over his shoulder, though he left this behind when he showed me over the barrack-like shelters that had been built for his patients. These shelters were occupied by people who, he told me, were not yet well enough to go home. Next to him on his mat, Bwanali had a copy of the Nyanja Bible.

He told me that for many years he had been a hunter in Portuguese East Africa, but that he had given this up some time back in order to become a 'doctor' (herbalist). His present work started in July 1946. Contrary to rumour, he asserted, he did not die and wake up again or have any revelations that God wanted him to do this work: he simply found that the number of his successful cures suddenly increased. From this he felt that God was helping him.

Referring to his general procedure, Bwanali said that if a person comes to him, he makes incisions in his skin on various parts of his body and rubs medicine into them. If a person wants medicine to take home, he gives it to him, but taking medicine home is not a condition of being treated. If people want to dig the medicinal roots for themselves, he tells them all they want to know – how to identify the trees, dig the roots, prepare and administer the medicine. Those with intelligence, he added, go back and become 'doctors' among their own people. He does not receive any payment for his work.

When I asked him to explain the relationship between Bonjisi (Mpulumutsi) and himself, Bwanali said that after Bonjisi had been killed by the witchcraft of his relatives, his corpse was brought to him [Bwanali] and he revived him. Bonjisi stayed on to learn all about the medicines, and then went back to his own area to do work similar to his [Bwanali's].

Asked whether people really confess their witchcraft to him, he said that they do. He emphasized that they do this before being given the medicine. He exhorts them to give up their evil practices. He points out to them that God did not create them bad, and that they should conduct themselves in a manner worthy of their creation. If they return to their tricks, he warns them, they will not continue to live. A return to witchcraft will make them feel ill, and this will be the sign that they are not behaving themselves as they should.

While I do not exclude the possibility that Bwanali was keeping information from me (our interview was rather a hurried one), the general impression I got of him was that he is very genuinely concerned with the growing incidence of man's wickedness (in the form of witchcraft) and that he considers it his divine calling to help man throw it off. His system of morality seems consistent with both Nyanja and Christian patterns. Though his belief in witchcraft and his encouragement in others of this belief would probably be condemned by certain missionaries, no one can say that he is not a deeply religious man. From the mental hygiene viewpoint he probably does more good than harm. His function is comparable with that of a father-confessor or a psychiatrist in our own society. Though, according to Western standards, he may be misguided, his sincerity seems striking.

For various reasons I was unable to pay a visit to Mpulumutsi and the nearest approach I have to a factual account of him is the following statement made to me by a man who had just returned from a visit to him.

We were ten days travelling before we arrived at his 'compound' which is at a place called Matenje in Portuguese territory. Mpulumutsi got his knowledge and technique from Ce Bwana Ali[2] who does similar work at a place near Blantyre. It was after he had died and risen again that he went to Bwanali. We arrived on the morning of the eleventh day, and at two o'clock that afternoon he called us and made us stand in a long queue – men and women together. He then started to make incisions in

2. *Ce* is the Yao equivalent of 'Mr'; *Bwana* is the Nyanja for 'master'.

our skins and rub medicine into them. He did this on our insteps, throats, chests and backs. He rubbed some medicine on our heads, gave us some to drink and some to take home with us. As he gave us the medicine, he told us to throw away all the medicines we had in our houses, especially those for killing people. Medicines not used for killing people, he said, should be thrown away, too, but fresh supplies of them might be dug without any danger – especially if they were mixed with some of the medicine he now gave us. That which he now handed to us we should use for this purpose, as well as for treating our relatives at home.

The person who gave these instructions was the one who died and woke up after his corpse had been two days in his house. After he had woken up he came with a book. It was a Christian book – the Nyanja Bible. This man was formerly a cook in Johannesburg. He is an Ngoni of Gomani's group, still quite young – about my age [between thirty and forty]. His name is Joni [John], but he admits to the name of Mpulumutsi. When we got there, he asked us, 'Why have you come here?' We replied, 'We heard that Mpulumutsi was here.' 'O.K.',[3] he said, 'you've found me today. But if you've come with two hearts, you won't get home again. You must come with one heart only.' 'We want people of good heart', he continued, 'we don't want people who kill one another. This season the people will not get their hoeing done easily because they'll be too busy carting one another back and forth [i.e. burying one another]. This is because many people will forget my warning and die as a result of returning to their practice of killing their fellow men by witchcraft or of eating human flesh [i.e. of people killed by other witches].'

After we had been treated and given medicine to take away with us, we retired. Some people woke up with headaches, and went and complained of them to Mpulumutsi. He said to them, 'You've been eating your fellow men.' One confessed: 'Yes, I've eaten two of my children.' Another said, 'I've eaten my mother-in-law and her husband.' A third admitted to having brought a human head with him and to having used flesh from it as a 'relish' to eat with his maize porridge on the very journey to Mpulumutsi! He had thrown it away just before arriving. Mpulumutsi warned these people that they should give up their evil practices. After that he gave them medicine to drink.

Those who, having been treated with Mpulumutsi's medicines, don't confess their witchcraft, or resume it after having confessed, are sure to die. Many die on the way home to their villages. [Q.] No, I didn't see any dead people, but on the way there I saw a number of trees from

3. The most adequate translation of the much-used Nyanja expression, *cabwino*.

which bark had been stripped in order to make coffins for those who had died by the way.

People don't have to pay anything: they simply receive treatment and medicine. Some bring castor oil and give it to Mpulumutsi for mixing with the medicine. Others don't bring anything. Why should they? Why should Mpulumutsi have a return for his work, seeing that God told him to do it?

A person on his return from being treated by Mpulumutsi should not touch his medicines but should get an untreated person to throw them away for him. They should be thrown away in water.

Mpulumutsi said nothing about beating a drum, but other people we met told us that he would beat a drum and all the witches would be forced by its sound to go to him and be caught.

The treatment given by Bwanali and Mpulumutsi is believed to have two functions, a protective one and a destructive one. There is a suggestion that the attraction of the first function causes witches to undergo the treatment and expose themselves to the dangers inherent in the second one. The belief in the destructive function of the medicine implies that it has a selective effect similar to that of the poison ordeal: it spares the innocent and kills the witches.

The reader will have noticed a number of similarities between the Bwanali-Mpulumutsi and Mcape[4] movements. Both started in Nyasaland and spread into adjoining territories. Both aimed at the complete removal of witchcraft from the country by the systematic destruction or reform of witches and by the protection of their potential victims. And the same beliefs have occurred in association with both: for instance, that the originator of the movement had died and been resurrected; that the medicine would lead to death in those who resumed their witchcraft; that on the 'second coming' or at some significant future date a drum would be beaten which would inexorably attract witches to their death; that Maria (Marya) would assist in the destruction of the witches; and that certain rules and taboos should be observed by persons who had been treated with the medicine.

The differences between the two movements are usually to be found in those activities to which European control might have been applied in the case of the Mcape movement. There were three ways in which the Mcape vendors threw themselves open

4. See previous Reading – *Ed.*

to European control. Firstly, they made their patients drink medicines said to have divining properties. This was bound to evoke opposition since it so clearly resembled the *mwabvi* poison ordeal, which had been suppressed. Secondly, not necessarily by administering medicines, but by using mirrors and other devices, they made direct accusations of witchcraft. This again was bound to conflict with the requirements of European Administrations whose concern to keep the peace had made them declare accusations of witchcraft illegal. Finally, they sold medicines and charms, a step that rendered them liable to prosecution for fraudulent dealing.

The most important differences between the Bwanali-Mpulumutsi and Mcape movements are in these three spheres. Firstly, the evidence suggests that, although it is not unknown for Bwanali and Mpulumutsi to administer medicines orally, they generally do this only after a confession has been made. Normally they apply the medicines to incisions made in the skin, a course of action that has no resemblance to the traditional poison ordeal. Secondly, judging from reports, they do not make a practice of openly accusing people of witchcraft; listening to confessions of witchcraft can hardly be an offence. Thirdly, the available evidence suggests that they do not receive any payment for their work. The movement of 1947 as compared with that of the 1930s is basically more like a religious movement than a commercial 'racket'. Its emphasis on divine inspiration, the sharing of sins by confession, and back-to-God moral rearmament classes it with a religious revival rather than with the patent medicine trade.

16 R. G. Willis

The Kamcape Movement

Excerpts from R. G. Willis, 'Kamcape: an anti-sorcery movement in south-west Tanzania', *Africa*, vol. 38, 1968, pp. 1–15.

While doing field-work among the Fipa of south-west Tanzania between December 1962 and June 1964 I collected evidence about an anti-sorcery cult or movement called Kamcape which was then active in the area.[1] The present article describes this evidence and seeks to assess its sociological significance. [. . .] The Fipa are a Bantu group inhabiting the high plateau at the south end of Lake Tanganyika [. . .]. They are primarily agriculturalists, with millet, maize and beans as the major crops. They also keep livestock: mainly cattle, goats and sheep. Many of the Fipa [. . .] inhabiting the Rukwa valley and Lake Tanganyika shore are fishermen. [. . .]

The Idiom of Mystical Belief

Traditionally, Fipa explained unfortunate or unusual events by reference to one of three kinds of mystical or invisible agency. There were the non-human divinities (*imyaao* or *amaleesa*) who were identified with some particular natural object and often reincarnated in pythons; there were the ancestral spirits (*imisimu*); and there was sorcery (*uloosi*). Which agency was responsible in any particular case was decided by divination. Against attack by sorcery, Fipa had two methods of defence: as individuals, they had recourse to magician-doctors for protective or countervailing medicine; and as communities, they periodically subjected those of their number who were suspected of being sorcerers to the ordeal of drinking a vegetable poison, *umwaafi*.[2] Those who vomited the poison were proved innocent;

1. The research was paid for by a generous grant from the Emslie Horniman Anthropological Scholarship Fund.
2. Village headmen obtained the poison on behalf of their villages from

those who did not were considered guilty and either died or were put to death. As a precautionary measure, poison was often administered to entire village populations, except children.

Seventy years of Christian missionary activity, and other Westernizing influences, have substantially eroded Fipa belief in the traditional divinities and, though to a lesser extent, in the ancestral spirits. On the other hand, belief in sorcery is general, even among many educated people. Fipa see the sorcerer (*unndoosi*; pl., *aloosi*) as a hereditary specialist analogous, in his own sinister way, to the magician-doctor (*siŋaanga*; pl. *asiŋaanga*). Like the magician-doctor, the sorcerer operates with a wide assortment of symbolic material ingredients which are divided into two categories: primary ingredients, *ifiti fikola*; and secondary ingredients, *ifisiimba* or *ifingila*, whose purpose is to augment and intensify the power of the primary ingredients. The primary ingredients are collected *ad hoc* by the magician-doctor (and supposedly by the sorcerer also). Secondary ingredients are kept by both classes of expert in a special bag, called *intaangala*. Sometimes Fipa implicitly recognize the similarity between sorcerers and magician-doctors by referring to the latter as 'doctors of life' (*asiŋaanga ya uumi*). The word for the lore and practice of magician-doctors, *ugaanga*, may also serve as a euphemism for sorcery.

A common image of a sorcerer is an old man who goes around his village naked at night, seeking to enter huts and remove head and pubic hair from their magically stupefied occupants, later using the hair to make noxious medicine. A more complex image consists of an old man and his wife, also naked, who carries her husband suspended upside-down from her shoulders, while she clasps his lower legs to her breasts.

Sorcerers are said to have many ways of injuring their victims at a distance. Sometimes they send a certain fly, whose bite is said to be fatal, or a mole, or a pigeon, or a kind of meteor called *ilyaŋoombe*. The most dreaded weapon of all is a preparation called *ulupekeso*, which is said to wipe out entire extended families.

Sorcerers are said to have means of turning their victims into zombies (*amasea*), which are then forced to work in their masters'

their district governor, who had custody of it. The poison ordeal was also employed to settle other disputed criminal cases, such as theft and murder.

gardens at night, sleeping on top of his hut by day. Certain experts in sorcery are said to have the power to metamorphose themselves (*ukusaangooka*) into the form of a ferocious animal, such as a lion or leopard, in which shape they attack and kill their human prey.

An Anti-Sorcery Movement in Action

The existence in Ufipa of an anti-sorcery cult first came to the notice of the authorities there near the end of 1963, when a man called Yasita Mtontela was severely beaten and injured by fellow villagers of Kapenta, a small settlement in the south-east corner of Ufipa. Four men and a woman were subsequently accused and convicted in the magistrate's court at Sumbawanga, central Ufipa, of assaulting Mtontela.

In their defence the accused said the assault on Mtontela followed a visit to Kapenta by adherents of a movement called Kamcape, whose object was to abolish sorcery. The visitors, who numbered about twenty, were led by the accused woman, Luse Pesambila, whose home was near Mpui, about thirty miles away. Her followers were all strangers to Kapenta.

The exponents of Kamcape required all the villagers to drink of a special potion and to have 'medicine' rubbed into incisions made in the centre of their foreheads and between the thumb and forefinger of their right hands. They were told that this treatment guaranteed immunity from sorcery. Several old men who were accused by the villagers of practising sorcery were similarly treated, and it was explained that if they reverted to sorcery afterwards the 'medicine' would kill them.

According to the five accused persons, Mtontela, who was believed to have killed a fellow villager by sorcery, refused to drink the Kamcape potion or submit to being cut. His hut was then searched and several animal horns were found concealed in the roof.

What happened next was described to me in an interview in prison with two of the convicted men:

The horns taken from Mtontela's hut were filled with a special medicine, made of zebra meat and oil, prepared by Luse Pesambila [the woman leader of the Kamcape party]. They were placed on a two-legged stool set upright in the ground in the middle of the *baraza* [a large open hut used for public and official business]. Three local headmen were among the crowd assembled there. Luse Pesambila then laid beads on the horns, which soon began to emit red smoke, of the kind sorcerers send to injure and kill their victims.

Confronted with this evidence of his guilt, Mtontela thereupon confessed his crime, describing how he had secretly taken samples of the dead man's excrement, spittle and urine and mixed them with medicine in order to kill him.

It was after this that we beat Mtontela.

The prisoners' statement added that the potion and medicine brought by the Kamcape cult members had originated in Nyasaland (Malawi), with a man called Icikanga, and had been brought from Unyamwanga (a tribal area to the south-east of Ufipa) by a certain Paulo Mombo.

In the following year, 1964, the Kamcape movement spread through southern Ufipa, giving rise to considerable and increasing concern among the officers of the local administration (as I learned from the then Area Commissioner, Mr Philip Mbogo).

There was a common pattern underlying Kamcape operations. The first move was for several cult members (referred to as 'scouts' by my informants) to visit a village and have secret conversations with the headman. The latter, it seems, could usually be persuaded that a Kamcape 'cleansing' operation in his village was desirable. A suitable fee was then agreed on. The visitors would spend the night in the headman's hut and disappear early the next morning.

Several days, or weeks, later, a party (which was always said to be 'large') of Kamcape cult members and supporters would arrive in the selected village and begin operations.

In March 1964 I visited several villages just after Kamcape had been there. In Kapele, a hamlet of about fifty inhabitants, seven old men had been accused of sorcery and 'branded' with deep razor or knife cuts in the centre of the forehead.

At this hamlet I saw a basket about two feet high and eighteen inches in diameter, which was full of animal horns, cowtails, pieces of wood, and animal bones. All these objects were said to have been removed from surrounding huts during the Kamcape operation. Near by was an earthen pot containing a pint-sized tin and an orange-coloured fluid said to have been made by boiling the bark of a tree called *nacifuumbi*.

One of the seven alleged 'sorcerers' in this hamlet, Mikaeli, told me he had been accused by Kamcape of killing five people and causing cattle to become lame. A young woman there admitted she had held the head of this old man, who was her mother's father, while he was 'branded'. Mikaeli vehemently denied his guilt to me, and publicly, and expressed his intention of going to Sumbawanga to complain to the police. A score or so people standing around, however, were apparently convinced of Mikaeli's guilt. The most vocal of these was a youth called Danieli who said he came from the village of Chianda, about five miles away. Mikaeli, he said, had made lethal medicine from the footprints of his victims. Asked how he knew this, he said he had been told by several people, whom he refused to name.

Danieli said that the object of Kamcape was to 'cleanse' the country and the villages. He claimed to possess official authorization to combat sorcery in the form of a certificate (*cheti*).

At another and larger settlement about three miles from the hamlet of Kapele, and on the same day, I saw a girl called Natalia whom I judged to be about sixteen years old and who was said to have taken a leading part in the Kamcape operation in Kapele. She admitted administering 'medicine' and making cuts on the foreheads and hands of alleged sorcerers, including Mikaeli.

Natalia said she had learned the technique of Kamcape from an elder sister who lived in the village of Mchima, about sixteen miles south-east of Kapele. The sister had in turn been instructed by a magician-doctor called Pita Ote, also of Mchima village, who was a disciple of Icikanga, the founder of the Kamcape movement.

How 'Icikanga' came to originate the Kamcape anti-sorcery movement is described in the following story:

Two brothers were at the seaside. They had collected a lot of money and one day the elder brother said he would go home, taking the money with him in a bag. The younger brother said he would follow him later. So the elder brother went home and a few days after arriving there he died, through sorcery. The other villagers buried him, together with the bag he had brought home.

Some time later the younger brother arrived and was told of his elder brother's death. Then he asked, 'What of the bag he brought with him?' and was told it had been buried with his brother. He then said he would dig up the corpse and recover the bag of money, and after considerable trouble obtained permission to disinter, the police coming along to watch. When he had been digging for a while there was a strange noise and the 'corpse' sat up, with the bag under its arm, and said: 'I have come back to rid the world of sorcery.'

Icikanga then arose and went and branded the man who had ensorcelled him, and that was the beginning of Kamcape.

The movement continued to spread northwards and westwards from its point of origin in south-eastern Ufipa throughout 1964. In November, according to my informants, Kamcape was active near and around the large village and port of Kirando, in the north-western corner of Ufipa. It was noticeable that the movement made no attempt to operate in the populous (and relatively well-policed) villages clustered around the administrative centre of Sumbawanga, but confined its activities to the more remote settlements. By the beginning of 1965 there were no more reports of such disturbances in any part of Ufipa.[3]

Earlier Movements

The anti-sorcery cult that flourished in Ufipa in 1964 was not the first movement of this kind to occur in the area or in this general region of central Africa. In 1933–4 a movement called *Mcape* (or *Mcapi*) swept from Nyasaland into Northern Rhodesia and later reached Southern Rhodesia, Mozambique and the Congo. The initiates of this movement or cult are said to have derived their authority and knowledge from a certain Kamwende of Mlanje in Nyasaland, who was resurrected after two days in the grave.[4]

3. According to an informant in contact with the administrative and judicial authorities at this time.
4. Richards (1935). According to an unpublished paper by Professor T. O. Ranger, who has drawn upon archival material in Dar es Salaam, this movement was active in south-west and southern Tanganyika, and particularly so in Ufipa.

In 1943–4 an anti-sorcery movement called Kamcape was active in some parts of Ufipa, particularly the Rukwa valley (eastern Ufipa).[5] In 1947 an anti-witchcraft movement called Bwanali-Mpulumutsi arose in Nyasaland and spread into Northern Rhodesia.[6] In 1954 a movement, or movements variously called Kamcape, *Wacilole*, or *WaCauuta*[7], flourished in Ufipa. The *Wacilole* (literally, 'People of the Mirror') employed a hand mirror with which they claimed to detect sorcerers, by studying the reflections in it of villagers lined up for the purpose.[8] The *WaCauuta* ('People of Cauuta') apparently recruited only women; members painted their faces white (this colour symbolizes spiritual power among the Fipa) and danced themselves into a state of dissociation, when they were supposed to be able to discover sorcerers.

Comparisons

The Kamcape anti-sorcery movement of 1963–4 in Ufipa bears certain obvious resemblances to earlier movements directed against mystical evil-doers in this part of Africa. The similarity between the name 'Kamcape' and the 'Mcape' (or 'Mcapi') movement of 1933–4 in Northern Rhodesia is at once apparent. According to Richards, 'Mcape' was derived from a Nyanja verb *ku-capa*, to rub or wash clothes. 'Kamcape' appears to be the same word prefixed by the common Bantu particle *ka*.[9] Like the Mcape and Bwanali-Mpulumutsi movements, the Kamcape movement of 1963–4 looked to an origin in Nyasaland (Malawi); and the return from the grave of Icikanga, Kamcape's supposed founder, recalls the 'resurrection' of Kamwende, originator of the 1933–4 movement.

5. I owe this information to missionary sources in Ufipa.

6. Marwick (1950). This movement, which was also associated with a resurrection myth, did not spread to Ufipa, as far as I know.

7. According to missionary and other informants. The 1954 Kamcape movement in Ufipa is also referred to in Marwick (1965, p. 94).

8. A similar method of divination was employed by the Mcape movement of 1933–4 (Richards, 1935).

9. In Fipa the particle *ka* is used to express a consequential action or end-result. 'Kamcape' might also be connected with a Swahili word *chapa*, a print or brand, in view of the Kamcape practice of 'branding' alleged sorcerers.

R. G. Willis

The methods employed by Kamcape to combat, or neutralize, the power of alleged sorcerers again resemble the procedure of Mcape[10] – and also of many Congolese anti-sorcery, or anti-witchcraft, cults.[11] The most recent Kamcape movement in Ufipa also resembled the Mcape cult of 1933–4 (and the Congolese cults too, apparently) in its insistence that villagers surrender (or submit to confiscation of) all objects of magico-medical significance.[12] Richards makes the point that most of the 'witch-craft objects' thus revealed were probably innocuous in both fact and purpose – though in the emotionally charged atmosphere of a witch-hunt the Bemba villagers found it hard to realize this (Richards, 1935). The same sort of thing seems to have happened during the Kamcape operations in Ufipa.

As well as administering an anti-sorcery potion, the Kamcape cultists of 1963–4 in Ufipa rubbed anti-sorcery 'medicine' into incisions made in the skin.[13] It may be that this combination of two traditional methods of introducing substances into the body represented some recognition of the apparent failure of earlier movements (including the Kamcape movements of 1943–4 and 1954 in Ufipa) and a consequent need to 'do better' this time.

Another feature of the most recent Kamcape movement in Ufipa was the conspicuous 'branding' of alleged sorcerers, who were compelled to submit to having large double crosses incised on their foreheads.

This combination of different techniques and practices appears to distinguish Kamcape from the recorded methods of other such movements in this part of Africa[14] and affords a clue to the complexity and variety of social factors involved.

10. Every villager had to drink a sip of Mcape medicine, 'a fine red powder which gave a soapy solution when shaken with water in a bottle' (Richards, 1935).

11. Referred to by Douglas (1963). The earliest of these cults was active about 1910, and Douglas suggests there may have been previous ones.

12. Douglas (1963, p. 158); Richards (1935). Similar demands were apparently made, with success, by some of the first European missionaries to arrive in Ufipa.

13. The Bwanali-Mpulumutsi movement of 1947 in Northern Rhodesia also used this latter technique.

14. The Mcape movement of 1933–4 relied on the administration of a potion and the Bwanali-Mpulumutsi movement of 1947 on a 'medicine'

Problems and Theories

In analysing a people's ideas and behaviour in the context of mystical evil-doing it seems important to distinguish between *beliefs* about witches and sorcerers – who and what they are, the conventional image or images of such figures[15] – and specific *accusations* of witchcraft or sorcery; the significance of the latter can only be assessed empirically, by observing the behaviour of a group over time. It may then be discovered that a pattern of accusations emerges which is more or less at variance with the accepted indigenous theory of witchcraft or sorcery.[16]

Like Zande witchcraft, day-to-day sorcery accusations among the Fipa are a function, firstly, of misfortune, and secondly, of personal relations (cf. Evans-Pritchard, 1937, p. 106). These inter-personal accusations are initiated by such events as sickness or death, or loss of crops or livestock, and occur between coevals in situations of sexual or status rivalry. Inter-generational accusations are rarely, if ever, heard. Moreover, the accusations that are made are essentially private and not of communal concern. Usually the alleged sorcerer does not know that he has been accused.

The accusations made during a Kamcape operation are of quite a different nature. The accusations are not a response to any particular personal misfortune (though personal sufferings, bereavements and losses may be retrospectively invoked by the accusers to substantiate their allegations). The accusations are public and the whole community participates in making them; and most of the accusers are of a different and junior generation to the accused.

It may be assumed, then, that the accusations made during a Kamcape operation relate primarily to general and social,

rubbed into incisions in the skin. Neither movement seems to have treated alleged witches or sorcerers differently from those presumed innocent.

15. In Monica Wilson's arresting phrase, 'the standardized nightmares of a group' (Wilson, 1951).

16. Thus although the official doctrine of the Cewa of eastern Zambia is that sorcerers are women, in nearly three-fifths of 101 cases reported, accusations were made against men (Marwick, 1965, p. 103).

rather than inter-personal conflicts within a village community. What are these conflicts, and how can the activities of Kamcape be thought of or felt by the Fipa as resolving or alleviating them?

It was seen earlier that in every Fipa village there is, or tends to be, a polarization of political opinion and sentiment into 'traditionalist' and 'progressive' parties. The 'traditionalists' draw their inspiration and ideology from their own village, its past and present, and their champion is the headman – the office-holder who represents the village to, and against, the outside world. The 'progressives' are involved intellectually and emotionally in a wider universe of interests and ideology, in the area and national organization and propaganda of TANU, Tanzania's governing party.

Economic conflict in Fipa villages is generated by a shortage of accessible land. Although Ufipa as a whole is quite sparsely populated, the stability of Fipa villages in space and time results in the exhaustion of nearby land, so that many villagers often have to go several miles to find suitable plots. Fipa cope with this problem by building hut-shelters of timber and turves in which they camp during specially busy times of year, such as tilling and harvesting. The more convenient plots adjacent to the village tend to be in the hands of a few elder men.

Both political and economic conflict in Fipa villages is thus to some extent also a conflict of generations: the 'traditionalists' are usually the elder (and largely illiterate) men who are also economically privileged; the 'progressives' tend to be younger and relatively better educated, but to have a smaller economic stake in the community.

Religious differences are another, if latent, source of conflict in many villages. The Christians tend to associate paganism with every kind of evil, including, and especially, sorcery; while the pagans tend to see the Christians as a divisive element opposed to the traditional ethos of village comradeship and unity.

Here then, in the different spheres of politics, economics and religion, are three of the commonest causes of intra-village conflict among the Fipa – and no doubt many other causes, potential and actual, could be discovered and enumerated. Although there is a tendency, noted earlier, for conflicts to follow generational lines, there is certainly much overlapping and even cross-cutting of age-groups and their respective political, economic and religious affiliations and interests.

Social and ecological factors combine to generate conflicts within village communities. Probably this has always been so, though in the more homogeneous society of pre-colonial Ufipa the causes of conflict may have been fewer and less complex. Even so, traditional Fipa society had several institutionalized means of coping with the problem.

If the headman of a village felt that sorcery had become a serious threat to the peace of his community, he could apply to his district governor (*umweene nkaandawa*) for *umwaafi* poison; this was then administered to suspects at a public ceremony. Often every adult member of a village had to participate (see above, p. 185).

Douglas has drawn attention to the formal and functional similarity between the mass administration of the poison ordeal to detect and eradicate mystical evil-doers (an institution found in many parts of Africa, and particularly common in central Africa and the Congo) with the techniques of modern movements directed against witches and sorcerers. An implication of Douglas's argument is that anti-witchcraft and anti-sorcery movements have emerged to fill the gap in society's defences against mystical enemies left by the suppression of the poison ordeal by colonial goverments. This is almost certainly part of the truth. In Ufipa the gap has been further widened by the suppression of the indigenous religion, in which village headmen played the role of priests at communal sacrifices. Another socially integrative institution of traditional Fipa religion, also suppressed, was that of public confession: a man who was conscious of having wronged his neighbours filled a winnowing tray with sand and shouted his confession, shaking the sand to the winds as he did so.

Modern Fipa village society has to make do without any of these integrative devices, in a situation in which external ideological influences, many of them destructive of traditional values, are stronger than ever. In such a situation it would seem that tensions and conflicts are likely to increase, in the absence of traditional palliative mechanisms, until they threaten the complete disruption of village society. To this problem there are two possible solutions: revolution, a radical change in the system of social relations; or millenarianism, a general attempt, in the form of a 'revivalist' movement, to reassert and re-establish the traditional ethos of communal solidarity.

What happens when Kamcape take over a village in a 'cleansing' operation has certain resemblances to a miniature revolution. The abrupt assumption of authority by young men and young women – those categories with least status in traditional and normal Fipa society – together with the degradation of members of the most prestigious class, the male elders, would seem to suggest that the old order has been overturned. But this reversal of social roles and values exists only for the hour or two that the Kamcape operation lasts. Afterwards the community returns to normal: the alleged 'sorcerers' become respected elders again and the youths and girls revert to their former subordinate status.

Kamcape shares with the Bwanali-Mpulumutsi movement, with Mcape, and with the Congolese movements described by Douglas, the millenarian intention of 'turning over a new leaf', of 'wiping the slate clean'. Moreover the whole tenor of a Kamcape operation, the explicit and implicit meaning of the entire performance, makes good sense in terms of indigenous social theory. As Fipa see it, the class or category of male elders, the *akombe* or *ayiikolo*, possess, by virtue of their privileged status, joint and collective responsibility for the whole village community, for its physical and spiritual integrity and harmony. If there is tension and conflict then, blame has to be levelled at this class or category of elders; or if not at the whole lot of them, then at a sub-group within that class or category who can be held to have betrayed their fellows and thus to be the enemies of the whole community. To identify this anti-social sub-group and ritually and magically render its members harmless is the purpose of the 'branding' by Kamcape of those accused of sorcery, coupled with the administration to them of anti-sorcery 'medicine'.

A Kamcape operation is thus a kind of ritual drama in which the whole community participates, in which a number of elder men play the scapegoat role of 'sorcerer', and in which the most active participants, appropriately, are those members of the community with least status, and therefore least responsibility for, and identification with, the old state of affairs. The purpose of this ritual drama is to effect a radical change in the moral climate of the community by abolishing what is felt to be the root cause of all social tensions and conflicts – the practice of sorcery.

Kamcape is then partly a magico-medical operation analogous to the traditional mass ordeal by poison; but it is also more than this, as is indicated by the Kamcape practice (superfluous if the object were merely the 'practical' one of eradicating sorcery) of publicly and conspicuously 'branding' those accused of being sorcerers. This act of 'branding' is the climax of the ritual drama of Kamcape, the purpose of which is moral and symbolic. In the acting-out of this drama the 'sorcerers' symbolize, visibly and concretely, the evil, destructive, disintegrative forces menacing village society. That the identification and 'branding' of the 'sorcerers' is a dramatic and symbolic act is further confirmed by the fact that those 'branded' are not banished or ostracized after the Kamcape operation is over but reassume their former place in village life.

The overt purpose of the Kamcape movement, its manifest function, is to eradicate sorcery. Its latent function is to effect a resolution at the psychic level of a generalized sense of internal conflict and to recreate the moral climate of village communities in accordance with the traditional ethos of unity and harmony. But the internal conflicts which give rise to this generalized sense of social unease are endemic in village communities. Therefore Kamcape can provide only a temporary, and not a permanent, solution of the problem. Eventually the social situation will be ripe for another 'millenarian' movement, perhaps employing new and more elaborate techniques, to appear on the scene. This cycle appears to have recurred several times in Ufipa, with anti-sorcery movements flourishing at roughly ten-yearly intervals in 1933–4, 1943–4, 1954 and 1964.

The quasi-revolutionary overtones of the Kamcape movement have already been remarked – the active leading part played in its operations by youths and girls, the temporary degradation of a segment of the dominant, prestigeful class of male elders. What are the prospects of such movements becoming genuinely revolutionary in aim and practice, of actually changing the pattern of social relations instead of playing at it?

Kamcape as it appeared in Ufipa could not have instituted a permanent change in social relations because it had no permanent organization of its own and no directing head: it had no existence as a political entity. Yet just as the ritual drama enacted by Kamcape in numerous villages contained in germ the idea of society remade, so the notion of a hierarchical political organization was also latently present in the ideology of Kamcape's followers. They looked to a founder in Malawi called Icikanga from whom the esoteric knowledge of Kamcape is said to have been obtained and handed down through a chain of disciples and followers to the local leaders in various parts of Ufipa. Whoever 'Icikanga' is, it seems unlikely that he knew what was being done in his name in south-west Tanganyika in 1963–4. What happened, I think, was that the exponents of the Kamcape movement in Ufipa found it convenient to invest their activities with a mystical authority by associating them with this renowned seer and eradicator of witchcraft and sorcery who is said to have experienced a Christ-like resurrection.

The idea of a hierarchical political organization under a mystical-religious head was certainly abroad in Ufipa at the time of the Kamcape movement of 1963–4, even though the movement itself, passing across the country in a wave of seemingly spontaneously generated action, had no such formal shape. Kamcape might be described as a proto-church with an incipiently revolutionary and totalitarian doctrine of millenarian revivalism, a more developed form of which could be seen in the Lumpa organization of Alice Lenshina in neighbouring Zambia.[17] When such movements achieve political organization they are likely, at any rate in the beginning, to turn their energies away from an internal struggle against witchcraft or sorcery and into resistance to, or even insurrection against, the established state power.[18]

17. The struggle against witchcraft was a central preoccupation of the cult and church founded by Alice Lenshina, who was said to have died and then returned to earth after a visionary experience. Those wishing to join her church had first to surrender their magical objects and confess their wrong doings. (See Rotberg, 1961; Fernandez, 1964.)

18. Rotberg (1961) notes that at a later stage such organized movements may lose much of their insurrectionary ardour and achieve a *modus vivendi*

The political potentialities of such seemingly non-rational movements as Kamcape have been noted by Simone Clemhout:

Nativistic movements represent a cultural innovation in that they try . . . to modify the institutionalized means to revitalize traditional values. These movements take mostly a religious form because they are innovations at the cathetic or symbolic level. These movements, as far as they involve political elements, are a very great help to rationalizing political leadership (Clemhout, 1966).

References
CLEMHOUT, S. (1966), 'The psycho-sociological nature of nativistic movements and the emergence of cultural growth', *Anthropos*, vol. 61, nos. 1–2.
DOUGLAS, M. (1963), 'Techniques of sorcery control in Central Africa', in J. Middleton and E. H. Winter (eds.), *Witchcraft and Sorcery in East Africa*, Routledge & Kegan Paul.
EVANS-PRITCHARD, E. E. (1937), *Witchcraft, Oracles and Magic among the Azande*, Clarendon Press.
FERNANDEZ, J. W. (1964), 'The Lumpa uprising: why?', *Africa Report*, November.
MARWICK, M. G. (1950), 'Another modern anti-witchcraft movement in East Central Africa', *Africa*, vol. 20, no. 2.
MARWICK, M. G. (1952), 'The social context of Cewa witch-beliefs', *Africa*, vol. 22, nos. 3–4.
MARWICK, M. G. (1965), *Sorcery in its Social Setting*, Manchester U.P.
RICHARDS, A. I. (1935), 'A modern movement of witch-finders', *Africa*, vol. 8, no. 4.
ROTBERG, R. (1961), 'The Lenshina movement of Northern Rhodesia', *Rhodes-Livingstone Journal*, vol. 29.
WILSON, M. Hunter (1951), 'Witch-beliefs and social structure', *American Journal of Sociology*, vol. 56.

with the state power, as happened with the Kibanguist movement in the Congo.

Part Three **Theories of Witchcraft**

With the exception of a few self-conscious, artificial cults, witches and sorcerers belong to modern man's fantasy-world. This may account for the considerable effort that has gone into explaining their existence in those societies where they were, or still are, experienced as real threats to life, health and property. This urge for reasonable comprehension is probably the mainspring of Margaret Murray's theory, here succinctly and fairly presented by Macfarlane before he tests it against the empirical evidence he won from the records of sixteenth and seventeenth-century Essex; but this motive seems less prominent in Elsie Clews Parsons's account of Pueblo witchcraft, which, in greater measure, is prompted by the sheer momentum of American anthropological diffusionism. With more comparative material at our disposal than she had, we can now be critical of some of her conclusions, especially her tendency to attribute to European influence many features since found to be nearly universal. A similar but more sober diffusionist approach is to be detected in some of Ewen's writings, not represented here but referred to in the Introduction (see p. 16). Psychological explanations of witchcraft, stemming from Freud's doctrine of the displacement of affect and mediated by Malinowski's general theory of magic (which draws some of its examples from Melanesian sorcery), are here represented most clearly by Kluckhohn. Krige's paper merits inclusion for its ethnographic richness alone, and could have gone into Part Two; but its penultimate paragraph contains a trenchant exposition of what we class as a psychological theory. Sociological theories, as we are reminded by the Readings from Wilson and Nadel, relate beliefs and attendant behaviour to the mesh of social relationships and to the moral values that keep it in workable shape. But, as no society is static, its shape is fluid, and these beliefs provide media for social dramas, which, in Turner's phrase, are either indices or vehicles of change (1957, p. 162). Accusations of witchcraft and sorcery punctuate and may even promote the discarding of the old order to make room for the new. This idea is central to the position of two writers working at the present growing point of the sociology of witchcraft and sorcery, Macfarlane and Crawford, whose contributions show a remarkable convergence, especially since they deal with societies widely separated in space and time and since the writers appear not to have been influenced by each other's work.

Reference
TURNER, V. W. (1957), *Schism and Continuity in an African Society*, Manchester U.P.

17 A. D. J. Macfarlane

Murray's Theory: Exposition and Comment

Excerpt from A. D. J. Macfarlane, *Witchcraft Prosecutions in Essex, 1560–1680: A Sociological Analysis*, D. Phil. thesis, University of Oxford, 1967, pp. 16–18.

The most radical attempt to provide a new explanation of witchcraft prosecutions was made by Miss Margaret Murray (1921).[1] Her work was based on the two assumptions that witchcraft beliefs cannot be profitably examined in isolation from other systems of ideas and that they cannot be dismissed as mere nonsense. These convictions were shared by G. L. Kittredge whose wide learning illuminated the subject (1929, pp. 372–3). Having decided that quite reasonable people really did fear witches and that others, without torture, freely confessed to this crime, Margaret Murray took what in many ways was a logical step and argued that there really must have been witches. They were, however, not the evil creatures described by their persecutors, but a highly organized pagan cult. She applied a number of Sir James Frazer's theories to English witchcraft, for instance the importance of rituals for increasing fertility in primitive religion, and thereby constructed a detailed picture of this 'witch-cult'. Witches, she claimed, met regularly at their 'Sabbats', they formed 'covens' of thirteen, each of which had a leader dressed in animal guise. They feasted, danced, and sang. This she termed 'ritual' witchcraft. Then the Christian inquisitors, in their attempt to stamp out paganism, turned this cult of pre-Christian gaiety into a deadly onslaught on the values of society. The leaders of the covens were transformed in their hands into the Devil, the innocent meetings were described as orgies. The 'witches' were believed to have made a secret or open compact with the Devil

1. As Professor Trevor-Roper recently pointed out, however, many of Murray's theories were anticipated by Jakob Grimm (Trevor-Roper, 1967, p. 15; excerpts from this paper will be found on pp. 121–50 of these Readings – Ed.).

whereby they exchanged their soul for transitory power and pleasure.

Miss Murray's work was immediately criticized and has continued to be attacked (Burr, 1922, pp. 780–83; Ewen, 1938, n.p.; Robbins, 1959, pp. 116–17; Rose, 1962). The major criticism is that by extracting and quoting out of context from the whole of European folklore she created a totally false picture. She mistook what people believed to be happening for what actually did happen. Though she showed that people thought there was a witch-cult, she failed to demonstrate that there actually was one. Her thesis will not be examined directly in the following pages. There are very few descriptions of the phenomena which she discusses in Essex witchcraft, for instance, the Sabbat, coven and diabolic compact are absent, except in the exceptional trials of 1645.[2] Nor does more detailed examination of those accused of witchcraft in Essex lend any support to the argument that there really was an underground pagan cult. Probably there were those who came to believe themselves to be witches, but there is no evidence that they formed a self-conscious organization. This is a negative conclusion and impossible to document. All that can be said is that the Essex evidence does not support her conclusions and, indeed, makes her picture of the witch-cult seem far too sophisticated and articulate for the society with which we are concerned. Yet her assumptions about the necessity to treat accusations as something more than intolerant superstition are subscribed to.

References

BURR, G. L. (1922), 'A review of M. A. Murray's *Witch-Cult in Western Europe*', *American Historical Review*, vol. 27, no. 4.

EWEN, C. L. (1938), *Some Witchcraft Criticisms: A Plea for the Blue Pencil*, n.p.

KITTREDGE, G. L. (1929), *Witchcraft in Old and New England*, Harvard U.P.

MURRAY, M. A. (1921), *The Witch-Cult in Western Europe*, Clarendon Press.

2. In another chapter of his thesis the author attributes the exceptional nature of these trials to the influence of the witchfinders, Hopkins and Stearne, and to tensions following the Civil War. Of over twelve hundred cases he reviews, only one is a clear instance of 'ritual witchcraft' though it could hardly be regarded as confirming Murray's theory–*Ed*.

ROBBINS, R. H. (1959), *Encyclopedia of Witchcraft and Demonology*, Crown.

ROSE, E. E. (1962), *A Razor for a Goat: Witchcraft and Diabolism*, University of Toronto Press.

TREVOR-ROPER, H. R. (1967), 'Witches and witchcraft', *Encounter*, vol. 28, nos. 5 and 6 (see Reading 12, ref. 7, p. 146 – *Ed.*).

18 Elsie Clews Parsons

Witchcraft among the Pueblos: Indian or Spanish?

Abridged from Elsie Clews Parsons, 'Witchcraft among the Pueblos: Indian or Spanish?', *Man*, vol. 27, 1927, pp. 106–12, 125–8.

Beliefs and Practices

In the Zuñi origin myth (Parsons, 1923, pp. 37–138) a witch pair, male and female, come up from the under worlds after the other people and bring with them two gifts – death to keep the world from being crowded, and corn. The tradition implies that in Zuñi opinion witchcraft is magical power which is not necessarily differentiated into good or evil. 'The best men of the pueblo may be witches', I have been told in Laguna, and there, as in Zuñi and in other pueblos, charges of witchcraft have been brought against high officials. The Pueblo curing societies work against witchcraft, but there are said to be society practices in black magic as well as in white, particularly among the clown societies. In short, although black magic is plainly distinguished from white magic and the witch is he or she who is habitually engaged in the practice of black magic, witchcraft may be practised by any person or by any group.

There is individualistic practice of witchcraft, but witchcraft also runs in families, and in several towns there is believed to be a society of witches which is organized like any other society, with the same officials. Members, it is said at Laguna, have to obey the orders of their officers, orders to go out and make people sick. To be initiated the candidate must sacrifice some one, i.e. bewitch some one to death. In the instances cited to me at Zuñi the sacrificed one has always been a member of the household of the candidate.

In the initiation, the candidate has to go under an arch or bow (Laguna). With him goes the member of the society whose type of animal transformation the candidate chooses for his own, i.e. if he wants to be a witch cat he goes under the bow with a witch cat – a variant of the familiar Pueblo pattern of society sponsor or ceremonial father. In Pueblo folk-tales going under a bow or through a ring or hoop to produce a metamorphosis is a common incident. A still more common means of metamorphosis is by putting on the skin of the creature one is to be changed into. The creatures most commonly mentioned for witch transformation are cats, dogs, burros, bears, owls.

Insects are controlled by witches as their agents. They can send caterpillars or grasshoppers to destroy crops, and they can send insects into the body of a victim similarly to destroy it.[1] Witches may also 'send in' a piece of flesh from a corpse or a shred of funeral cloth or a splinter of bone; any sharp or pointed thing is serviceable, thorn, cactus point, glass, etc. Sending things into the body is the commonest form of witch attack, but, at Zuñi at least, witches may also attack through the ghosts (*ahoppa*) of members of the family they are persecuting.

Epidemic is always imputed to witchcraft; but not every individual ailment. The ailment from which recovery is rapid is much less likely to be attributed to a witch than that which is lingering, on and off.

Besides causing sickness, individual and epidemic, and insect plague, witches can control the weather, keeping the rain off[2] or causing wind.

Bewitching is very commonly the result of a grievance, since a witch who feels injured will retaliate. Now as you never know who is a witch, you are always careful not to give offence – unless you are yourself a witch. A reckless attitude towards others, 'not caring what you say', seems to be one indication of witchhood. I cannot help but connect the very striking social timidities of the Pueblos with their witchcraft theories. Father Dumarest had the same impression. 'Why are the Pueblo Indians so pacific?' he writes. 'Why do they not try even to defend themselves in quarrels? Because from their youth their elders have taught them

1. For such use of a centipede see Parsons (1917, part 2, p. 270, no. 2).
2. Feathers of the owl and the crow are associated with witchcraft because, I was told at Zuñi, these birds keep away other birds and hence keep away the rain.

that nobody can know the hearts of men. There are witches everywhere' (1919, p. 162).

Envy is a very common motive in witchcraft.

The most abusive and the most dreadful charge you can bring against anyone is that of being a witch. In some towns such charges are quite commonly bandied about; although how much colour an accused has to lend it by his behaviour in general it is difficult to determine. Besides reckless speech, dishonesty in regard to property, or, still more, the possession of wealth from sources unknown[3] and roaming about at night or looking into windows seem to be characters or habits open to suspicion. Lurking at night about the house where a person is sick is particularly questionable and the house of an invalid will be watched in order to catch the operating witch.

Persons may labour under the suspicion of witchcraft for years without decisive action being taken against them. They are said to be more or less shunned.

Decisive action is taken against witches in case of a public misfortune like an epidemic or a grasshopper plague or a drought. Then some person, either long under suspicion or but freshly suspected, is likely to be tried. Formerly at Zuñi the suspect was hung by his arms tied behind his back to a projecting beam of the Catholic Church until he confessed. Nowadays, he is 'talked to' by the bow-priests. This nagging is felt to be very trying [and he may be advised to] tell them something to get rid of them.

In individual cases of bewitchment the curing societies are called upon. The particular doctor is invited by a relative of the invalid to make the cure.

The use of arrow points on altars and attached to fetishes is a charm against witchcraft.

The animal paws which figure on altars are also charms against witches or agents in fighting them. In this turning of the wild animals against the witches who can themselves become wild animals, may be seen the conceptual closeness between witches and medicine-men, of which we have already spoken. The con-

3. For example, a certain member of the council at Taos is reputed a witch since without working he wears good clothes and, an extra touch, 'he looks under his eyes'.

nexion appears again in the sucking cure of the medicine-man, he sucking out of the invalid's body what the witch has sent into it.

Ashes are also a charm or prophylactic against witchcraft.

It is believed in Zuñi and Taos, probably elsewhere, that witches can use hair cuttings in their black magic, so hair cuttings are burned or thrown into the river.

[In a Tewa folk-tale Coyote marries Yellow Corn Girl and teaches her how to transform herself into an animal by jumping through a ring. He then helps her to kill her mother and brother by witchcraft.] 'After this there were witches. There were never witches before the girl married Coyote. That is the reason why people are witches now. They have been taught by Coyote.'

Indian or Spanish?

In Pueblo folk tales, as in Plains Indian tales, Coyote is frequently the arch trickster, so holding him responsible for the introduction of witchcraft is characteristically Indian; but what of other features in this tale as well as in the foregoing account in general: causing sickness by image or by injection, killing relatives, the witch assembly, transforming into animal form by putting on an animal skin, or jumping through a ring or under a bow, – are these European or Indian features? Belief in animal metamorphosis is certainly both European and Indian; transformation by ring seems more European, by skin, more Indian (although this can be found as a medieval belief). The witch assembly is, of course, a European idea, but it is so thoroughly worked into the Pueblo idea of ceremonial organization that it would be rash to hold that it was not a pre-Spanish idea. Killing relatives is European, although killing by taking out the 'heart' (soul) is Indian. Causing sickness is both European and Indian, but causing it by sending something into the body is Indian;[4] whereas the use of an image to represent the invalid seems European.

Is the use of ashes as a witch prophylactic Spanish or native, or both? Marking a cross on the head with ashes on Ash Wednesday

4. See R. H. Lowie (1924, pp. 176–80), for the distribution among Indians of the theories of sickness from intrusion and from soul-kidnapping.

is a prevalent Catholic rite, one that seems to be the origin of rubbing ashes on a baby at Laguna and at Zuñi. But is it also the origin of the practice at Laguna of a medicine-man rubbing his legs that he may not tire in his witch contest, or of the use of ashes in the exorcising rite of waving around the head, familiar at Zuñi and among the Hopi? Probably not.

Again, what is European and what is native in the belief that persons in high office are open to the charge of witchcraft? In early days the Spaniards were continually abusing the medicine-men as witches, the very kind of abuse and suspicion the Indians are quick to indulge in today. And yet even before the advent of the Spaniards, medicine [-men] may have been suspected of black magic.

In contrast with these dubieties certain miscellaneous witch beliefs and practices may be mentioned as plainly European: the belief in Taos and Laguna that witches travel as balls of fire, and the related belief that a light which is seen to vanish betokens a death in the family (Laguna, Zuñi); to catch a witch, the practice of turning one's clothes inside out, trousers, coat, etc. (Zuñi); the belief that the footfall of a witch animal is inaudible (Laguna and Santa Clara). The belief that the witch animal which is wounded is subsequently found as a wounded person I would also classify as European, together with the belief about hair cuttings and the practice in the Eastern towns of burning anti-witch root. The burning of the witch with green wood in the Tewan folk-tale appears to point back to the witch executions which actually took place in New Mexico under Spanish administration.

In conclusion, I venture this general reconstruction. In pre-Spanish days the ceremonial groups were considered capable of black as well as of white magic, they could cause the same inflictions they could cure and, in particular, their members could send harmful substances into the human body. Their members got their medicines through the prey animals, and, by wearing portions of the animal, were endowed with the powers of the animals, by putting on the whole skin of the animal might even transform into it. All these beliefs (except that of sending things into the body, which belief is unfamiliar to the Mexican neighbours of the Pueblos) were enriched by Spanish witchcraft theory, which also spread, if it did not introduce, the idea that anybody might practise witchcraft. In this connexion it is significant that among the Hopi there is much less reference to witchcraft in the daily life or of its practice on the part of any evilly disposed person than there is at Zuñi or in the east. Here, I infer, as in other particulars, the Hopi are a touch-stone of Spanish influence. In other words, where Spanish influence has prevailed, witchcraft has been secularized and witch notions have tended to permeate the daily life.

References

DUMAREST, NOËL (1919), 'Notes on Cochiti, New Mexico', *Memoirs of the American Anthropological Association*, vol. 6.

LOWIE, R. H. (1924), *Primitive Religion*, Boni & Liveright.

PARSONS, E. G. (1917), 'Notes on Zuñi', *Memoirs of the American Anthropological Association*, vol. 4, no. 4.

PARSONS, E. C. (1923), 'The origin myth of Zuñi', *Journal of American Folk-Lore*, vol. 36, pp. 37–138.

19 Bronislaw Malinowski

Magic, Science and Religion

Excerpts from Bronislaw Malinowski, *Magic, Science and Religion and Other Essays*, edited by Robert Redfield, Doubleday, 1954, pp. 70–84; Free Press, 1948. The essay from which these excerpts are taken was first published in 1926.

Let us have a look at a typical act of magic, and choose one which is well-known and generally regarded as a standard performance – an act of black magic. Among the several types which we meet in savagery, witchcraft by the act of pointing the magical dart is, perhaps, the most widespread of all. A pointed bone or a stick, an arrow or the spine of some animal, is ritually, in a mimic fashion, thrust, thrown, or pointed in the direction of the man to be killed by sorcery. We have innumerable recipes in the oriental and ancient books of magic, in ethnographic descriptions and tales of travelers, of how such a rite is performed. But the emotional setting, the gestures and expressions of the sorcerer during the performance, have been but seldom described. Yet these are of the greatest importance. If a spectator were suddenly transported to some part of Melanesia and could observe the sorcerer at work, not perhaps knowing exactly what he was looking at, he might think that he had either to do with a lunatic or else he would guess that here was a man acting under the sway of uncontrolled anger. For the sorcerer has, as an essential part of the ritual performance, not merely to point the bone dart at his victim, but with an intense expression of fury and hatred he has to thrust it in the air, turn and twist it as if to bore it in the wound, then pull it back with a sudden jerk. Thus not only is the act of violence, or stabbing, reproduced, but the passion of violence has to be enacted.

We see thus that the dramatic expression of emotion is the essence of this act, for what is it that is reproduced in it? Not its end, for the magician would in that case have to imitate the death of the victim, but the emotional state of the performer, a state which closely corresponds to the situation in which we find it and which has to be gone through mimetically.

I could adduce a number of similar rites from my own experience, and many more, of course, from other records. Thus, when in other types of black magic the sorcerer ritually injures or mutilates or destroys a figure or object symbolizing the victim, this rite is, above all, a clear expression of hatred and anger. Or when in love magic the performer has really or symbolically to grasp, stroke, fondle the beloved person or some object representing her, he reproduces the behavior of a heartsick lover who has lost his common sense and is overwhelmed by passion. In war magic, anger, the fury of attack, the emotions of combative passion are frequently expressed in a more or less direct manner. In the magic of terror, in the exorcism directed against powers of darkness and evil, the magician behaves as if himself overcome by the emotion of fear, or at least violently struggling against it. Shouts, brandishing of weapons, the use of lighted torches, form often the substance of this rite. Or else in an act, recorded by myself, to ward off the evil powers of darkness, a man has ritually to tremble, to utter a spell slowly as if paralysed by fear. And this fear gets hold also of the approaching sorcerer and wards him off.

All such acts, usually rationalized and explained by some principle of magic, are *prima facie* expressions of emotion. The substances and paraphernalia used in them have often the same significance. Daggers, sharp-pointed lacerating objects, evil-smelling or poisonous substances, used in black magic; scents, flowers, inebriating stimulants, in love magic; valuables, in economic magic – all these are associated primarily through emotions and not through ideas with the end of the respective magic.

Besides such rites, however, in which a dominant element serves to express an emotion, there are others in which the act does forecast its result, or, to use Sir James Frazer's expression, the rite imitates its end. Thus, in the black magic of the Melanesians recorded by myself, a characteristic ritual way of winding-up the spell is for the sorcerer to weaken the voice, utter a death rattle, and fall down in imitation of the rigor of death. It is, however, not necessary to adduce any other examples, for this aspect of magic and the allied one of contagious magic has been brilliantly described and exhaustively documented by Frazer.

Sir James has also shown that there exists a special lore of magical substances based on affinities, relations, on ideas of similarity and contagion, developed with a magical pseudo-science. [. . .]

Magic is not born of an abstract conception of universal power, subsequently applied to concrete cases. It has undoubtedly arisen independently in a number of actual situations. Each type of magic, born of its own situation and of the emotional tension thereof, is due to the spontaneous flow of ideas and the spontaneous reaction of man. It is the uniformity of the mental process in each case which has led to certain universal features of magic and to the general conceptions which we find at the basis of man's magical thought and behavior. It will be necessary to give now an analysis of the situations of magic and the experiences which they provoke. [. . .]

Now we must analyse this belief from the point of view of the sociological observer. Let us realize once more the type of situation in which we find magic. Man, engaged in a series of practical activities, comes to a gap; the hunter is disappointed by his quarry, the sailor misses propitious winds, the canoe builder has to deal with some material of which he is never certain that it will stand the strain, or the healthy person suddenly feels his strength failing. What does man do naturally under such conditions, setting aside all magic, belief and ritual? Forsaken by his knowledge, baffled by his past experience and by his technical skill, he realizes his impotence. Yet his desire grips him only the more strongly; his anxiety, his fears and hopes, induce a tension in his organism which drives him to some sort of activity. Whether he be savage or civilized, whether in possession of magic or entirely ignorant of its existence, passive inaction, the only thing dictated by reason, is the last thing in which he can acquiesce. His nervous system and his whole organism drive him to some substitute activity. Obsessed by the idea of the desired end, he sees it and feels it. His organism reproduces the acts suggested by the anticipations of hope, dictated by the emotion of passion so strongly felt.

The man under the sway of impotent fury or dominated by thwarted hate spontaneously clenches his fist and carries out imaginary thrusts at his enemy, muttering imprecations, casting words of hatred and anger against him. The lover aching for his unattainable or irresponsive beauty sees her in his visions, addresses her, and entreats and commands her favors, feeling himself accepted, pressing her to his bosom in his dreams. The anxious fisherman or hunter sees in his imagination the quarry enmeshed in the nets, the animal attained by the spear; he utters their names, describes in words his visions of the magnificent catch, he even breaks out into gestures of mimic representation of what he desires. The man lost at night in the woods or the jungle, beset by superstitious fear, sees around him the haunting demons, addresses them, tries to ward off, to frighten them, or shrinks from them in fear, like an animal which attempts to save itself by feigning death.

These reactions to overwhelming emotion or obsessive desire are natural responses of man to such a situation, based on a universal psycho-physiological mechanism. They engender what could be called extended expressions of emotion in act and in word, the threatening gestures of impotent anger and its maledictions, the spontaneous enactment of the desired end in a practical impasse, the passionate fondling gestures of the lover, and so on. All these spontaneous acts and spontaneous works make man forecast the images of the wished-for results, or express his passion in uncontrollable gestures, or break out into words which give vent to desire and anticipate its end.

And what is the purely intellectual process, the conviction formed during such a free outburst of emotion in words and deeds? First there surges a clear image of the desired end, of the hated person, of the feared danger or ghost. And each image is blended with its specific passion, which drives us to assume an active attitude towards that image. When passion reaches the breaking point at which man loses control over himself, the words which he utters, his blind behavior, allow the pent-up physiological tension to flow over. But over all this outburst presides the image of the end. It supplies the motive-force of the reaction, it apparently organizes and directs words and acts towards a definite purpose. The substitute action in which the passion finds it vent, and which is due to impotence, has subjectively all the value of a real action, to which emotion would, if not impeded, naturally have led.

213

As the tension spends itself in these words and gestures the obsessing visions fade away, the desired end seems nearer satisfaction, we regain our balance, once more at harmony with life. And we remain with a conviction that the words of malediction and the gestures of fury have traveled towards the hated person and hit their target; that the imploration of love, the visionary embraces, cannot have remained unanswered, that the visionary attainment of success in our pursuit cannot have been without a beneficial influence on the pending issue. In the case of fear, as the emotion which has led us to frenzied behavior gradually subsides, we feel that it is this behavior that has driven away the terrors. In brief, a strong emotional experience, which spends itself in a purely subjective flow of images, words, and acts of behavior, leaves a very deep conviction of its reality, as if of some practical and positive achievement, as if of something done by a power revealed to man. This power, born of mental and physiological obsession, seems to get hold of us from outside, and to primitive man, or to the credulous and untutored mind of all ages, the spontaneous spell, the spontaneous rite, and the spontaneous belief in their efficiency must appear as a direct revelation from some external and no doubt impersonal sources.

When we compare this spontaneous ritual and verbiage of overflowing passion or desire with traditionally fixed magical ritual and with the principles embodied in magical spells and substances, the striking resemblance of the two products shows that they are not independent of each other. Magical ritual, most of the principles of magic, most of its spells and substances, have been revealed to man in those passionate experiences which assail him in the impasses of his instinctive life and of his practical pursuits, in those gaps and breaches left in the ever-imperfect wall of culture which he erects between himself and the besetting temptations and dangers of his destiny. In this I think we have to recognize not only one of the sources but the very fountainhead of magical belief.

To most types of magical ritual, therefore, there corresponds a spontaneous ritual of emotional expression or of a forecast of the desired end. To most features of magical spell, to the commands, invocations, metaphors, there corresponds a natural flow of words, in malediction, in entreaty, in exorcism, and in the descriptions of unfulfilled wishes. To every belief in magical efficiency there can be laid in parallel one of those illusions of subjective experience, transient in the mind of the civilized rationalist, though even there never quite absent, but powerful and convincing to the simple man in every culture, and, above all, to the primitive savage mind.

Thus the foundations of magical belief and practice are not taken from the air, but are due to a number of experiences actually lived through, in which man receives the revelation of his power to attain the desired end. We must now ask: What is the relation between the promises contained in such experience and their fulfillment in real life? Plausible though the fallacious claims of magic might be to primitive man, how is it that they have remained so long unexposed?

The answer to this is that, first, it is a well-known fact that in human memory the testimony of a positive case always overshadows the negative one. One gain easily outweighs several losses. Thus the instances which affirm magic always loom far more conspicuously than those which deny it. But there are other facts which endorse by a real or apparent testimony the claims of magic. We have seen that magical ritual must have originated from a revelation in a real experience. But the man who from such an experience conceived, formulated and gave to his tribesmen the nucleus of a new magical performance – acting, be it remembered, in perfect good faith – must have been a man of genius. The men who inherited and wielded his magic after him, no doubt always building it out and developing it, while believing that they were simply following up the tradition, must have been always men of great intelligence, energy, and power of enterprise. They would be the men successful in all emergencies. It is an empirical fact that in all savage societies magic and outstanding personality go hand in hand. Thus magic also coincides with personal success, skill, courage and mental power. No wonder that it is considered a source of success.

This personal renown of the magician and its importance in enhancing the belief about the efficiency of magic are the cause of an interesting phenomenon: what may be called the *current mythology* of magic. Round every big magician there arises a halo made up of stories about his wonderful cures or kills, his catches, his victories, his conquests in love. In every savage society such stories form the backbone of belief in magic, for, supported as they are by the emotional experiences which everyone has had himself, the running chronicle of magical miracles establishes its claims beyond any doubt or cavil. Every eminent practitioner, besides his traditional claim, besides the filiation with his predecessors, makes his personal warrant of wonderworking.

Thus myth is not a dead product of past ages, merely surviving as an idle narrative. It is a living force, constantly producing new phenomena, constantly surrounding magic by new testimonies. Magic moves in the glory of past tradition, but it also creates its atmosphere of ever-nascent myth. As there is the body of legends already fixed, standardized and constituting the folklore of the tribe, so there is always a stream of narratives in kind to those of the mythological time. Magic is the bridge between the golden age of primeval craft and the wonder-working power of today. Hence the formulas are full of mythical allusions, which, when uttered, unchain the powers of the past and cast them into the present.

With this we see also the role and meaning of mythology in a new light. Myth is not a savage speculation about origins of things born out of philosophic interest. Neither is it the result of the contemplation of nature – a sort of symbolical representation of its laws. It is the historical statement of one of those events which once for all vouch for the truth of a certain form of magic. Sometimes it is the actual record of a magical revelation coming directly from the first man to whom magic was revealed in some dramatic occurrence. More often it bears on its surface that it is merely a statement of how magic came into the possession of a clan or a community or a tribe. In all cases it is a warrant of its truth, a pedigree of its filiation, a charter of its claims to validity. And as we have seen, myth is the natural result of human faith, because every power must give signs of its efficiency, must act and be known to act, if people are to believe in its virtue. Every belief engenders its mythology, for there is no faith without miracles, and the main myth recounts simply the primeval miracle of the magic.

20 Clyde Kluckhohn

Navaho Witchcraft

Excerpts from Clyde Kluckhohn, *Navaho Witchcraft*, Beacon Press, 1962, pp. 67–121 (first published as Papers of the Peabody Museum of Archaeology and Ethnography, Harvard University, 1944).

[The next section] will [...] be given over to structural analysis. The hypothesis will be developed that the euphoric effects of the witchcraft pattern assemblage are considerable, perhaps even outweighing the dysphoric effects at the present moment. It is hoped that this may influence anthropologists more frequently to examine without prejudice the contributions of any pattern assemblage to the total social system and to resist the tendency to label 'witchcraft' or 'sorcery' as 'evil' – in accord with the connotations which such words as 'witchcraft' and 'sorcery' have in our language, conformant to our system of sentiments. It is also hoped that this exercise in structural analysis may contribute to the general understanding of some aspects of Navaho social structure which have perhaps been insufficiently appreciated. At the same time, the emphasis upon structure will by no means preclude other kinds of interpretation.[1] Thus witchcraft as an expression in fantasy for the culturally disallowed, but unconsciously wanted, will be considered because

1. These interpretations were partially developed in the course of participation in the seminar on Culture and Personality conducted by A. Kardiner and R. Linton in Columbia University, 1939–40. For the opportunity of sharing in this seminar I am grateful to the Carnegie Corporation. While I benefited markedly from association with Dr Kardiner, it is only fair to him to state that few of his psychoanalytic interpretations of Navaho witchcraft material are here incorporated, and that he has not commented upon many of the hypotheses in this section because they have been formulated subsequent to the time of my contact with him. Membership in Dr Sandor Rado's seminar on psychoanalytic theory at the New York Psychoanalytic Institute during the same period should also be mentioned as an important influence underlying the type of analysis attempted.

But for direct revisions of this section I am most indebted to a painstaking criticism (both factual and theoretical) by David Aberle.

such wish fulfilments are of obvious utility to individuals in the preservation of their equilibrium. [. . .]

A structural analysis (an investigation of 'functional dependences') is a study in the interrelation of parts. All of the parts must be described before their interrelationships can be understood. A description of many aspects of Navaho social structure will, therefore, be a necessary background to comprehension of the workings of witchcraft. This becomes clear immediately when we ask the question which is actually most central to our conceptual scheme: why have witchcraft patterns (whatever their historical source!) survived through the periods to which our material relates? If we look at a few features of the Navaho socialization process and at some conditions of Navaho life which the child early experiences, we at once gain a partial (though by no means complete) enlightenment.

Early Life as Background for the Survival of Belief in Witchcraft

Let us observe, first of all, how socialization implements the persistence of witchcraft beliefs. The child, even before he is fully responsive to verbalizations, begins to get a picture of experience as potentially menacing. He sees his parents, and other elders, confess their impotence to deal with various matters by technological or other rational means in that they resort to exoteric prayers, songs and 'magical' observances and to esoteric rites. When he has been linguistically socialized, he hears the hushed gossip of witchcraft and learns that there are certain fellow tribesmen whom his family suspect and fear. One special experience of early childhood which may be of considerable importance occurs during toilet training. When the toddler goes with mother or with older sister to defecate or urinate, a certain uneasiness which they manifest (in most cases) about the concealment of the waste matter can hardly fail to become communicated to the child. The mother, who has been seen not only as a prime source of gratification but also as an almost omnipotent person, is now revealed as herself afraid, at the mercy of threatening forces. The contrast must be uncommonly great between the picture of the world which the child had during what the psychoanalysts call the period of 'oral mastery' and the picture of the world which he gets from the words and acts of his elders during the period when he is being obliged to give up the 'instinctual gratifications' of unrestricted urination and defecation.

Other early experiences of the child help to create a soil fertile for the implanting of belief in such a phenomenon as witchcraft. What with a diet which no longer has even the advantages of being a trial and error adaptation over many generations to the peculiar conditions of Navaho life, with no skills for combatting the disease introduced by Europeans, with drafty hogans and wet clothing and other inadequate protections, it is hardly surprising that Navaho children are frequently ill. The threats to health which were characteristic of the aboriginal culture are still largely present, but additional threats arising out of unwise adoption of our dietary habits, and from other European borrowings, have been added. In short, it is inevitable that the Navaho child experiences discomfort and pain – without quick or satisfactory means of alleviation. The child likewise sees others ill and suffering. Hunger, too, is an early experience. Not many Navaho have attained adulthood without knowing starvation for short periods and hunger rations for long periods. Since the child soon discovers that even his mother cannot control these things and since the doings and sayings of his elders make it plain that all of these privations occur even when people work very hard and very skilfully, it is small wonder that experience has a capricious and malevolent component for most Navahos.

Thus we see, in a very general way, how a belief in witches fits with what the young Navaho very soon comes to expect of living. But as yet we have learned little as to why these particular forms of belief in *witchcraft* should be perpetuated. The learning of urine and faeces concealment may act as a conditioning mechanism specific to witchcraft belief. Otherwise, however, the only thing which seems demanded by the conditions listed is fear of *some* sort of malevolent forces. To get beyond the demonstration of a social matrix favourable to the survival of beliefs of the generic type of witchcraft, we must examine systematically the contributions which the witchcraft pattern assemblage makes to the maintenance of personal and social equilibrium. [. . .]

What are the 'functions', the sociological *raison d'être*, of belief in (and perhaps practice of) witchcraft by the Navaho? It will be convenient to consider this question first from the standpoint of the adjustive responses which such beliefs and practices make possible for the individual. We shall then see how they constitute, up to a point, adaptive responses for the society. Since a society is made up of individual organisms, the two categories inevitably merge, but an emphasis upon the two angles of perspective will show the 'functions' in sharper focus.

Manifest 'Functions' of Witchcraft for the Individual Navaho

The manifest 'functions' are limited in number. So far as practice is concerned, witchcraft is obviously a means of attaining wealth, gaining women, disposing of enemies and 'being mean'. In short, witchcraft is a potential avenue to supernatural power. Power seems to be an important central theme in Navaho culture of which gaining wealth, disposing of enemies, and even, to some extent, obtaining possession of women are merely particular examples.

An inadequate memory, lack of the fees for teachers (the teacher of witchcraft needs to be paid only by the sacrifice of a sibling!), or other factors prevent some Navahos from attaining supernatural power through the socially approved route of becoming a singer. For such persons learning witchcraft is a manifest antidote to deprivation. Indeed, the presence of the witchcraft patterns must be a constant 'temptation' to Navahos who lust for power but have not attained it by other means. The practice of witchcraft similarly supplies an outlet to those Navaho in whom aggressive impulses are peculiarly strong. Old Navahos often comment that the men who used to organize war parties were of a special personality type: 'they were the ones that always like to stir up trouble.' One may speculate that personalities who found leading a war party an especially congenial occupation would find becoming a witch the most congenial substitute in the contemporary Navaho world.

But since most of the data evidence belief in witchcraft rather than practice of witchcraft, our major attention must be given to seeing how witchcraft 'functions' in the lives of Navahos who are not witches. At the manifest level, it may be pointed out, first of all, that witchcraft stories have the obvious value of the dramatic – the exciting story. They partially fulfil the 'functions' which books and magazines, plays and moving pictures carry out in our culture. In the second place, it must be realized that witchcraft ideology gives a partial answer to the problems which disturb the Navaho as well as other peoples – stubborn illness without apparent etiology, death without visible cause. One of man's peculiarities is that he requires 'reasons' for the occurrence of events.[2] One of the manifest 'functions' of belief in witchcraft is that such belief supplies answers to questions which would otherwise be perplexing – and because perplexing, disturbing. More specifically, the availability of witchcraft as an explanation helps to maintain the Navaho's conviction in the efficacy of the curing ceremonials. If a chant which has been performed without a hitch by a singer of great reputation fails, nevertheless, to cure, the Navaho need not wonder: 'Are the chants really any good? Or are we perhaps, after all, hopelessly at the mercy of the forces that cause illness?' A culturally acceptable alternative explanation is at hand: 'The disease was caused by witchcraft, *that's why* the chant didn't work.' This line of reasoning also

2. Lee (1940, pp. 356–7) has argued that 'An analysis of Trobriand behaviour and language shows that the Trobriander, by custom, focuses his interest on the thing or act in itself, not on its relationships . . . he deduces no causal connexion from a sequence. . . . The Trobriander has no linguistic mechanism for expressing a relationship between events or acts. Culturally, causation and teleology are either ignored or non-existent.' She is, however, careful to say, 'By this I mean, not that the individual Trobriander cannot understand causality, but that in his culture, the sequence of events does not automatically fall into the mould of causal or telic relationship.'

Whether or not all peoples employ a category which may be roughly equated with our 'causation' or even our 'mutual interdependence', all human beings whom I have known or read about seem to go to considerable trouble to find and to express 'reasons' for what they say and do. The giving of justifications which are 'rational' with reference to the logics of that culture seems to be one of the most universal of adjustive responses. This does not mean, of course, that 'the function' of such behaviour is usually that of 'satisfying intellectual curiosity', although this motivation must not be too dogmatically and cavalierly excluded in every case (cf. Kluckhohn, 1942, p. 56, fn. 46).

So far as the Navaho are concerned, the statement hardly needs qualification. For the Navaho language is marked by elaboration and refinement of causative categories.

221

gives an obvious out for the singer who has failed. Unless he feels the situation to be of a kind that voicing such a suspicion will be a boomerang against himself, he may say, 'Well, my friends, I have done my best and my chant is very powerful. But your unfortunate kinsman has clearly been witched. As you know, only Evil Way chants will do any good against those who have been witched. And the best medicine is not a chant but a prayer ceremonial. That is why I have failed. I am sure that the man who did divination should have found out that a witch was behind this illness.'

But would the convenience of witchcraft as an explanation be, of itself, sufficient to ensure the survival of such beliefs at the expense of more rational modes of explanation? It must be remembered that acculturated Navahos characteristically continue to fear witches after they have lost all trust in Navaho medicine. Even in a more complex culture like our own which prides itself upon its rationality, belief in 'black magic' is by no means totally extinct. After all, until comparatively recent times, the Christian Church taught – not that witchcraft was untrue but that it was an evil religion. Our culture hardly needs witchcraft as explanation. The tenacity of such beliefs must have additional supports. To understand fully why witchcraft belief has such survival value among the Navaho, we must look at the latent 'functions' of belief in witchcraft for the individual.

Latent 'Functions' of Witchcraft for the Individual Navaho

The most obvious of these is that the individual can capitalize on the credence of his fellows in these patterns to gain the center of the stage for himself. It is difficult to know how often Navahos complain of the symptoms of witchcraft as a device for getting attention. But close analysis of some cases where the personal context is well known indicates that this mechanism is sometimes employed. A high proportion of those who have suddenly 'fainted' or gone into a semi-trance state at 'squaw dances' or other large gatherings are women or men who are somewhat neglected or occupy low status. The rich and powerful (who are usually, of course, somewhat aggressive types) tend to announce or to have it discovered by a diagnostician in the privacy of their homes that they are victims of witchcraft. But, out of seventeen cases where I have the relevant facts, eleven of those who collapsed at large gatherings were women and thirteen of those were persons known to receive a minimum of prestige responses in the normal run of things. These facts fit well with similar phenomena which have been reported from other cultures. It is a commonplace that European and New England witch trials were frequently started by publicity seekers, often children. It is probable that in the South frustrated women make up a considerable proportion of the accusations which get Negroes lynched. Linton points out that among the Tanala of Madagascar 'most of those subject to *tromba* [a neurotic seizure indicated by an extreme desire to dance] are persons of minor importance' (Kardiner, 1939, p. 270). Mead's material on the differential participation in certain trance states in Bali suggests somewhat similar interpretations (1939).

A second latent 'function' of the corpus of witchcraft lore for individuals is that of providing a socially recognized channel for the expression (in varying degrees of obliquity) of the culturally disallowed. Certain aberrant impulses (such as those toward incest and necrophilia) may achieve some release in phantasy. Of course, a man can have a day dream involving intercourse with a dead woman without recourse to a witchcraft setting. But he is then likely to have his pleasure dampened by worry over the abnormality of his phantasy. In the Navaho phrase 'he will wonder if he is losing his mind'. He will probably feel under the necessity of having Blessing Way sung over him at once. Whereas, if the phantasy takes the form of repeating (or manufacturing) a witchcraft tale involving this incident or visualizations while listening to another telling such a story, the psychological mechanisms of identification or projection permit the outlet in phantasy without conflict.

Quantitatively more significant as adjustive responses are the ways in which witchcraft beliefs and practices allow the expression of direct and displaced antagonisms. The Leightons found that into their category of 'difficulties with other Navahos' fell 26 per cent of the 859 'threats' which were mentioned in their interview material. They note that intra-tribal friction ranks second only to the disease-accident and injury-religious beliefs as a source of the worries which Navahos reported to them (Leighton and Leighton, 1942, p. 206). My own material abundantly confirms this indication of the importance of the problem of aggression in Navaho society at the present time. Witchcraft is, of course, only one of many possible ways of handling this problem and is indeed only one of a number of ways utilized by the Navaho. Fights occur; aggression is expressed against dead relatives as ghosts; there are other cultural devices for meeting the hostility problem which will be discussed in due course. But if myths and rituals provide the principal means of *sublimating* the Navaho individual's anti-social tendencies, witchcraft provides one of the principally socially understood means of *expressing* them. [. . .]

The two most important latent 'functions' of Navaho witchcraft for the individual relate to the crucial Navaho problems of aggression and anxiety. These latent 'functions' seem to be less related to individual status than to certain general pressures which affect (to varying degrees) all Navahos. Let us briefly review the picture. The intra-societal tensions which are present in every society (Dollard, 1938) are aggravated in the case of the Navaho by their uncushioned dependence upon a capricious physical environment, by emotional inbreeding, by insecurity consequent upon the pressure of our culture and society, by restrictions upon various methods for discharge of aggressive impulses. Non-aggressive ways of handling hostile feelings are inadequate. Most direct forms of intra-group aggression constitute too great a challenge to social solidarity and to subsistence survival. Under these circumstances the beliefs and practices related to witchcraft constitute eminently adjustive cultural solutions for Navaho individuals.

Displacement of aggression

There are few socially legitimated hostilities among the Navaho. The witch is the person whom the ideal patterns of the culture say it is not only proper but necessary to hate. Instead of saying all the bitter things one has felt against one's stingy and repressive father-in-law (which would threaten one's own economic security as well as bring down upon one's head unpleasant social disapproval), one can obtain some relief by venting one's spleen against a totally unrelated witch in the community. This displaced aggression does not expose one to punishment so long as one is discreet in the choice of the intimates to whom one talks. And if one rages against a witch who isn't even in the locality but lives over the mountain a safe hundred miles away one is perfectly assured against reprisals.

The fact that a high proportion of witchcraft gossip refers to *distant* witches makes Navaho witchcraft much more adaptive than most patterns which center witch activity within the group. At Zuni where everyone knows everyone else the effect appears to be much more destructive. But in a Navaho story the witch can be specified as a Navaho – with a gain to the imaginative reality of the tale – and yet never have been seen by narrator and hearers, or perhaps seen only rarely when he visited the community to conduct a ceremonial. In such cases the social visibility is sufficient for credence but the social distance great enough to make the origin of feuds unlikely. Since Navaho witches (with the partial exception of the de Chelly and Cañoncito populations) are a distributive rather than a segmental minority, persistive sadism of the type directed against Jews in Germany does not appear. [. . .]

Direct aggression

Witchcraft, however, not only provides 'scapegoats' against whom hostile impulses may be displaced. Under some circumstances, witchcraft provides a means for attack upon the actual targets of my hostile feelings. If I am a singer and smarting under professional jealousy of another singer I can whisper accusations of witchcraft against my rival (cf. Newcomb and Reichard, 1937, p. 16; Reichard, 1939, pp. 7, 8). Or I can mitigate the burning of my envy of a rich neighbor by suggesting that perhaps the way his riches were obtained would not bear too careful scrutiny. If my wife runs off with another man, I can often say to my relatives 'Oh, he got her by Frenzy Witchcraft.' This both permits intensified and socially justified indignation on my part and also reduces my shame: it is not that the seducer is a better man than I – *he* used magical powers.

Nor does witchcraft belief merely channelize antagonisms between one individual and another. The feuds between different extended family groups (which perhaps often actually rest primarily upon a realistic conflict over land or water resources) are frequently given a formulation in witchcraft terms (cf. Kluckhohn, 1962, p. 208). For instance, one group had complained to the Indian agent of the drinking and fighting of some of their neighbors; these retaliated by threatening to kill an old man of the accusing group as a witch.

Witchcraft belief also permits a limited amount of direct verbal expression of aggression against relatives. Guarded gossip about a tyrannical maternal uncle is a useful safety valve! On several occasions I have had a Navaho in a communicative mood say to me, 'Yes, my maternal uncle is a big singer all right. But some people say he is a witch too.' Such gossip about close blood relatives is relatively rare, but cases of direct accusation against affinal relatives are not infrequent (cf. Kluckhohn, 1962, Part I, section 10, para. 10). My material confirms Morgan's suggestion that such accusations are notably more frequent among patrilocal consumption groups.

This is doubtless partly because such patrilocal residence creates new strains in social relationships within a social organization which is still dominantly matrilineal and matrilocal. [. . .]

In summary, witchcraft is one Navaho means of handling the hostility problem. The existence of this belief in Navaho culture permits the socially tolerated expression of direct and displaced aggression. It channels the expression of aggression. It possibly forces the expression of aggression. But my thesis is not that given the amount and kind of aggression which exists in Navaho society witchcraft belief *must* exist. My thesis is only that given these conditions some forms of release must exist. When other forms are inadequate, and when the witchcraft patterns were historically available, witchcraft belief is a highly adjustive way of releasing not only generalized tension but also those tensions specific to Navaho social structure. [. . .]

It is almost inevitable that Navaho life today should be anxiety ridden. But nothing is more intolerable to human beings than being persistently disturbed without being able to say why or without being able to phrase the matter in such a way that some relief or control is potentially available. It is worth noting that man not only craves reasons and explanations, but in most cases these reasons involve some form of personification, some human-like agency either natural or supernatural. It seems that only a small minority among highly sophisticated peoples can fairly face impersonal forces and the phenomena of chance. Doubtless the explanation for this attitude is that during the years of dawning consciousness practically everything that happens is mediated by human agents – the parents or their substitutes.

Witchcraft belief allows the verbalization of anxiety in a framework that is understandable and which implies the possibility of doing something. Witches (who are living individuals) are potentially controllable by the society; the caprices of the environment are not. Likewise, it is important for the adjustment of the individual that witchcraft is a focus of anxiety which the culture recognizes as valid. The symptoms of anxiety which the members of different societies manifest under conditions of stress are characteristically different. For a Navaho, witchcraft is something in terms of which he can acceptably justify his anxiety to his fellows. It is a peculiarly adjustive response in that he can justify his anxiety without taking any blame himself. For in the case of those illnesses which are normally treated by Holy Way chants the ultimate etiology from the Navaho point of view rests in the infraction of some cultural prohibition. To some degree, it is the individual's own fault that he is sick. However, the Navaho consider the witch victim as guiltless. Thus, between various possibilities for the objectification of anxiety, witchcraft is one of those which is most wholly advantageous. But the cultural validity is the issue which concerns us immediately here. [. . .]

To sum up: witchcraft is a major Navaho instrument for dealing with aggression and anxiety. It permits some anxiety and some malicious destructiveness to be expressed directly with a minimum of punishment to the aggressor. Still more anxiety and aggression is displaced through the witchcraft pattern assemblage into channels where they are relatively harmless or where, at least, there are available patterns for adjusting the individuals to the new problems created. Individual adjustment merges with group adaptation.

Witchcraft as an Adaptive Structure for the Local Group and for Navaho Society

That most Navahos believe in witchcraft is, up to a point, a danger not merely to the solidarity but to the very existence of the society. The informant's remark, 'If the white people hadn't stopped us, we'd have killed each other all off' has more than a grain of truth in it. Paradoxically, however, belief in witchcraft, so long as other forces hold the disruptive tendencies in check, is an adaptive structure of a high order. The principal manifest 'function' is that witchcraft lore affirms solidarity by dramatically defining what is bad: namely, all secret and malevolent activities against the health, property and lives of fellow tribesmen. This sanction is reinforced by attributing to witches all the stigmata of evil: incest, nakedness and other kinds of forbidden knowledge and act.

But credence in witchcraft likewise has many specific latent 'functions' which make for the preservation of the group's and the society's equilibrium. It tends, along with other social mechanisms, to prevent undue accumulation of wealth and tempers too rapid a rise in social mobility. A rich man knows that if he is stingy with his relatives or fails to dispense generous hospitality to all and sundry he is likely to be spoken of as a witch. Individuals know also that if they accumulate wealth too rapidly the whisper will arise that they got their start by robbing the dead of their jewelry. In a society like the Navaho which is competitive and capitalistic, on the one hand, and still familistic on the other, any ideology which has the effect of slowing down economic mobility is decidedly adaptive. One of the most basic strains in Navaho society arises out of the incompatibility between the demands of familism and the emulation of European patterns in the accumulating of capital. The rich tend to have considerable prestige, but they are also much hated. The reasons for this are many-sided. Among others, there is the association between polygyny and wealth. 'I might lose my wife because rich people can have more than one wife.' One is tempted to speculate on the associations between Frenzy Witchcraft, polygyny and wealth, but in the absence of fuller information about the history of the various sub-patterns of polygyny and of any historical knowledge of Frenzy Witchcraft, such speculations would be empty. To return to the point at issue, the best hope for the preservation of the coherence of Navaho culture and the integrity of the Navaho way of life seems to rest in there being a gradual transition between the familistic type of social organization and a type more nearly resembling our own. A man cannot get rich very fast if he does his full duty by his extended family. Any pattern, such as witchcraft, which tends to discourage the rapid accumulation of wealth makes, therefore, for the survival of the society.

Similarly, the threat of an accusation of witchcraft acts as a brake upon the power and influence of ceremonial practitioners. They are effectively warned that their capacity for influencing the course of events by supernatural techniques must be used only to accomplish socially desirable ends. The fact that witches are depicted as using whistles, pollen, turquoise, sandpainting, songs (cf. Kluckhohn, 1962, pp. 54, 77, 81, 97) and that there are many other highly specific parallels between witchcraft and chant practice (e.g., sorcerers bearing [burying?] materials under a tree struck by lightning[3] indicates that witchcraft is thought of as *bad* ceremonialism (Kluckhohn, 1962, fn. 1, Appendix 9). The whole association of practitioners and ceremonial practices with witchcraft reflects the central ambivalence of feeling which the Navaho have for this sector of the culture. Singers are valued – but distrusted. Witchcraft gossip and potential trials and executions guarantee the lay Navaho that practitioners will think twice before they abuse their powers. How this works in the concrete is well illustrated by an incident which occurred at Red Rock in 1937. A man went to his maternal uncle and asked him to sing over his wife. The uncle was not satisfied with the number of sheep offered and evaded performing the chant. The wife died. The nephew first accused his uncle as a witch but was unable to muster family or community support for disciplining. He thereupon killed the uncle himself. Such events must surely reinforce the disposition of singers to be liberal to their kin and prompt in acceding to requests for ceremonial help.

3. cf. 'disposal' in chants.

229

Witchcraft as a Technique of Social Control

Accusation of witchcraft is, indeed, a threat which Navaho social organization uses to keep all 'agitators', all individuals who threaten to disrupt the smooth functioning of the community, in check. When Manuelito in 1884 brought about the execution of more than forty 'witches' (Van Valkenburgh, 1938, p. 47), there is good evidence that this was a very astute way of silencing leaders throughout the Navaho country who were beginning to advocate another armed resistance to the whites. Manuelito was convinced that the only hope for his tribe lay in peace. He knew that if he caused the troublemakers to be arrested and turned over to the United States government his own prestige would suffer and possibly be destroyed. But they could be tried and killed as witches with full social approval. I may here be attributing undue prescience to Manuelito, but the interpretation has the support both of Navaho informants and qualified white observers. Perhaps, all of this is rationalization after the fact; I merely report what Navahos and whites who either knew Manuelito personally or knew some member of his immediate family have told me. Certainly, however, the use of this device for social control is in most cases less consciously carried out. The introduction of the Ghost dance cult among the Navaho was blocked by spreading the word that proponents of the new religion were witches (cf. Kluckhohn, 1962, p. 232). Any powerful instigator of trouble in a local Navaho group simply tends to be talked about as a probable witch, and this tendency operates to reduce intra-group friction. Realization that someone who 'acts mean' is likely to be accused as a witch acts as a deterrent of hostile acts. The corollary is that an offended person may avenge himself by witchcraft.

There are other respects in which witchcraft belief is an effective sanction for the enforcement of social co-operation.[4] The aged, whether they have a claim as relatives or not, must be fed or they will witch against one. The disposition to aid siblings who are ill is reinforced by the realization that the death of siblings may give rise to suspicion that a survivor is learning

4. For an excellent discussion of witchcraft as a device for social control see Gayton (1930, pp. 409–11).

witchcraft. The effectiveness of leaders is sometimes increased by the fear that they are witches and that if they are disobeyed they will use witchcraft against those who fail to follow them. While this sometimes doubtless has the consequence of perpetuating bad leadership, it has its good side too in that the anarchistic tendencies of Navaho society make it peculiarly vulnerable when facing a society organized like our own. The survival of Navaho groups is favored by any sanctions which assist a united front behind leaders of some permanence. The singer's care and best efforts for his patients are reinforced by his knowing what the consequences of his losing too many patients will be: suspicion of witchcraft, perhaps open accusation, possibly trial and execution. Even the fear of going about at night has social value. One of the principal sources of friction among Navahos is sexual jealousy. Fear of witches at night acts to some slight extent as a deterrent of extra-marital sex relations because night-time would otherwise provide favorable conditions for a secret rendezvous. [...]

Discussion and Summary

After presenting patterned cultural theory and practice relating to one sector of Navaho culture which may be referred to in English by the one word 'witchcraft',[5] an attempt at 'explanation' has been made. That is, I have tried to show that certain available data bear a determinate relationship to other data and to generalized propositions. In particular, we have seen that the data did not bear a haphazard relationship to the physical environment, economic problems, health conditions, the concrete

5. It is true that I have not found any single Navaho word which lumps together Witchery, Sorcery, Wizardry and Frenzy Witchcraft. So far as 'conceptual category' is concerned, the category 'witchcraft' is probably the observer's and not a native category. I do think that evidence has been presented that the Navaho do treat the separate varieties as a 'feeling category'. In any case from the standpoint of the observer attempting a structural analysis, there can be no doubt that all of these patterns are crystallized around a common focus: private manipulation of the supernatural for socially disapproved ends. Moreover, there are more explicit elements common to each. For example, the use of the personal name enters in all four techniques. As one informant remarked, 'They used to say you can't witch a person until you know his name.'

situation of the individual and to such other sectors of culture as the forms of habit training and general social organization.

The study of Navaho witchcraft does not stop, then, with the bringing to light of bits of curious and sometimes terrible belief. Systematic analysis of observed behaviours and of the latent and manifest content of interview material suggests clues as to the stresses and strains of Navaho social organization and the dynamics of social process generally. The outstanding conclusions specific to the Navaho may now be briefly reviewed.

Burke has remarked, 'Human beings build their cultures, nervously loquacious, upon the edge of an abyss.' This is even more true of the Navaho than of many human societies. Witchcraft supplies a partial answer to some of the deeper uncertainties supplementing the answers provided by myths and rituals. If myths and rituals are the principal integrative and instrumental patterns for meeting the need-persistive (cf. Rosenzweig, 1941) reactions to frustration, witchcraft patterns are instruments of no mean importance in adjusting to the ego-defensive (Rosenzweig, 1941) reactions to deprivation. Those substitute responses which do not constitute aggressive acts in the social sense cannot, for the Navaho, discharge the cumulative tensions. In a society where the relative strength of anticipations of punishment for overt aggression is high, witchcraft allows imaginary aggression. Witchcraft channels the displacement of aggression, facilitating emotional adjustment with a minimum of disturbance of social relationships. Even direct aggression through witchcraft helps to maintain societal inhibitions consonant with the old native culture. Likewise, the witch is a convenient anxiety object. Anxieties may be disguised in ways which promote individual adjustment and social solidarity. The threat of accusation of witchcraft is a check upon the strong and powerful. The belief that the destitute, the aged – and even animals – may, if treated too unkindly, turn with witchcraft upon those who neglect or oppress them is, up to a point, a protection for these unfortunates. Many sorts of cultural values are reinforced by the corpus of witchcraft lore. It is probably no accident that the bogeymen who are used to socialize children have so many characteristics in common with the were-animals dreaded by adults (cf. Kluckhohn, 1962, part 1, section 3, fn. 8).

The extent to which Navahos avail themselves of these cultural instruments is related to place in the social structure, temporary social situation and probably to constitutional factors. All of these are determinants of the level of tolerance of frustration. 'If the tolerance is poor, then some aggressor must be fabricated. A thwarted individual would then displace the aggression onto a system or onto any group representing a constellation of ideas that evoked hostility, no matter how mild, in the previous experience of the individual' (Levy, 1941, p. 356). With the Navaho – as with, I suspect, all peoples – beliefs and practices related to witchcraft are, to some extent, infantile, regressive instrumental patterns differentially invoked by those persons who are more 'on the spot' or more under the stress of misfortune than others, or by those who for constitutional or whatever factors are less able to 'take it' than others.

Similarly, those who are suspected or accused of witchcraft do not constitute a random sample of the Navaho population generally. A large majority consist of two groups of people: the rich,[6] and old and powerful singers. Gossip against the rich almost always takes the form of the rationalization that they got their start by stealing jewelry and other valuables from the dead.[7] But actually the prevalence of this rationalization acts

6. cf. Horney (1937, pp. 171–5). Power, prestige and possessions serve not only as a reassurance against anxiety but also as a means of releasing hostility.

7. The constant association of witchcraft with the dead is a problem which can be regarded at present as only partially understood. The explanation is doubtless historical, in part. That is, the generalized complex of witchcraft idea patterns which has been transmitted to the Navaho contains this as one element – for the witch-ghoul notion has a very wide distribution. But the Navaho have intensified and reified the association. The linking of almost all types of witchcraft activity with the dead or with objects connected with the dead is approximately to be explained as part of the pattern which attributes all the Navaho 'worst things' to witches. Likewise, the association is to be understood on the ground of the partial equivalence of witches and ghosts (ghost = witch from the company of the dead). In this connexion, Opler's (1936) hypotheses of ambivalence may, in my opinion, profitably be invoked.

The peculiarly morbid Navaho fear of the dead, however, is a topic which deserves an essay of its own. Among other things, this almost pathological (as it seems to the observer from our culture) fear may perhaps be related to the configuration of individualism and its sub-configuration

as a kind of economic leveler. The rich feel pressure to be lavish in hospitality, generous in gifts to needy relatives and neighbors and prodigal in the ceremonies they sponsor. Otherwise, they know the voice of envy will speak out in whispers of witchcraft which would make their life in society strained and unpleasant. Similarly, the existent mechanism regulates the power and influence of the singer. Feeling toward singers always tends to be somewhat ambivalent. On the one hand, they have great prestige, are much in demand and may obtain large fees. On the other hand, they are feared, and the border of active distrust is always close. A singer must not lose too many patients. He must also be more generous and hospitable than the model Navaho. It is also well documented that at various crucial times in the history of the Navaho clever leaders have used the accusation of witchcraft as an effective means of social control. During the post-Fort Sumner period, the chiefs in power took care of advocates of renewed resistance to the whites by spreading the word that these persons were witches. Many were killed. There seems evidence that a correlation exists between the amount of fear and talk about witches and general state of tension prevailing among the Navaho. Thus, during the last difficult years of controversy over the stock reduction programme, there has been appreciably more witchcraft excitement than for some time past. The resentment over stock reduction must itself be seen in the context of the general disequilibrium of the Navaho economy. The 'depression' of the 'thirties had much more direct and sharply felt effects upon the Navaho than did earlier down shifts in American business cycles – because, prior to 1929, Navaho economy was

of modesty. These are manifested in many other witchcraft data. Note that modesty and privacy are to some extent preserved even in a witchcraft context (Kluckhohn, 1962, p. 54, where the boy is allowed to be apart while he urinates and thus escapes).

I suggest that such dread of the dead is likely to be at a maximum in a culture which glorifies the individual. The later Middle Ages where the salvation of the individual was the great goal and where St Thomas Aquinas expressed the dominant attitude as 'persona est, quod est perfectissimum in natura' is a good parallel. Here also the macabre, the gruesome, the dismal aspects of death seem to have been deliberately exploited (cf. Huizinga, 1927, esp., chap. 11, 'The Vision of Death'). One may contrast cultures where societies are extended by generations as in India and China.

much less fully integrated with American economy generally. Since Navahos suffered as a result of the fall in the price of sheep and wool, the loss of market for their craft products, unemployment at wage work, this factor alone helps us understand increased antagonism against the rich during the last decade.

But witchcraft is not something which need be viewed with naïve abhorrence. It has been seen to have its manifest and its latent 'functions' both for the individual and for social groups. At the same time, witchcraft has its *cost*[8] for the individual and for the group. Given the conditions of Navaho life and the Navaho socialization process, given the guarantee in the background that the Indian Service will prevent wholesale slaughter of 'witches', Navaho witchcraft does constitute an adjustive and an adaptive structure. Its *cost* is projected aggression and some social disruption. Probably, as a natural consequence of the insistence that witchcraft *does* have important adaptive and adjustive effects, the *cost* has been too little stressed. In many cases witchcraft belief undoubtedly does more to promote fear and timidity than to relieve aggressive tendencies. The fears consequent upon witchcraft tend to restrict the life activities of some persons, to curtail their social participation. Perhaps the witchcraft pattern assemblage tends to be mainly adjustive for individuals who tend to be aggressive, mainly disruptive for those who tend to be non-aggressive. Such a view would fit well with the suggestions which have been made of the relationship between witchcraft patterns and war patterns (Kluckhohn, 1962, part 2, section 3, paras. 3 and 4).

Another aspect of the *cost* of witchcraft belief to which attention should be drawn is that probably this is a basis for unwillingness to undertake or to continue the burdens of leadership. For example, a young Navaho who has made a splendid record during the past two years as a judge has told his friends that he was resigning because he felt that his father's serious illness was traceable to witchcraft activities occasioned by resentment at some of the judge's decisions. Likewise, to counterbalance the tendency to economic leveling, there is to be reckoned the power and instrument for domination which accrues to the rich in so far

8. I am indebted to David Aberle for suggesting to me this concept of 'cost' to balance that of 'function'.

as they are dreaded as witches. A statement in *Son of Old Man Hat* is a classic in this connexion:

Bunch of Whiskers wasn't a headman, but everybody knew him and feared him. He was the richest Navaho on the reservation. They used to say, 'He's a witch. That's why he has lots of sheep, horses and cattle, and beads of all kinds, and all kinds of skins.' He had everything, and by that everyone knew him and was afraid of him (Dyk, 1938, p. 357).

References

DOLLARD, J. (1938), 'Hostility and fear in social life', *Social Forces*, vol. 17.

DYK, W. (1938), *Son of Old Man Hat: A Navaho Autobiography*, New York.

GAYTON, A. H. (1930), 'Yokuts-Mono chiefs and shamans', *University of California Publications in American Archaeology and Ethnology*, vol. 24.

HORNEY, K. (1937), *The Neurotic Personality of Our Time*, New York.

HUIZINGA, J. (1927), *The Waning of the Middle Ages*, Arnold; Penguin Books, 1955.

KARDINER, A. (1939), *The Individual and His Society: The Psychodynamics of Primitive Social Organization*, New York.

KLUCKHOHN, C. (1942), 'Myths and rituals: a general theory', *Harvard Theological Review*, vol. 35, no. 1.

KLUCKHOHN, C. (1962), *Navaho Witchcraft*, Beacon Press.

LEE, D. (1940), 'A primitive system of values', *Philosophy of Science*, vol. 7, no. 3.

LEIGHTON, A. H. and LEIGHTON, D. C. (1942), 'Some types of uneasiness and fear in a Navaho Indian community', *American Anthropologist*, n.s., vol. 44.

LEVY, D. M. (1941), 'The hostile act', *Psychological Review*, vol. 48, no. 4.

MEAD, M. (1939), 'Researches in Bali', *Transactions of the New York Academy of Sciences*, series 2, vol. 2, no. 1.

NEWCOMB, F. J., and REICHARD, G. A. (1937), *Sandpaintings of the Navaho Shooting Chant*, New York.

OPLER, M. E. (1936), 'An interpretation of ambivalence of two American Indian tribes', *Journal of Social Psychology*, vol. 7.

REICHARD, G. A. (1939), *Navajo Medicine Man: Sandpaintings and Legends of Miguelito*, New York.

ROSENZWEIG, SAUL (1941), 'Need-persistive and ego-defensive reactions to frustration as demonstrated by an experiment on repression', *Psychological Review*, vol. 48, no. 4.

VAN VALKENBURGH, R. F. (1928), *A Short History of the Navaho People*, Window Rock.

21 J. D. Krige

The Social Function of Witchcraft

J. D. Krige, 'The social function of witchcraft', *Theoria*, vol. 1, 1947, pp. 8–21.

Introduction

My objective is to show that witchcraft is something more than meaningless superstition. I can do so most effectively by restricting myself to a single Bantu tribe, the Lobedu of the far N.E. Transvaal. For in this way I shall be able to analyse some of its relations to the ideas and values of the society and perhaps also to achieve my aim of making some sense of an institution which, owing to its associations among ourselves, seems to be utterly devoid of sense.

Among the Lobedu, just as of course among other Bantu people, witches and sorcerers, so far from playing the role of unreason, make a rational contribution to the fulfilment of men's needs and purposes. This is almost immediately evident when we remember that witchcraft and sorcery are explanations of evil in the universe. They enable men to account for their failures and frustrations. Moreover, since the evil operates only through the medium of human beings, it can also be brought under human control. The parts assigned to these characters, the witches and sorcerers, presuppose a just world, ordered and coherent, in which the evil is not merely outlawed but can be overcome by man-made techniques. In the result men feel secure and the moral order is upheld.

I cannot undertake the task of demonstrating the validity of the underlying conceptions and presuppositions, because the whole setting is entirely different from anything with which we are familiar. I have to limit myself to a small segment of the circle circumscribing the magical background against which witchcraft assumes meaning. But I shall have failed in my purpose if I fashion the witch to a shape that cannot be articulated with ordinary human needs such as we ourselves have.

Let us at the outset see how the Lobedu phrase the roles of those arch-enemies of society, the witches and sorcerers. They picture witchcraft as criminality incarnate, an intrinsically evil influence in the universe which can manifest itself only through a human being; it is independent of all the other supernaturals, but it is not a capricious power; and it is thought to be set into motion only by malice, hatred and similar motives and generally only against some specific individual.

The phraseology used indicates that the Lobedu make a major distinction between witchcraft proper, which is the wickedness, sometimes without overt rhyme or reason, of the night-witch, and sorcery, which is the destructive technique of the day-witch; witchcraft implies personal relationships with the supernatural, sorcery means manipulation of magic which is not supernatural by Lobedu conceptions. An elaborate moral grading of magic indicates, however, that many other distinctions are drawn. At the one extreme good magic or medicine – the two conceptions are identical – safeguards the moral order and is approved; for it is the application in the public interest of the properties of matter, as when the queen, transformer of the clouds, makes rain or the doctors heal disease. At the other extreme, evil magic or sorcery is bad and frowned upon. Between these extremes there are several grades of magic (or rather uses of magic since magical power in itself is generally neutral) some within the law but ethically disapproved and some about which opinions differ. Often enough the victim places an interpretation upon his misfortunes which differs from that of his fellows: he may try to incriminate a sorcerer, but they will tell you that he is merely blaming others to escape a sense of his own inadequacy or incompetence. Perhaps I shall be able to turn later to some of these complications in the moral scheme. At the moment my point is that it is essential to understand that sorcery which falls into the category of magic is entirely different from witchcraft proper. Sorcery is neither wonderful nor above ordinary matter-of-fact physical laws; but witchcraft involves supercausation, is mysterious and transcends the operation of natural cause and effect.

The night-witch is accordingly a sinister character. He belongs to an unholy fraternity, whose members meet at night to deliberate upon their deeds of darkness. For these deeds are always mysterious in the sense that no one knows how they are done, and they are physically impossible by natural means. The idea is that he disposes of the powers of darkness rather than that he does his evil work by night. The night-witch uses no medium of destruction such as poison; he himself has inborn powers to ride through the air, prowling over villages like night bombers over our cities, but invisible, infiltrating unobserved into the defences and insinuating himself through the smallest crevices. He uses no spells or incantations; nor indeed does he employ medicines or send his soul on these miraculous excursions. But he has familiars who have various functions: he may send them out as vampires or leave them at his home in his own image as an alibi. No one, however, knows precisely what his methods are except that they are all supernatural.

It is his mystical presence which paralyses you when you wake in a sweat after a terrifying nightmare. He maliciously excises parts of your body in order to insert sand or millet, which accounts for the excruciating pains familiar to anyone who has experienced foreign matter impinging upon exposed tissues. When unaccountably your bones ache or you feel tired as on the morning after the night before, you know that it is a night-witch who has set you to hoe all night in his garden. Nowadays, in the more sophisticated culture-contact situation, you ascribe lassitude for which no ostensible reason exists to such new devices of night-witches as causing you in your sleep to cycle aimlessly up hill and down dale.

Night-witches, like the succubi of medieval times, are almost invariably women, not men, but the rationalization incriminating the gentler sex is rather different. According to popular opinion as reflected, e.g., in Dr Wier's disquisition in 1563 on the credulity and fragility of the female sex, medieval women were considered to be peculiarly susceptible to evil influences owing to their mental and moral infirmities. The Lobedu have a much higher estimate of women's nature and role, for women are the supreme rulers, the high priests, the great go-betweens in quarrels, the final adjudicators in questions of inheritance and succession and, as may be suspected in a society that does not rely on force or coercion, the guarantors of the effectiveness of all the major sanctions. Nevertheless, the Lobedu seem to have succumbed to the masculine illusion that what is feminine is often inexplicable, instinct with inscrutability. With such credentials Lobedu women both become psychological substitutes on whom people tend to project their failures and frustrations and are believed to be endowed with inscrutable powers such as the night-witch disposes of.

The province of the night-witch is not limited to destruction by disease and death. Among other things, barrenness, marked differences in the productivity of adjoining fields, the wind that breaks the growing crops, are attributed to witchcraft of this brand. And rather more sinister is the power to enslave souls and to send familiars and vampires upon nefarious errands. The addition of the familiar to the scheme permits of its further elaboration; but I have to content myself by saying that the relationship between witch and familiar is not invoked as an explanation of frigidity in women as is the case among some Xhosa tribes. Lobedu familiars are often obnoxious animals such as polecats and hyenas, though the most fearful of them all is the *khidudwane*, a human being killed in such a way that when he is buried only his shadow is interred, the real personality being imprisoned in a large earthen pot by day and dispatched by its mistress upon sinister missions by night. Quite unlike the *khipago*, a conception borrowed, as the name indicates, from the European spook, which is comparatively harmless and can easily be laid by appeasing his complaint or pouring medicine on his grave, this fearful familiar of the witch causes one to faint, waste away and die, and nothing will avail except discovery of and a direct attack upon the witch.

There is a great deal more to the witch than this, for the analysis of wickedness is taken far back and is closely articulated with conscious as well as subconscious, hidden, human motivations. The night-witch, e.g., is born not made; but, since criminality is by Lobedu conceptions a product of both nature and nurture, the potentialities with which the witch is born unfold apace as she imbibes the evil secretions in her mother's milk. Moreover she must learn how to put her power into practice. This learning process begins on the second or third day after birth when mother-witch flings infant-witchling up against the wall to which it will cling like a bat and so learn its first lesson in flying.

The sorcerer by Lobedu conceptions is an entirely different character. He is usually a man whose machinations involve the use of medicines and incantations, ordinary natural techniques 'of the day' as they phrase it, not the inscrutable and supernatural devices 'of the night'. Sorcery operates by natural laws. It is not the nature of its power that is evil, but only its perverted application. Its essence is the criminal use of the potency of medicines, which can be and usually are in the service of legitimate ends. The sorcerer's techniques are simply those of lawful medical practice; but they are lawful means put to unlawful ends. Spells are not essential, since the destructive potency is usually inherent in the poisons used, not in the sorcerer himself. For the sorcerer is not evil incarnate: he belongs to no criminal gang, does not inherit either his knowledge or his sinful propensities, and has no power to tame and teach familiars. The Lobedu have in mind a normal human being, a man even of good character and generous instincts, who owing to some temporary aberration succumbs to the temptation of injuring an enemy by using some poison – an extract of the ordinary properties of material things, which he may acquire from another. Unlike the night-witch who might send a hyena to take up its abode in your body and eat your food, the sorcerer's method is to cause you to eat some indissoluble toxic substance which clings to your oesophagus and from there poisons your whole system. There is no known antidote to the internal hyena, except of course the long-range attack upon the unknown witch; but the foreign substance introduced by the sorcerer can be removed by means of an emetic.

A favourite technique of the sorcerer is to challenge enemies by pitting the potency of his poisons against the drugs they use to protect themselves. This conception of medicines warring against one another, like our toxins and anti-toxins, is the reason why everyone must be inoculated with anti-sorcery serum, just as we guard ourselves in anticipation by vaccination. It is also obvious that such techniques as placing poisoned thorns in your path, or pointing a medicated forefinger are used by sorcerers not night-witches. It suffices to ground an imputation of sorcery when a man menaces you with the words *u do bona* (you will see) and evil subsequently befalls you.

241

The Moral Grading of Magic

Since sorcery is simply lawful means put to unlawful ends, the same techniques may be moral and approved in one context but immoral and outlawed in another. And a study of these different contexts casts considerable light upon a number of underlying conceptions. Take, e.g., the technique of challenging or in Lobedu phraseology 'trying' others with medicines. The medicines are called *malego* and the technique *hu lega*, and *hu lega* is sorcery and illegal except when employed by doctors against one another. It is legal in this context not merely because the trial of strength has social value and the quacks are discredited, but also for a much subtler reason. Lobedu society is fundamentally co-operative and frowns upon all forms of rivalry. Even when the good things of life, the prizes, or the means for achieving desired ends such as land, are, objectively considered, limited, the scarcity is rephrased in such a manner that rivalries are avoided. It is as if everything for which people might compete is made to fall into the category of free commodities, or rather, since psycho-logical principles are involved, objective facts are reinterpreted in a way that shifts the problem to a subjective setting in which the scarcity no longer appears as a significant factor. The popula-tion, e.g., presses hard upon the natural resources but the periodi-cal threat of starvation, even the scarcity of relishes, is attributed not to the limited resources, but to some shortcoming in men such as indolence; and the virtue of rephrasing the difficulty in this way is that rivalries for the scarce things are obviated while the merit of, say, industry is stressed. This is naturally only part of the explanation, for the functioning of the culture relies on co-operativeness: aggressiveness and the measurement of one's achievement against that of another are never rewarded, the social structure places barriers between potential competitors and, among a multitude of other cultural arrangements tending in the same direction, the whole educational system – the absence of any comparison of the attainments of children, the insistence upon sharing (even the head of a locust, as the Lobedu say), the team work and mutuality that are given a high cultural rating, the disapproval of any form of personal display – all this inculcates values that are incompatible with competitiveness.

Now when one doctor tries another with *malego*, the intention to injure does not constitute sorcery. I have said that the Lobedu themselves rationalize what appears to be an inconsistency by saying that this licence, that is allowed doctors, is a guarantee of the effectiveness of their medicines, since if they cannot immunize themselves against the poisons of others, they are little use as guardians of the public health. But partly also *lega*ing is the projection of rivalries into the magical world since it is disallowed in ordinary life. There cannot be competition for clients or their custom, for any rivalry on the economic level is simply inconceivable. Nevertheless, the implications of scarcity of clients are inescapable. The attention is, however, diverted from the objective situation of a limited clientele to the warring of medicines in the magical world, and this vicarious outlet for, instead of complete repression of, competition is condoned not merely because it is to the public benefit but also because it is compartmentalized, as completely segregated from the conception of rivalry as heroic deeds in war involving the killing of the enemy are among us segregated from foul murder in peace.

Many other uses of the power which we call magic are moral and hence medicinal, or immoral and hence sorcery according as the motive is approved or not. Some of them, curiously enough in a co-operative society, are concessions to the impulse of revenge; some are methods of frustrating an enemy by making his objective invisible; and there are today also techniques to secure the favour of others, like love-magic or medicine to attract trade customers but these are introductions from other tribes, incompatible with the Lobedu pattern, and hence always reprehensible. The power is in itself neutral; it is the objective which makes it moral or immoral. That, of course, is not the whole story; the handling of human motivations is much subtler; but I must content myself with this over-simplification, which at all events is a sufficient approximation to Lobedu conceptions to enable us to take our analysis a little further.

One type of vengeance magic is *madabi* which is the use of powers – really certain properties of matter – to transmute the thing to which it is applied, e.g., *madabi* will enable you to turn pieces of the skin of an animal into the animal itself. A deserted husband may legitimately so manipulate *madabi* as to frighten his erring wife into running back to him, for instance, by causing monkeys to appear whenever his unfaithful spouse cooks or draws water for her new-found lover. Among us mice rather than monkeys might occasion misgivings in a conscience-stricken wife. But the use of *madabi* for purely personal ends is sorcery and hence criminal, as when a man takes revenge upon a girl, whom he has seduced and who subsequently jilts him, by changing her sex whenever the child is about to be born, and thereby endangering her life. In the first instance *madabi* functions as a moral sanction and its psychological effect reflects the effective internalization of a sense of guilt which nothing will remove except repentance and restitution; in the second, it conceptualizes a sense of frustration seeking an outlet in unlawful revenge. Like other vengeance or rather justice magic, *madabi* continues to act unless and until the person who dispenses it reverses its power. To apply *madabi* is *hu dabeka*; to arrest or reverse its action is *hu dabekulla*; and this reversal has been very neatly linked up with conceptions of fair play and the ultimate triumph of justice. Let me illustrate from the technique called *mutsikela*, the most dreaded form of vengeance magic which, even when lawfully used, is considered to be so drastic that preliminary public warning of its being put into operation is necessary.

Mutsikela, or working on the grave of a victim killed by sorcery or witchcraft, is lawful if directed against the criminal murderer, even though its effects are so deadly that it destroys not merely the criminal but also his relatives; for either they are accomplices or the homicidal propensity is inherent in them and has been nurtured in the same home. While medicine to reanimate the spirit of the deceased victim is being poured down a hole in the grave, the most diabolical spell known to the Lobedu – it is *ex tempore* but follows a familiar pattern – is uttered sending the spirit on its mission of stern justice. Spirit and medicine are instructed to search for and strike down the homicidal witch, the phraseology I heard on one occasion being, 'to cause them to follow you to the grave; and we say not one of them but the whole brood of culprits'. There are, however, dangers in using this method of restituting a wrong. It is perfectly legal in untainted hands, though its morality is doubted. It must be preceded by the public warning, *hu ebela*, which consists in a warning shouted out from some vantage point, within earshot of the suspected witch, that, unless he desists and makes amends, retaliatory action will be taken. One must remember that in the Lobedu pattern of justice, the repressive sanctions, such as penalties, fines, punishments, indeed any measure involving physical coercion, are practically unknown; all wrongs fall under the restitutive sanction and the procedure given the highest cultural rating is *hu khumelwa*, mutual reconciliation. The criminal, even if he has murdered your son, is wherever possible converted into a kinsman: he gives his daughter and so becomes a son-in-law who has many obligations to you and in return receives beer, the bond *par excellence* of brotherhood, from you.

Mutsikela, like all justice magic, searches for the evildoer and passes judgement upon him; but if the culprit has made suitable restitution and you neglect to recall the forces you have set into operation, or if the witch who has caused the death himself *tsikela*'s for you in an attempt to disarm suspicion against him, the omniscient medicine will seek the culprit in vain and returning will strike down the guilty sender. And so the engineer of evil is hoist with his own petard; the criminal use of this kind of magic not merely constitutes sorcery of the worst brand but also rebounds upon the criminal. It is, however, more than suspected that the cleverest sorcerers and witches have methods of confusing these medicines, though in the last resort the greatest magicians, the specialists whose function it is to protect the society against witchcraft and sorcery, are superior and the operation of their medicines cannot be circumvented.

Anti-Witchcraft Defences

As *mutsikela* indicates, the Lobedu have effective anti-witchcraft defences. Of course a victim may always consult the divinatory dice, those specially prepared bones that take the place of our stethoscopes and X-rays in diagnosis. No one believes, as we naïvely imagine, that bones are in themselves endowed with perspicacity; but properties and powers can be imparted to them by subjecting them to certain treatments. I am not concerned to explain how such a conception can be justified, except to say that at the level of observation, technology, and scientific verification of these people it is impossible to demonstrate its invalidity. Now, if the bones have identified the witch, it is open to the victim to accuse him and risk the legal proceedings that follow. But resort to law is not altogether satisfactory: it tends to harden animosities in this case whereas appeasement is the accepted function of law; the court is liable to dismiss the accusation as based on idle gossip, or to procrastinate in the hope that the parties will forget their grievances in letting off steam again and again as the case drags on; and there is the danger that the attempt to invoke legal sanctions against a witch will spur him to greater activity against you. It depends entirely upon a man's estimate of the total situation whether he will rely mainly on legal justice or other means to deal with harm caused by the witch or sorcerer; but in any case anticipatory protective measures are always taken. The type of defence is determined by the kind of attack that is feared. A few examples will suffice to indicate the general principles of anti-witchcraft defences.

Protection against the parachutists that ride through the air, the night-flying witches, not unnaturally takes the form of camouflaging the village or other objective of the enemy. Hence the *diphaba*, medicine encircling the village or placed at strategic points, such as the gates. This medicine masks the village, making it appear like an expanse of water so that the witch is deluded and concludes that he has come to the wrong place. Logically enough, the camouflaging effect is obtained by using the properties of products of the ocean, such as whale-oil and sea sand. Medicated pegs around the village block the passage of poisoned shafts hurled by sorcerers. So-called witch-doctors of various kinds, for some establish contact with the forces involved through the diagnostic bones, some through their own innate powers and some others through the medium of ancestral spirits, are the detectors and predictors. They divine the nature and direction of the attack, smell out the quislings and send back with interest the death and destruction. Vengeance-magic with its preliminary warning to the enemy is nothing else than the legitimate reprisal.

The usual defences are unavailing against the witch within the village, since he probably knows the disposition and nature of the precautions taken. There are, therefore, methods of dealing with fifth-columnists. Traitors within the gates may be expelled but a much more favoured solution than physical coercion, which is always regarded as objectionable, is to *fera* the witch. *Fera*ing consists in surreptitiously introducing into his system, through his food or beer, a drug which calms the irritation impelling him to bewitch. It stops that itching of the fingers which constrains him to commit crimes and causes him to forget his frustrations and to seek compensation in day-dreaming or loquacity instead of in action. He may become gossipy and guileless. An examination of the ingredients of the medicine used throws a good deal of light upon the conceptions that they are handling in this case, but the thought-pattern can hardly be explained here and I must content myself by saying that the objective is to convert the compulsion to do evil into conduct that is aimless and harmless.

The Incidence and Function of Witchcraft

I have so far confined myself to description and have mentioned a few of the Lobedu rationalizations. But it is necessary to pursue the analysis very much further in order to understand the real role of witchcraft and sorcery and to show to what needs in human nature the institution is a response. I need hardly reiterate that witches and sorcerers are considered to be the embodiment of malignant forces ever on the alert to enter into unholy matrimony with the criminal impulses of the human heart. Witchcraft particularly is the essence of evil, vicious and inscrutable, that whirls through the universe and seeks asylum in sinful souls in which the germs of wickedness lie ready to be quickened into life. Sorcery is not transmitted in the germ-plasm: a child can never be guilty of sorcery, but the kind of precocity in him which enables him to circumvent an adult or the accepted code is a sure sign of incipient witchcraft. Both vices are, however, identified with the malice and jealousies that motivate anti-social conduct. Both of them occur only where you find stresses and strains in life, where, in other words, there are tensions, actual or potential, between people. Hence it is relatives and neighbours, but never strangers, who use witchcraft or sorcery against one another.

Merely to say that we have here the projection of conflicts

that in a non-aggressive social environment are driven underground because they are not permitted to find expression in open dissension, is not enough. Some kinds of tension are rather differently canalized; they are given other avenues of vicarious expression. There are, e.g., relatives such as the father's sister towards whom, according to the behaviour patterns of the Lobedu, onerous obligations and an extreme delicacy of conduct are enjoined; they are easily aggrieved and readily nurse grievances; and they may have concealed complaints, repressed and subconscious wants. A father's sister's subconscious grievance is actually conceptualized as *mahava*, which may cause illness in the family of her brother's home. And when he calls her, as he may, to remove the cause, she often uses the phraseology (in the conciliation rite she performs): 'if I have been aggrieved and am harbouring ill-will in my heart, I am quite unaware of it. . . .' The interesting point is not merely this conception of hidden frustrations, but also that *mahava* is in quite a different category from witchcraft or sorcery. The position is that the father's sister's displeasure or frustrations cannot be projected as witchcraft or sorcery; and the technique of handling tensions of this kind is entirely different.

It is, however, not merely the incidence of witchcraft and sorcery as between persons, i.e., the types of personal tensions involved, that raises numerous interesting problems; there is a different problem in attempting to explain why these evils are invoked for only a limited range of situations. Why, e.g., can you never ascribe the cracking of your pot in the process of burning to these destructive forces, while you do so when the crops in your garden, also the fruits of your labour, unaccountably fail? Why, when you are caught out telling lies, cannot you incriminate a witch maliciously intent upon discrediting you? After all the Lobedu have a technique, *hu nielela*, which can quite legitimately be used to cause a thief who has escaped detection to repeat his thieving so that he may be caught redhanded. A criminal may be made the victim of an obsessive compulsion to relapse into crime so that he will once more be tried for an offence for which he has, say, been let off with a light sentence in our European courts; for as the Lobedu see things, our justice causes criminals to multiply and witches to become more aggressive and the clemency we exercise to reform the offender presents itself as a challenge to which they respond by magically constraining him to crime. *Hu nielela* is never anti-social and hence can never fall in the category of sorcery; and while it will take me too far afield into Lobedu cultural arrangements, orientations of values and conceptual categories to demonstrate the good sense and coherence of these apparent incongruities, I can say, generally, that when the total situation considered against the background of the knowledge and control of nature available demands an explanation in terms of lack of skill, incompetence or other inadequacy, a man is not permitted to attribute his misfortune or failure to sorcery or witchcraft. Moreover the fundamental presupposition, that the social order is dominated by moral forces, must not be invalidated by the interpretation of causes that a man invokes to account for his shortcomings.

Leaving on one side these difficult questions, let us for a moment revert to the incidence as between persons of witchcraft and sorcery. A statistical analysis reveals that some relatives never bewitch one another, even though their relationship is subject to the severest conflicts. A brother can, for instance, never impute witchcraft or sorcery to his cattle-linked sister, that is, the sister through whose marriage he obtains the cattle for his own marriage. She is the builder of his home and can intervene in it; indeed, he can never divorce the wife obtained with his sister's cattle unless she consents; and in the last resort she may give refuge to that wife if he drives her away and so can prevent the annulment of the marriage and cause the wife to bear children by anyone she likes: the children will still be his and she may still require one of the daughters to marry her son (or if she has none, a supposititious son) so as to become her daughter-in-law who will care for her in her old age. The situation is obviously one that is pregnant with potential stresses and strains. Yet, as I have seen, the ill-conceived idea of a brother to impute witchcraft or sorcery to this sister is ridiculed as a mental aberration or treated as a psychopathic compensatory adjustment. The Lobedu rationalization is usually that brother and sister know one another's medicines and hence cannot harm one another in this way, but underlying this rationalization is the realization that to admit the possibility of witchcraft between these two relatives would endanger the whole social structure, the delicately-balanced edifice built upon the *lobola* exchanges.

On the other hand the most prolific source of witchcraft and sorcery is the conflict of co-wives. They become entangled (if I may use the metaphor of the eternal triangles of our monogamy) in the polygons of jealousy that arise in polygamy. The specific cause of the frustration that is projected may be neglect or favouritism of the husband, status of one wife relative to the other co-wives, indeed any kind of differential treatment or attempt by the husband to benefit the house of one wife at the expense of another. Sexual jealousies do not, however, take a prominent place, since the structure of the family is such that the husband-wife relationship is primarily the link holding together two larger groups, the intermarrying lineages whose interlocking rights and duties constitute the basis of social solidarity as well as of the political organization. A very considerable portion of the total cultural energy goes to devices for ensuring the smooth running of these crucial institutions; and the solutions for difficulties that are ranked highest are always compromise, give and take, conciliation. Dissension and open conflict between co-wives is severely frowned upon, while agreement even in the humblest home receives royal recognition, which means a great deal since the queen is divine and only rarely accessible to ordinary mortals. The consequence is that co-wives can express their resentments only indirectly in some substitute activity. This is, of course, good soil for the growth of grievances for which witchcraft and sorcery provide a very natural vicarious outlet – hence the high incidence among co-wives of vicarious fights in the world of fantasy.

It would serve no good purpose to analyse the various conflict situations in which imputations of witchcraft and sorcery arise. They are quite unintelligible in our setting since the different ways in which men account for their failures and frustrations are always relative to the functioning and values of their society. But a few facets of these situations can be dealt with fairly generally. The first is the psychological function of witchcraft and sorcery. They enable men to believe that their failures are due not to any fault of their own, but to the machinations of others; and it is very necessary, in a world in which the technology is inadequate for the satisfaction of the complex culturally created needs, that men should be able to compensate for their inadequacy and continue to feel that they are masters of their own fate. Moreover, witchcraft and sorcery provide avenues of vicarious achievement to those who, because of their aggressive temperaments or disharmonious conditioning, find it impossible or extremely irksome to conform to the pattern of co-operativeness and reciprocity.

Another point worth mentioning is that witchcraft and sorcery do not operate automatically, as a number of other forces do; they must always be set into motion by a specific individual; and consequently there must be some theory incriminating such an individual. Part of the theory is that there are people with innate perverse impulses, and since the values and institutional arrangements of the society reflect an ultimate and universal sanity, they are abnormal and can have intimate relations with the supernormal. Their techniques therefore override ordinary physical laws. But it is impossible to impute witchcraft or sorcery to certain individuals, since they cannot have the necessary evil motivations, or a logical inconsistency would be involved: the society has found it useful to convert the misfortune suffered into a social sanction. There is, in other words, a good deal more in witchcraft and sorcery than meets the eye, and they can be shown to be intelligent responses to man's fundamental needs in the context of the society in which they are found.

22 Monica Hunter Wilson

Witch-Beliefs and Social Structure

Monica Hunter Wilson, 'Witch-beliefs and social structure', *American Journal of Sociology*, vol. 56, 1951, pp. 307–13. The first draft of this paper was delivered as a lecture to the Chicago Anthropological Society in April 1950.

Many anthropologists are concerned just now with the relation between values and social structure. My subject is a facet of that problem. I shall try to show that witch beliefs are one expression of the values of a society and that these vary with the social structure. My analysis is based on the comparison of two African peoples among whom I have done field work, the Nyakyusa of Tanganyika (G. Wilson, 1936a, 1936b, 1938; M. Wilson, 1937, 1950, 1951) and the Pondo of South Africa (cf. Hunter, 1936).

These peoples are similar in many respects: they are both cattle people and cultivators, traditionally having had a subsistence economy but now drawn into the world economy, the Pondo as migrant laborers in the gold mines of South Africa, the Nyakyusa as migrant laborers on the mines and sisal plantations of Tanganyika and as peasant producers of coffee and rice. Both peoples were, and still are, organized under chiefs and have well-developed legal institutions; both peoples are patrilineal, and marriage is legalized by the transfer of cattle from the groom's group to that of the bride; both speak a Bantu language, with all that that implies in similarity of concepts and categories of thought; and both have the type of religion so general in Bantu Africa, viz., an elaborate ancestor cult, a belief in the power of medicines (that is, in mystical power residing in certain material substances), and a belief in witchcraft.

I am using 'witchcraft' in the sense in which Professor Evans-Pritchard uses it for the belief in a mystical power innate in certain individuals and exercised by them to harm others, and I distinguish it from sorcery, which is the illegal use of medicines to harm others. In doing so, I follow precisely the Nyakyusa verbal usage, for they distinguish between *ubulosi*, an innate power used to work evil, and *ubutege*, the illegal use of destructive medicines. The distinction is an important one; for sorcery, as I have defined it, is practised, that is, people use medicines (which are sometimes poisons) with the object of harming others, while few anthropologists would admit the reality of witchcraft – the exercise of an innate power to harm others directly. But, though both Nyakyusa and Pondo have a lively fear of witchcraft, there are marked variations in the forms of their beliefs and in the incidence of accusations, and it is these differences which I wish to discuss.

The Nyakyusa believe that witches exist as pythons in the bellies of certain individuals. They are something tangible, discoverable at an autopsy, and inherited. The incentive to witchcraft is said to be the desire for good food. Witches lust for meat and milk – the prized foods of the group – and it is this which drives them to commit witchcraft. They delight in eating human flesh and gnaw men inside, causing death to their victims. The witches also steal milk, sucking the udders of cows, so that the cows dry up and later abort. All this happens in dreams. Nightmares of being throttled, of being chased, of fighting, and of flying through the air are taken as evidence of an attack by witches; and, if a man wakes up suddenly at night in fear and sweating, he knows that 'they' – the witches – have come to throttle him. The witches are thought to fly by night on their pythons or 'on the wind'; they attack either singly or in coverns; and they feast on human flesh.

Though the first incentive to witchcraft is said to be the lust for food, witches select as their victims those against whom they have a grudge; they act illegally and immorally but not without cause. They attack those with whom they have quarreled, so that the good man who keeps on friendly terms with his neighbors has little to fear from the witches. Children are warned not to be quarelsome or boastful or brusque in their manners, lest they arouse the anger of witches. People also fear to be conspicuously successful, lest, exciting envy, they bring upon themselves the attack of a witch. One can show off a bit, but not too much. Thus a man may safely hoe a garden bigger than that of his neighbors, but it must not be too conspicuously bigger, and he must not boast of its size; a woman may carry home a heavier load of faggots than her fellow, but it must not be too conspicuously heavier; and so on. To be a Don Juan, carrying on many intrigues, or the favorite wife of one's husband is also dangerous, provoking jealousy. Above all, witches are thought to attack those who are stingy with food, and a direct connexion is made between feeding potential witches on beef and protecting one's self against attack. Well-fed pythons stay quiet.

The kind of person accused of being a witch is very like the person thought to be attacked. He (or she) is proud and boastful, morose, or aloof and unsympathetic to neighbors in trouble. The 'strong, silent man' depicted as a hero by Hollywood would very likely be labeled a witch in African society. The unusually successful man, the go-getter, is also liable to be accused of practicing witchcraft or sorcery, for it is argued that his success can only have come through some mystical power and *at the expense of his fellows*.

The Nyakyusa believe that witchcraft is extremely dangerous but that the danger is limited in two ways: first, witchcraft rarely operates beyond the village – a private person can be attacked only from within his own village – and, second, the good man is defended by his neighbors. It is thought that in every village there are 'defenders' (*abamanga*) who see the witches in dreams and fight them and drive them off. The leader of 'the defenders' is the headman of the village.

But not only do 'the defenders' protect the innocent, they also punish the guilty. They bring upon a wrongdoer a chilling breath which paralyses him or causes him to sicken with a fever or some debilitating disease. The supposed victim of such an attack will complain angrily of 'witchcraft' (*ubulosi*), but other people will speak of his sin and the just retribution that has fallen upon him through 'the breath of men' or 'the curse'. The source of this power of defense and punishment is almost identical with that of witchcraft: it comes from pythons in men's bellies, though, curiously, defenders have only one python, whereas witches have several, and the defender's python is not visible at an autopsy like that of a witch. The sins which are believed to bring down the anger of the defenders are many, but the commonest are failure to provide feasts on certain specified occasions, disrespectful behavior toward parents or by a woman toward her husband or parents-in-law, incest, and a breach of conventions regarding the limitation of pregnancies. Ill health in man and beast and field was directly linked to sin by our informants; Job, who suffered misfortune, though he was righteous, is foreign to Nyakyusa thought. Hence a study of cases of misfortune provided concrete data on values; it shows very clearly what was judged good and what evil.

The categories of people suspected by the Nyakyusa of practising witchcraft are, first and foremost, village neighbors – more than a third of the cases of witchcraft we collected were of this type – second, fellow-workers in a mining camp, and, third, wives. Only very rarely is an accusation of practising witchcraft lodged against a kinsman.[1]

The Pondo ideas about witchcraft are rather different. First, they think that a witch always works by means of a familiar – a fabulous hairy being with exaggerated sexual characteristics called *Tikoloshe*, or a baboon, a wild cat, a snake or a lightning bird. The familiar is of opposite sex to that of the witch and is often spoken of as taking the form of a beautiful girl or a handsome man, very light in color, and the witch and familiar have sexual relations. Usually the familiar is acquired by inheritance (Hunter, 1936). The basis of these beliefs is again dreams, sex dreams being frequently interpreted in terms of witchcraft. The Pondo do not distinguish so sharply between witchcraft and sorcery as the Nyakyusa do; nevertheless, they speak of two types of power used illegally, viz., familiars and medicines. Familiars are regarded as altogether and utterly evil, and there is no idea of their being used in defense or to punish a wrongdoer. A homestead is defended against witches by its ancestors and by medicines placed round about it, not by some of its members who see and fight the witches in dreams. And the range of witchcraft is not limited in the way in which it is among the Nyakyusa; nowadays it is even said to be sent by post.

I know much less about the kind of behavior thought to excite the attacks of witches or to lead to an accusation against one

1. This account is based on the general statements of our Nyakyusa friends and an analysis of ninety-one cases of misfortune, all of which were attributed to mystical causes.

among the Pondo than among the Nyakyusa, for I was less interested in this problem when I was in Pondoland than I became later on and also I was less intimate with the Pondo than with the Nyakyusa. I do know, however, that envy, roused by conspicuous success, is a cause very commonly cited. I am inclined to think that misfortune is less closely linked with morality among the Pondo than among the Nyakyusa, that is, that they conceive of the witches acting without cause in a way in which the Nyakyusa do not; but I have not the evidence to substantiate this. Further investigation will be necessary to prove or to disprove such a hypothesis. But, even though witchcraft and morality may not be so closely linked by the Pondo as by the Nyakyusa, a study of Pondo witch beliefs throws a good deal of light on Pondo morality.

The typical accusations of witchcraft in Pondoland are between mother and daughter-in-law who live in the same homestead and between fellow-employees in the mines or elsewhere. Accusations against neighbors, people of other homesteads, occur but are less frequent. I have no figures to support this impression of the incidence of accusations among the Pondo, but it is largely confirmed by the analysis of accusations now being made by a young anthropologist, Miss Selma Kaplan, in another Xhosa-speaking area, the Keiskama Valley, which is culturally very similar to Pondoland.

Now the differences between the Nyakyusa and Pondo ideas about witchcraft are not absolute; there is some overlapping between them. There are some hints among the Nyakyusa of sex associations with witchcraft, though they have no theory of familiars with whom the owner has sex relations and do not interpret sex dreams in terms of witchcraft, and there is some suggestion among the Pondo of witches seeking food – the baboon familiar is said sometimes to milk cows. There is also some overlapping in the type of behavior thought to anger the witches in the two societies and in the relationships within which accusations occur. But the difference in emphasis is very great. I went straight to the Nyakyusa after working with the Pondo, and I was puzzled by the contrast. What was the reason for it? Why should the Nyakyusa always talk about the witches lusting for food and the Pondo talk about witch lovers? Why do the

Nyakyusa have this theory of a power akin to witchcraft used in defense and to punish evildoers, and not the Pondo?

With the reports of the dreams of men in half-starved prisoner-of-war camps in mind, I began, first, to reflect on the differences in Nyakyusa and Pondo diet, but I found no answer there. The Nyakyusa have long been among the best-fed people in Africa (Lugard, 1893, vol. 1, p. 131; Thomson, 1881, vol. 1, pp. 268–74), while the Pondo are nowadays very badly fed. The Nyakyusa eat only a limited amount of meat but have a good deal of milk and ample supplies of bananas and plantains, maize, beans, finger-millet, groundnuts, sweet potatoes, pumpkins and greens; and many of them get fish and rice. The Pondo, on the other hand, have no more meat than the Nyakyusa and almost certainly less milk, while their supplies of fruit, grains, pulses, greens and fish are much more limited in quantity and variety. It is true that a century ago the Pondo probably had much more meat and milk than they have today; but, if meat hunger really produces the idea that witches kill to get flesh, then it would have appeared among the Pondo long before this. There is no tradition of cannibalism among either people, though it may conceivably have been resorted to by both in periods of extreme privation. Neither people have ever had the reputation among their neighbors of being cannibals, as the Azande had.

What, then, are the other conspicuous differences between Nyakyusa and Pondo societies? The Nyakyusa are peculiar in that they live not in kinship villages, like most African peoples, but in age-villages. A group of boys build a village when they are still quite young – about ten or eleven years old – and they remain together through life, bringing their wives to this village when they marry. Tremendous emphasis is laid on enjoying the company of age-mates, on eating and drinking with them, and avoiding quarrels with them. Until he marries, a boy is fed by his mother, though he sleeps in the boys' village and spends his spare time there, but he does not come home alone for meals. Instead, a group of boys visits the mother of each member in turn, and this habit of eating in a group is ideally maintained all through life. A man cannot eat with women, and he cannot eat with his sons; to do so would imply a familiarity wholly immoral in Nyakyusa eyes; but he should eat with neighbors who are age-mates of his own standing. Generosity with food and hospitality to neighbors is the first virtue and the basis of prestige in the society. The village is the landholding group and joins in common defense under the leadership of the village headman in the 'war by day and war by night' (*ubwite pa musi nobwite pa kelo*), 'war by night' meaning the war against witches. Traditionally, also, the members of a village have certain responsibilities for torts committed by one of their fellows.

In spite of living and fighting with his age-set, however, a Nyakyusa man has very close ties with his kinsmen. He is bound to them by a supposed mystical interdependence and the performance of rituals directed to common ancestors, on which health and fertility are thought to depend, and by interest in the cattle owned by members of his agnatic lineage. I have not space now to go into the very complicated system by which cattle are acquired and distributed; it must suffice to say that they circulate within agnatic lineages and between lineages; a man acquires cattle primarily through kinship connexions, and his kinsmen have certain claims on the cattle he holds. Fellow-villagers have no claims on his cattle other than food; they do not inherit from him or get cattle from him with which to marry, but they do expect to receive a share of his milk and to feast on beef upon certain recognized occasions, when he should kill cattle for a ritual. There are no clans or large exogamous groups. Descendants of a common grandparent cannot marry, and those with a common great-grandparent should not marry; but, since kinsmen are scattered, the limitation on choice within one neighborhood is small.

Nyakyusa country has been under European control since 1893 and, as we saw earlier, some of the men are in European employment, but relations between Nyakyusa and European are still fairly tenuous; the atmosphere is that of a frontier, and the caste system has not solidified as it has in South Africa. Racial segregation is not taken as an ultimate value by any group.

The Pondo social structure is quite different. Among them the local group, the homestead (*umzi*), is a kinship group, comprising an agnatic lineage, together with wives and unmarried daughters. The men of a homestead form a close-knit group, commonly eating in company and formerly being jointly responsible for each other's torts and fighting as a unit in the army of the district. A number of lineages make up a clan, which, though not strictly a territorial group, has a territorial headquarters, a substantial proportion of the men in any one area being of the same clan, that of the chief of the area. Tremendous emphasis is laid on clan exogamy and not marrying into the clan of one's mother or of either grandmother. Clans are large; they may have three thousand or four thousand members; and, since they tend to concentrate in different areas, a great many girls in one neighborhood are classed as sisters by a young man of the neighborhood. The emotional content of this taboo on clan incest is tremendous; it survives even among urbanized people, and it is one of the main cultural differences separating the Xhosa- and Zulu-speaking people from the Sotho, with whom they mingle in Johannesburg and other centers of employment.

Second, the Pondo are members of a color-caste society, in which one of the ultimate values is the exclusion of sex relations between members of different castes. They are in much closer contact with whites than the Nyakyusa are, and the emphasis on endogamy within each colour group is much greater in South Africa than in Tanganyika. Sex relations between white and black, whether marital or extra-marital, are now a criminal offense in South Africa.

Now my hypothesis is that the differences between the Nyakyusa and Pondo ideas of witchcraft are directly connected with these differences in their social structure. The Nyakyusa emphasize the virtue of feeding village neighbors and regard the lust for meat and milk as the main incentive to witchcraft *because* they live not with kinsmen but with neighbors, and yet cattle, the main form of wealth, are controlled by kinship groups. Jealousy of a neighbor's wealth is common enough, but it is peculiarly keen among the Nyakyusa because nonrelatives live close together in villages and the poor cannot help being aware when the rich feast on good food. Our Nyakyusa friends spoke of the witches *smelling* meat roasting or *smelling* milk, and that, I think, is very significant. A share in feasts is the only benefit a non-relative can expect to have from the wealth in cattle of a fellow-villager.

The Pondo setup is quite different. Among them, only kinsmen live together, and kinsmen can expect to benefit from the herd of their wealthy relatives either through inheritance or by assistance with marriage cattle, so every man has a personal interest in the increase of cattle belonging to the kinsmen with whom he lives. Pondo also crave meat feasts, but they speak of the pressure to kill cattle as coming from the ancestors, not from neighbors. When a sacrifice is made on behalf of a kinsman who is ill the Pondo say: *Balambile, bafuna ukudla ngaye*, meaning 'they are hungry, they want to eat with him', and 'they' refers to the ancestors, not to witches or neighbors. Neighbors play no necessary part in the ritual at all, and even if they do not come to share in the feast the patient will recover, whereas, if a Nyakyusa has been ill and sacrifices, the neighbors *must* eat of the meat of the sacrifice and bless him.

And what of the Pondo emphasis on sex in witchcraft? Are they a much more inhibited people than the Nyakyusa? At first sight it appears that they are not. There is, in fact, much greater freedom of premarital relations between the sexes among the Pondo than among the Nyakyusa, for the marriage age of girls is much higher and the marriage age of men rather lower. In Pondoland there is a large group of nubile girls who dance and flirt and cuddle with the young men, whereas among the Nyakyusa there is no such group. Among the latter most girls are bethrothed well before puberty, and, once a girl is betrothed, any sex contact with her (outside the puberty ceremonies) is treated as adultery. But the Pondo prohibit sex relations with a much wider group of persons than do the Nyakyusa. I relate the emphasis on sex in witchcraft among the Pondo to the system of clan exogamy, which excludes large categories of individuals living in the same neighborhood from marrying or flirting with one another, and the idea that the familiar is a light-colored person to the caste system which almost excludes sex relations between persons of different colors. In short, I suggest that the familiar is a symbol of forbidden sex attraction and that such attraction is common in a society in which large categories of people who live in close contact with one another are forbidden to marry.

The belief in 'the breath of men', that is, in a power akin to witchcraft used in defense and to punish wrongdoers is also, I suggest, related to the age-village organization. It is matched in a kinship village by the belief that the ancestors are a shield against misfortune to the group and that senior living relatives have a mystical power over their descendants and juniors. The concept of 'the breath of men' gives a Nyakyusa village headman a power over the members of his village comparable to that of a headman in a Pondoland village. The fact that the power of the one is thought to derive from a python in his belly and the power of the other from his ancestors does not materially affect his relationship with members of his village.

The difference in the incidence of accusations of witchcraft in Nyakyusa and Pondo societies is also related to the differences in the social structure of the two groups. A Pondo bride joins the homestead of her husband and lives, often for many years, under the control of her mother-in-law. Friction between them is very common. Moreover, she is long regarded as a stranger and so is suspect because she is a member of another clan. The Nyakyusa wife, on the other hand, lives in a different village from her mother-in-law and does not necessarily see much of her. Nor is she an outsider in a closely knit kin group as the Pondo woman is. In Nyakyusa society friction is most likely between neighbors who live close together, and it is between them that accusations of witchcraft are most frequent. Both societies are polygynous, and, in both, accusations are fairly frequent between co-wives. Individuals from both societies work for Europeans, and accusations are very common between fellow-workers.

There are indications that, as these two societies are drawn into closer relationship with the outside world, there is a change in the forms of belief, as well as in the incidence of accusations. Among the Nyakyusa, for example, the more sophisticated fear sorcery while denying belief in witchcraft. Sorcery is felt by them to be compatible with Western science in a way in which witchcraft is not, for *ubutege*, the word I have translated as 'sorcery', is usually interpreted as 'poisoning' by those Nyakyusa who know some English. It is quite true that it includes poisoning, but it also includes burying a medicine under an enemy's doorstep or in the thatch of his hut, and no consistent distinction is made by the Nyakyusa between these different types of *ubutege*.

But, though the forms of belief change, belief in witchcraft or sorcery of one kind or another continues, and this, I think, is the crux of our problem. What are the social conditions which produce a general belief in witchcraft and sorcery? Granted that accusations of practising witchcraft or sorcery are an expression of conflict and that they are likely to be many when conflict is acute, as in a Johannesburg slum or a mining camp in Tanganyika, we still have to explain why such accusations are not common in London slums or Tyneside collieries. For example, what were the social conditions in seventeenth-century England that produced beliefs so very similar to contemporary beliefs in Pondoland – the parallels to the Pondo belief in familiars are very close indeed in seventeenth-century England – and what were the effective causes of the decline of these beliefs? I long to read an adequate analysis of this problem by some social historian aware of anthropological theory. The decline in belief in witchcraft and sorcery is not purely a matter of extending scientific knowledge – our answer must cover the astute Pondo teacher, who said to me: 'It may be quite true that typhus is carried by lice, but who sent the infected louse? Why did it bite one man and not another?'

I have suggested elsewhere (Wilson and Wilson, 1945) that witch beliefs are general in small-scale societies with inadequate control of their environment and dominated by personal relationships, societies in which people think in personal terms and seek personal causes for their misfortunes. This hypothesis may or may not prove to be part of the answer; but, even if it is true, it does not take us far enough. Innumerable other questions crop up. For example, is the close connexion which the Nyakyusa make between witchcraft and morality, between misfortune and sin, characteristic of all very small societies or of all relatively stable societies, or is it related to other, quite different factors? Supposing that I am right in thinking that the Pondo tie misfortune less closely to morality than the Nyakyusa do, what is the reason for this difference?

And when the belief in witchcraft in the sense in which I have defined it disappears, what takes its place? Are the witches but the primitive form of the scapegoat who is always with us? Are men with pythons in their bellies and those who ride baboons by night indeed a true parallel to the red agents of McCarthy's fevered dreams?

Understanding of these problems will, I think, proceed from a close analysis of the relation between witch-beliefs and other aspects of society, such as I have tried to paint on a very small canvas in this paper. I see witch-beliefs as the standardized nightmare of a group, and I believe that the comparative analysis of such nightmares is not merely an antiquarian exercise but one of the keys to the understanding of society.

References

HUNTER, M. (1936), *Reaction to Conquest*, Oxford U.P. for International Institute of African Languages and Cultures.

LUGARD, F. D. (1893), *The Rise of our East African Empire*, Blackwood.

THOMSON, J. (1881), *To the Central African Lakes and Back*, Sampson Lowe, Marston, Searle & Rivington.

WILSON, G. (1936a), 'An African morality', *Africa*, vol. 9.

WILSON, G. (1936b), 'An introduction to Nyakyusa society', *Bantu Studies*, vol. 10.

WILSON, G. (1938), *The Land Rights of Individuals among the Nyakyusa*, Rhodes-Livingstone Papers.

WILSON, G., and WILSON, M. H. (1945), *The Analysis of Social Change*, Cambridge U.P.

WILSON, M. Hunter (1937), 'An African Christian morality', *Africa*, vol. 10.

WILSON, M. Hunter (1950), 'Nyakyusa Kinship', in A R. Radcliffe-Brown and D. Forde (eds.), *African Systems of Kinship and Marriage*, Oxford U.P. for International African Institute.

WILSON, M. Hunter (1951), *Good Company: A Study of Nyakyusa Age-Villages*, Oxford U.P. for International African Institute.

23 S. F. Nadel

Witchcraft in Four African Societies

S. F. Nadel, 'Witchcraft in four African societies: an essay in comparison', *American Anthropologist*, vol. 54, 1952, pp. 18–29.

In this paper[1] it is proposed to present a small-scale model of a comparative analysis, more precisely, of an analysis of 'concomitant variations' (to borrow Durkheim's term), such as any enquiry concerned with the explanation of social facts must employ. The facts in question are particular variants of the belief in witchcraft. Indirectly, the study will also refer to a much discussed hypothesis, the assumption that infantile experiences represent a paramount determinant of culture.

The comparison concerns two pairs of societies – the Nupe and Gwari in Northern Nigeria, and the Korongo and Mesakin tribes in the Nuba Mountains of the Central Sudan. Each pair shows wide cultural similarities combined with a few marked divergencies, one of these being the diversity in witchcraft beliefs. This discussion will proceed on two assumptions:

1. That any one relevant cultural divergence entails further, concomitant, divergences in the respective cultures.

2. That witchcraft beliefs are causally related to frustrations, anxieties or other mental stresses precisely as psychopathological symptoms are related to mental disturbances of this nature.

Witchcraft in Nupe and Gwari

The two societies are neighbors in an identical environment and also maintain frequent contacts. They speak closely related languages and have an identical kinship system, based on patrilineal succession, patrilocal residence, and localized extended families.

1. In slightly abridged form and under the title 'A comparative study of witchcraft', the paper was presented at the Berkeley meeting of the A.A.A. For a fuller account of some of the ethnographical material see Nadel (1942, esp. ch. 9; 1935; 1947).

Political organization and the regulation of male adolescence are closely similar in both tribes; so is their economy, though marketing and trade are on a much larger scale in Nupe. The religion of Nupe and Gwari is again closely similar (ignoring here the more recent spread of Islam), and the conceptions of life and death, of a body possessed of a double soul ('shadow-' and 'life-soul'), or of the reincarnation of ancestral souls, are identical even as regards nomenclature.

Both groups, too, firmly believe in witchcraft; several grave incidents showing the strength of the beliefs occurred even during the period of field work among the two tribes. Both conceive of witchcraft as unequivocally evil, as destroying life, mainly through mysterious wasting diseases, and as implying the power of witches to 'eat' the 'life-soul' of their victims. Witches are active at night and cannot be seen or discovered by ordinary means. Everything connected with witchcraft takes place in a fantasy realm which is, almost *ex hypothesi*, intangible and beyond empirical verification. This is shown most clearly in the tenet that it is only the 'shadow-souls' of witches which roam about and attack victims, while their bodies remain asleep at home, thus deceiving any ordinary attempts at proving, or disproving, these mystic activities.

The two beliefs, however, differ radically in the ascription of sex to the witch. In Nupe witches are always women (called *gáci*, from *egá*, 'witchcraft'). They are thought to be organized in a society closely modelled on similar human associations and headed by the woman who is also, in real life, the titled official head of the women traders. It may be noted that this is the only instance of the fantasy world of witchcraft projecting into and becoming tangible in concrete, everyday life. The woman said to preside over the association of witches occupies an exceptional position also in another sense; for she is the only 'good' female witch, sometimes a 'reformed' witch, and hence a person willing and able to control the sinister activities of her companions.

The men fit into this pattern in an ambiguous way. Certain individuals are said to possess a power similar to witchcraft, which enables them to see and deal with witches. This power is known by a different name (*eshe*) and is essentially good; so that the men possessed of it can control and combat the women witches. At the same time the female witches need the co-operation of the men, for only when the female and male powers are joined does female witchcraft become fully effective, that is, deadly. Here again, the men are said to use their power not to assist, but to restrain the female witches, by withholding the required aid. The ambiguity referred to, then, lies in this: men are necessary for the fullest effect of witchcraft; but as a class, they also stand aloof and are not themselves evil; rather do they attempt to block evil witchcraft. Even so, the fatal effects of female witchcraft are admitted to occur; in which case one argues that a few evil individuals among the men (whom no one can name) have betrayed their own sex and become the helpers of a woman witch. The general picture is that of a sharp sex-antagonism, which assigns the evil intentions to the female, and to the male a benevolent and ideally decisive – if somewhat Utopian – role.

Characteristically, the men are never blamed or accused of witchcraft, and the main collective weapon against witchcraft lies in the activities of a male secret society which, by threats and torture, 'cleanses' villages of witchcraft. The same idea that the men alone have the secret power of defeating female witchcraft is expressed in the legends on the origins of witchcraft and anti-witchcraft. The case studies collected add a further twist to this sex-antagonism; for in the majority of cases the alleged witch is a woman, usually an older and domineering female, who would attack a younger man who somehow fell under her dominance; which situation is again pictured in the legends. The men, therefore, though on the Utopian or fantasy plane the masters of female witchcraft, are, on the plane of 'real' incidents and fears, its main victims.

One case history and one legend may be quoted. The former concerns a young man from a village on the river Niger who one night suddenly disappeared. A body which the police had good reason to believe was his was later fished out of the river; but the people refused to accept this 'natural' explanation, maintaining that the young man had been spirited away by a witch. Suspicion at once fell on an elderly wealthy woman whose house the young man had frequently been visiting; he had, in fact, been something like a protégé of that woman or, in Nupe parlance, her *egi kata* – 'son of the house' – which term is applied to any individual who seeks the patronage of some influential older person and becomes dependent upon his patron's advice and material help.

The legend tells of a young king 'in ancient times', whose mother was an overbearing old woman, constantly interfering with her son's plans and actions. At last the son decided to rid himself of her influence. He consulted a (male) diviner, who told him the secret of a certain cloth mask, which would drop on his mother and remove her from the earth. Thus, it is said, originated the Nupe anti-witchcraft cult *ndakó gboyá*, which is today vested in the male secret society mentioned before and employs the cloth masks as its main paraphernalia.

As regards the Gwari beliefs, a brief outline will suffice. They involve no sex-antagonism or sex-polarity. Witches and their victims are indiscriminately male and female. Witchcraft is discovered by ordinary divination, practised by both men and women, and anti-witchcraft measures consist in the main in an annual 'cleansing' ritual which embraces the whole community, again irrespective of sex.

So much for the general picture of the two cultures and their divergent conceptions of witchcraft. Turning now to the search for 'concomitant' divergences, and taking our lead from psychoanalysis, we might start with infantile experiences and the techniques of child-rearing. Here we meet with one relevant difference only, concerning children of two and over. Until a newborn child has reached the age of two or three the parents in both tribes refrain from cohabitation. Afterwards, when cohabitation is resumed, the Nupe wife visits the husband's hut, the children staying in her sleeping quarters, while in Gwari the husband visits the wife, so that cohabitation takes place in the presence of the young children. The people have no doubt that the children do in fact witness the sexual act. Assuming, with Freudian psychology, that this fact entails deeply unsettling psychological effects, it should foster the oedipus trauma and definite tensions between child (perhaps more specifically son) and father.[2] Assuming further that these tensions, normally

2. Gwari informants in fact claimed that a marked hostility between father and son was a common feature of their family life. The writer's material on the Gwari, however, is not sufficiently full to permit any more definite statement.

repressed or blocked in overt behavior, might find an outlet in the fantasy of witchcraft beliefs, we should expect these to reveal some bias towards sex-antagonism and towards identifying the evil witches either with males (the hated father image) or perhaps, by a more devious transference, with females (the mother avenging herself on all males). In fact, neither assumption is borne out by the evidence, the sex-antagonism occurring in the tribe where the traumatic experience is absent.

Certain other cultural divergences, however, concerning adult life, seem to be congruent with the diversity in witchcraft beliefs. They resolve upon marriage, which, generally speaking, is without serious complications and relatively tension-free in Gwari, but full of stress and mutual hostility in Nupe. Two facts may be mentioned.

1. The economic position of the Nupe wives, many of whom are successful intinerant traders, is generally much better than that of their peasant husbands. Thus husbands are often heavily in debt to their wives, and the latter assume many of the financial responsibilities which should rightly belong to the men as fathers and family heads, such as finding bride-price for sons, paying for the children's education, bearing the expenses of family feasts and the like. This reversal of the institutionalized roles is openly resented by the men, who are, however, helpless and unable to redress the situation.

2. As has been said, many married women become itinerant traders. According to the tenets of Nupe morality, this occupation should be reserved for childless women, in whose case one also excuses the moral laxity which, in that society, goes together with this livelihood. But in fact mothers too become itinerant traders, leaving their children once they are four or five years old; more importantly, women also refuse to have children, practising abortion and using alleged contraceptives, in order to be free to choose this occupation. Again, the men are helpless; they can only brand this voluntary sterility as the gravest possible form of immorality.

In practice, then, the men must submit to the domineering and independent leanings of the women; they resent their own helplessness, and definitely blame the 'immorality' of the women-folk. The wish to see the situation reversed is expressed in

nostalgic talk about 'the good old days' when all this was un-
heard of (and which are disproved by all genealogies and concrete
records of the past). Equally, it can be argued, the hostility
between men and women *plus* this wish-fulfilment are projected
into the witchcraft beliefs with their ambivalent expression of
sex-antagonism, in which men are the 'real' victims but the
'Utopian' masters of the evil women. A final item of evidence,
mentioned before, lies in the identification of the head of the
witches with the official head of the women traders. It relates
the 'projection' in a direct and overt manner to the conscious
hostility and the concrete situations evoking it. The psychological
'symptom', we might say, and the anxieties and stresses which
are its cause are connected by a clear thread of meaning.

Witchcraft in Korongo and Mesakin

These two tribes are once more neighbors in the same environment; though speaking different languages they know one another
and are often bilingual. They share the same economy, political
organization, and religious beliefs and practices. Both reckon
descent in the mother's line and have the same kinship system
and domestic arrangements; more particularly, in both groups
children of six or seven are free to leave their father's house,
where they were born, for that of their mother's brother to grow
up under his tutelage. A detailed census showed that in each
tribe this change of residence and affiliation occurred in about
half of all cases. In all other respects, too, child-rearing is
identical in the two societies.

So is the regulation of male adolescence, with one exception
to be discussed later. It may be pointed out here that male
adolescence and, indeed, the whole life-cycle of the men, revolve
upon a highly formalized division into age classes, each of which
is characterized by the right to engage in particular sporting
contests, which are exhibitions of virility as well. These sports
are light wrestling, wrestling of a more strenuous kind, and
fighting with spears. In the first, lowest, age class, before puberty,
no sports are practised. The severe variety of wrestling marks
the peak of physical vigor, attained towards the end of adolescence; while spear-fighting, which implies more skill than bodily

strength, is considered appropriate to an age of already declining physical vigor. After the spear-fighting stage, the tests or exhibitions of virility cease altogether, the men having become 'too old'. At the same time the men give up sleeping in the cattle camps out in the bush, which more arduous mode of life is once more regarded as appropriate for youths only. This decline in physical vigor at the end of adolescence is attributed to the cumulative effects of sexual activity, especially to the sex life involved in marriage and procreation. In both groups, finally, the first part of the sporting contests after puberty is celebrated with much ceremony and is made the occasion for an important gift on the part of the boy's mother's brother. This consists of an animal taken from the mother's brother's herd, the same herd which the sister's son is in due course bound to inherit. The gift therefore represents something like an 'anticipated inheritance', and is in fact known by the term 'inheritance', a point which is of crucial importance for the understanding of the witchcraft beliefs.

To turn now to the contrast between the two groups. The Korongo have no witchcraft beliefs at all; the Mesakin are literally obsessed by fears of witchcraft (known as *torogo*) and witchcraft accusations, entailing violent quarrels, assaults, and blood revenge, are frequent. Witchcraft itself is a mysterious, malignant and often deadly power, emanating directly from evil wishes, though it is subject to two significant restrictions. Mesakin witchcraft is believed to operate only between maternal kin, especially between a mother's brother and sister's son, the older relative assailing the younger. Mesakin witchcraft further operates only if there is a reason, some legitimate cause for resentment or anger; and the latter is almost invariably a quarrel over the 'anticipated inheritance' mentioned before. As has been said, both tribes acknowledge this particular duty of the mother's brother. But in Korongo it is never refused. The gift can be postponed, but is also sometimes made twice, and rarely raises any serious difficulty. In Mesakin the exact opposite is true. The gift is always refused to begin with and has often to be taken by force, a procedure which is fully sanctioned by public opinion. The gift cannot be postponed, nor is it ever repeated. Quarrels over it between the youth and his mother's brother are the rule; and if by any chance the former falls ill, dies, or suffers some other misfortune, the older man is invariably suspected of having employed witchcraft.

Practices of child-rearing, being identical in the two tribes, offer no clue either to the sharply divergent attitude towards the anticipated inheritance or to the witchcraft beliefs which, in one of the two groups, come into play in this connexion. The clue seems to lie, rather, in certain cultural differences shaping the adult attitudes towards life and, more especially, towards the fate of growing old.

To begin with, the two tribes deal differently with pre-marital sex relations. Both groups, as will be remembered, firmly believe that regular sexual intercourse is physically weakening for the male, yet also glorify physical vigor and manliness. In both groups, for example a 'born' coward or weakling is called by the name normally given to the male homosexuals (who invariably turn transvestite), is treated with the same contempt, and is often forced to join their ranks. In both groups, too, the men hate growing old, which means, above all, withdrawing from the 'manly' pursuits and admitting their physical debility; thus the 'old men' will always try to join the sports for which they are supposed to be no longer fit, even at the risk of being ridiculed, or sneak out for a night in the cattle camps to join the company of the younger men. Yet while among the Korongo pre-marital and highly promiscuous sex relations are fully accepted and openly engaged in, among the Mesakin they are carefully concealed; indeed, the Mesakin insisted that formerly pre-marital chastity was rigidly observed. In other words, the Korongo accept the 'dissipation' of strength through sexual intercourse as something one can do nothing about; the Mesakin at least believe that it should be restricted and postponed, and face the failure of the ideal with all the symptoms of a feeling of guilt.[3]

Furthermore, the two tribes schematize their age classes differently, thus establishing a different correspondence between 'social age', as indicated in the age class, and physical age.[4]

3. There is an interesting trace of this also among the Korongo; for here the fiancée of a young man will refuse to have pre-marital relations with him (and with him only), thus avoiding responsibility for the dissipation of strength of her beloved (Nadel, 1947, p. 289).

4. See Table 1 (overleaf).

Table 1
Korongo and Mesakin Age Classifications and Activities

272

Approx. age	Korongo			Mesakin		
	Age class	Activities	General circumstances	Age class	Activities	General circumstances
Up to 12–13	1. belad	None	Pre-puberty	1. nate	None	Pre-puberty
13–16	2. dere	Light wrestling	Post-puberty; first sex-relations	2. kaduma	Light wrestling; severe wrestling; spear-fighting; live in cattle camps	Post-puberty; pre-marital sex relations; later marriage
17–20	3. adere	Severe wrestling; live in cattle camps	Unmarried; pre-marital sex relations			
21–25	4. adumok	Severe wrestling; later spear-fighting; live in cattle camps part of the time	Married			

Approx. age	Korongo			Mesakin		
	Age class	Activities	General circumstances	Age class	Activities	General circumstances
26–50	5. asnda-gan	Spear-fighting; visits to cattle camps; both end after 3–4 years	Fathers, family heads	3. mede	None	Fathers, family heads; including physically old men
50–	6. tgif	None	Physically old men			

273

The Korongo have six age classes, as against three among the Mesakin, so that in the former tribe the various phases of individual life are much more faithfully represented; also, the rights and responsibilities changing with age are more evenly spaced. Above all, the pursuits typical of youth, tribal sports and life in the cattle camps, are discarded gradually, allowance being made for transitional stages. Thus the severe wrestling, indicative of the peak of physical vigor, is assigned to the third age class, of as yet unmarried youths, but lasts into the next grade, when marriage, at the age of twenty–twenty-two, and regular sexual relations are expected to show their weakening effect. At this stage spear-fighting is the appropriate sport, again lasting into the next higher grade. This, the fifth grade, starts with parenthood and the assumption of the responsibilities of a family head; but the final farewell to sports and life in the cattle camps does not take place until a few years afterwards, at the age of twenty-eight–thirty. The Korongo also specifically name their sixth and last grade the age class of 'old men', the criterion now being the visible physical decline of the really old. In short, the Korongo accept a gradual process of growing old, the social 'old age' being only one of many steps and congruent with physical age.

The Mesakin, on the other hand, distinguish explicitly only between boys before puberty, youths (unmarried and married) before parenthood, and 'men', without further separation of the really old. Wrestling, spear-fighting, and life in the cattle camps all cease together, at the end of the second grade, that is, at the age of about twenty-two–twenty-four. The Mesakin, therefore, introduce the indices of social 'old age' early in life, and expect men to renounce the cherished privileges of youth abruptly and on purely conventional grounds, which take little account of physical age.

Let us now return to the demand for the anticipated inheritance which figures so prominently in Mesakin witchcraft beliefs. In both tribes the mother's brother must see in this insistent demand a reminder that he has definitely grown old; not only has he by then probably begotten children (which fact would merely announce his declining youth), but he has now a ward sufficiently old to claim his 'inheritance', that is, a gift explicitly anticipating the donor's impending death. Now, among the Korongo the older man is prepared for the gradual decline of age and accepts its onset, which coincides with sex life, with good grace or at least without struggle; furthermore, since among the Korongo the anticipated inheritance can be postponed, the mother's brother may by then be an older or old man also in the physical sense. Among the Mesakin, who know no such gradual transition to old age and idealize pre-marital chastity (which would postpone its onset), the 'reminder' must find the donor mentally unprepared; and since the gift cannot be postponed it will often be demanded of men still physically young. Hence the violent resentment on the part of the mother's brother when the demand is made and his invariable first refusal.

The resentment and refusal merely express the older man's envy of youth and virility, the loss of which is brought home to him by the very request for the anticipated inheritance. Clearly, every man in the tribe has gone through this phase or knows about it in the case of others; everybody also knows that the mother's brother's refusal is bound to be abortive in the end, that he can be forced to yield the gift, and that tribal morality is against him. It is suggested that the belief in the mother's brother's power to use witchcraft against his would-be heirs arises from this knowledge. The hostility which, one knows, the older man feels but should not feel, and which he has no means of realizing finally and successfully, is accepted as operating in the sphere of secret as well as anti-social aims, that is, in the sphere of witchcraft. Differently expressed, every man projects his own frustrations of this nature into the allegations that others are guilty of witchcraft. In punishing them, the accuser vicariously wipes out his own guilt, unadmitted or admitted.

The picture just drawn is to some extent over-simplified. For the Mesakin believe that witchcraft may also be practised by a sister's son against his mother's brother or by full brothers against one another. Here, too, there must be a legitimate motive, which lies again in a grievance over inheritance; but this may be ordinary as well as 'anticipated' inheritance. Nor need the alleged witch attack only the kinsman by whom he feels he has been injured; he may equally attack a close relative (patrilineal or matrilineal) of that kinsman or any one of the latter's matrilineal kin, thus venting his anger almost at random. These facts, however, seem significant: the belief in the powers of witchcraft of a sister's son over his mother's brother is pure 'theory', for which the people themselves can cite no concrete cases; in all the remaining instances, too, including that of brothers bewitching one another, it is invariably the older man who is accused; and finally, even where witchcraft is believed to strike at random, both victim and assailant are always males.[5] If, then, the accusations of witchcraft are not invariably directed against a mother's brother resentful of his kinship obligations, they are always directed against a person likely to feel the resentment and anxieties that go with mature age; and though the motives imputed to the witch are less single-minded than the previous discussion would suggest, and the occasions thought to provoke them less conspicuously 'reminders' of the loss of virility, the witchcraft accusations remain a projection of the hostility of the old towards the young and of the frustrations springing from such envy of youth. This is perhaps borne out most strikingly by the following, admittedly atypical, instance. In one of the witchcraft cases recorded the alleged witch was a transvestite homosexual who had no livestock property, so that the question of inheritance did not arise; he was said to have bewitched his sister's young boy for no reason other than 'envy of a true male'.

Conclusions

Before attempting to summarize our findings, some general remarks may be interjected. The correlations suggested in the preceding discussion, between witchcraft beliefs and particular features of the cultures in which they appear (or fail to appear), are not the only ones that can be discovered, even in the few societies here considered. These other correlations have been neglected mainly because they seem to be of lesser relevance; more precisely, they appear to belong only to the background of

5. Only in one case, said to have occurred 'a long time ago' a woman was accused of having bewitched her brother's young son. But the people considered this a most unusual case, which they themselves were at a loss to explain. Nor were they certain of the circumstances.

facilitating or impeding conditions, and not to the core of basic causes and determinants. Two examples may be given.

The Korongo, who have no witchcraft, possess a full and explicit mythology concerned with explaining all the things in the world – the creation of man and animals, the origin of death and disease, the invention of fire, and so forth. The witchcraft-ridden Mesakin, on the other hand, have nothing of the kind. Now it may be argued that an explicit explanatory mythology presents a picture of the universe less obscure and puzzling than does a religion backed by no such intellectual efforts; their absence, therefore, may be taken to foster anxieties and a sense of insecurity, and hence, indirectly, to predispose people toward also accepting the mysterious and malevolent powers of witches. Yet it seems clear that this factor can only have contributory significance since too many instances could be quoted of cultures combining an explicit mythology with belief in witchcraft.

The second example refers to the dualistic nature of the Nupe witchcraft beliefs, which occur in a culture and idea system generally characterized by a marked bias for dichotomous conceptions. Among the Gwari, where the witchcraft beliefs ignore the polarity of the sexes, the idea system is similarly devoid of any dualistic trend. Witchcraft beliefs, then, and that wider orientation hang together logically. Here we are once more dealing merely with predispositions of a general kind – with ways of thinking about the universe and of ordering its phenomena. Nor, in fact, does this last correlation exhibit any causal nexus, however indirect or contributory, but only a general 'fit', a logical consistency, linking witchcraft beliefs with a general mode of thought.

Even so, an exhaustive analysis must obviously include these and further, additional factors also. More generally speaking, in any inquiry like ours, based upon 'concomitant variations', we must be prepared to reckon with several concomitants and multiple forms of interdependence, rather than with simple one-to-one correlations. That only studies of this far-reaching order can do justice to the complexity of social situations, need hardly be defended. As regards the present inquiry, this ideal degree of completeness was beyond its scope. Perhaps, too, such completeness will often remain an ideal, unattainable in the present stage of our science.[6]

To turn to the conclusions proper:

1. The witchcraft beliefs here examined are causally as well as conspicuously related to specific anxieties and stresses arising in social life. The word 'conspicuously' is relevant because the witchcraft beliefs also indicate the precise nature of the social causes of which they are the symptoms – marriage-relations in Nupe, and the relationship between mother's brother and sister's son in Mesakin.

2. The anxieties and stresses need not arise from infantile experiences alone; rather, the present evidence tends to show that adult experiences, too, may be responsible for their emergence, and hence for the emergence also of the particular cultural features indicative of the anxieties and stresses.

3. The witchcraft beliefs of the Nupe and Mesakin seem to represent two basic potentialities or types. In Nupe, the witch is identified with the person openly and successfully setting aside the social values and thus denying the state of society desired and thought 'good'; attacks against witches are thus attacks upon the successful enemies of the ideal society. In Mesakin, the witch is identified with the person who cannot live up to the social values yet cannot openly rebel against them; the attacks upon witches are attacks upon the victims of the ideal society. In the first case one punishes the human agents responsible for the frustrations suffered by the believers in the ideal; in the second, one punishes and tries to obliterate the very fact that submission to the social ideal can give rise to frustration. In both types, then, the imputation of witchcraft serves to uphold the desired, if Utopian, state of society by identifying the witch with the transgressor – whether in successful action or in unadmitted, suppressed desire. Gwari witchcraft, so far as the somewhat incomplete data go, seems to stand halfway between these extremes. We may note in passing that if the Mesakin belief in witchcraft wielded by aggrieved brother's and sister's sons were more than 'theory', this would illustrate a third type of witchcraft in which the witch is identified with the victim of the 'transgressor' and the act of witchcraft with

6. The methodological issues touched upon above have been treated more fully in Nadel (1951, pp. 234, 258 ff.).

punitive action – though of a disproportionate and unlawful kind.

4. It is sometimes said that witchcraft beliefs 'canalize' hostility or 'deflect' hostile impulses into socially relatively harmless channels, that is, help society to function. Our evidence does not quite bear out this assumption. The witchcraft fears and accusations only accentuate concrete hostilities and in fact give them free rein. The concrete hostilities *are* 'canalized', in the sense that they are directed against a few scapegoats rather than against more numerous victims. But every witchcraft accusation or punishment of witches adds to the stresses of the society, through causing a serious disturbance of social life, entailing blood revenge, and the like. The accusations of witchcraft *do* deflect tensions and aggressive impulses; these are deflected, as it were, from the maladjusted institutions which cause them – marriage and the economic system in Nupe, kinship relations and the regulation of adolescence in Mesakin – so that these institutions can continue to operate. But they remain maladjusted and their continued operation only creates further tensions. Each persecution of witches no doubt relieves the tensions and stresses in a cathartic manner; but the relief is itself creative of new difficulties; equally, it is short-lived, for witchcraft cases go on happening all the time.

In brief, the witchcraft beliefs enable a society to go on functioning in a given manner, fraught with conflicts and contradictions which the society is helpless to resolve; the witchcraft beliefs thus absolve the society from a task apparently too difficult for it, namely, some radical readjustment. But from the observer's point of view it is doubtful if this is more than a poor and ineffectual palliative or can be called a solution 'less harmful' than open hostility or even the break-up of the existing institutions and relationships.

References

NADEL, S. F. (1935), 'Nupe witchcraft and anti-witchcraft', *Africa*, vol. 8.

NADEL, S. F. (1942), *A Black Byzantium*, Oxford U.P. for International Institute of African Languages and Cultures.

NADEL, S. F. (1947), *The Nuba*, Oxford U.P. for International African Institute.

NADEL, S. F. (1951), *The Foundations of Social Anthropology*, Free Press of Glencoe.

24 Max Marwick

Witchcraft as a Social Strain-Gauge

Excerpts from M. G. Marwick, 'Witchcraft as a social strain-gauge', *Australian Journal of Science*, vol. 26, 1964, pp. 263–8. Presidential Address, Section F, Australian and New Zealand Association for the Advancement of Science, Canberra Congress, January 1964.

I have decided to examine some aspects of the sociology of witch-craft and sorcery that appear to me to be in need of clearing up and pruning if we are to make further progress in this field. I am encouraged to attempt this task because I now find myself better situated geographically for the exploration of a problem that has interested me for some time, and among colleagues better fitted to advise me on it. The problem to which I am referring is the fact that, in Oceania, one of the well-founded propositions of the sociology of sorcery and witchcraft does not seem to apply.

Elsewhere, especially in Africa, it has been repeatedly recorded (for instance Evans-Pritchard, 1937, pp. 105–6; Krige and Krige, 1943, p. 263; Hunter, 1936, p. 307; Schapera, 1952, p. 49) that both believed attacks and accusations of witchcraft and sorcery occur only between persons already linked by close social bonds; but in Oceania it is more often reported (for instance, Elkin, 1937, *passim*; Hogbin, 1935, *passim*; Lawrence, 1952, p. 342, and 1955, p. 12; Meggitt, 1962, pp. 249, 325) that the sorcerer, who seems to be commoner here than the witch, is believed to direct his destructive magic *outside* his own group; and Oceanian accusations of sorcery, in the rare instances where they are recorded, seem to be consistent with this belief. A corollary to the generalization supported by the African material is that the relationship between alleged witch or sorcerer and believed victim is not only close but also strained; and this fact gives us a means of detecting the tension-points of a social structure by the frequency with which attacks of witchcraft and sorcery are believed to occur between persons standing in various relationships. Thus among the South-Eastern Bantu-speaking peoples of Africa accusations of witchcraft are reported to be directed against the women who have been brought in as wives into the patriarchal, virilocal settlement; and this is taken as a pointer to the peculiar difficulty of adjusting affinal relationships in a society dominated by the twin principles of patrilineal descent and polygny associated with the house property complex (Hunter, 1936, p. 307; Gluckman, 1956, p. 98; Middleton and Winter, 1963, pp. 10, 11). The fact that, in different societies, different types of persons accuse each other of witchcraft and sorcery provides us with what I am here calling a social strain-gauge. Thus Wilson has discovered a different incidence of accusations of witchcraft among the South African Mpondo, who typically accuse their daughters-in-law, and the East African Nyakyusa, who typically accuse their un-related village neighbours. She has attributed the difference to the differing social conditions resulting from the fact that the Mpondo live in small hamlets with their paternal kinsmen and the latter's wives; and the Nyakyusa, in villages with unrelated age-mates (Wilson, 1951b, *passim*).

My main objective in this paper will be to examine the problems that arise if we try to apply this social strain-gauge, developed largely in Africa, to detecting the characteristic tensions of Oceanian societies, and from this exercise, as well as from retrospective glances at some of the inadequacies of my own fieldwork in Africa, to formulate some hints for future investigators in this field. [. . .]

I have already mentioned one of the differences that seem to exist between Oceania and the rest of the world, but particularly Africa, in reports on the social directions believed to be taken by witchcraft and sorcery. In Africa these belief systems seem to reflect tensions within a community, whereas in Oceania they more commonly express tensions between communities. The question arises whether this difference is a real one or one resulting, in part at least, from different definitions of terms and different conventions of field-work. As my knowledge of Oceanian ethnography is still very limited, I shall inevitably ask questions rather than answer them. In any event a consideration of this difference will serve as a starting point for an examination of how field-work methods might be developed to meet the need for wider comparability of data and consequently more soundly established generalizations.

To ensure that field material is comparable between societies and regions, anthropologists have to be in agreement on what they propose to observe, and they have to be explicit about the steps they take in making and recording their observations. I would add that, in presenting the final results of the analysis of their material, they should ingenuously take the reader into their confidence rather than employ literary forms that obscure the nature of the sources of their information.

To be in agreement about what we are to observe we must first agree on definitions. In investigating the difference I have mentioned between the reported actions, real or believed, of Oceanian sorcerers and witches and those of other regions, I have encountered a difference in definition. With a few notable exceptions,[1] Oceanianists usually equate the term 'sorcery' with destructive magic in general and do not apply it exclusively, as Africanists do, to destructive magic applied anti-socially or illegitimately. The precedents for the different usage of terms by anthropologists in these two regions go back 30 or 40 years. In Oceania, Melanesia in particular, Malinowski (1926, pp. 93, 94) and Fortune (1932, pp. 167, 176) used the term 'sorcery' to mean destructive magic in all its possible applications, socially approved or not, and this wider definition has been followed by other writers dealing with this wider region, for example, Firth (1956, p. 156), Hogbin (1934, pp. 221, 223), R. M. Berndt (1962, pp. 208, 211) and Meggitt (1962, p. 325), although some of the more recent writers, such as Berndt and Meggitt, explicitly recognize two categories of sorcery, on the one hand legal or retaliatory and on the other illegitimate or socially condemned. In contrast to this, anthropologists working in Africa have found it profitable to follow the usage established by Evans-Pritchard (1931, p. 26; 1937, p. 21) when, with apparently no necessary intention of standardizing terminology for the whole continent, or for the whole anthropological profession, he used terms such as 'witchcraft', 'sorcery' and 'magic' as the English equivalents

1. For instance, Spencer and Gillen (1899, pp. 532–3) distinguish between the roles of medicine-man and sorcerer even if they recognize that these roles are sometimes combined in the same person; and Burridge (1960, pp. 59–71) uses the term 'sorcerer' exclusively for the person among the Tangu of New Guinea whose evil machinations are blamed for misfortunes.

of clearly distinguished native concepts. Important for our present purposes is the fact that, faithfully translating Zande terms, he differentiated between witches and sorcerers on the score of personality types, motivation and method, and threw them together on the score of social or moral status. He reported that, whereas the Azande believe witches to have aberrant personalities permanently addicted to evil-doing and harming others by mystical means, they look upon sorcerers as ordinary folk driven by possibly passing fits of anger or envy and employing destructive magic to attain their anti-social ends. He summed up their important social or moral similarity in the statement, 'Both alike are enemies of men' (Evans-Pritchard, 1937, p. 387). In other words, the activities of both are deemed anti-social or illegitimate.

Thus it has come about that, where Oceanianists refer to 'legal sorcery' or 'retaliatory sorcery', Africanists refer to 'destructive magic put to legitimate use', as in the protection of property or the prevention of adultery, or to 'vengeance magic', and they reserve the term 'sorcery' for the illegitimate applications of destructive magic.

Even with questions of definition settled, different results can be obtained from different methods of field-work. Even in the same society there are, as we all know, differences between what informants tell us and what, when we are fortunate enough to have the opportunity, we see actually happening. More than that, there are different degrees of generality and specificity in informants' statements in those fields of enquiry, such as opinion and belief, in which we are obliged to rely heavily on them because the object of investigation eludes direct observation. The existence of these different and divergent sources and levels of information in the same society is, of course, recognized in the injunction by the writers of *Notes and Queries on Anthropology* (Committee of the R.A.I., 1951, p. 36) that the direct observation of events and the interrogation of informants are complementary and interdependent methods. The fact that varied and conflicting information can be wrung from the same society by different approaches was brought home to me when I was among the Ceŵa of east-central Africa. It was brought home to me in a number of ways, of which I shall mention two that are relevant to my present theme. I found that the informants whom I consulted casually and non-systematically were in close agreement on two points relating to the mystical evil-doers of their society, *nfiti*, a term I translate as 'sorcerers' rather than 'witches'. They affirmed (a) that virtually all deaths resulted from sorcery; and (b) that most sorcerers were women. When I put this informal consensus of opinion to quasi-statistical investigation by having one of my African assistants interview ten men and nine women individually, the picture was not greatly altered. The averages of the estimates of this small sample of informants showed no significant sex differences, and were to the effect that (a) 93 per cent of 20 hypothetical deaths would have been the result of sorcery, and (b) the sex ratio of 20 hypothetical sorcerers would have been 27 per cent male to 73 per cent female.

I later compared these estimates with the proportions obtained from another source. During the course of my field-work I collected nearly 200 explanations given for actual cases of misfortunes, mostly deaths. The main features of these cases were tabulated and the totals gave very different answers to these two questions.

1. Only 55 per cent of the misfortunes were attributed to sorcery.

2. Within these, 58 per cent of the alleged sorcerers were male and 42 per cent female.

Informants may thus make very different statements about the same phenomenon when they are speaking generally and when they are referring to a series of specific instances.

Another source of variation is to be found in the different levels of reality of aspects of the phenomenon being investigated, this being a point of some importance in the sociology of witchcraft and sorcery. In this field, the primary data of the field-worker are behaviour episodes such as accusations, protective measures and (conceivably but rarely) malevolent rites. From these he can infer a secondary order of data, viz., the beliefs themselves, whose existence helps to explain the behaviour. He can confirm his conclusions about the nature of these beliefs by noting what informants may say about them when asked, or in some other way moved, to introspect and describe them. When we record the relationship between an alleged witch or sorcerer on the one hand and his believed victim on the other, we are clearly in the secondary realm of informants' beliefs, and the degree of reality we attribute to what we are recording will depend on the extent to which we may or may not share such beliefs. Assuming that we are entirely sceptical of the existence of witchcraft and that we have reservations about the frequency with which sorcery is actually practised, we are, when we consider the witch or sorcerer *vis-à-vis* his believed victim, dealing more or less with an imaginary relationship. As Berndt (1962, p. 224) remarks, this does not mean that we should disregard it because it is imaginary: 'If people believe these things occur, that is sufficient reason to consider them. We are not, as anthropologists, concerned primarily with the empirical 'reality' of the situation, with whether or not it actually takes place; local belief in it gives that degree of reality which is required for our purposes.' By this he presumably means that we are justified in studying beliefs because they have real social concomitants.

I agree with this approach to the extent that a record of people's beliefs about the relationship between alleged witches or sorcerers and their victims provides us with an interesting summary of their insights into their own social system. By noting the frequency with which persons in various categories of social relationship come together as witch and victim or as sorcerer and victim, we are reading the society's home-made strain-gauges, which in my experience are more reliable in their assessment of tension-points than are the general statements of informants. What I would like to emphasize, however, is that there is no need to be satisfied with the study of the realm of belief alone. There are many real manifestations of these imaginary beliefs, such as accusations and protective measures, and therefore more objective strain-gauges for exploring social tensions can be employed. Some of us in Africa (Wilson, 1951a, pp. 198–205; Marwick, 1952, 1963, 1965; Mitchell, 1956, pp. 156 ff.; Turner, 1957, *passim*) mainly at Mitchell's instigation, have come to concentrate our attention on that important and hitherto somewhat neglected character in a witchcraft or sorcery drama, the accuser. Whereas the relationship between alleged sorcerer or witch and believed victim is usually an imaginary one, that between accuser and alleged sorcerer or witch is one with a greater degree of reality, belonging to the primary order of data I have referred to. Though the person designated as a witch or sorcerer may in fact be entirely innocent of any of the actions or characteristics implied in such a charge, the relationship between him and the accuser is nevertheless real. It is real enough for the field-worker to observe it on occasion, and, if the accusation takes place in his absence, to feel reasonably certain of establishing the existence of the relationship from informants' statements. It is true that this external, more objective strain-gauge gives recordings of tensions that are often similar to those indicated by the way in which persons of various relationships are brought together in the roles of witch and victim or sorcerer and victim, by, that is, what I have called the homemade strain-gauges; but some interesting differences may appear. For instance, my Cewa case material shows a statistically significant difference in the relative age of alleged sorcerers, their believed victims and their accusers. Sorcerers are older than their believed victims and accusers are younger than those whom they accuse, this relative age distribution reflecting in part the fact that an accusation of sorcery is often involved in a younger man's bid for leadership of one of the segments into which a Cewa matrilineage usually divides.

Once again the application of these more objective measures, such as an examination of the kinds of social relationships between accuser and accused or even accused and believed victim, may give a picture of social tensions very different from that derived from informants' general statements. There is a saying among the Cewa, *ŋombe ndi cipali cikutha ẁanthu*, 'Cattle and polygyny finish people', meaning that quarrels over the ownership and inheritance of cattle (which are relatively recent additions to Cewa culture) and over polygyny are frequent, and often culminate in believed attacks of sorcery. When the first part of this statement is put to the more precise test of the strain-gauges I have mentioned, it is confirmed, though in rather small measure; for cattle are the objects of competition in about 15 per cent of the 80-odd cases in my sample of believed attacks by sorcery said to have been preceded by quarrels. The second part of the statement is not confirmed by the case material; for cases involving polygyny account for only 1 per cent of the total relationships between sorcerer and victim and for only 2 per cent of those between accuser and sorcerer.

This experience of having obtained different results from different research procedures in the same society has made me very interested in the precise source of an investigator's information and correspondingly sceptical of arguments he may put forward to account for the tensions he believes he has found to be characteristic of the social system concerned. If he claims that witchcraft is believed to operate between half-brothers in a patrilineal society and proceeds to explain this in terms of a house property complex, we are entitled, before we examine his argument, to ask whether the data it seeks to explain are derived from informants' statements, introspective or otherwise, or from records of a series of believed attacks by witches.

My experience of finding that different methods of enquiry yielded different answers to the same questions seems to have been shared by the late Professor Kluckhohn. In *Navaho Witchcraft* (1944, p. 55) he reported a tendency for distant and totally unrelated witches to be blamed for people's misfortunes. However, in a commentary he was kind enough to send me on one of my papers, he stated that his more recent data had not confirmed his earlier conclusions in this respect, and that gossip about local witches was commoner than his first impressions had led him to believe. I get the impression that his earlier finding may have been based on informants' general statements; and his later one, on the examination of specific instances. It may be that both answers are right: that people put the blame for misfortunes in general on to distant witches and for a specific misfortune on to someone within the community who is a natural choice because he is eccentric in some way or because the believed victim offended him.

Middleton and Winter (1963, pp. 10–11), suggest that, if witchcraft is invoked for explaining one type, e.g. generalized misfortune, sorcery will be invoked for the other type. I believe that this might fit Kluckhohn's material and I find a hint of it in my own. I feel, however, that the argument of Middleton and Winter depends too heavily on taking Evans-Pritchard's distinction to its logical conclusion, and is not sufficiently concerned with the comparability of the terminological usage of those whose works they review.

If within a single society, such as that of the Cewa or the Navaho, different estimates of the incidence of social tensions accrue from different ways of collecting data, how much more likely are there to be differences and inconsistencies between different ethnographic regions where terms are differently defined and where different conventions of field-work methods may have developed. I say 'may have developed' because it is not always possible to judge from an anthropologist's writings what methods he in fact used. Too much attention to euphony of prose in general, and too much concern with the dilemma between repetition and elegant variation in particular, sometimes drive anthropological writers into possibly graceful but certainly obscure statements that hide from their readers the sources of their data and the bases of their conclusions. Thus when Kuper (1947, p. 175) writes in reference to the Swazi that 'witchcraft and sorcery ... are usually selective and take toll of people between whom bonds already exist', we are entitled to ask her a few questions about how she came to this conclusion. It might be a rather hair-splitting revocation of the licence we would readily grant someone of her literary grace to ask whether her statement implies that she herself believes in Swazi witchcraft and sorcery. It would not, however, be an unfair question to ask whether this dramatic sentence rests on informants' general statements about witchcraft and sorcery, whether it summarizes their beliefs about a series of specific cases or whether it represents the pattern of accusations revealed by case material.

Similarly when Berndt (1962, p. 217), in discussing the position of a person who practises sorcery against a member of his own political unit, writes '... in spite of examples to the contrary the assumption is that sorcery is, and should be, directed outside the district', one wishes he were more explicit about whose assumption he is referring to and about the extent of the disagreement between this assumption and the examples to the contrary. And though the following passage from Fortune (1932, p. 127) is a reminder that the role of the anthropologist is empathetic exploration, in the sense of feeling himself in the position of a member of the society he is studying and then reporting on his feelings, one could wish for an indication of a more objective basis for so important a conclusion:

The whole life of the people is strongly coloured by a thorough absence of trust in neighbours and the practice of treachery beneath a show of friendliness. Every person goes in fear of the secret war, and on frequent occasion the fear breaks through the surface.

Any comparative sociology built on the comparison of in-comparables is doomed to failure. We cannot judge whether our comparisons are safe unless field workers are more explicit on how they collected their data and how they came to their conclusions.

In my cursory search through Oceanian ethnography for references to witchcraft and sorcery, I have found that most anthropologists in this region have not made a practice of systematically collecting specific instances of either believed attacks of sorcery or witchcraft or of observed or observable accusations of these. For instance, in an otherwise admirable analysis of the position of the sorcerer among the Tangu, Burridge (1960, pp. 59–71) offers only hypothetical cases and, apart from saying (on p. 64) that 'first suspects are those most strange or distant', omits any information on how the believed sorcerer was related to his accuser and to his believed victim. Of the authors whose works I have examined, Berndt (1962, pp. 214–28) offers the most detailed illustrative cases; but only seven of these have to do with sorcery, and he does not indicate to which of the three periods mentioned in his Introduction (pp. 8–9) each case belongs.

A common failing in the case reports I have encountered in the Oceanian literature is an omission to specify the social relationships between the main characters concerned. This may be partly the result of the fact that most cases of sorcery reported are ones in which it is believed to have taken its traditional social direction, i.e. between members of different groups rather than of the same group; and in this type of case, if the ethnographer gives the group affiliations of the main characters, he is providing most of what is material to their social relationships. This applies to six of Berndt's seven cases. However, in the seventh case, which involves people in the same village (Berndt, 1962, p. 223), no details of social relationships are mentioned except that the sorcery was used by men to punish two women who had trespassed on an exclusively male preserve.

Sometimes Oceanian authors' incidental references to specific

cases of sorcery do not necessarily confirm more general statements about the direction that attacks are believed usually to
take. Thus Meggitt (1962, p. 325), who explicitly states that,
among the Walbiri, it is usually someone outside the local community who is suspected of sorcery (though it can be a relative),
happens to give two instances, one real and one hypothetical, of
the believed operation of sorcery, and neither happens to fit the
general pattern. The first (p. 176) involves an accusation between
two women in the same community, the potential co-wives of an
intended polygynist; and the second (p. 246) describes how a
punitive party in pursuit of a wrong-doer from their own community who is seeking refuge in the territory of another community might confine itself to performing sorcery against him
from a distance.

On the other hand there are a number of instances where the
incidental illustration does confirm the general Oceanian belief
that sorcery operates between communities rather than within
the same community. Spencer and Gillen (1899, p. 533) report:

News was brought into the camp that a very celebrated old man had
died far away out to the west. His death was due simply to senile decay,
but along with the news of his decease word was brought that he had
been killed by a charmed stick pointed at him by a man of a distant
group, the locality of which was stated with certainty.

Reay (1959, pp. 136 ff.) makes some references to the witch's
being suspected of cooperating with an enemy group. The Kuma
witch is therefore in the interesting position of resembling the
African witch or sorcerer by being the enemy within the community; and yet he conforms to the general Oceanian trend for
beliefs in witchcraft or sorcery to provide a medium of inter-
community strife. Two of the cases that occurred when Hogbin
(1935) was on Wogeo, and the majority of other cases reported to
him there, were ones in which a person from another district was
held to have been responsible for the death of the victim. The
Garia sorcery-feud reported by Lawrence (1952, p.343) is
consistent with his general finding (1955, pp. 11, 14) that sorcery
is usually suspected outside one's 'security circle' of close kinsmen
and in this respect it resembles the blood feud. Oliver (1955, pp.
241, 242), on the other hand, cites a case in illustration of his

statement that 'suspicion is not limited to persons living *outside* the village'.

From this inadequate array of case material that I have picked up in my hasty and superficial examination of Oceanian literature, it would appear that the general statement that Oceanian sorcerers are usually believed to be outside the communities of their victims and presumably of their accusers, though at present sometimes supported by undisclosed if not dubious evidence, is likely to be sustained by more systematically collected case material. It may well be that social strain-gauges which in Africa have usually detected tensions within a community may serve in this region as measures of relationships between different social groups. As Berndt (1962, p. 209) puts it (although his definition of sorcery is wider than mine), 'Sorcery, like warfare, can throw into relief all those conflicts which are an accompaniment of inter-district relations'.

There certainly seems to be a close intertwining in this region of the mystical aggression of sorcery and the real aggression of war. Berndt (1962, p. 223) uses the presence or absence of associated physical aggression as the criterion for distinguishing his two major categories of sorcery in the Eastern Highlands of New Guinea; and the Australian Aboriginal techniques of sorcery are often described as though they were actual physical attacks on the victim (e.g. Spencer and Gillen, 1899, p. 536; Warner, 1937, pp. 194–206). In the Australian literature the sorcerer is sometimes referred to as the 'murderer' (Elkin, 1937, *passim*), and his dispatch by the emu-padded allies of the victim is an important part of sorcery-lore. It may be that the association between physical aggression and sorcery has had a part in the emergence of the wider definition of sorcery adopted by Oceanianists; for whether the destructive magic used is illegitimate or not depends upon the viewpoint of one or other of the groups concerned.

But all this is speculation. So far as I am aware, no book comparable with Evans-Pritchard's study of Azande witchcraft nor even Kluckhohn's of Navaho witchcraft has yet been written on the sorcery and witchcraft of an Oceanian people. Despite its title, Fortune's book on Dobu is largely confined to description of sorcerers' techniques and contains remarkably little that could be used for the detailed sociological analysis of sorcery. It is to be hoped that when such an analysis is made of the sorcery and witchcraft of an Oceanian people, the material used will include specific cases as well as informants' general estimates of the ways of sorcerers and witches, and that the style will not prevent the reader from judging which line of evidence is being led.

One of the problems relating to the use as strain-gauges of statistics derived from cases of accusation arises from the fact that the incidence of accusations of sorcery or witchcraft in various relationship categories is of complex determination. A high absolute frequency of accusations in a particular category, say that between matrilateral parallel cousins in a matrilineal society, is an index, not only of the degree of tension characteristic of the relationship, but also of the sheer frequency of interaction in it. Thus, to argue that a high frequency of accusations in a given relationship-category indicates a high degree of social tension in it is as naïve as contending that divorce is a more serious problem in the United Kingdom than among South African whites because the absolute number of divorces in any one year is greater in the former than in the latter population. Just as divorces can be compared only when considered as rates, i.e. in relation to the universe in which they occur, such as the total population or the total married population, so must accusations of sorcery and witchcraft somehow be related to the universe of social inter-actions in which they occur. In short, a person may accuse a cousin more frequently than a brother simply because he has far more cousins than brothers with whom he interacts; and the higher frequency for cousins does not necessarily indicate a tenser relationship with them than with brothers unless the differing sizes of the two universes of interaction can somehow be con-trolled. I cannot offer a solution to this problem which I have set out more fully elsewhere (Marwick, 1961, 1963, 1965), but I commend it to statistically minded social scientists.

What lessons are to be learned from the comparison I have attempted and from my experience and that of some of my colleagues in Africa? I suggest that the person who carries out field-work in preparation for the book on the sociology of Oceanian sorcery or witchcraft for which we are waiting might bear the following points in mind. Firstly, terms such as sorcery or witchcraft must be clearly defined and the differentiation between destructive magic socially approved and that socially condemned should be maintained; for the difference between them is for obvious reasons material to sociological analysis. Secondly, the well-established principle of comparing the ideal with the real applies in this field of inquiry as much as in any other, and should not be forgotten simply because it is obvious. The general statements that informants make about sorcerers and witches must be compared with specific ones they make in reference to particular cases and with what the ethnographer may observe of their and other people's actions. Thirdly, beliefs in sorcery and witchcraft invariably have a social setting in the sense that they mediate, though they sometimes complicate, the living together of people in the on-going process we call a society. They do this by providing a means of expressing tense social relationships. Sometimes they relieve the tension. Sometimes they end the relationship when it has become redundant and insupportable and yet, because of emotional investment in it, indissoluble by the quiet process of closing a contract. They also mediate social living by dramatizing moral values both in the retrospective reconstructions of disturbed relationships between the believed victim and his alleged attacker and in the negative example of the witch or the sorcerer who, by the African definition at least, is someone beyond the pale, the personification of evil, and a bogey man with which to frighten naughty children.

These considerations mean that, fourthly, the field-worker, in collecting his material, has to pay particular attention to the three central characters, the accuser, the alleged sorcerer or witch and the believed victim, and to the social relationships, the rivalries and the alliances between them.

Finally, the ethnographer should again apply a well-established canon of field-work to his particular topic, i.e. when he cannot observe the relationships believed to be involved in a particular instance of misfortune, and even when he can, and wishes to supplement his observations, he should not rely on only one informant for each case, but should record the interpretations of different persons differently placed in relation to the central characters.

I feel that, if the strain-gauge I have described is used according to these prescriptions, it may, through making field material from different societies more profitably comparable, advance our knowledge of the sociology of tension and conflict and once again demonstrate that the role of anthropology is the pursuit of exotic customs not merely for their own sake but for what they can contribute to the understanding of human behaviour in general.

References

BERNDT, R. M. (1962), *Excess and Restraint*, University of Chicago Press.

BURRIDGE, K. (1960), *Mambu*, Methuen.

COMMITTEE OF THE ROYAL ANTHROPOLOGICAL INSTITUTE (1951), *Notes and Queries on Anthropology*, R.A.I., 6th edn.

ELKIN, A. P. (1937), 'Beliefs and practices connected with death in north-eastern and western South Australia', *Oceania*, vol. 7.

EVANS-PRITCHARD, E. E. (1931), 'Sorcery and native opinion', *Africa*, vol. 4, no. 1.

EVANS-PRITCHARD, E. E. (1937), *Witchcraft, Oracles and Magic among the Azande*, Clarendon Press.

FIRTH, R. (1956), *Human Types*, Nelson, rev. edn.

FORTUNE, R. F. (1932), *Sorcerers of Dobu*, Routledge.

GLUCKMAN, M. (1956), *Custom and Conflict in Africa*, Blackwell.

HOGBIN, H. I. (1934), *Law and Order in Polynesia*, Christophers.

HOGBIN, H. I. (1935), 'Sorcery and administration', *Oceania*, vol. 6.

HUNTER (now WILSON), M. (1936), *Reaction to Conquest*, Oxford U.P. for International Institute of African Languages and Cultures.

KLUCKHOHN, C. (1944), *Navaho Witchcraft*, Papers of the Peabody Museum of American Archaeology and Ethnology, Harvard University, vol. 22; Beacon Press, 1962.

KRIGE, E. J. and KRIGE, J. D. (1943), *The Realm of a Rain Queen*, Oxford U.P. for International Institute of African Languages and Cultures.

KUPER, H. (1947), *An African Aristocracy*, Oxford U.P. for International African Institute.

LAWRENCE, P. (1952), 'Sorcery among the Garia', *South Pacific*, vol. 6.

LAWRENCE, P. (1955), *Land Tenure among the Garia*, Australian National University, Social Science Monographs, no. 4.

MALINOWSKI, B. (1926), *Crime and Custom in Savage Society*, Kegan Paul, Trench, Trubner.

MARWICK, M. G. (1952), 'The social context of Ceŵa witch-beliefs', *Africa*, vol. 22.

MARWICK, M. G. (1961), 'Some problems in the sociology of sorcery and witchcraft', Paper contributed to Third International African Seminar, Salisbury, Rhodesia, December (subsequently published as ch. 9 of M. Fortes and G. Dieterlen (ed.), *African Systems of Thought*, Oxford U.P. for International African Institute, 1965).

MARWICK, M. G. (1963), 'The sociology of sorcery in a central African tribe', *African Studies*, vol. 22.

MARWICK, M. G. (1965), *Sorcery in its Social Setting*, Manchester U.P.

MEGGITT, M. J. (1962), *Desert People*, Angus & Robertson.

MIDDLETON, J., and WINTER, E. H. (eds.) (1963), *Witchcraft and Sorcery in East Africa*, Routledge & Kegan Paul.

MITCHELL, J. C. (1956), *The Yao Village*, Manchester U.P. for Rhodes-Livingstone Institute.

OLIVER, D. L. (1955), *A Solomon Island Society*, Harvard U.P.

REAY, M. (1959), *The Kuma*, Melbourne U.P. for the Australian National University.

SCHAPERA, I. (1952), 'Sorcery and witchcraft in Bechuanaland', *African Affairs*, vol. 51, no. 41.

SPENCER, B., and GILLEN, F. J. (1899), *The Native Tribes of Central Australia*, Macmillan.

TURNER, V. W. (1957), *Schism and Continuity in an African Society*, Manchester U.P. for Rhodes-Livingstone Institute.

WARNER, W. L. (1937), *A Black Civilization*, Harper.

WILSON (née HUNTER), M. (1951a), *Good Company*, Oxford U.P. for International African Institute.

WILSON (née HUNTER), M. (1951b), 'Witch-beliefs and social structure', *American Journal of Sociology*, vol. 56, p. 307.

25 A. D. J. Macfarlane

Witchcraft and Conflict

A. D. J. Macfarlane, *Witchcraft in Tudor and Stuart England*, Routledge &
Kegan Paul, 1970, chapter 15, 'Witchcraft Beliefs as an Explanation of
Suffering and a Means of Resolving Conflict'.

Those who stormed against the folly of believing in witchcraft
stated that nearly every strange or painful event was blamed on
witches. Ady (1656, p. 114) complained that:

seldom hath a man the hand of God against him in his estate, or health
of body, or any way, but presently he cryeth out of some poor innocent
Neighbour, that he, or she hath bewitched him.

Reginald Scot (1584) also remonstrated (see also Gaule, 1646,
p. 85):

that fewe or none can (nowadaies) with patience indure the hand and
correction of God. For if any adversitie, greefe, sicknesse, losse of
children, corne, cattell, or libertie happen unto them; by & by they
exclaime upon witches.

Analysis of the Essex prosecutions, however, and particularly
comparison of death and sickness in the sample villages with
known cases of witchcraft, has shown that witchcraft was suggested as a cause of misfortune in only a small proportion of the
accidents occurring during our period. This poses the problem of
why people blamed certain misfortunes and not others on witches.
Several possibilities have already been ruled out. Although there
was sometimes an emphasis on the strangeness of an event, for
instance, when a woman was suddenly covered by lice which
'were long, and lean, and not like other Lice' (pamphlet, 1645,
p. 23), strangeness, in itself, was not enough to produce a suspicion of witchcraft. Likewise, witches were not merely sought
when there was a gap in contemporary medical knowledge or
when a death was particularly sudden, painful, or unexpected. It
is true that individual witchcraft only explained particular, as
opposed to general, misfortunes. While witches, in theory, were
believed 'to raise winds and tempests' and cause 'thunder and

lightning', the actual court prosecutions show that they were only blamed for specific damage (Gifford, 1587, sig. H4^v; Ady, 1656, p. 113).[1] But the variety of the damage blamed on witches, and the many misfortunes which were not attributed to their power, suggests that there was another, determining, factor. This factor, it will be argued, was the relationship between witch and victim.

When witchcraft was used as an 'explanation' of a misfortune, this did not necessarily preclude other explanations. For analytic purposes, therefore, we need to distinguish between natural and supernatural explanation: thus witchcraft was a supernatural cause of an illness, while syphilis, for example, was a 'natural' cause. Since the interpreters of an accident might be seeking to 'explain' a variety of things, the supernatural and natural might coexist. Thus a villager might recognize quite clearly the series of events leading up, on the physical side, to an accident. He might see that a child died 'because' it fell from a chair and broke its neck. 'Because' here meant 'how' it died, the outward, observable, reasons. Explanation was also needed as to 'why' it died. Why *this* child, on *this* day, died.[2] This would explain to an anxious parent why her child, rather than that of a neighbour, had died. Thus witchcraft could be the 'cause' in the sense that it explained the purpose, motive, or will behind an injury, while the 'cause', in another sense, was a perfectly well understood disease or accident. This distinction meant that the same symptoms might be interpreted in very different ways, depending on the attitude of the sufferer. The two levels of causation were recognized by the Essex witch-finder Matthew Hopkins, who distinguished between a natural illness and supernatural malice:

God suffers the Devill many times to doe much hurt, and the devill doth play many times the deluder and imposter with these Witches, in perswading them that they are the cause of such and such a murder wrought by him with their consents, when and indeed neither he nor they had any hand in it, as thus: We must needs argue, he is of a long

1. Thus there seems to have been a direct relationship between the dimensions of the misfortune and the size of the enemy blamed. Ady (1656, p. 104) noted that general misfortunes (tempests, plagues) were blamed on the large company of dead witches, rather than on specific living ones.

2. This classic distinction is discussed on pp. 300ff., below.

standing . . . and so have the best skill in *Physicke*, judgment in *Physiognomie*, and knowledge of what disease is reigning or predominant in this or that man's body (and so for cattel too) . . . as *Plurisie*, *Imposthume*, &c.

The Devil waits until a person is nearly dead, then offers to kill him for his enemy, a witch. He dies, and everyone believes that the witch has done it 'when and indeed the disease kills the party, not the witch, nor the Devill' (Hopkins, 1647, pp. 59–61 of 1928 edn.).

Hopkins implied that the disaster would have happened in any case. Here he was probably more sceptical than the majority of the Essex population, as well as many other writers. While they would have agreed that the misfortune might occur, on occasions, without being sent by a witch, yet they stressed that it happened more often and more horribly because of the will of evil people. This was the opinion of Sir Thomas Browne when asked for his advice at a witchcraft trial in 1664. He stated that the witches and Satan only worked on natural causes, but such natural causes were exacerbated by supernatural methods (*A Tryal*, 1664). This view was echoed by William Perkins. The Devil, he wrote, was the principal agent of evil, but the witch was rightly punished, 'because if the devill were not stirred up, and provoked by the Witch, he would never do so much hurt as he doth' (1608, p. 253). A similar view seems to have been held by Essex villagers. They were convinced that many accidents would never have happened if there had been no witch. Gifford (1587, sig. H3) expressed this popular attitude with clarity:

men looke no further then unto ye witch: they fret and rage against her: they never looke so high as unto God: they looke not to the cause why ye devil hath powers over them: they seeke not to appease Gods wrath. But they fly upon ye witch: they think if shee were not, they should doo well enough: shee is made the cause of all plagues & mischiefes.[3]

Thus witchcraft was an explanation which involved the idea that pain was not random, but caused by the motive or will of a person. An event which could, from one angle, be seen as the culmination of a series of uncontrollable physical circumstances would, from another, be examined for origins in human or divine planning.

3. This is an almost exact paraphrase of Richard Bernard (1627, pp. 202–3), and was therefore presumably well known to the jury-men for whom Bernard wrote and who tried witchcraft cases.

It is very difficult to estimate what percentage of accidents in our period demanded an interpretation in terms of personal will. It has been suggested that in a small-scale, 'face-to-face' society where there are few specialized relationships and where close personal bonds serve most men's interests, 'all events tend to be explained by what occurs in those relationships' (Gluckman, 1963, p. 95).[4] The many deaths by 'misfortune' listed in the Essex coroner's inquisitions suggest that English society may have already passed beyond this stage and people may have accepted that illness and death often occurred without purpose.[5] Yet the comments of Puritan writers show clearly that a connexion between sin and disease, or between suffering and human failure, was often drawn. The difference between the Puritans and those they castigated was merely in the details of the connexion Once a person sought to relate an injury to personal motivation there were three alternatives from which to choose. He could either blame himself, his neighbours, or God. While those who advocated the punishment of witches chose the middle solution, Puritans laid stress on the first and last of the three alternatives. George Gifford's complaint was that people would not face up to the responsibility of admitting that misfortune was their own fault: 'They can by no means see, that God is provoked by their sinnes to give the devill such instruments to work withall, but rage against the witch' (1593, sig. D3^v). Persons thinking themselves bewitched will find on self-examination, William Perkins declared, 'that their owne sinnes are the true and proper causes of these evills' (1608, p. 230). Ady commented that 'no Inchantment can hurt us, but the only thing that can hurt any man is sinning against God' (1656, p. 53). If such an interpretation had been widely accepted it would have led to an enormous weight of guilt for the individual, since all natural misfortunes would have had to be related back to personal failure. Others would have been in the position of Ralph Josselin, who blamed his own unseason-

4. This topic is further discussed on pp. 300ff., below. There is a statistical analysis of the proportion of injuries attributed to witches in Marwick (1965, pp. 15, 37, 73).

5. This probably constitutes one of the major differences between English and Zande society, and hence their systems of witchcraft. The Azande say, 'Death has always a cause, and no man dies without a reason' (Evans-Pritchard, 1937, p. 111).

able chess-playing for the death of his infant son.[6] The alternative offered by the Puritans was based on the story of Job and stressed patience in the face of the testing hand of God. This might, however, face the individual with a contradiction between a benign and loving Father, and the idea of a torturing and cruel task-master.[7] Moreover, this interpretation lacked one great advantage of the other alternatives, the possibility of counter-action, of taking active steps to avoid future suffering and end present misery.

It is arguable that the Catholic Church in England before the Reformation provided a more satisfactory answer to the problem of explaining suffering. Catholic ritual, with its dramatization of the expulsion of evil and communal propitiation of God, may have offered a solution to the misfortunes of daily life which did not involve the blame being centred on either the individual or his neighbours. Prayers and activities offered people satisfactory counter-action in times of distress and also the hope that their environment might be controlled. At the Reformation, it might be suggested, the misfortunes and worries continued, but the whole ritual framework designed to deal with them was destroyed. This huge topic cannot be dealt with satisfactorily in a sociological analysis of prosecutions in one county starting in 1560;[8] but Essex material does suggest that witchcraft beliefs were one method of dealing with problems of human suffering, and hence they pose the question: How were such problems solved in previous centuries?

In the classic instance of witchcraft being used as an explanation of *why* a misfortune happens, people suffer an injury first and then look round to see who might have bewitched them.[9] Individuals are not permanently thought of as witches and the incident is soon forgotten. In Essex prosecutions the process

6. This point in Josselin's diary is cited in Notestein (1962, p. 152).

7. This problem is further discussed elsewhere in the book from which this excerpt is taken – *Ed*.

8. The forthcoming book by Keith Thomas (in press) will deal comprehensively with this problem.

9. 'A Zande is interested in witchcraft only as an agent on definite occasions and in relation to his own interests, and not as a permanent condition of individuals', writes Evans-Pritchard (1937, p. 26).

seems to have been different; once a suspicion had arisen about a certain person future injuries were blamed on her. Someone first offended a neighbour, and subsequently suffered. In fact, the links were more complicated than this. Often, it seems, a person would not remember that he had denied a neighbour until some tragedy happened. Yet there is little doubt that the stress was on the motive for the bewitching, not on the strangeness of the injury. What was being explained, in fact, was the feeling between two people rather than a physical injury. When a person felt that he had angered someone, he himself felt angry and worried. The subsequent hostility could be interpreted in the ideology of witchcraft. The victim would feel justified in hating someone because she was an evil witch and had injured him physically: her rage was felt to be the rage of a wicked woman. This interpretation also accords with the conclusion that only certain injuries were blamed on witches and that these misfortunes were not necessarily exceptional in any way. It was the social context which determined the interpretation. A man who knew he had deeply offended a neighbour and that she had reason to curse him would interpret subsequent events differently from the man who felt no particular malice towards, or from, his co-villagers. Furthermore, it has been argued that it was often the victim who felt the hostility and guilt and projected this on to the witch. It was only when hatred was known to be prevalent that people would feel precarious enough, angry enough, and anxious enough to press a charge of witchcraft. Thus witchcraft was not just an automatic explanation of all, or specific, types of misfortune. Rather, it was combined solution to why a certain painful event had happened, and why a person felt a certain painful emotion. To both types of uncertainty it promised relief.

Witchcraft prosecutions, we have seen, were usually between people who knew each other intimately – that is, between village neighbours. They almost always arose from quarrels over gifts and loans in which the victim refused the witch some small gift, heard her muttering under her breath or threatening him, and subsequently suffered some misfortune. It was usually the person who had done the first wrong under the old ideals of charity who felt himself bewitched. The weight of these traditional ideals, as well as the belief that a moral offence would be afflicted by physical punishment, is excellently illustrated by Thomas Ady (1656, p. 130):

God hath given it as a strict Command to all men to relieve the poor, *Levit*. 25.35. and in the next Chapter it followeth, vers. 14, 15. *Whosoever hearkneth not to all the Commandments of the Lord to do them* (whereof relieving the poor is one), *the Lord will send several crosses and afflictions, and diseases upon them*, as followeth in the Chapter, and therefore men should look into the Scriptures, and search what sins bring afflictions from God's hands, and not say presently, what old man or woman was last at my door, that I may hand him or her for a Witche; yea we should rather say, Because I did not relieve such a poor body that was lately at my door, but gave him harsh and bitter words, therefore God hath laid this Affliction upon me, for God saith, *Exod*. 22.23, 24. *If thou any way afflict widows, and fatherless, and they at all cry unto me, I will surely hear their cry, and my wrath shall wax hot against thee*.

Physical afflictions were the punishment for social deviation and men might well tremble when they heard a widow's curse, backed, as it was said to be in the Bible, by God's power. But by suggesting that the widow was a witch the power of the old sanctions to neighbourly behaviour, especially cursing, was broken. As Ady recognized, an accusation of witchcraft was a clever way of reversing the guilt, of transferring it from the person who had failed in his social obligation under the old standard to the person who had made him fail. Through the mechanism of the law, and the informal methods of gossip and village opinion, society was permitted to support the accuser.

From a certain viewpoint, therefore, witchcraft prosecutions may be seen as a means of effecting a deep social change; a change from a 'neighbourly', highly integrated and mutually interdependent village society, to a more individualistic one. Both the necessity and dangers of such a change are illustrated by Thomas Cooper when he warned the godly in 1617 to forgo indiscriminate charity and to be especially hard on suspected witches, 'to bee straight-handed towards them, not to entertaine them in our houses, not to relieve them with our morsels': not to fear the spiritual consequences, to 'use a *Christian courage* in all our *Actions*, not to *feare their curses*, nor seeke for their blessings'

(1617, p. 288). Among the counter-actions against witches a number have already been noted that would have the effect of severing relationships between neighbours. The danger was again emphasized by an Elizabethan preacher who told his congregation that 'we may see how experience, and the very confessions of witches, agree that the merciful lenders and givers are preserved of God, and unmerciful usurers and covetous Nabals are vexed and troubled of Satan' (Haweis, 1844, p. 244). Thus witchcraft beliefs provided both the justification for severing contact, and an explanation for the guilt and fear still felt by the individual when he did so: he might expect to be repaid on the spiritual plane for his lack of charity, but could be satisfied that this was witchcraft, and thus evil, rather than punishment for his own shortcomings. In one sense, witchcraft beliefs can be seen as a form of reciprocal relationship. One neighbour injures another, both on the physical level, by refusing a gift, but also, more generally, by denying the existence of a mutual relationship. The witch reciprocates on two levels also, through a physical attack which is accompanied by a malice equivalent to that of the victim. All this occurred within the context of village life where there were immense difficulties facing those who wished to deny the existence of a neighbourly bond. Christianity, as we have seen from Ady's quotation from the Bible, still upheld communal values. There was no code to which a person who felt the need to cut down or re-direct his relationships could appeal. Yet, through the idiom of witchcraft prosecutions, the older values were undermined or changed, while, on the surface, they were maintained. Witchcraft prosecutions, therefore, may have been principally important as a radical force which broke down the communal pattern inherited from the medieval period. Anthropologists, perhaps because they tend to make static studies, usually stress the conservative effects of witchcraft beliefs. They argue that such beliefs maintain and reinforce social relationships.[10] A historical study suggests that prosecutions may just as well be a means of destroying old relationships and ideals.

10. For example, Marwick (1965, p. 221) argues that 'sorcery and witchcraft emerge as conservative social forces; and their conservative character is brought into sharp relief when they operate under conditions of social change'.

Yet this explanation leaves many unanswered problems. Some villages were free of witchcraft accusations in Essex. Clearly witchcraft accusations were not the necessary or only mechanism for dealing with a conflict between an ideal of neighbourliness and the practical consequences of social and economic change. Nor does it seem probable that disputes between neighbours were absent before 1560, or that they ended abruptly in the middle of the seventeenth century. This leads us directly to the problems surrounding the rise and decline of witchcraft accusations.

References

ADY, T. (1656), *A Candle in the Dark: or, A Treatise Concerning the Nature of Witches and Witchcraft.*

BERNARD, R. (1627), *A Guide to Grand Jury Men.*

COOPER, T. (1617), *The Mystery of Witchcraft.*

EVANS-PRITCHARD, E. E. (1937), *Witchcraft, Oracles and Magic among the Azande*, Clarendon Press.

GAULE, J. (1646), *Select Cases of Conscience Touching Witches and Witchcraft.*

GIFFORD, G. (1587), *A Discourse of the Subtill Practices of Devilles by Witches and Sourcerers.*

GIFFORD, G. (1593), *A Dialogue Concerning Witches and Witchcrafts.*

GLUCKMAN, M. (1963), *Custom and Conflict in Africa*, Blackwell.

HAWEIS, J. O. W. (1844), *Sketches of the Reformation and Elizabethan Age.*

HOPKINS, M. (1647), *The Discovery of Witches*, 1928 edn, M. Summers (ed), Cayme Press.

MARWICK, M. G. (1965), *Sorcery in its Social Setting*, Manchester U.P.

NOTESTEIN, W. (1962), *English People on the Eve of Colonization*, Harper.

Pamphlet (1645), *A True and Exact Relation of the Several Informations, Examinations, and Confessions of the late Witches, Arraigned and Executed in the County of Essex.*

PERKINS, W. (1608), *A Discourse of the Damned Art of Witchcraft*, Cambridge.

SCOT, R. (1584), *The Discoverie of Witchcraft*, p. 25 of the 1964 edn, Preface by H. R. Williamson, Centaur Press.

THOMAS, K. (in press), *Religion and the Decline of Magic*, Weidenfeld & Nicolson.

A Tryal of Witches at Bury St Edmunds on the Tenth Day of March 1664, in *A Collection of Rare and Curious Tracts relating to Witchcraft*, 1838.

26 J. R. Crawford

The Consequences of Allegation

Excerpts from J. R. Crawford, *Witchcraft and Sorcery in Rhodesia*, Oxford University Press for International African Institute, 1967, pp. 160–61, 278–90.

Introduction

There are a number of aspects of wizardry allegations. [...] One problem is the extent to which fear of an allegation of wizardry assists to ensure conformity with the social norms of the community. Another, and perhaps greater problem, is whether allegations of wizardry are mere manifestations of social tensions or whether they are something more than this. Some social anthropologists write of wizardry allegations as if they were of little more significance than signposts to social friction – almost like a rash in the case of measles. On this aspect of the matter I shall let the case material speak for itself. Over and over again it is difficult not to come to the conclusion that the sequence of events related could not have come about had the accusation which was made not been made in the idiom of wizardry. Then there is the question as to whether persons deliberately or unconsciously make use of the wizardry allegation in the manipulation of the structure of society to their own advantage. Are wizardry allegations, in other words, 'merely a stereotyped response to misfortune' or are they 'an instrumental technique'? (see Beattie in Middleton and Winter, 1963, p. 31). Do wizardry allegations resolve social tensions or intensify them? There are no doubt many other questions also. To some it is possible to suggest an answer, but more often the material at my disposal is insufficient or ambiguous. It may, perhaps, be wrong to assume that there is any very clear-cut answer. It is probable, for example, that among the Shona an allegation of wizardry is often no more than a stereotyped response to misfortune. It would, I think, be quite wrong to deduce from this that it can never be used as an instrumental technique. In certain circumstances, for example, in the case of rivalry for political office, accusations of wizardry are clearly used as an instrumental technique.

In the following pages I shall give an account of a number of wizardry allegations, mostly taken from cases which have come before the courts. The accounts will give an illustration of the nature of the material used by me, the manner in which accusations may take place and, I hope, something of the atmosphere surrounding an accusation. It is very easy to discuss wizardry accusations in the clinical atmosphere of a sociological study, but it is as well to keep in mind the emotions of hate and terror, the feelings of doubt and of certainty, the moments of rationality and irrationality which accompany an allegation and of the brutality which may eventuate. [. . .]

The Normative Aspects of Wizardry Belief

A number of cases have been referred to where a breach of the social norms has been followed by an accusation of wizardry. In some cases it would seem that the breach has something to do with the accusation, in other cases after the allegation has been made the fact that the person accused has acted in an improper manner is seen as evidence confirming the truth of the accusation. On the face of it, if accusations follow breaches of the social norms, the fear of an accusation might be expected to operate as a sanction against the breach of these norms. Obviously it is important to establish whether, in fact, the fear of an accusation is a sanction against anti-social behaviour. Many anthropologists assume that it must be such a sanction. While, however, it is usually easy enough to decide why people depart from the social norms of the community in which they live, it is less easy to establish the reasons why people conform to those norms, although it is easy enough to appreciate that a group of persons can hardly live together as a group unless they do conform to certain standards of conduct. A large part is notoriously played by informal sanctions such as public opinion, reciprocity and so forth. Of course formal sanctions are, on occasion, necessary. In our own society the thief no doubt ordinarily appreciates the anti-social effect of his conduct but the financial rewards of his crime are such as to render this sort of conduct attractive notwithstanding this. It is, for this reason, necessary to impose an institutionalized sanction in the form of criminal punishment. A formal sanction such as this is no less a sanction because the chances of punishment for any particular offence are small as they are, in our own society, in the case of certain driving offences. It is, therefore, not fatal to the theory that wizardry accusations serve as a social sanction, that an accusation by no means necessarily, or even usually, follows certain sorts of anti-social conduct. What does, however, create a measure of doubt is that the types of anti-social conduct in respect of which the allegation of wizardry is supposed to serve as a social sanction are, among the Shona, the types of conduct which Shona society has not singled out as being actionable wrongs. It is this very class of conduct which rural communities throughout the world control effectively whether or not they believe in wizardry. When I have discussed political or other matters with a Shona it is usually clear that public opinion or, as he would express it 'what the people say or think' is a matter which plays a considerable part, and often a conscious part, in the formation of his own views and attitudes. It is abundantly clear that, whether or not the fear of a wizardry allegation is, among the Shona, a sanction against social conduct, it is possible to explain the high degree of social conformity which exists among the Shona without invoking wizardry beliefs. Sorcery however is a sanction which can be of importance, particularly in the enforcement of a contract or in quasi-contractual relationships. If an employee, for example, finds a replacement while away on holiday, fear of sorcery may ensure that he regains his post on return.

Manipulating Public Opinion

While there may be a measure of doubt as to whether wizardry beliefs are an effective social sanction there can be no doubt that such beliefs can be used as a means of manipulating public opinion in much the same manner as allegations of heresy in medieval Europe or Communism in modern America and Southern Africa were, and are, used. Malice can be expressed as an allegation of wizardry and will find credence if the person against whom hostility is expressed is unpopular, particularly if he has also acted in an unusual manner. It is thus easy to marshal public opinion against the social non-conformist. The person manipulating public opinion in this manner need not do so consciously. If one person dislikes another he is likely to attribute to him evil ways. After all, everyone knows himself to be a reasonable person and he is hardly likely to dislike someone unless he merits this dislike! If the person has evil ways, one tends to define these in terms of one's social stereotype of an evil person, for most of us do our thinking in stereotypes. If one is a Shona, the stereotype is that of a wizard. When the suspect's behaviour is examined, it is found that he has acted suspiciously in disregarding social norms, and who of us always does everything he should do? This confirms one's views and, that being so, it is one's plain duty to tell one's friends of the danger in their midst. Whether or not one's friends will believe what they are told will depend in part on whether other people want to believe the accusation and whether reasonable grounds for suspicion exist. It is obviously easier to turn public opinion against an unpopular than a popular person. If the accusation is believed the accuser has successfully marshalled public opinion against the object of his dislike which is what he, consciously or unconsciously, set out to do. A person is most likely to dislike persons who are sexually, economically or politically in competition with him and the accusation of wizardry affords a technique for marshalling public opinion against the rival in what is, essentially, a private quarrel. It is suggested that beliefs in wizardry are more important as a means of social manipulation than as a sanction against anti-social conduct. An allegation of wizardry by a diviner is, however, not necessarily such an attempt at social manipulation but – in common with other accusations of wizardry – I see it as an attempt to associate the community as a whole with an event. There can be no doubt that the effect of an allegation of wizardry by a diviner is to make the divination the concern of the community as a whole. If this is the effect, it is probable that this is also the end desired. In the case of a professional diviner, the motive for the allegation may, no doubt, be primarily to enhance his prestige. An allegation of wizardry is, therefore, an appeal to the moral feelings of the community in an attempt to involve the community emotionally in a certain state of affairs. The reasons for making the appeal depend on the person making it and the events of the moment.

Cathartic Effect?

It is frequently suggested that wizardry allegations have a 'cathartic effect' in resolving the social tensions of a community. A moment's thought will convince one that this cannot be entirely true. A mere accusation of wizardry can do nothing except worsen social relationships. Immediately, of course, it will worsen relationships between the accuser and the accused. If some believe the accusation and some do not, then the community is likely to be divided into opposing groups, normally no doubt, into groups reflecting a pre-existing segmentation or potential segmentation in the community. It is only 'proof' of an accusation – and, what is more, 'proof' of a nature which will convince everyone in the community or in a section of it – which can serve to resolve social tensions whether by the finding of a scapegoat, by the crystallization of the various interest groups or the exculpation of the suspect from all guilt. It is, therefore, vitally important to distinguish between the accusation of wizardry and the 'proof' of wizardry. Here, there can be no doubt that, in the past, the most convincing 'proof' of wizardry was, in the case of the Shona, the poison ordeal. Shona attitudes were very similar to those of a number of other African peoples. Douglas (in Middleton and Winter, 1963, p. 123) has a suggestion of some interest about the poison ordeal amongst groups in Central Africa north of the Zambesi and, in particular, about the Lele of the Kasai. She states that, in the past, the poison ordeal was the only sure way of indicating a sorcerer. If suspicion fell upon a young man he could move away from his village but the position was not the same with an old man who found it less easy to move and whose village became a closed community. If his quarrel built up cumulatively he could easily 'acquire the reputation of a fully committed sorcerer, responsible for every death in the village'. An ordinary oracle could not clear the name of such a person but the poison oracle could. In the absence of such an oracle he faces social extinction and, probably, social exile. In addition, if his name was not cleared his clansmen were faced with the payment of blood compensation. The ordeal provided a solution to the problem. If the person concerned survived the ordeal he could demand compensation and make a new start. If he did not survive and died, his kin and supporters had no option but to pay compensation and, when this was done, there could again be a new start. With the prohibition of the ordeal by the Colonial Administration there remained no way of resolving social tensions by recourse to the ordeal and no one could be certain who was, and who was not, a sorcerer. The situation became intolerable. A way out of the problem was found in the various anti-sorcery cults which spread through Lele country at various intervals from 1910 onwards. By initiation into the cult, of which the *Kabenga-Benga* is the most recent, a person was cleansed of sorcery. Should a person, once initiated, practise sorcery again it was believed he would die. The cults, therefore, enabled a person to be cleansed of suspicion and to re-integrate himself into the community and also removed the tensions and suspicions which were making community life increasingly intolerable. Inevitably these cults collapse in the end as the theory that only sorcerers who have been initiated die becomes inadequate to account for the deaths of, for example, small children. Each cult becomes, in turn, discredited.

Divinatory Role of Pentecostal Churches

Among the Shona, diviners have never been supposed to be infallible, although they may have considerable reputations. The only way a person could finally clear himself of suspicion of wizardry was by means of the poison ordeal. I have already shown how women, in areas where the ordeal still survived may, of their own volition, seek the ordeal as a means of freeing themselves from an intolerable situation. Now that the ordeal is prohibited, recourse to it is, in most parts of the country, impossible. The Shona solution to the problem has not been, however, the development of cults on the lines of the *Kabenga-Benga* cult or of those described by Marwick (1950, p. 2) or Richards (1935, pp. 448–61) although the *muchapi* movement, when it first spread to Rhodesia before the last war, was probably very similar. *Muchapi* is still known and persons still administer it; but the movement has long ago spent its force. Instead, the role of the anti-sorcery movements among the Lele is, among the Shona, largely taken by the Pentecostal Churches. I have previously described the manner in which these churches cleanse initiates of wizardry and divine wizardry. Some churches have even developed new forms of the ordeal; here the manner in which the churches have tried to make good the vacuum occasioned by the prohibition of the poison ordeal is particularly evident. If one accepts, as a believer must, that a Pentecostal prophet is speaking with the voice of God, his pronouncements are clearly infallible, unlike those of a doctor diviner. A prophet accepts no money for his services – at any rate directly – and that he has no obvious reason to tell lies is an added reason for credence. The prophet in his bright robes, with a mitre on his head and a crozier in his hand, is a much more impressive figure than the ordinary Shona diviner and his psychological impact on his congregation correspondingly greater. The Pentecostal Churches do not, of course, afford an entirely satisfactory alternative to the poison ordeal because many of them are comparatively small and not everyone belongs to them. Even if the church is large, the congregations are often widely scattered and their followers are seldom dominant in any particular community. Because of this, and because they cannot convince everyone of their power, the churches are probably less effective than the *Kabenga-Benga* cult or the poison ordeal in resolving social tensions. On the other hand, if a person becomes disillusioned with the church he can always transfer his allegiance to another. One does not, therefore, in Mashonaland get the widespread cycles of belief and disbelief which occur among the Lele, although there is undoubtedly a pattern of growth and decay among the individual Pentecostal Churches. From the point of view of the person suspected of wizardry the joining of a Pentecostal Church may not free him of suspicion as far as non-believers are concerned; but at least he is joining a group with whom normal social relationships can be established.

It should be stressed that the Pentecostal Churches are more than an anti-wizardry cult, for they manifestly have other social roles as well. Of these, perhaps the most important is their role in helping the Shona to adapt to the modern world and to provide an acceptable *tertium quid* between the beliefs of the past, and the beliefs of the various European-sponsored Christian Missions with their discipline, prohibition of polygamy and their European background. The Pentecostal Churches have often an advantage over the Mission Churches, merely because they are African.

The Shona have developed a reasonably coherent cosmology and wizardry beliefs are in accord with their general religious beliefs. The religious beliefs do not, however, appear to be essential for the existence or survival of wizardry beliefs. If the religious framework of Shona wizardry beliefs were an essential part of those beliefs one would expect wizardry beliefs in societies with religious beliefs differing from those of the Shona to take a very different form. This is not the case. Again, if the religious aspect of Shona wizardry beliefs were an essential part of these beliefs they would be abandoned on the acceptance of Christianity. This is not so – the various spirits which the Shona believe are associated with wizardry are simply transformed into Biblical devils. It is because wizardry, although explained in terms of Shona religious beliefs, is not dependent for survival upon those beliefs that it shows such remarkable resilience to social change. As long as children and young people continue to die it is unlikely that belief in wizardry will be abandoned. The main importance of Shona religious ideas today (as far as we are concerned with them in this book), at least in the case of persons who no longer find these beliefs adequate for their needs, is that – being essentially belief in various forms of spirit possession – they prepare a person seeking fresh religious experience for the reception of beliefs of Pentecostal type. Traditional Shona beliefs also ensure that, where a church of essentially non-Pentecostal type is joined, it will tend, if controlled to any extent by the Shona, to conform increasingly to the Pentecostal pattern. The life of most of the Shona is today rather drab and in the circumstances, and even without the background of traditional beliefs, the colour and excitement of ceremonies of Pentecostal character would undoubtedly prove attractive.

Witchcraft and the Moral Community

An element which Shona witchcraft beliefs share with the beliefs of many other societies is the ascribing to a witch of perverted conduct or conduct which is an inversion of that approved of by society. An example of perverted conduct is the Shona witch's predilection for human meat; a food strongly disliked by ordinary men. It has been suggested by Winter (Middleton and Winter, 1963, p. 292) when discussing a similar situation among the Ambo that one of the reasons why it is believed that a witch can only harm persons within the village or neighbourhood is to be found in the fact that a witch's conduct is believed to be an inversion of socially acceptable conduct. The local community is a moral community where persons must conduct themselves in their relations with one another in an acceptable way and in accordance with the concepts of the society in regard to good neighbourliness. It is, therefore, unnatural for a person living in the community to seek to harm it. On the other hand, communities living outside the neighbourhood are, among the Ambo, essentially hostile and, therefore, there is nothing unnatural about an attempt to harm a member of these groups. No question of inverted conduct and no question of witchcraft arises.

However probable this theory may seem among the Ambo it gives rise to difficulties if one attempts to apply it to the Shona. In the past the moral community of the Shona embraced at least the tribe and it is probably wider now. One was expected to conduct oneself in a proper way with other tribesmen even if they were not members of the village. In fact, members of the same tribe usually regarded one another as kinsmen even if blood relationship could not be established. Witchcraft allegations, however, as among the Ambo, are confined to the village or neighbourhood. While I am not suggesting that Winter's theory is wrong, for society is complex and there is often no single cause for any observed pattern of conduct, I think that, at least among the Shona, the reason for the confining of witchcraft allegations to a comparatively small territorial area is best explained – not in terms of any 'moral' community – but in the fact commented upon by many social anthropologists that accusations are most likely in situations of intimate personal contact where the status of the persons concerned is more or less equal. In rural areas one only normally comes into intimate personal contact of this nature with persons living in the same locality. Wizardry allegations also occur in factories and rural schools which cannot be regarded as 'moral communities' save in a rather extended sense of the term. The concept of the 'moral community' does not, in any event, explain why accusations are made against certain members of the community and not against others. It is surely best to apply Occam's razor and find the explanation for both the pattern of accusations within the community and the limitation of accusations to a village or neighbourhood in inter-personal contact and rivalry rather than to find a different reason for each. Even if Winter's theory is unsatisfactory the concept of the moral community is not without relevance as far as the study of Shona wizardry allegations is concerned. There is, among the Shona, nothing improper in the use of sorcery or magic to destroy a member of a hostile group. The person who uses such means against an enemy is not a wizard, as would be the case if he turned his supernatural weapons against one of his own community. Indeed, the ability to fortify one's own group magically against the machinations of an enemy group is obviously a socially desirable ability. In the past, no army would have set out to attack another group without being adequately fortified by means of magic.

Shona wizardry beliefs throw light upon what the Shona conceive the 'moral community' to be; but I am a little doubtful if the concept of the 'moral community' has any great effect as far as the pattern of wizardry allegations are concerned.

There is no need to say much here about the distinction the Shona make – but do not well express – between witchcraft and sorcery. I believe, however, that I have shown that this distinction is vital for the understanding of the nature of witchcraft allegations. The importance of the distinction arises from the fact that witchcraft allegations are made against women and sorcery allegations, which are less serious, are made against men. In a patrilineal society with virilocal marriage this inevitably means that witchcraft allegations are, in the main, made against the wives and mothers of lineage members and that sorcery allegations are made against lineage members. In other words, the solidarity of the lineage is maintained at the expense of non-lineage members. It is essential for my argument in this respect to show that witchcraft allegations against women are socially of greater consequence and are more serious from the point of view of the person accused of witchcraft than is the case where a sorcery allegation is made against a man. The figures given previously show, with very little doubt, that allegations resulting in serious consequences to the person accused are more often made against a woman than a man. This, of course, does not establish my case as one might, for example, argue that this does not mean that allegations made against a woman are, in themselves, more serious that those made against a man; all that is shown is that women are in a position of inferiority in Shona society and are thus less capable of coping with the situation which arises. There may be something in this argument; but in the few court records where a witchcraft allegation, as opposed to a sorcery allegation was made against a man, the consequences to that man appear to have been as serious as is frequently the case in allegations made against women. In any event, even if an able-bodied Shona man can avoid the consequences of a believed allegation of witchcraft or sorcery by moving elsewhere, an old man, unless he is a chief or headman, is hardly in a better position to cope with his environment than a woman. In the result, therefore, the evidence in my opinion supports the view that the consequences of an allegation against a woman are more serious that against a man because the allegation against a woman is a more serious allegation, rather than the view that the differing consequences are merely the direct consequence of a difference in social status.

Accusations and Social Tension

I have referred on a number of occasions to allegations of wizardry which I have stated have arisen from or been generated by social conflicts of various sorts. The question now arises as to whether this is an altogether accurate statement of the origin of the accusation of wizardry and also whether it is entirely correct to regard an accusation of wizardry as an expression of social conflict. Where co-wives are competing for the favours of their husband and accuse one another of wizardry, it is very difficult not to regard the accusation as being a reflection of social conflict – although it may be other things as well. In such circumstances it would appear to be not incorrect to state that the allegation arises from the conflict. Where, however, the diviner is consulted about the death of a child and divines the cause of the death to be wizardry, naming a particular person to be a wizard, it is clear that the allegation does not arise directly from any social conflict. The diviner may, of course, be acquainted with, or may discover, the social conflicts in the community from which his consultants come and may make use of this knowledge when indicating a wizard; but it is clearly not correct to regard the accusation as arising from any particular social conflict. In both the case of the accusation by a co-wife and the accusation by a diviner the accusation will reflect social conflict in the community; but in the first case there is a direct causal link between the conflict and the accusation. In the second there is not. The diviner need not have divined the presence of wizardry at all and, if wizardry were divined, need not have named the person he did name as a wizard. A social conflict may have guided, but it did not determine, the diviner's choice. Although the two types of accusation have a different origin they both, as I suggested previously, are in essence an appeal to the community with the intention of involving the community as a whole emotionally in some particular occurrence.

Too much emphasis on the allegation of wizardry as being the reflection of social tension leads one into the error of supposing that an allegation is a mere symptom of social malaise and is not, in itself, a dynamic force in the community. There are, indeed, many social anthropologists who would appear to overlook the dynamic importance of wizardry allegations. An allegation of wizardry may originally reflect a state of enmity between two persons but, once made, a chain of events may be set in motion which can lead rapidly to the most unforeseen and often tragic consequences. There is no reason to suppose that any other form of expression of hostility would ordinarily result in the tragedies occasioned by an allegation of wizardry, nor is it easy to think, in the context of Shona society, of any other type of accusation which can so readily embitter social relations and increase social tension. One can no more regard wizardry allegations as a mere expression of social conflict than the all too common beer drink stabbings among the Shona. The accusation, as in the case of the stabbing, reflects social conflict; but the deed itself may entirely alter the nature of the conflict and, in any event, adds to it an entirely new dimension.

If the allegation of wizardry is primarily a device for involving the community as a whole in some particular happening then the reason why some sorts of social conflict result in a wizardry allegation is – at least in part – explained. One would really only expect allegations to occur in situations where the marshalling of public opinion against an offender serves a useful purpose. If, for example, one's daughter is seduced, a Shona man's primary interest is in obtaining recompense. The marshalling of public opinion against the offender, particularly if he is a member of another community (for public opinion is most effective within the community) does not serve any very real purpose, as the only reasonable way to recover damages, if the seducer will not willingly pay them, is action in the chief's court. What is primarily required is not emotion, but a good case. Of course, if legal proceedings become frustrated, as we have seen, an appeal to public opinion made in the idiom of wizardry is not unlikely. I would also suggest one reason why a commoner would not normally make an allegation of wizardry against a chief, and that is that the marshalling of public opinion against a chief would not only serve no useful purpose, but would be distinctly dangerous.

If any reason is to be sought for the limitation of wizardry allegations to a village or neighbourhood other than that allegations result from intense inter-personal relationships, it lies in the nature of the wizardry allegation as a device for controlling public opinion. If a person is a stranger from outside one's community the marshalling of public opinion in one's own community against the man serves little purpose and, indeed, is probably unnecessary. The views of the members of one's own community about the conduct of the stranger will probably coincide with one's own.

The use of the allegation of wizardry as a device for directing public opinion against a person is particularly obvious in a struggle for political power within a community in which each contestant tries to involve as many persons as possible in the dispute and get them on his side. The weapon is, of course, a two-edged weapon and is as useful in securing the retention of power in the face of a challenge as in securing the advantage of a person seeking to challenge established power. The use by the Ndebele kings of wizardry allegations to remove those who were politically dangerous is notorious. It would seem that this device was not entirely unknown in the Shona chieftaincies also.

References

MARWICK, M. G. (1950), 'Another modern anti-witchcraft movement in East Central Africa', *Africa*, vol. 20, no. 2.

MIDDLETON, J., and WINTER, E. H. (eds.) (1963), *Witchcraft and Sorcery in East Africa*, Routledge & Kegal Paul.

RICHARDS, A. I. (1935), 'A modern movement of witch-finders', *Africa*, vol. 8, no. 4.

Part Four
Witch-Beliefs Throw Light on Other Problems

Anthropologists have long been preoccupied with the problem why beliefs in magic, witchcraft and sorcery, though palpably false, nevertheless continue to have influence. One of the most systematic resolutions of this problem is to be found in Evans-Pritchard's description of the protective devices, or secondary elaborations, by means of which failures can be explained away and successes emphatically recorded (Evans-Pritchard, 1937, p. 330). The steps non-literate peoples take to protect their beliefs from falsification give rise to closed circular systems of thought which, though starting from different premises, are no less logical than ours. Such systems are of considerable relevance to the discussion of scientific methodology (see the Readings from Gluckman (p. 321) and Polanyi (p. 332). Horton's paper (p. 342), though not dealing solely with the logic of witchcraft, is important for the clarification it brings to the distinction between the 'closed' and the 'open' predicaments first systematically discussed by Popper over twenty years ago (Popper, 1966, vol. 1, ch. 10). On a more empirical plane, Cardozo's paper (p. 369) on McCarthyism shows the gains that accrue from applying to the analysis of a modern political movement the generalizations emerging from the study of witch-crazes.

References
EVANS-PRITCHARD, E. E. (1937), *Witchcraft, Oracles and Magic among the Azande*, Clarendon Press.
POPPER, K. R. (1966), *The Open Society and its Enemies*, 5th edn, Routledge & Kegan Paul.

27 Max Gluckman

The Logic of African Science and Witchcraft

Excerpts from Max Gluckman, 'The logic of African science and witchcraft: an appreciation of Evans-Pritchard's *Witchcraft, Oracles and Magic among the Azande* of the Sudan', *Human Problems in British Central Africa*, vol. 1, 1944, pp. 61–71.

I have selected this book for the first appreciation in our journal, because it is one of the most notable contributions to the scientific understanding of African problems. Though the researches on which it is based were made in the Sudan, the general argument applies to all African tribes who believe in witchcraft, oracles or divination, and magic. The author describes clearly the functioning of witchcraft and magic in a book that is fascinating to the specialist, and is also written so simply and vividly that every layman who begins it will not be able to leave it till he has followed the argument to its close. For an understanding of the behaviour of Africans, and, as will be seen, of ourselves where we do not act on scientifically valid grounds, it is a work which everyone should read. Since the book explains to us not only customs of the Sudan Azande, but also the basis of such wide fields of human behaviour, I shall here set out the general lessons which it teaches, and then touch on the differences between the Azande and our own peoples. However, as Evans-Pritchard does not consider in detail aspects of Zande behaviour other than what he calls the mystical, I begin by referring to these.

The title of this review poses the question: is there a fundamental difference between African and European logic, and if so, is it due to physical differences, or to psychological ones related to the different social conditions in which Africans and Europeans live? Without entering into the arguments for and against, I may say that the consensus of scientific opinion is that there is no proof of any great difference between the brains of various races. If there are any differences, they are altogether insufficient to account for the great differences between cultures and modes

321

of thought, and above all, they cannot account for the rapid spurts in cultural development which some countries achieved in very short time. That is, if we have to explain London and an African village, we cannot do so by bodily differences between Londoners and Africans: we must investigate their history and struggles, especially their contacts with other peoples, and other social factors. For if an African were brought up from birth by a Londoner, he would be a Londoner. We know that shipwrecked European children were distinguishable from their African foster-people only by their colour.

Therefore, if the mind of the African differs from the European's, it is because he has grown up in a different society, where from birth his behaviour and ideas are moulded by those of his parents and fellows. If he inherits a 'mind', he inherits it socially, and not physically. [. . .]

In technological and administrative matters [. . .] [the African] reasons much as we do, though within much narrower ranges of facts, and of course without testing his theories by scientific experiment. This ability to reason clearly also appears where he works with beliefs and ideas that are different from ours, notably those about witchcraft and magic, a system of ideas which our civilization abandoned some 150 years ago. Many Europeans, particularly peasants, still hold them. That these beliefs subsisted till so recently in educated Europe and America, shows that they are not innate in Africans, but are part of their culture, as they were of ours. Anyone who follows Evans-Pritchard's exposition of the intellectual aspect of Zande magic and witchcraft will be fascinated by their logical skill. [. . .]

The fundamental point is that the African is born into a society which believes in witchcraft and therefore the very texture of his thinking, from childhood on, is woven of magical and mystical ideas. More important still, since magic and witchcraft are lived, far more than they are reasoned about, his daily actions are conditioned by these beliefs, till at every turn he is confronted by the threat of witchcraft and meets it with divination and magic. The weight of tradition, the actions and behaviour of his elders, the support which chiefs give to the system, all impress on the African the truth of the system, and since he cannot measure it against any other system, he is continually caught in the web of its making. Evans-Pritchard stresses too, that the African does not go about his business in constant terror of witchcraft nor does he approach it with an awesome fear of the supernatural; when he finds it is working against him he is angry against the witch for playing a dirty trick on him.

These points emerge from a brief analysis of the essential characteristics of the system of witchcraft-divination-magic beliefs and behaviour. The Azande, like many other Central African tribes, believe witchcraft to be a physical condition of the intestines (as found in a corpse, it is probably a passing state of digestion), which enables the soul of the witch to go out at night and harm his fellows. There is also sorcery (which is more commonly believed in in Southern Africa) which is the use of magical substances for anti-social purposes. A man may have witchcraft in his body, and yet not use it: his witchcraft may be 'cool'. Africans are not interested in witchcraft as such, but in the particular witch who is bewitching them at a certain moment. They do not get the idea that they are being bewitched and are therefore going to suffer some misfortune, such as to fall ill and die. What happens is that they suffer misfortune and after it has occured blame it on a witch: and if it is not a misfortune past and done with, they find out who the witch is and get him to withdraw his evil influence or tackle it with magic. Therefore Evans-Pritchard says he knows of no Zande who would die in terror of witchcraft, and this is confirmed by other trained observers.

The problem which the African answers with his belief in witchcraft is this: why misfortune to me? He knows that there are diseases which make people ill; he knows that hippos upset dugouts and drown people. But he asks himself: 'why should I be ill and not other people?' The man whose son has drowned when a hippo upset his dugout, in effect says, 'My son frequently travelled by dugout on the river where there are always hippo, why on this one occasion should the hippo have attacked and drowned him?' This he answers: 'because we were bewitched'. He knows full well that his son was crossing the river to visit his mother's family, and that the hippo, irritable because it had a calf, was migrating upstream when it met the dugout. We say that it was providence or ill-luck which brought the hippo and the son together so that the son died, as we do when a man crossing the road from one shop to another is run over by a car; when the African says it is witchcraft that caused these deaths, he is explaining a coincidence which science leaves unexplained, except as the intersection of two series of events. The African is fully aware that his son drowned because his lungs filled with water: but he argues that it was a witch, or a sorcerer by his medicines, who brought together the paths of dugout and an angry mother hippo to kill the son. The Azande explain it by a hunting simile. The first man who hits a buck shares the meat with the man who puts the second spear in it. 'Hence if a man is killed by an elephant Azande say that the elephant is the first spear (existing in its own right) and witchcraft is the second spear and that together they killed the man. If a man spears another in war the slayer is the first spear and witchcraft is the second spear and together they killed him.' [...]

Immediately they suffer misfortune Africans think that a witch has been working against them. Every kind of accident or of ill may be ascribed to witchcraft. But this does not mean that the African does not recognise lack of skill and moral lapses. For an unskilled potter to say that his pots broke in firing because he was bewitched, would not convince his fellows if he had left pebbles in the clay; but the skilled potter who had followed all the rules of his craft would be supported in saying this. It would not be a sound defence for a criminal to plead that he did wrong because he was bewitched to do so, for it is not believed that witchcraft makes a man lie, steal, betray his chief, or commit adultery.

This is how witchcraft works as a theory of causes. The African goes further. Witchcraft does not harm people haphazardly, for the witch wants to hurt people he hates, has quarrelled with, of whom he is envious. So that when a man falls ill, or his crops fail (for on good soil crops should not fail), he says that someone who envied him his many children, the favour of his chief, or his good employment by Europeans and his fine clothes, therefore hated him and has used medicines or evil power to do him ill. Witchcraft is thus a moral theory for witches are bad people, hating, grudging, envious, spiteful. A witch does not just attack his fellows, he attacks those whom he has reason to hate. There is a clear distinction between the man who has witchcraft in him but is a good man and does not use it against his fellows, and the man who wants to do others harm but has not the power of witchcraft or cannot get the evil medicines of sorcery, and the witch himself, the man who has the power to bewitch and uses that power. Since people are only interested in whether their fellows are witches when they suffer misfortunes, they seek among their enemies for those who may have this power. They think of someone with whom they have quarrelled, and suspect him of the evil deed. We find thus that witchcraft as a theory of causes of misfortunes is related to personal relations between the sufferer and his fellows, and to a theory of moral judgments as to what is good and bad.

When a man suffers a misfortune which he cannot remedy, such as the breaking of his pots in firing, he may just accept it, as witchcraft, just as we would say, 'Bad luck'. But when witchcraft is making him ill and may cause him to die, when it is blighting his crop, or when by divination he finds that it is threatening him in the future, he does not sit down hopelessly under it. He has to scotch its evil working. This he does by using medicines against it, which will stop the witchcraft and possibly kill the witch, or by calling in a diviner to find out who is the witch so that he can be put out of business, or persuaded to remove his witchcraft. The diviner does not seek for the witch haphazardly. Most methods of divination allow one of two possible answers, yes or no, to a stated question. For example, the Azande give a 'poison' (of course they do not know it is a poison) with strychnine properties to fowls which die or do not die to say 'yes' or 'no' to a question of the form: is A the witch who is harming me? Thus a man, seeking for the witch among the people he thinks wish him ill, must eventually get the answer 'yes' to one of them. This particular oracle is out of human control; others, including witchdoctors, are less trusted by the Azande as being subject to human manipulation. But even the Zande witchdoctor, though he works on his knowledge of local gossip, does not often deliberately cheat. He may seek, or be asked by his client to seek, for the witch among say four names: these are the names of enemies of the client, and though the witchdoctor may choose from these, or others whom he knows wish his client ill, by unconscious selection, there is a moment when by bodily

325

sensation he knows that the medicines, which give him his divining power, say: it is A who is the witch, and not B. Or the diviner will indicate someone generally without specifying a name – e.g. 'one of your wives', 'an old woman' – and the client will fix on some definite person, among his neighbours, who is thus described and whom therefore he thinks has reason to wish him ill. Charges of witchcraft thus reflect personal relations and quarrels. Often a man accuses not someone who hates him, or who is envious of him, but someone whom he hates or envies. The African knows this, and may stress it when he is not involved in the case or when he is the accused, but he forgets it when he is making the accusation. In Zululand a man accused his brother of having bewitched him because he was jealous of him. An old diviner, aware of psychological projection, told me: 'Of course, it is obvious that it is the complainant who hates his brother, though he thinks it is his brother who hates him'. But that diviner believed firmly in his own power to detect witchcraft.

Evans-Pritchard stresses that the Azande cannot thus set out the intellectual basis of their theory; this is what he has worked out from an observation of hundreds of situations involving charges of witchcraft, discussions about it, and so on. [...]

Since personal relations and spites determine who shall be accused of bewitching a man, we find that in different societies different types of people accuse each other of witchcraft. As witchcraft is hereditary, Zande princes who are all related, do not accuse each other of witchcraft, nor do other kinsmen, though an accuser of his brother could escape the imputed taint on himself by saying that his brother is a bastard. In all African societies courtiers suspect each other, and the jealousy of polygynous households breaks out thus. While the Azande do not accuse kinsmen, the Lozi almost always do, for reasons I have given in my *Economy of the Central Barotse Plain*. Among the southeastern Bantu, for determinable reasons, it is the daughter-in-law who is often accused. If a sociologist can find where charges of witchcraft in a particular society fall, he can almost reconstruct the social relationships of the society.

The theory of witchcraft is thus seen to be reasonable and logical, even if it is not true. Since it explains the intersection of two chains of events by the enmity of people with evil power, it works in fields our modern science leaves unexplained. Thus the African cannot see that the system is untrue and moreover he has to reason with the system as we do with our scientific beliefs. Wherever the system might conflict with reality its beliefs are vague, and deal with transcendant non-observable facts: the witch works at night with his soul, the soul of the poison oracle (which is not personified, but has consciousness) finds out the witchcraft. The theory is a complete whole, in which every part buttresses every other part. Illness proves that a witch is at work, he is discovered by divination, he is persuaded to withdraw his witchcraft. Even though he may feel himself that he is not the real witch, he will at least show that he intends no harm to the sick man. Or he is attacked with magic. It is difficult for the African to find a flaw in the system. Scepticism exists, and is not socially repressed, and Evans-Pritchard writes that the

absence of formal and coercive doctrine permits Azande to state that many, even most, witch-doctors, are frauds. No opposition being offered to such statements, they leave the main belief in the prophetic and therapeutic powers of witch-doctors unimpaired. Indeed, scepticism is included in the pattern of belief in witchdoctors. Faith and scepticism are alike traditional. Scepticism explains failures of witch-doctors, and being directed towards particular witchdoctors even tends to support faith in others.

Even the witch-doctor who works by sleight of hand believes that there are doctors who have the magic to make this unnecessary.

In this web of belief every strand depends upon every other strand, and a Zande cannot get out of its meshes because this is the only world he knows. The web is not an external structure in which he is enclosed. It is the texture of his thought and he cannot think that his thought is wrong. Nevertheless, his beliefs are not absolutely set but are variable and fluctuating to allow for different situations and to permit empirical observation and even doubts.

Within this web, the African may reason as logically as we do within the web of scientific thought. If your house, which you have protected with lightning-conductors, is nevertheless struck by lightning you say that the workman was bad, the wires poor, or there was a break in the wiring. If the African has had his village protected with medicines against storms and it is struck by lightning, he says the magician was bad, his medicines poor, or a taboo was broken. [. . .]

Evans-Pritchard's analysis of witchcraft illuminates the working of human thought in other spheres. For instance, he makes this comparison. The Azande as we have seen exclude witchcraft as a cause of moral lapses.

As in our own society a scientific theory of causation, if not excluded, is deemed irrelevant in questions of moral and legal responsibility, so in Zande society the doctrine of witchcraft, if not excluded, is deemed irrelevant in the same situations. We accept scientific explanations of the causes of diseases, and even of the causes of insanity, but we deny them in crime and sin because here they militate against law and morals which are axiomatic. The Zande accepts a mystical explanation of the causes of misfortune, sickness, and death, but he does not allow this explanation if it conflicts with social exigencies expressed in law and morals.

I make one final point here, in answer to the oft-made statement that witchcraft charges are based on cheating. Evans-Pritchard emphasises that the patient, who wishes to abolish the witchcraft harming him, above all people does not wish to cheat: for what good is it to him if he detects the wrong person as witch? But he does accuse his personal enemies.

When the African, with these beliefs, comes to deal with Europeans, there are many ways in which they affect his behaviour so that it seems incomprehensible to us. For example, he queries: it is true that the White doctors are very good in treating disease, but while they cure the disease they don't treat the witchcraft which caused the disease, and that will continue to do harm. Evans-Pritchard shows that the Zande's oracles are 'his guide and councillor', whom he consults about every enterprise. Evans-Pritchard himself lived thus, and found it as good a way as any other of ordering his affairs. But because of it, Europeans often cannot understand Zande behaviour: why a Zande will suddenly move from his home to shelter in the bush (because of witchcraft), why a homestead will suddenly be moved (because of witchcraft attacking them in that spot), and so on. Frequently his guests suddenly departed without bidding him farewell, and he was angry till he realized that the oracles had told them that witchcraft was threatening them.

I found that when a Zande acted towards me in a manner that we would call rude and untrustworthy his actions were often to be accounted for by obedience to his oracles. Usually I have found Azande courteous and reliable according to English standards, but sometimes their behaviour is unintelligible till their mystical notions are taken into account. Often Azande are tortuous in their dealings with one another, but they do not consider a man blameworthy for being secretive or acting contrary to his declared intentions. On the contrary they praise his prudence for taking account of witchcraft at every step. . . . With the European it is different. We only know that a Zande has said he will do something and has done nothing, or has done something different, and we naturally blame the man for lying and being untrustworthy, for the European does not appreciate that Azande have to take into account mystical forces of which he knows nothing.

Evans-Pritchard gave a feast to which a prince promised to come; he sent to tell that he would not come. Suddenly he arrived. He arranged to stay the night; in the night he disappeared. He had been told that witchcraft threatened him, and it was a great compliment to the sociologist that he attended the feast; his wayward actions were to deceive the witches. I myself had a favoured informant in my employ who kept replying to my summonses, that he would come; but stayed away until I moved my home. He had been threatened with witchcraft at the one spot, not the other. For notions of place and time in witchcraft thought vary from ours; witchcraft may threaten a man now from the future, so the future is in the present, and has to be avoided by not adopting a line of action which was contemplated, as going on a journey; or a man will decide to build his homestead on a certain spot, by eliminating other spots where witchcraft will threaten him, though he has not yet built on them.

There is a second way in which witchcraft behaviour may affect Africans when we deal with them. Under these beliefs, people who produced good crops while their neighbours' harvests were meagre; who had large healthy families while all around was illness; whose herds and fishing prospered exceedingly; these fortunate people were sometimes believed to make good by magic and witchcraft at the expense of their fellows. We have seen in a quotation above that they believed themselves open to attack from witches. The Zande knows that if he becomes rich the poor will hate him, that if he rises in social position his inferiors will be jealous of his authority, that if he is handsome the less favoured will envy his looks, that if he is talented as a hunter, a singer, a fighter, or a rhetorician, he will earn the malice of those less gifted, and that if he enjoys the regard of his prince and of his neighbours he will be detested for his prestige and popularity.

These are the motives that lead to witchcraft. Such beliefs were only possible in a society with nowhere to sell surplus goods, no profit motives, without storable goods, with no luxuries so that there was no heavy pressure on any member to produce more than he required for his own needs. Africans have come from a society with these beliefs into our economic system where they are expected to work long and hard, trying to outdo their fellows, and perhaps the beliefs deter them in this struggle and affect their efficiency. I know Africans who blame their misfortunes on witches envious of their higher wages, or their fine would-be European-style houses. It is possible that fear of witchcraft prevents Africans developing what skill and capacity they have, in their work for Europeans, though this fear would be unimportant in comparison with other factors preventing their development, such as disease and social barriers.

I have given part of the argument of Evans-Pritchard's book to set out the main framework of magic-witchcraft thought. I hope I have shown how skilfully the argument is set out. In my short review I am unable to do more than indicate its unlimited riches of delight, which make reading and re-reading it an unfailing fascination. Everyone who is interested in human problems in this region should own the book. But I must warn the layman that in applying its conclusions to our own tribes, he must do so with care. The central argument applies absolutely, but there are certain important differences. Among the Azande, witchcraft was not a crime but a delict, for which compensation was paid only on a death. In many Southern African tribes witchcraft is a crime, and the state punished witches by killing them. Also in Southern Africa sorcery (the deliberate use of evil magic) was believed to be at work, rather than witchcraft (causing ill by inherent evil power plus malice). This produces important changes in the whole system, which can be traced, e.g. in Hunter's *Reaction to Conquest* on the Mpondo.

In quoting Evans-Pritchard to show how beliefs in witchcraft affect Africans' behaviour and thought, I have emphasized that often their minds work in the same logical patterns as ours do, though the material with which they think is different, so that it is clear that if they were given the same education and cultural background as we have, they would think with the same materials and in the same way as we do.

28 Michael Polanyi

The Stability of Scientific Theories against Experience

Excerpts from Michael Polanyi, *Personal Knowledge*, University of Chicago Press, 1958, pp. 286–94.

Implicit Beliefs

The limitations of doubting as a principle can be elaborated [...] by extending our inquiry to the beliefs held in the form of our conceptual framework, as expressed in our language. Our most deeply ingrained convictions are determined by the idiom in which we interpret our experience and in terms of which we erect our articulate systems (Polanyi, 1958, p. 80). Our formally declared beliefs can be held to be true in the last resort only because of our logically anterior acceptance of a particular set of terms, from which all our references to reality are constructed.

The fact that primitive people hold distinctive systems of beliefs inherent in their conceptual framework and reflected in their language was first stated with emphasis by Lévy-Brühl earlier in this century. The more recent work of Evans-Pritchard on the beliefs of Azande has borne out and has given further precision to this view (Evans-Pritchard, 1937). The author is struck by the intellectual force shown by the primitive African in upholding his beliefs against evidence which to the European seems flagrantly to refute them. An instance in point is the Zande belief in the powers of the poison-oracle. The oracle answers questions through the effects on a fowl of a poisonous substance called *benge*. The oracle-poison is extracted from a creeper gathered in a traditional manner, which is supposed to become effective only after it has been addressed in the words of an appropriate ritual. Azande – we are told – have no formal and coercive doctrine to enforce belief in witch-doctors and their practice of the poison-oracle, but their belief in these is the more firmly held for being embedded in an idiom which interprets all relevant facts in terms of witchcraft and oracular powers. Evans-Pritchard gives various examples of this peculiar tenacity of their implicit belief.

Suppose that the oracle in answer to a particular question says 'Yes', and immediately afterwards says 'No' to the same question. In our eyes this would tend to discredit the oracle altogether, but Zande culture provides a number of ready explanations for such self-contradictions. Evans-Pritchard lists no less than eight secondary elaborations of their beliefs by which Azande will account for the oracle's failure. They may assume that the wrong variety of poison had been gathered, or a breach of taboo committed, or that the owners of the forest where the poisonous creeper grows had been angered and avenged themselves by spoiling the poison; and so on.

Our author describes further the manner in which Azande resist any suggestion that *benge* may be a natural poison. He often asked Azande, he tells us, what would happen if they were to administer oracle-poison to a fowl without delivering an address, or if they were to administer an extra portion of poison to a fowl which has recovered from the usual doses.

The Zande [he continues] does not know what would happen and is not interested in what would happen; no one has been fool enough to waste good oracle-poison in making such pointless experiments which only a European could imagine. . . . Were a European to make a test which in his view proved Zande opinion wrong they would stand amazed at the credulity of the European. If the fowl died they would simply say that it was not good *benge*. The very fact of the fowl dying proves to them its badness (Evans-Pritchard, 1937, pp. 314–15).

This blindness of Azande to the facts which to us seem decisive is sustained by remarkable ingenuity. 'They reason excellently in the idiom of their beliefs, but they cannot reason outside, or against, their beliefs because they have no other idiom in which to express their thoughts' (Evans-Pritchard, 1937, p. 338).

Our objectivism, which tolerates no open declaration of faith, has forced modern beliefs to take on implicit forms, like those of Azande. And no one will deny that those who have mastered the idioms in which these beliefs are entailed do also reason most ingeniously within these idioms, even while – again like Azande – they unhesitatingly ignore all that the idiom does not cover. I shall quote two passages to illustrate the high stability of two modern interpretative frameworks, based on these principles:

My party education had equipped my mind with such elaborate shock-absorbing buffers and elastic defences that everything seen and heard became automatically transformed to fit a preconceived pattern (Koestler, 1950, p. 68.)

The system of theories which Freud has gradually developed is so consistent that when one is once entrenched in them it is difficult to make observations unbiased by his way of thinking (Horney, 1939, p. 7.)

The first of these statements is by a former Marxist, the second by a former Freudian writer. At the time when they still accepted as valid the conceptual framework of Marx or of Freud – as the case may be – these writers would have regarded the all-embracing interpretative powers of this framework as evidence of its truth; only when losing faith in it did they feel that its powers were excessive and specious. We shall see the same difference reappear in our appraisals of the interpretative power of different conceptual systems, as part of our acceptance or rejection of these systems.

Three Aspects of Stability

The resistance of an idiom of belief against the impact of adverse evidence may be regarded under three headings, each of which is illustrated by the manner in which Azande retain their beliefs in the face of situations which in our view should invalidate them. Analogous cases can be adduced from other systems of beliefs.

The stability of Zande beliefs is due, in the first place, to the fact that objections to them can be met one by one. This power of a system of implicit beliefs to defeat valid objections one by one is due to the circularity of such systems. By this I mean that the convincing power possessed by the interpretation of any particular new topic in terms of such a conceptual framework is based on past applications of the same framework to a great number of other topics not now under consideration, while if any of these other topics were questioned now, their interpretation in its turn would similarly rely for support on the interpretation of all the others. Evans-Pritchard observes this for Zande beliefs in mystical notions. 'The contradiction between experience and one mystical notion is explained by reference to other mystical notions' (Evans-Pritchard, 1937, p. 339).

So long as each doubt is defeated in its turn, its effect is to strengthen the fundamental convictions against which it was raised. 'Let the reader consider (writes Evans-Pritchard) any argument that would utterly demolish all Zande claims for the power of the oracle. If it were translated into Zande modes of thought it would serve to support their entire structure of belief' (Evans-Pritchard, 1937, p. 319). Thus the circularity of a conceptual system tends to reinforce itself by every contact with a fresh topic.

The circularity of the theory of the universe embodied in any particular language is manifested in an elementary fashion by the existence of a dictionary of the language. If you doubt, for example, that a particular English noun, verb, adjective or adverb has any meaning in English, an English dictionary dispels this doubt by a definition using other nouns, verbs, adjectives and adverbs, the meaningfulness of which is not doubted for the moment. Inquiries of this kind will increasingly confirm us in the use of a language.

Remember also what we have found about the axiomatization of mathematics; namely that it merely declares the beliefs implied in the practice of mathematical reasoning. The axiomatized system is therefore circular: our anterior acceptance of mathematics lends authority to its axioms, from which we then deduce in turn all mathematical demonstrations. The division of mathematical formulae, or of the asserted sentences of any deductive system, into axioms and theorems is indeed largely conventional, for we can usually replace some or all of the axioms by theorems and derive from these the previous axioms as theorems. Every assertion of a deductive system can be demonstrated by, or else shown to be implied as axioms of, the others. Therefore, if we doubt each assertion in its turn each is found confirmed by circularity, and the refutation of each consecutive doubt results in strengthening our belief in the system as a whole. [. . .]

A second aspect of stability arises from an automatic expansion of the circle in which an interpretative system operates. It readily supplies elaborations of the system which will cover almost any conceivable eventuality, however embarrassing this may appear at first sight. Scientific theories which possess this self-expanding capacity are sometimes described as epicyclical, in allusion to the epicycles that were used in the Ptolemaic and Copernican theory to represent planetary motions in terms of uniform circular motions. All major interpretative frameworks have an epicyclical structure which supplies a reserve of subsidiary explanations for difficult situations. The epicyclical character of Zande beliefs was shown above by the ready availability of eight different subsidiary assumptions for explaining a point-blank self-contradition in two consecutive answers of an oracle.

The stability of Zande beliefs is manifested, thirdly, in the way it denies to any rival conception the ground in which it might take root. Experiences which support it could be adduced only one by one. But a new conception, e.g. that of natural causation, which would take the place of Zande superstition could be established only by a whole series of relevant instances, and such evidence cannot accumulate in the minds of people if each of them is disregarded in its turn for lack of the concept which would lend significance to it. The behaviour of Azande whom Evans-Pritchard tried to convince that *benge* was a natural poison which owed none of its effectiveness to the incantations customarily accompanying its administration, illustrates the kind of contemptuous indifference with which we normally regard things of which we have no conception. 'We feel neither curiosity nor wonder', writes William James, 'concerning things so far beyond us that we have no concepts to refer them to or standards by which to measure them.' The Fuegians in Darwin's voyage, he recalls, wondered at the small boats, but paid no attention to the big ship lying at anchor in front of them (James, 1890, p. 110). A more recent instance of this occurred when Igor Gouzenko, cypher clerk of the Soviet Embassy in Canada, tried in vain for two days in succession (5 and 6 September 1945) to attract attention to the documents concerning Soviet atomic espionage which he was showing round in Ottawa at the risk of his life.

This third defence mechanism of implicit beliefs may be called the principle of suppressed nucleation. It is complementary to the operations of circularity and self-expansion. While these protect an existing system of beliefs against doubts arising from any adverse piece of evidence, suppressed nucleation prevents the germination of any alternative concepts on the basis of any such evidence.

Circularity, combined with a readily available reserve of epicyclical elaborations and the consequent suppression in the germ of any rival conceptual development, lends a degree of stability to a conceptual framework which we may describe as the measure of its completeness. We may acknowledge the completeness or comprehensiveness of a language and the system of conceptions conveyed by it – as we do in respect to Azande beliefs in witchcraft – without in any way implying that the system is correct.

The Stability of Scientific Beliefs

We do not share the beliefs of Azande in the power of poison-oracles, and we reject a great many of their other beliefs, discarding mystical conceptions and replacing them by naturalistic explanations. But we may yet deny that our rejection of Zande superstitions is the outcome of any general principle of doubt.

For the stability of the naturalistic system which we currently accept instead rests on the same logical structure. Any contradiction between a particular scientific notion and the facts of experience will be explained by other scientific notions; there is a ready reserve of possible scientific hypotheses available to explain any conceivable event. Secured by its circularity and defended further by its epicyclical reserves, science may deny, or at least cast aside as of no scientific interest, whole ranges of experience which to the unscientific mind appear both massive and vital.[1]

The restrictions of the scientific outlook which I summed up as objectivism have been recurrent themes throughout this book. My attempt to break out of this highly stabilized framework and

1. I have described similar stabilities before, when showing that two alternative systems of scientific explanation are separated by a logical gap and thus give rise to passionate controversy in science (Polanyi, 1958, pp. 150–59, 112–13).

to enter avenues of legitimate access to reality from which objectivism debars us will be presently pursued further. At the moment I only wish to give some illustrations to show how, *within science itself*, the stability of theories against experience is maintained by epicyclical reserves which suppress alternative conceptions in the germ; a procedure which in retrospect will appear right in some instances and wrong in others.

The theory of electrolytic dissociation proposed in 1887 by Arrhenius assumed a chemical equilibrium between the dissociated and the undissociated forms of an electrolyte in solution. From the very start, the measurements showed that this was true only for weak electrolytes like acetic acid, but not for the very prominent group of strong electrolytes, like common salt or sulphuric acid. For more than thirty years the discrepancies were carefully measured and tabulated in textbooks, yet no one thought of calling in question the theory which they so flagrantly contradicted. Scientists were satisfied with speaking of the 'anomalies of strong electrolytes', without doubting for a moment that their behaviour was in fact governed by the law that they failed to obey. I can still remember my own amazement when, about 1919, I first heard the idea mooted that the anomalies were to be regarded as a refutation of the equilibrium postulated by Arrhenius and to be explained by a different theory. Not until this alternative conception (based on the mutual electrostatic interaction of the ions) was successfully elaborated in detail, was the previous theory generally abandoned.

Contradictions to current scientific conceptions are often disposed of by calling them 'anomalies'; this is the handiest assumption in the epicyclical reserve of any theory. We have seen how Azande make use of similar excuses to meet the inconsistencies of poison-oracles. In science this process has often proved brilliantly justified, when subsequent revisions of the adverse evidence or a deepening of the original theory explained the anomalies. The modification of Arrhenius's theory for strong electrolytes is a case in point.

Another example may illustrate how a series of observations which at one time were held to be important scientific facts, were a few years later completely discredited and committed to oblivion, without ever having been disproved or indeed newly tested, simply because the conceptual framework of science had meanwhile so altered that the facts no longer appeared credible. Towards the end of the last century numerous observations were reported by H. B. Baker on the power of intensive drying to stop some normally extremely rapid chemical reactions and to reduce the rate of evaporation of a number of commonly used chemicals (Baker, 1894, p. 611). Baker went on publishing further instances of this drying effect for more than thirty years (Baker, 1922, p. 568; 1928, p. 1051). A large number of allegedly allied phenomena were reported from Holland by Smits (1922)[2] and some very striking demonstrations of it came from Germany (Coehn and Jung, 1923, p. 695; Coehn and Tramm, 1923a, p. 456, 1923b, p. 356 and 1924, p. 110)[3]. H. B. Baker could render his samples unreactive sometimes only by drying them for periods up to three years; so when some authors failed to reproduce his results it was reasonable to assume that they had not achieved the same degree of desiccation. Consequently, there was little doubt at the time that the observed effects of intensive drying were true and that they reflected a fundamental feature of all chemical change.

Today these experiments, which aroused so much interest from 1900 to 1930, are almost forgotten. Textbooks of chemistry which thoughtlessly go on compiling published data still record Baker's observations in detail, merely adding that their validity 'is not yet certainly established' (Philbrick, 1949, p. 215), or that 'some (of his) findings are disputed by later workers, but the technique is difficult' (Partington, 1946, p. 483; Thorpe, 1947)[4]. But active scientists no longer take any interest in these phenomena, for in view of their present understanding of chemical processes they are convinced that most of them must have been spurious, and that, if some were real, they were likely to have been due to trivial causes.[5] This being so, our attitude towards

2. Baker's experiments are referred to (p. vii) as 'the most beautiful means of establishing the complexity of unary phases' postulated by the author.

3. These authors reported the stopping of the photochemical combination of hydrogen and chlorine by intense drying.

4. Thorpe reports Baker's 'interesting discovery' without any qualification.

5. Other examples of this procedure in which its results subsequently

these experiments is now similar to that of Azande towards Evans-Pritchard's suggestion of trying out the effects of oracle-poison without an accompanying incantation. We shrug our shoulders and refuse to waste our time on such obviously fruitless enquiries. The process of selecting facts for our attention is indeed the same in science as among Azande; but I believe that science is often right in its application of it, while Azande are quite wrong when using it for protecting their superstitions.[6]

I conclude that what earlier philosophers have alluded to by speaking of coherence as the criterion of truth is only a criterion of *stability*. It may equally stabilize an erroneous or a true view of the universe. The attribution of truth to any particular stable alternative is a fiduciary act which cannot be analysed in non-committal terms. [...] There exists no principle of doubt the operation of which will discover for us which of two systems of implicit beliefs is true – except in the sense that we will admit decisive evidence against the one we do not believe to be true, and not against the other. Once more, the admission of doubt proves here to be as clearly an act of belief as does the non-admission of doubt.

References

BAKER, H. B. (1894), *Journal of the Chemical Society of London*, vol. 65.

BAKER, H. B. (1922), *Journal of the Chemical Society of London*, vol. 121.

BAKER, H. B. (1928), *Journal of the Chemical Society of London*, part I.

COEHN, and JUNG, C. (1923), *Ber. deutsch. Chem. Ges.*, vol. 56.

COEHN, and TRAMM, (1923a), *Ber. deutsch. Chem. Ges.*, vol. 56.

---

proved erroneous were given before in section 4 of this chapter to illustrate the equivalance of belief and doubt (Polanyi, 1958).

6. The wise neglect of awkward facts may be of value even for the development of the deductive sciences. Greek mathematicians allowed themselves to be discouraged from developing algebra by the impossibility of representing the ratio of two incommensurable line segments in terms of whole numbers. B. L. Van der Waerden (1954, p. 266) says that 'it does honour to Greek mathematics that it adhered inexorably to such logical consistency'. But had their successors been as exacting in their logical scruples, mathematics would have died of its own rigor.

COEHN, and TRAMM (1923b), *Zeitschr. f. Phys. Chem.*, vol. 105.

COEHN, and TRAMM, (1924), *Zeitschr. f. Phys. Chem.*, vol. 110.

EVANS-PRITCHARD, E. E. (1937), *Witchcraft, Oracles and Magic among the Azande*, Clarendon Press.

HORNEY, K. (1939), *New Ways of Psychoanalysis*, Routledge.

JAMES, W. (1890), *Principles of Psychology*, vol. 2, New York.

KOESTLER, A. (ed.) (1950), *The God that Failed*, Hamilton.

PARTINGTON, J. R. (1946), *General and Inorganic Chemistry*, n.p.

PHILBRICK, F. A. (1949), *Textbook of Theoretical and Inorganic Chemistry*, rev. edn, London.

POLANYI, M. (1958), *Personal Knowledge*, University of Chicago Press.

SMITS (1922), *The Theory of Allotropy*.

THORPE, E. (1947), 'Benzene and its homologues', *Dictionary of Applied Chemistry*, n.p.

VAN DER WAERDEN, B. L. (1954), *Science Awakening*, Gröningen.

29 Robin Horton

African Traditional Thought and Western Science[1]

An abridgement of Robin Horton, 'African traditional thought and Western science', *Africa*, vol. 37, 1967, pp. 50–71, 155–87.

Part 1: Features Common to Modern Western and Traditional African Thought

The first part of this paper[2] seeks to develop an approach to traditional African thought guided by the conviction that an exhaustive exploration of features common to modern Western and traditional African thought should come before the enumeration of differences.

I shall start by setting out a number of general propositions on the nature and functions of theoretical thinking. These propositions are derived, in the first instance, from my own training in Biology, Chemistry and Philosophy of Science. But, as I shall show, they are highly relevant to traditional African religious thinking. Indeed, they make sense of just those features of such thinking that anthropologists have often found most incomprehensible.

The quest for explanatory theory is basically the quest for unity underlying apparent diversity; for simplicity underlying apparent complexity; for order underlying apparent disorder; for regularity underlying apparent anomaly

Typically, this quest involves the elaboration of a scheme of entities or forces operating 'behind' or 'within' the world of common-sense observations. These entities must be of a limited

1. This abridgement is about a third of the length of the original and cannot do justice to the consistent richness, clarity and relevance of this outstanding paper. We hope that what is presented here will whet the reader's appetite and lead him to read the original – *Ed*.

2. I am grateful to the Institute of African Studies, University of Ibadan, for a grant towards the publication of this paper. The Institute is, however, in no way responsible for the opinions expressed.

number of kinds and their behaviour must be governed by a limited number of general principles. Such a theoretical scheme is linked to the world of everyday experience by statements identifying happenings within it with happenings in the everyday world.

Some modern writers deny that traditional religious thinking is in any serious sense theoretical thinking. In support of their denial they contrast the simplicity, regularity and elegance of the theoretical schemas of the sciences with the unruly complexity and caprice of the world of gods and spirits (Beattie, 1966). But this antithesis does not really accord with modern fieldwork data. Indeed, one of the lessons of recent studies of African cosmologies is precisely that the gods of a given culture do form a scheme which interprets the vast diversity of everyday experience in terms of the action of a relatively few *kinds* of forces.

Modern work gives the lie to the old stereotype of the gods as capricious and irregular in their behaviour. For it shows that each category of beings has its appointed functions in relation to the world of observable happenings. The gods may sometimes appear capricious to the unreflective ordinary man. But for the religious expert charged with the diagnosis of spiritual agencies at work behind observed events, a basic modicum of regularity in their behaviour is the major premiss on which his work depends. Like atoms, molecules, and waves, then, the gods serve to introduce unity into diversity, simplicity into complexity, order into disorder, regularity into anomaly.

Theory places things in a causal context wider than that provided by common sense

When we say that theory displays the order and regularity underlying apparent disorder and irregularity, one of the things we mean is that it provides a causal context for apparently 'wild' events. Putting things in a causal context is, of course, one of the jobs of commonsense. But although it does this job well at a certain level, it seems to have limitations. To say of the traditional African thinker that he is interested in supernatural rather than natural causes makes little more sense, therefore, than to say of the physicist that he is interested in nuclear rather than natural causes. In fact, both are making the same use of theory to trans-

343

cend the limited vision of natural causes provided by common sense.

Modern Western medical scientists had long been distracted from noting the causal connexion between social disturbance and disease by the success of the germ theory. It would seem, indeed, that a conjunction of the germ theory, of the discovery of potent antibiotics and immunization techniques, and of conditions militating against the build-up of natural resistance to many killer infections, for long made it very difficult for scientists to see the importance of this connexion. Conversely, perhaps, a conjunction of no germ theory, no potent antibiotics, no immunization techniques, with conditions favouring the build-up of considerable natural resistance to killer infections, served to throw this same causal connexion into relief in the mind of the traditional healer. If one were asked to choose between germ theory innocent of psychosomatic insight and traditional psychosomatic theory innocent of ideas about infection, one would almost certainly choose the germ theory. For in terms of quantitative results it is clearly the more vital to human well-being. But it is salutary to remember that not all the profits are on one side.

Common sense and theory have complementary roles in everyday life

All theories take their departure from the world of things and people, and ultimately return us to it. In this context, to say that a good theory 'reduces' something to something else is misleading. Ideally, a process of deduction from the premisses of a theory should lead us back to statements which portray the common-sense world in its full richness.

I suggest that in traditional Africa relations between common sense and theory are essentially the same as they are in Europe. That is, common sense is the handier and more economical tool for coping with a wide range of circumstances in everyday life. Nevertheless, there are certain circumstances that can only be coped with in terms of a wider causal vision than common sense provides. And in these circumstances there is a jump to theoretical thinking. The Kalabari people of the Niger Delta recognize many different kinds of diseases, and have an array of herbal specifics with which to treat them. Sometimes a sick person will be treated by ordinary members of his family who recognize the disease and know the specifics. Sometimes the treatment will be carried out on the instructions of a native doctor. When sickness and treatment follow these lines the atmosphere is basically commonsensical. Often, there is little or no reference to spiritual agencies.

Sometimes, however, the sickness does not respond to treatment, and it becomes evident that the herbal specific used does not provide the whole answer. The native doctor may rediagnose and try another specific. But if this produces no result the suspicion will arise that 'there is something else in this sickness'. In other words, the perspective provided by common sense is too limited. It is at this stage that a diviner is likely to be called in (it may be the native doctor who started the treatment). Using ideas about various spiritual agencies, he will relate the sickness to a wider range of circumstances – often to disturbances in the sick man's general social life.

Again, a person may have a sickness which, though mild, occurs together with an obvious crisis in his field of social relations. This conjunction suggests at the outset that it may not be appropriate to look at the illness from the limited perspective of common sense. And in such circumstances, the expert called in is likely to refer at once to certain spiritual agencies in terms of which he links the sickness to a wider context of events.

What we are describing here is generally referred to as a jump from common sense to mystical thinking. But, as we have seen, it is also, more significantly, a jump from common sense to theory. And here, as in Europe, the jump occurs at the point where the limited causal vision of common sense curtails its usefulness in dealing with the situation on hand.

Level of theory varies with context

A person seeking to place some event in a wider causal context often has a choice of theories. Like the initial choice between common sense and theory, this choice too will depend on just how wide a context he wishes to bring into consideration. Where he is content to place the event in a relatively modest context, he will be content to use what is generally called a low-level theory – i.e. one that covers a relatively limited area of experience. Where he is more ambitious about context, he will make use of a higher-level theory – i.e. one that covers a larger area of experience.

Once again, we find parallels to this in many traditional African religious systems. It is typical of such systems that they include, on the one hand, ideas about a multiplicity of spirits, and on the other hand, ideas about a single supreme being. Though the spirits are thought of as independent beings, they are also considered as so many manifestations or dependants of the supreme being. The spirits provide the means of setting an event within a relatively limited causal context. They are the basis of a theoretical scheme which typically covers the thinker's own community and immediate environment. The supreme being, on the other hand, provides the means of setting an event within the widest possible context.

All theory breaks up the unitary objects of common sense into aspects, then places the resulting elements in a wider causal context. That is, it first abstracts and analyses, then re-integrates

Numerous commentators on scientific method have familiarized us with the way in which the theoretical schemas of the sciences break up the world of common-sense things in order to achieve a causal understanding which surpasses that of common sense. But it is only from the more recent studies of African cosmologies, where religious beliefs are shown in the context of the various everyday contingencies they are invoked to explain, that we have begun to see how traditional religious thought also operates by a similar process of abstraction, analysis, and reintegration. A good example is provided by Fortes's recent work on West African theories of the individual and his relation to society. Here we have a theoretical scheme which, in order to produce a deeper understanding of the varying fortunes of individuals in their society, breaks them down into three aspects by a simple but typical operation of abstraction and analysis.

In evolving a theoretical scheme, the human mind seems constrained to drawn inspiration from analogy between the puzzling observations to be explained and certain already familiar phenomena

In the genesis of a typical theory, the drawing of an analogy between the unfamiliar and the familiar is followed by the making of a model in which something akin to the familiar is postulated as the reality underlying the unfamiliar. Both modern Western and traditional African thought-products amply demonstrate the truth of this. Whether we look amongst atoms, electrons and waves or amongst gods, spirits and entelechies, we find that theoretical notions nearly always have their roots in relatively homely everyday experiences, in analogies with the familiar.

In complex, rapidly changing industrial societies the human scene is in flux. Order, regularity, predictability, simplicity, all these seem lamentably absent. It is in the world of inanimate things that such qualities are most readily seen. This is why many people can find themselves less at home with their fellow men than with things. And this too, I suggest, is why the mind in quest of explanatory analogies turns most readily to the inanimate. In the traditional societies of Africa, we find the situation reversed. The human scene is the locus *par excellence* of order, predictability, regularity. In the world of the inanimate, these qualities are far less evident. Here, being less at home with people than with things is unimaginable. And here, the mind in quest of explanatory analogies turns naturally to people and their relations.

Where theory is founded on analogy between puzzling observations and familiar phenomena, it is generally only a limited aspect of such phenomena that is incorporated into the resulting model

When a thinker draws an analogy between certain puzzling observations and other more familiar phenomena, the analogy seldom involves more than a limited aspect of such phenomena. And it is only this limited aspect which is taken over and used to build up the theoretical schema. Other aspects are ignored; for, from the point of view of explanatory function, they are irrelevant.

Many writers have considered this sort of abstraction to be one of the distinctive features of scientific thinking. But this, like so many other such distinctions, is a false one; for just the same process is at work in traditional African thought. Thus when traditional thought draws upon people and their social relations as the raw material of its theoretical models, it makes use of some dimensions of human life and neglects others. The definition of a god may omit any reference to his physical appearance, his diet, his mode of lodging, his children, his relations with his wives and

347

so on. Asking questions about such attributes is as inappropriate as asking questions about the colour of a molecule or the temperature of an electron. It is this omission of many dimensions of human life from the definition of the gods which gives them that rarefied, attenuated aura which we call 'spiritual'. But there is nothing peculiarly religious, mystical, or traditional about this 'spirituality'. It is the result of the same process of abstraction as the one we see at work in Western theoretical models: the process whereby features of the prototype phenomena which have explanatory relevance are incorporated into a theoretical schema, while features which lack such relevance are omitted.

A theoretical model, once built, is developed in ways which sometimes obscure the analogy on which it was founded

In its raw, initial state, a model may come up quite quickly against data for which it cannot provide any explanatory coverage. Rather than scrap it out of hand, however, its users will tend to give it successive modifications in order to enlarge its coverage. Sometimes, such modifications will involve the drawing of further analogies with phenomena rather different from those which provided the initial inspiration for the model. Sometimes, they will merely involve 'tinkering' with the model until it comes to fit the new observations. By comparison with the phenomena which provided its original inspiration, such a developed model not unnaturally seems to have a bizarre, hybrid air about it.

Examples of the development of theoretical models abound in the history of science. One of the best documented of these is provided by the modern atomic theory of matter.

In studying traditional African thought, alas, we scarcely ever have the historical depth available to the student of European thought. So we can make few direct observations on the development of its theoretical models. Nevertheless, these models often show just the same kinds of bizarre, hybrid features as the models of the scientists. Since they resemble the latter in so many other ways, it seems reasonable to suppose that these features are the result of a similar process of development in response to demands for further explanatory coverage. The validity of such a supposition is strengthened when we consider detailed instances: for these show how the bizarre features of particular models are indeed closely related to the nature of the observations that demand explanation.

In treating traditional African religious systems as theoretical models akin to those of the sciences, I have really done little more than take them at their face value. Although this approach may seem naïve and platitudinous compared to the sophisticated 'things-are-never-what-they-seem' attitude more characteristic of the social anthropologist, it has certainly produced some surprising results. Above all, it has cast doubt on most of the well-worn dichotomies used to conceptualize the difference between scientific and traditional religious thought. Intellectual versus emotional; rational versus mystical; reality-oriented versus fantasy-oriented; causally oriented versus supernaturally oriented; empirical versus non-empirical; abstract versus concrete; analytical versus non-analytical: all of these are shown to be more or less inappropriate. If the reader is disturbed by this casting away of established distinctions, he will, I hope, accept it when he sees how far it can pave the way towards making sense of so much that previously appeared senseless.

One thing that may well continue to bother the reader is my playing down of the difference between non-personal and personal theory. The point I have sought to make is that the difference is more than anything else a difference in the idiom of the explanatory quest. Grasping this point is an essential preliminary to realizing how far the various established dichotomies used in this field are simply obstacles to understanding. Once it is grasped, a whole series of seemingly bizarre and senseless features of traditional thinking becomes immediately comprehensible. Until it is grasped, they remain essentially mysterious. Making the business of personal versus impersonal entities the crux of the difference between tradition and science not only blocks the understanding of tradition. It also draws a red herring across the path to an understanding of science.

Part 2: The 'Closed' and 'Open' Predicaments

In Part 1 of this paper, I pushed as far as it would go the thesis that important continuities link the religious thinking of traditional Africa and the theoretical thinking of the modern West. I showed how this view helps us to make sense of many otherwise puzzling features of traditional religious thinking. I also showed how it helps us to avoid certain rather troublesome red herrings which lie across the path towards understanding the crucial differences between the traditional and the scientific outlook.

In Part 2, I shall concentrate on these differences. I shall start by isolating one which strikes me as the key to all the others, and will then go on to suggest how the latter flow from it.

What I take to be the key difference is a very simple one. It is that in traditional cultures there is no developed awareness of alternatives to the established body of theoretical tenets; whereas in scientifically oriented cultures, such an awareness is highly developed. It is this difference we refer to when we say that traditional cultures are 'closed' and scientifically oriented cultures 'open'.[3]

One important consequence of the lack of awareness of alternatives is very clearly spelled out by Evans-Pritchard in his pioneering work on Azande witchcraft beliefs. Thus he says:

I have attempted to show how rhythm, mode of utterance, content of prophecies, and so forth, assist in creating faith in witch-doctors, but these are only some of the ways in which faith is supported, and do not entirely explain belief. Weight of tradition alone can do that.... There is no incentive to agnosticism. All their beliefs hang together, and were a Zande to give up faith in witch-doctorhood, he would have to surrender equally his faith in witchcraft and oracles.... In this web of belief every strand depends upon every other strand, *and a Zande cannot get out of its meshes because it is the only world he knows. The web is not an external structure in which he is enclosed. It is the texture of his*

3. Philosophically minded readers will notice here some affinities with Karl Popper, who also makes the transition from a 'closed' to an 'open' predicament crucial for the take-off from tradition to science (Popper, 1945). For me, however, Popper obscures the issue by packing too many contrasts into his definitions of 'closed' and 'open'. Thus, for him, the transition from one predicament to the other implies not just a growth in the awareness of alternatives, but also a transition from communalism to individualism, and from ascribed status to achieved status. But as I hope to show in this essay, it is the awareness of alternatives which is crucial for the take-off into science. Not individualism or achieved status: for there are lots of societies where both of the latter are well developed, but which show no signs whatever of take-off. In the present context, therefore, my own narrower definition of 'closed' and 'open' seems more appropriate.

thought and he cannot think that his thought is wrong (Evans-Pritchard, 1937, p. 194).

And again:

And yet Azande do not see that their oracles tell them nothing! Their blindness is not due to stupidity, for they display great ingenuity in explaining away the failures and inequalities of the poison oracle and experimental keenness in testing it. It is due rather to the fact that their intellectual ingenuity and experimental keenness are conditioned by patterns of ritual behaviour and mystical belief. Within the limits set by these patterns, they show great intelligence, but it cannot operate beyond these limits. Or, to put it in another way; *they reason excellently in the idiom of their beliefs, but they cannot reason outside, or against their beliefs, because they have no other idiom in which to express their thoughts* (Evans-Pritchard, 1937, p. 338).

Yet again, writing more generally of 'closed' societies in a recent book, he says:

Everyone has the same sort of religious beliefs and practices; and their generality, or collectivity, gives them an objectivity which places them over and above the psychological experience of any individual, or indeed of all individuals. . . . *Apart from positive and negative sanctions, the mere fact that religion is general means, again in a closed society, that it is obligatory, for even if there is no coercion, a man has no option but to accept what everybody gives assent to, because he has no choice, any more than of what language he speaks. Even were he to be a sceptic, he could express his doubts only in terms of the beliefs held by all around him* (Evans-Pritchard 1965, p. 55).

In other words, absence of any awareness of alternatives makes for an absolute acceptance of the established theoretical tenets, and removes any possibility of questioning them. In these circumstances, the established tenets invest the believer with a compelling force. It is this force which we refer to when we talk of such tenets as sacred.

A second important consequence of lack of awareness of alternatives is vividly illustrated by the reaction of an Ijo man to a missionary who told him to throw away his old gods. He said: 'Does your God really want us to climb to the top of a tall palm tree, then take off our hands and let ourselves fall?' Where the established tenets have an absolute and exclusive validity for those who hold them, any challenge to them is a threat of chaos, of the cosmic abyss, and therefore evokes intense anxiety.

With developing awareness of alternatives, the established theoretical tenets come to seem less absolute in their validity, and lose something of their sacredness. At the same time, a challenge to these tenets is no longer a horrific threat of chaos. For just as the tenets themselves have lost some of their absolute validity, a challenge to them is no longer a threat of absolute calamity. It can now be seen as nothing more threatening than an intimation that new tenets might profitably be tried. Where these conditions begin to prevail, the stage is set for change from a traditional to a scientific outlook.

Here, then, we have two basic predicaments: the 'closed' – characterized by lack of awareness of alternatives, sacredness of beliefs, and anxiety about threats to them; and the 'open' – characterized by awareness of alternatives, diminished sacredness of beliefs, and diminished anxiety about threats to them.

Now, as I have said, I believe all the major differences between traditional and scientific outlooks can be understood in terms of these two predicaments. In substantiating this, I should like to divide the differences into two groups: those directly connected with the presence or absence of a vision of alternatives; and those directly connected with the presence or absence of anxiety about threats to the established beliefs.

Differences Connected with the Presence or Absence of a Vision of Alternatives

Magical versus non-magical attitude to words

A central characteristic of nearly all the traditional African world-views we know of is an assumption about the power of words, uttered under appropriate circumstances, to bring into being the events or states they stand for.

To know the name of a being or thing is to have some degree of control over it. In the invocation of spirits, it is essential to call their names correctly; and the control which such correct calling gives is one reason why the true or 'deep' names of gods are often withheld from strangers, and their utterance forbidden to all but a few whose business it is to use them in ritual. Similar ideas lie behind the very widespread traditional practice of using euphemisms to refer to such things as dangerous diseases and wild animals: for it is thought that use of the real names might secure their presence. Yet again, it is widely believed that harm can be done to a man by various operations performed on his name – for instance, by writing his name on a piece of paper and burning it.

This last example carries me on to an observation that at first sight contradicts what we have said so far: the observation that, in a great deal of African magic, it is non-verbal symbols rather than words that are thought to have a direct influence over the situations they represent. Bodily movements, bits of plants, organs of animals, stones, earth, water, spittle, domestic utensils, statuettes – a whole host of actions, objects and artefacts play a vital part in the performances of traditional magic. But as we look deeper the contradiction seems more apparent than real. For several studies of African magic suggest that its instruments become symbols through being verbally designated as such.

This interpretation, which reduces all forms of African magic to a verbal base, fits the facts rather well. One may still ask, however, why magicians spend so much time choosing objects and actions as surrogate words, when spoken words themselves are believed to have a magical potential. The answer, I would suggest, is that speech is an ephemeral form of words, and one which does not lend itself to a great variety of manipulations. Verbal designation of material objects converts them into a more permanent and more readily manipulable form of words. Considered in this light, magical objects are the pre-literate equivalents of the written incantations which are so commonly found as charms and talismans in literate but prescientific cultural milieux.

The scientist's attitude to words is, of course, quite opposite. He dismisses contemptuously any suggestion that words could have an immediate, magical power over the things they stand for. Indeed, he finds magical notions amongst the most absurd and alien trappings of traditional thought. Though he grants an enormous power to words, it is the indirect one of bringing control over things through the functions of explanation and prediction. Words are tools in the service of these functions – tools which like all others are to be cared for as long as they are useful, but which are to be ruthlessly scrapped as soon as they outlive their usefulness.

With the change from the 'closed' to the 'open' predicament, then, the outlook behind magic becomes intolerable; and to escape from it people espouse the view that words vary independently of reality. Smug rationalists who congratulate themselves on their freedom from magical thinking would do well to reflect on the nature of this freedom!

Ideas-bound-to-occasions versus ideas-bound-to-ideas

Many commentators on the idea-systems of traditional African cultures have stressed that, for members of these cultures, their thought does not appear as something distinct from and opposable to the realities that call it into action. Rather, particular passages of thought are bound to the particular occasions that evoke them.

If ideas in traditional culture are seen as bound to occasions rather than to other ideas, the reason is one that we have already given in our discussion of magic. Since the member of such a culture can imagine no alternatives to his established system of ideas, the latter appear inexorably bound to the portions of reality they stand for. They cannot be seen as in any way opposable to reality.

In a scientifically oriented culture such as that of the Western anthropologist, things are very different. The very word 'idea' has the connotation of something opposed to reality. Nor is it entirely coincidental that in such a culture the historian of ideas is considered to be the most unrealistic kind of historian. Not only are ideas dissociated in people's minds from the reality that occasions them: they are bound to other ideas, to form wholes and systems perceived as such. Belief-systems take shape not only as abstractions in the minds of anthropologists, but also as totalities in the minds of believers.

Here again, this change can be readily understood in terms of a change from the 'closed' to the 'open' predicament. A vision of alternative possibilities forces men to the faith that ideas somehow vary whilst reality remains constant. Ideas thus become detached from reality – nay, even in a sense opposed to it. Furthermore, such a vision, by giving the thinker an opportunity to 'get outside' his own system, offers him a possibility of his coming to see it *as a system*.

Unreflective versus reflective thinking

At this stage of the analysis there is no need for me to insist further on the essential rationality of traditional thought. In Part 1, indeed, I have already made it out far too rational for the taste of most social anthropologists. And yet, there is a sense in which this thought includes among its accomplishments neither Logic nor Philosophy. Despite its elaborate and often penetrating cosmological, sociological, and psychological speculations, traditional thought has tended to get on with the work of explanation, without pausing for reflection upon the nature or rules of this work. Thinking once more of the 'closed' predicament, we can readily see why these second-order intellectual activities should be virtually absent from traditional cultures. Briefly, the traditional thinker, because he is unable to imagine possible alternatives to his established theories and classifications, can never start to formulate generalized norms of reasoning and knowing. For only where there are alternatives can there be choice, and only where there is choice can there be norms governing it. As they are characteristically absent in traditional cultures, so Logic and Philosophy are characteristically present in all scientifically oriented cultures. Just as the 'closed' predicament makes it impossible for them to appear, so the 'open' predicament makes it inevitable that they must appear. For where the thinker can see the possibility of alternatives to his established idea-system, the question of choice at once arises, and the development of norms governing such choice cannot be far behind.

Mixed versus segregated motives

This contrast is very closely related to the preceding one. As I stressed in Part 1 of this essay, the goals of explanation and prediction are as powerfully present in traditional African cultures as they are in cultures where science has become institutionalized. In the absence of explicit norms of thought, however, we find them vigorously pursued but not explicitly reflected upon and defined. In these circumstances, there is little thought about their consistency or inconsistency with other goals and motives. Hence wherever we find a theoretical system with explanatory and predictive functions, we find other motives entering in and contributing to its development.

Despite their cognitive preoccupations, most African religious systems are powerfully influenced by what are commonly called 'emotional needs' – i.e. needs for certain kinds of personal relationship. In Africa, as elsewhere, all social systems stimulate in their members a considerable diversity of such needs; but, having stimulated them, they often prove unwilling or unable to allow them full opportunities for satisfaction. In such situations the spirits function not only as theoretical entities but as surrogate people providing opportunities for the formation of ties forbidden in the purely human social field.

There is little doubt that because the theoretical entities of traditional thought happen to be people, they give particular scope for the working of emotional and aesthetic motives. Here, perhaps, we do have something about the personal idiom in theory that does militate indirectly against the taking up of a scientific attitude; for where there are powerful emotional and aesthetic loadings on a particular theoretical scheme, these must add to the difficulties of abandoning this scheme when cognitive goals press toward doing so. Once again, I should like to stress that the mere fact of switching from a personal to an impersonal idiom does not make anyone a scientist, and that one can be unscientific or scientific in either idiom. In this respect, nevertheless, the personal idiom does seem to present certain difficulties for the scientific attitude which the impersonal idiom does not.

Where the possibility of choice has stimulated the development of Logic, Philosophy, and norms of thought generally, the situation undergoes radical change. One theory is judged better than another with explicit reference to its efficacy in explanation and prediction. And as these ends become more clearly defined, it gets increasingly evident that no other ends are compatible with them. People come to see that if ideas are to be used as efficient tools of explanation and prediction, they must not be allowed to become tools of anything else. (This, of course, is the essence of the ideal of 'objectivity'.) Hence there grows up a great watchfulness against seduction by the emotional or aesthetic appeal of a theory – a watchfulness which in twentieth-century

Europe sometimes takes extreme forms such as the suspicion of any research publication not written out in a positively indigestible style.

Differences Connected with the Presence or Absence of Anxiety about Threats to the Established Body of Theory

Protective versus destructive attitude towards established theory

Both in traditional Africa and in the science-oriented West, theoretical thought is vitally concerned with the prediction of events. But there are marked differences in reaction to predictive failure.

In the theoretical thought of the traditional cultures, there is a notable reluctance to register repeated failures of prediction and to act by attacking the beliefs involved. Instead, other current beliefs are utilized in such a way as to 'excuse' each failure as it occurs, and hence to protect the major theoretical assumptions on which prediction is based. This use of *ad hoc* excuses is a phenomenon which social anthropologists have christened 'secondary elaboration'.[4]

The process of secondary elaboration is most readily seen in association with the work of diviners and oracle-operators, who are concerned with discovering the identity of the spiritual forces responsible for particular happenings in the visible, tangible world, and the reasons for their activation. Typically, a sick man goes to a diviner, and is told that a certain spiritual agency is 'worrying' him. The diviner points to certain of his past actions as having excited the spirit's anger, and indicates certain remedial actions which will appease this anger and restore health. Should the client take the recommended remedial action and yet see no improvement, he will be likely to conclude that the diviner was either fraudulent or just incompetent, and to seek out another expert. The new diviner will generally point to another spiritual agency and another set of arousing circumstances as responsible

4. The idea of secondary elaboration as a key feature of prescientific thought-systems was put forward with great brilliance and insight by Evans-Pritchard in his *Witchcraft, Oracles and Magic*. All subsequent discussions, including the present one, are heavily indebted to his lead (Evans-Pritchard, 1937).

for the man's condition, and will recommend fresh remedial action. In addition, he will probably provide some explanation of why the previous diviner failed to get at the truth. He may corroborate the client's suspicions of fraud, or he may say that the spirit involved maliciously 'hid itself behind' another in such a way that only the most skilled of diviners would have been able to detect it. If after this the client should still see no improvement in his condition, he will move on to yet another diviner – and so on, perhaps, until his troubles culminate in death.

What is notable in all this is that the client never takes his repeated failures as evidence against the existence of the various spiritual beings named as responsible for his plight, or as evidence against the possibility of making contact with such beings as diviners claim to do. Nor do members of the wider community in which he lives ever try to keep track of the proportion of successes to failures in the remedial actions based on their beliefs, with the aim of questioning these beliefs. At most, they grumble about the dishonesty and wiles of many diviners, whilst maintaining their faith in the existence of some honest, competent practitioners.

In these traditional cultures, questioning of the beliefs on which divining is based and weighing up of successes against failures are just not among the paths that thought can take. They are blocked paths because the thinkers involved are victims of the closed predicament. For them, established beliefs have an absolute validity, and any threat to such beliefs is a horrific threat of chaos. Who is going to jump from the cosmic palm-tree when there is no hope of another perch to swing to?

Where the scientific outlook has become firmly entrenched, attitudes to established beliefs are very different. Much has been made of the scientist's essential scepticism toward established beliefs; and one must, I think, agree that this above all is what distinguishes him from the traditional thinker. But one must be careful here. The picture of the scientist in continuous readiness to scrap or demote established theory contains a dangerous exaggeration as well as an important truth. The scientist is, as it were, always keeping account, balancing the successes of a theory against its failures. And when the failures start to come thick and fast, defence of the theory switches inexorably to attack on it.

This underlying readiness to scrap or demote established

theories on the ground of poor predictive performance is perhaps the most important single feature of the scientific attitude. It is, I suggest, a direct outcome of the 'open' predicament. For only when the thinker is able to see his established idea-system as one among many alternatives can he see his established ideas as things of less than absolute value. And only when he sees them thus can he see the scrapping of them as anything other than a horrific, irretrievable jump into chaos.

Faced with a theory postulating several possible causes for a given event, and no means of inferring the actual cause from observable evidence, divination goes, as it were, 'over the head of' such evidence. It elicits a direct sign from the realm of those unobservable entities that govern the causal linkages it deals with – a sign that enables it to say which of the several sequences indicated by the theory is the one actually involved.

Divination techniques share two basic features. First, as I have said, they are means of selecting one actual causal sequence from several potential sequences. Secondly, they all carry a subtle aura of fallibility which makes it possible to 'explain everything away' when remedial prescriptions based on them turn out not to work. Thus many divination procedures require an esoteric knowledge or faculty which the client does not share with the operator. Hence the client has no direct check on the operator; and in retrospect there is always the possibility of the latter's dishonesty or sheer incompetence. Again, nearly all of these procedures are thought to be very delicate and easily thrown out of kilter. Among other things, they may be affected by pollution, or by the machinations of those who have a grudge against the client.

So, whereas the positive features of the divining process make it possible to arrive at a definite causal verdict despite a converging-sequence theory, the aura of fallibility provides for the self-protecting action of such a theory by making it possible, in the event of a failure, to switch from one potential sequence to another in such a way as to leave the theory as a whole unimpugned. In the last section, we noted that the context of divination provided some of the clearest illustrations of the defence-mechanism known as 'secondary elaboration'. Now, I think, we can go further: that is, we can say that divination owes its very existence to the exigencies of this mechanism.

Where the 'open' predicament prevails, anxieties about threats to the established theories decline, and previously blocked thought-paths become clear. We now witness the development of theories that assign distinctive effects to differing causes; and in the face of this development the type of theory that assumes converging sequences tends to disappear. Nowadays, of course, it is more fashionable to talk of covariation than to talk of cause and effect. But the continuous-covariation formula of the type $d\mathrm{s} =$ f. $d\mathrm{t}$, so prominent in modern scientific theory, is in fact an instance of the tendency I am referring to. For, spelled out, the implication of such a formula is that, to an infinite number of values of a cause-variable, there correspond an infinite number of values of an effect-variable.

Where this type of theory comes into the ascendant, the diviner gives place to the diagnostician. The latter, whether he is concerned with bodily upsets or with aeroplane disasters, goes to work in a way which differs in important respects from that of his traditional counterpart. Dealing as he does with theories that postulate non-converging causal sequences, he has a task altogether more prosaic than that of the diviner. For, given non-convergence, a complete and accurate observation of effect, plus knowledge of the relevant theory, makes it possible for him to give an unambiguous causal verdict. Once these conditions have been fulfilled, there is no need for the additional operations of the diviner. No need for special mechanisms to elicit signs from the realm of unobservable entities. No need for a way of going 'over the head of' observable evidence in order to find out which of several potential causes is the actual one.

Divination versus diagnosis

Earlier in this essay I drew certain parallels between the work of the traditional African diviner and the work of the Western diagnostician.[5] In particular, I showed how both of them make much the same use of theoretical ideas: i.e. as means of linking observed effects to causes that lie beyond the powers of common sense to grasp. I now propose to discuss certain crucial differences between these two kinds of agent.

5. Not included in this abridgement. See pp. 55 ff. of the original paper – *Ed.*

A theory which postulates converging causal sequences,[6] though self-protective to a high degree, faces serious problems in its application to everyday life. For the man who visits a diviner with misfortune E does not want to be told that it could be due to any one of four different kinds of spirits, activated by circumstances A, B, C or D. He wants a definite verdict and a definite remedial prescription.

Far from being an integral part of any mechanism for defending theory, then, the diagnostician often contributes his share to the circumstances that lead to the abandonment of old ideas and the adoption of new ones.

Absence versus presence of experimental method

Anyone who has read Part 1 of this paper should be in little doubt as to how closely adjusted traditional African theoretical systems often are to the prevailing facts of personality, social organization, and ecology. Indeed, although many of the causal connexions they posit turn out to be red herrings when subjected to scientific scrutiny, others turn out to be very real and vital. Thus an important part of traditional religious theory posits and attempts to explain the connexion between disturbed social relationships and disease – a connexion whose reality and importance Western medical scientists are only just beginning to see. Nevertheless, the adjustments of these systems to changing experience are essentially slow, piecemeal, and reluctant. Nothing must happen to arouse public suspicion that basic theoretical models are being challenged.

Scientific thought, by contrast, is characteristically 'one jump ahead' of experience. It is able to be so because of that distinctive feature of the scientist's calling: the Experimental Method. This method is nothing more nor less than the positive extension of the 'open' attitude to established beliefs and categories which we referred to on pp. 358–9. For the essence of experiment is that the holder of a pet theory does not just wait for events to come along and show whether or not it has a good predictive performance. He bombards it with artificially produced events in

6. i.e. the possibility that a result, E, is attributable to any of a set of causes, A, B, C, D, etc. – *Ed*.

such a way that its merits or defects will show up as immediately and as clearly as possible.

We can say, then, that, whereas in traditional thought there is continual if reluctant adjustment of theories to new experience, in science men spend much of their time deliberately creating new experience in order to evaluate their theories. Whilst in traditional thought it is mostly experience that determines theory, in the world of the experimental scientist there is a sense in which theory usually determines experience.

The confession of ignorance

The European anthropologist working in a traditional African community almost never finds a confession of ignorance about the answer to some question which the people themselves consider important. Scarcely ever, for instance, does he come across a common disease or crop failure whose cause and cure people say they just do not know.

Given the basic predicament of the traditional thinker, such an admission would indeed be intolerable. For where there are no conceivable alternatives to the established theoretical system, any hint that this system is failing to cope must be a hint of irreparable chaos, and so must rouse extreme anxiety.

In the case of the scientist, his readiness to test every theory to destruction makes it inevitable that he will have to confess ignorance whenever a theory crumbles under testing and he has no better one immediately available. Indeed, it is only in a culture where the scientific attitude is firmly institutionalized that one can hope to hear the answer 'we don't know' given by an expert questioned on the causes of such a terrible human scourge as cancer.

Coincidence, chance, probability

Closely related to the development of a capacity to tolerate ignorance is the development of concepts which formally recognize the existence of various kinds of limitation upon the possible completeness of explanation and prediction. Important among such concepts are those of coincidence, chance, and probability.

Let us start with the idea of coincidence. In the traditional cultures of Africa, such a concept is poorly developed. The tendency is to give any untoward happening a definite cause. When a rotten branch falls off a tree and kills a man walking underneath it, there has to be a definite explanation of the calamity. Perhaps the man quarrelled with a half-brother over some matter of inheritance, and the latter worked the fall of the branch through a sorcerer. Or perhaps he misappropriated lineage property, and the lineage ancestors brought the branch down on his head. The idea that the whole thing could have come about through the accidental convergence of two independent chains of events is inconceivable because it is psychologically intolerable. To entertain it would be to admit that the episode was inexplicable and unpredictable: a glaring confession of ignorance.

It is characteristic of the scientist that he is willing to face up to the inexplicability and unpredictability of this type of situation, and that he does not shrink from diagnosing an accidental convergence of different chains of events. This is a consequence of his ability to tolerate ignorance.

As with the idea of coincidence, so with that of probability. Where traditional thought is apt to demand definite forecasts of whether something will or will not happen, the scientist is often content to know the probability of its happening – that is, the number of times it will happen in a hypothetical series of, say, a hundred trials.

When it was first developed, the probability forecast was seen as a makeshift tool for use in situations where one's knowledge of the factors operating was incomplete, and where it was assumed that possession of all the relevant data would have made a definite forecast possible. This is still an important context of probability forecasting, and will continue to be so. Nevertheless, the assumption remains that if all the relevant factors could be known and observed, the probability forecasts could be replaced by unequivocal predictions.

From one angle, then, the development of the scientific outlook appears more than anything else as a growth of intellectual humility. Where the prescientific thinker is unable to confess ignorance on any question of vital practical import, the good scientist is always ready to do so. Again, where the prescientific thinker is reluctant to acknowledge any limitation on his power to explain and predict, the scientist not only faces such limitations with equanimity, but devotes a good deal of energy to exploring and charting their extent.

This humility, I suggest, is the product of an underlying confidence – the confidence which comes from seeing that one's currently held beliefs are not the be-all and end-all of the human search for order. Once one has seen this, the difficulty of facing up to their limitations largely dissolves.

Protective versus destructive attitude to the category-system

If someone is asked to list typical features of traditional thinking, he is almost certain to mention the phenomenon known as 'taboo'. 'Taboo' is the anthropological jargon for a reaction of horror and aversion to certain actions or happenings which are seen as monstrous and polluting. It is characteristic of the taboo reaction that people are unable to justify it in terms of ulterior reasons: tabooed events are simply bad in themselves. People take every possible step to prevent tabooed events from happening, and to isolate or expel them when they do occur.

Taboo has long been a mystery to anthropologists. Of the many explanations proposed, few have fitted more than a small selection of the instances observed. It is only recently that an anthropologist has placed the phenomenon in a more satisfactory perspective by the observation that in nearly every case of taboo reaction, the events and actions involved are ones which seriously defy the established lines of classification in the culture where they occur.[7]

Perhaps the most important occasion of taboo reaction in traditional African cultures is the commission of incest. Incest is one of the most flagrant defiances of the established category-system: for he who commits it treats a mother, daughter, or sister like a wife. Another common occasion for taboo reaction is the birth of twins. Here, the category distinction involved is that of human beings versus animals – multiple births being taken as characteristic of animals as opposed to men. Yet another very generally tabooed object is the human corpse, which occupies, as

7. This observation may well prove to be a milestone in our understanding of traditional thought. It was first made some years ago by Mary Douglas, who has developed many of its implications in her recent book *Purity and Danger* (Douglas, 1966). Though we clearly disagree on certain wider implications, the present discussion is deeply indebted to her insights.

it were, a classificatory no-man's land between the living and the inanimate. Equally widely tabooed are such human bodily excreta as faeces and menstrual blood, which occupy the same no-man's-land between the living and the inanimate.

Just as the central tenets of the traditional theoretical system are defended against adverse experience by an elaborate array of excuses for predictive failure, so too the main classificatory distinctions of the system are defended by taboo avoidance reactions against any event that defies them. Since every system of belief implies a system of categories, and vice versa, secondary elaboration and taboo reaction are really opposite sides of the same coin.

From all this it follows that, like secondary elaboration, taboo reaction has no place among the reflexes of the scientist. For him, whatever defies or fails to fit in to the established category-system is not something horrifying, to be isolated or expelled. On the contrary, it is an intriguing 'phenomenon' – a starting point and a challenge for the invention of new classifications and new theories. It is something every young research worker would like to have crop up in his field of observation – perhaps the first rung on the ladder of fame. If a biologist ever came across a child born with the head of a goat, he would be hard put to it to make his compassion cover his elation. And as for social anthropologists, one may guess that their secret dreams are of finding a whole community of men who sleep for preference with their mothers!

The passage of time: bad or good?

On the major time-scale of the typical traditional culture, things are thought of as having been better in the golden age of the founding heroes than they are today. On an important minor time-scale, the annual one, the end of the year is a time when everything in the cosmos is run-down and sluggish, overcome by an accumulation of defilement and pollution.

A corollary of this attitude to time is a rich development of activities designed to negate its passage by a 'return to the beginning'. Such activities characteristically depend on the magical premiss that a symbolic statement of some archetypal event can in a sense recreate that event and temporarily obliterate the passage of time which has elapsed since its original occurrence.

Where the traditional thinker is busily trying to annul the passage of time, the scientist may almost be said to be trying frantically to hurry time up. For in his impassioned pursuit of the experimental method, he is striving after the creation of new situations which nature, if left to herself, would bring about slowly if ever at all.

Once again, the scientist's attitude can be understood in terms of the 'open' predicament. For him, currently held ideas on a given subject are one possibility amongst many. Hence occurrences which threaten them are not the total, horrific threat that they would be for the traditional thinker.

So much, then, for the salient differences between traditional and scientific thought. The concept of the 'closed' predicament not only provides a key to the understanding of each one of the eleven salient traits of traditional thought, it also helps us to see why these eleven traits flourish and perish as a set.

What are the circumstances tending to promote awareness of alternatives to established theoretical models? Three relevant factors of this kind suggest themselves at once: the development of written transmission of beliefs; the development of culturally heterogeneous communities; and the development of the trade-travel-exploration complex.

In naming these three factors as crucial for the development of the 'open' predicament, I am not implying that wherever they occur, there is a sort of painless, automatic, and complete transition from 'closed' to 'open' thinking. On the contrary, the transition seems inevitably to be painful, violent, and partial.

Why should the transition be so painful? Well, a theme of this paper has been the way in which a developing awareness of alternative world-views erodes attitudes which attach an absolute validity to the established outlook. But this is a process that works over time – indeed over generations. Throughout the process there are bound to be many people on whom the confrontation has not yet worked its magic. These people still retain the old sense of the absolute validity of their belief-systems, with all the attendant anxieties about threats to them. For these people, the confrontation is still a threat of chaos of the most horrific kind – a threat which demands the most drastic measures. They respond in one of two ways: either by trying to blot out those responsible for the confrontation, often down to the last unborn child; or by trying to convert them to their own beliefs through fanatical missionary activity.

Again, as I said earlier, the moving, shifting thought-world produced by the 'open' predicament creates its own sense of insecurity. Many people find this shifting world intolerable. Some adjust to their fears by developing an inordinate faith in progress toward a future in which 'the Truth' will be finally known. But others long nostalgically for the fixed, unquestionable beliefs of the 'closed' culture. They call for authoritarian establishment and control of dogma, and for persecution of those who have managed to be at ease in a world of ever-shifting ideas. Clearly, the 'open' predicament is a precarious, fragile thing.

In modern western Europe and America, it is true, the 'open' predicament seems to have escaped from this precariousness through public acknowledgement of the practical utility of the sciences. It has achieved a secure foothold in the culture because its results maximize values shared by 'closed-' and 'open-' minded alike. Even here, however, the 'open' predicament has nothing like a universal sway. On the contrary, it is almost a minority phenomenon. Outside the various academic disciplines in which it has been institutionalized, its hold is pitifully less than those who describe Western culture as 'science-oriented' often like to think.

The layman's ground for accepting the models propounded by the scientist is often no different from the young African villager's ground for accepting the models propounded by one of his elders. In both cases the propounders are deferred to as the accredited agents of tradition. As for the rules which guide scientists themselves in the acceptance or rejection of models, these seldom become part of the intellectual equipment of members of the wider population. For all the apparent up-to-dateness of the content of his world-view, the modern Western layman is rarely more 'open' or scientific in his outlook than is the traditional African villager.

References

BEATTIE, J. (1966), 'Ritual and social change', *Journal of the Royal Anthropological Institute*, vol. 1, no. 1.

DOUGLAS, M. (1966), *Purity and Danger*, Routledge & Kegan Paul.

EVANS-PRITCHARD, E. E. (1937), *Witchcraft, Oracles and Magic among the Azande*, Clarendon Press.

EVANS-PRITCHARD, E. E. (1965), *Theories of Primitive Religion*, Oxford U.P.

POPPER, K. R. (1945), *The Open Society and its Enemies*, Routledge.

30 A. Rebecca Cardozo

A Modern American Witch-Craze

Abridged version of A. Rebecca Cardozo, *Witches: Old and New*, 1968, original MS.

Common Features of Crazes

Social, political, economic and religious upheaval makes a society especially vulnerable to a craze. In an atmosphere of confusion and uncertainty, people become intolerant toward change; and it is primarily social, political and religious intolerance that provides the initial impetus for a craze. Influential members of society single out and identify an 'enemy of the people', e.g. the witch, the heretic, the Communist, the Jew. This infamous 'enemy' is then blamed for all evil and uncertainty. Malinowski describes this tendency as universally human and persistent. It permits the concentration of blame and hatred to fall 'on certain clearly defined groups suspected of causing evils for which one otherwise would have to blame all the members of the community, its government, the decrees of destiny, or other elements against which immediate reaction is not possible' (Malinowski, 1945, p. 97).

A myth is created about this diabolical threat to society. And the 'truth' of the myth is soon substantiated by evidence obtained in confessions of the accused. It is important to note, particularly in relation to the crazes to be discussed in this paper, that the persecutors obtain official authority or an influential position that enables them to proceed with the persecutions. Society, in effect, implicitly sanctions their efforts to eradicate the 'enemy'.

As a craze develops, a climate of fear and suspicion permeates throughout the society; and the consequence of the widespread fear and intolerance is the madness of 'the hunt'. Accompanying 'the hunt' are false accusations, torture, forced confessions, ruined reputations and death.

369

Crazes do not die out overnight. Rather, they can and have lasted for centuries. The perpetuation of the hysteria associated with a craze can be accounted for in a number of ways. The mythological 'truths' stating the nature of the threatening enemy are disseminated throughout society and passed to succeeding generations in the language of local folklore. In modern times, the Press serves a similar purpose. However, it is fear itself that is primarily responsible for perpetuating a craze. Fear suppresses open dissent and resistance in the midst of widespread hysteria. Skeptics, in speaking out against the persecutors, risk their own persecution. In resisting persecutors' efforts to exterminate the 'enemy', skeptics are often accused of consorting with that enemy. Resistance easily leads to guilt-by-association. Thus, the persecutions continue, shielded from the skeptics' attacks.

At some point, however, the craze is brought to an end. Somehow the spell is broken. The ideology of the craze no longer suffices to justify the hunt. The breakdown may occur as a result of an Enlightenment such as Europe saw in the eighteenth century, or the spell may be broken by newly found courage of a country's leaders.

It is the purpose of this paper to examine the causes, development, consequences and decline of two crazes – the European witch-craze of the sixteenth and seventeenth centuries and McCarthyism from 1950 to 1954. Although these crazes are widely divergent with respect to the time, place, duration and circumstances of their occurrence, they are nevertheless strikingly similar.

The European Witch-Craze

It was religious intolerance that provided the initial impetus for the European witch-craze. Although, in the Middle Ages, beliefs in witchcraft seemed to be declining and were discouraged by both legal and ecclesiastical enactments, they were, from the twelfth century onwards, revived in the struggles between Western Catholicism and heretics in mountain areas such as the Alps and the Pyrenees (Trevor-Roper, 1967a, p. 9). The Dominicans soon began pressing for a revision of official Church policy towards witchcraft which they saw as inseparable from the heresies for the combatting of which their order had been founded. Their earlier attempts were resisted by the Church, but, by the late fifteenth century, the Inquisitors of the day were influential enough to induce Pope Innocent VIII to issue his famous bull, *Summis Desiderantes Affectibus* (1484), authorizing two of them, Heinrich Institor (Krämer) and Jakob Sprenger, to extirpate witchcraft in Germany. Two years later these two Dominicans issued the first great printed encyclopedia of demonology, the *Malleus Maleficarum* (the 'Hammer of Witches'), which consolidated the mythology of, and gave impetus to, a campaign that was to continue for two centuries (1967a, pp. 4, 8). Thus, as Trevor-Roper puts it, 'By 1490, after two centuries of research, the new, positive doctrine of witchcraft would be established in its final form. From then on it would be simply a question of applying this doctrine: of seeking, finding, and destroying the witches whose organization had been defined' (1967a, p. 4).

The fear of witches spread. The 'hunt' now had the official blessing of the Church; and people began to associate all deviant behavior with witchcraft. 'Those who believed that there were devil-worshipping societies in the mountains soon discovered that there were devil-worshipping individuals in the plains' (1967a, p. 20). In the course of time Dominicans and other Catholics were followed by Protestants and lay politicians in the war against witchcraft.

The consequences of these hunts were appalling. The fear was so great that judicial torture was allowed in the Courts of the Inquisition in order to force confessions from the accused. Of course people confessed even though they had been falsely accused; and, in the course of their confessions, set about 'creating witches where none were and multiplying both victims and evidence' (1967a, p. 17). If convicted, the victims were usually sentenced to burn. Thousands did burn.

It should be noted that the widespread confusion and fear prevailing during a craze is easily exploited, not only by the persecutors. Other members of society take advantage of 'the hunt' for purposes of personal and political revenge. To note one example, to accuse Joan of Arc of witchcraft was indeed a convenient way to get rid of her.

The European witch-hunt lasted for centuries. People continued to believe the 'truths' expounded in the *Malleus Maleficarum*. The ideology reached and influenced all of society, since it was disseminated in the language of local folklore and passed to succeeding generations.

It was not everyone, however, who believed that the persecutions could be justified. There were political and religious leaders as well as artists who opposed the massive witch-hunt (Trevor-Roper, 1967a, p. 21; 1967b, pp. 15ff.). These skeptics were appalled at the false accusations and sentencing of innocent people to death. John Weyer, for example, attributed the actions of many of the accused to 'melancholia' rather than to witchcraft (Trevor-Roper, 1967b, pp. 15–16). But open dissent and resistance in the midst of the craze was a dangerous endeavor. 'Until the middle of the seventeenth century the orthodox always prevailed. The voice of dissent was powerless to stay the persecution. It could hardly be uttered in safety' (1967a, p. 23). Skeptics in their efforts to stop the 'hunt' were often accused of consorting with the Devil. Thus fear of accusation did a great deal to suppress resistance movements.

There was some skepticism which did reach and influence large numbers of people. It was apparently not this, however, that brought about the end of the craze. Trevor-Roper offers the following explanation of how the spell was broken: 'What ultimately destroyed the witch-craze, on an intellectual level, was not the arguments of the sceptics ... [but] the new philosophy, a philosophical revolution which changed the whole concept of Nature and its operations. [It was the Enlightenment] in which the duel in Nature between a Hebrew God and a medieval Devil was replaced by the benevolent despotism of a modern, scientific "Deity" ' (1967b, pp. 29–30). It is difficult to tell what exactly he means by 'a modern scientific "Deity" ', but his point is that the widespread belief expressed in witch-mythology, that there were witches consorting with the Devil, lent mass support to the persecutions, making 'the hunt' possible; but, as soon as certain fundamental beliefs changed in the eighteenth century, the fear of witches subsided – and with it the craze.

McCarthyism: 1950–1954

The United States in 1950 was hardly Europe in the late Middle Ages. But the causes, development, consequences and decline of McCarthyism closely resemble those of the European witch-craze. Political intolerance provided the initial impetus for the movement. To America and her allies in the 1950s, the threat of Communist infiltration was a mysterious but very real threat. At the time, very little was understood about the Communist movement, its tactics and its direction, and fear of it was considerable.

McCarthyism was possible because of this fear and ignorance of Communism. However, Joe McCarthy's initial reason for seeking out the 'Communists in government' was hardly as patriotic as it sounded. Actually, his own political ambitions prompted his first accusations. 'Communists in government' would make a good campaign issue for the 1952 election (Rovere, 1959, p. 119). His first attack on these 'enemies of the people' came on 9 February 1950, when, in a speech in Wheeling, West Virginia, he told the people: 'I have here in my hand a list of 205 names that were made known to the Secretary of State [Dean Acheson] as being members of the Communist Party and who nevertheless are still working and shaping policy in the State Department' (Anderson and May, 1952, p. 174). He made similar accusations on the floor of the Senate a few days later (*Congressional Record*, 20 February 1950).

That McCarthy was a Senator made a difference. As a Senator, he had access to information he might not have otherwise had. The American people therefore took heed of his accusations. Most important in relation to his advantage as a Senator is the fact that Senators speaking in Congress are immune from libel suits. Undoubtedly this immunity gave McCarthy a certain amount of courage in making such serious accusations (Anderson and May, 1952, p. 205).

The myth of Communists in government created fear and suspicion throughout the country. The hunt for Reds was on. 'In [McCarthy's] demonology the Democratic leaders, the liberal intelligentsia, and a supposedly decadent Eastern aristocracy played the accomplice role that Hitler assigned to the Jews' (Rovere, 1959, p. 19). The accusations continued, becoming more personal and ugly. McCarthy said once, for example, 'The Democratic label is more the property of men and women who have . . . bent to the whispered pleas from the lips of traitors . . . men and women who wear the political label stitched with the idiocy of a Truman, rotted by the deceit of an Acheson, corrupted by the red slime of a [Harry Dexter] White' (Rovere, 1959, p. 11).

A Senate committee was appointed in February of 1950 to investigate the charges being made by McCarthy (Anderson and May, 1952, p. 174). 'Doggedly, Joe pursued the elusive "proof" he needed to back up his charges. He chased pink shadows through the maze of government bureaus and agencies; he set up his own private spy system; and he pestered newspapermen and petty officials for leads. He also telephoned Congressman Richard Nixon . . . then a big gun on the House Unamerican Activities Committee . . . and pleaded . . . over the phone for a peek at the Unamerican Activities Committee's secret files . . .'. (p. 191).

The 'Tydings Committee' called in the State Department to testify to the validity of the charges against its employees (U.S. Senate, 1950, p. 151). Out of approximately eighty-one cases investigated, not one of the accused was proved to be a Communist. In effect, the members of the Committee were disgusted with McCarthy and his unfounded accusations. Senator Tydings in his report said the following: 'We have seen the technique of the "Big Lie", elsewhere employed by the totalitarian dictator with devastating success, utilized here for the first time on a sustained basis in our history. We have seen how, through repetition and shifting untruths, it is possible to delude great numbers of people' (pp. 151–2).

But McCarthy continued his search for Communists in government. And he was given the chance again to have the charges investigated by another Senate Committee. This time the chairman of the Sub-Committee on Internal Security was Pat McCarran, friend and supporter of McCarthy (Anderson and May, 1952, p. 340). An all-out effort was made to gather 'proof' by legal and illegal means. The story of how McCarthy and his aides obtained files belonging to his victims is much too complicated to relate here (Anderson and May, 1952, p. 208).

The McCarran hearings also failed to prove the existence of

card-carrying Communists in the government. Yet, in spite of the findings of the Committee, McCarthyism endured. How was it that McCarthy was allowed to continue making outlandish accusations with little forceful resistance outside the hearing room? The Senators were 'scared stiff'. They believed McCarthy could in some way determine their political futures, particularly if they openly criticized his tactics (Rovere, 1959, p. 35). Tydings had spoken out against McCarthy; and, in the 1952 election campaign, McCarthy set out to discredit Tydings and ensure his defeat. Tydings, who had been in the Senate for many terms, was defeated; and many other Senators attributed his defeat to McCarthy (Anderson and May, 1952, p. 295). Even by 1954, McCarthy was still considered powerful. As Rovere, a newspaper-man, puts it, 'Evidence was not conclusive ... but politicians cannot afford to deal in finalities and ultimate truths; they abide, by and large, by probabilities and reasonable assumptions and the law of averages, and there was nothing unreasonable, in 1954, in assuming that McCarthy held enormous power in his hands, when it came to the question of deciding who should and should not sit in the United States Senate' (1959, p. 35).

Numerous other examples seemed to back up this assumption. It is now thought that McCarthy's influence on the electorate was considerably less than believed at the time; and that the defeat of several of McCarthy's enemies can be attributed as easily to the Eisenhower landslide as to McCarthy (Polsby, 1963, p. 820). But the Senators' fears nevertheless greatly suppressed open opposition to McCarthy, and their timid behavior, as well as that of influential members of society, directly aided in perpetuating McCarthyism.

The Press was also a vital force in helping McCarthyism to endure (Anderson and May, 1952, p. 266). Newspapers played up McCarthy's accusations in big headlines. McCarthy craved publicity, and he got it. More importantly, newsmen and editors also feared the Senator. A news article critical of McCarthy's efforts could leave the author wide open to accusation. Editorial opposition was suppressed because of these fears. Thus, what could have been a vital force against McCarthyism turned out as a force in his favor. It is said that 'if Joe McCarthy [was] a political monster, then the Press [had] been his Dr Frankenstein'

(Anderson and May, 1952, pp. 266–7). Of course many people did believe that the Senator was doing the ultimate good for America; and, following news reports of his campaign against traitors, money poured into his office (p. 180). Indirectly, the Press was indeed an agent in McCarthy's favor, that is, until some newspapers regained their courage and openly condemned 'the hunt'.

Finally, in 1952, some Senators took a forceful stand against McCarthy. Senator Hubert Humphrey was one of these. After declaring that accusing people and demanding that they prove their innocence was 'Anglo-Saxon jurisprudence upside down', he added: 'I think it is time we stated that we are not going to let people be ruined, their reputations destroyed, and their names defiled because we happen to be in the great game of American politics' (Anderson and May, 1952, p. 330).

The United States Senate had regained its courage. For many, their renewed courage was too late in coming. 'The real victims of McCarthyism [had] been the men and women who had their careers damaged by being unjustly labeled "security" risks, or who were punished for "crimes" which were defined by no law and without being given an opportunity to fight back against their accusers' (Lubell, 1956, p. 242).

But the final assault against McCarthy was testimony to Americans' faith in the due process of law. In July 1954, Senator Flanders introduced a resolution to censure Senator Joseph McCarthy (U.S. Senate, 1954a, p. 8). Hearings followed to investigate the charges against him; and, on 22 December 1954, following recommendations by the Investigating Committee, McCarthy was censured by the Senate on two of the original five charges, one, for 'contempt of the Senate or Senatorial Committee, and two, for ridiculing a witness in a hearing and for violating certain rules of that committee' (U.S. Senate, 1954b, p. 67).

Censure destroyed McCarthy, and with him the era of McCarthyism. He became a thoroughly dejected man and died three years later. America began her recovery from a craze not unlike the European witch-craze at the close of the Middle Ages.

References

ANDERSON, J., and MAY, R. (1952), *McCarthy: The Man, The Senator, The 'Ism'*, Beacon Press.

Congressional Record, 20 February 1950.

LUBELL, S. (1956), *Revolt of the Moderates*, Harper.

MALINOWSKI, B. (1945), *The Dynamics of Culture Change*, Yale U.P.

POLSBY, N. (1963), 'Toward an explanation of McCarthyism', in N. Polsby *et al.*, *Politics and Social Life: An Introduction to Political Behavior*, Houghton Mifflin.

ROVERE, R. (1959), *Senator Joe McCarthy*, Harcourt, Brace.

TREVOR-ROPER, H. R. (1967a), 'Witches and witchcraft: an historical essay', *Encounter*, vol. 28, no. 5, pp. 3–25.

TREVOR-ROPER, H. R. (1967b), 'Witches and witchcraft: an historical essay', *Encounter*, vol. 28, no. 6, pp. 13–34.

U.S. SENATE (1950), *Report of the Committee on Foreign Relations, Pursuant to Senate Resolution 231, State Department Loyalty Investigation*.

U.S. SENATE (1954a), *Hearings on Senate Resolution 301, Hearings Before a Select Committee to Study Censure Charges*, parts 1 and 2.

U.S. SENATE (1954b), *Senate Report no. 2508 on Censure Hearings*.

Postscript

The Decline of Witch-Beliefs in Differentiated Societies[1]

A postscript to a volume of Readings is unusual enough to call for an explanation. This one appears for two reasons. Firstly, compiling the subject index has given me a familiarity with the Readings far closer than the one I had over a year ago when I selected them and wrote the introduction. Secondly, since there were delays in my securing, or even hearing about, materials I might consider using, some papers reached me too late for inclusion. Among these was a paper by Swartz (1969), for which I certainly would have made room had I come by it sooner; and a logical consequence of using it would have been to include also the important paper by Mitchell (1965), on which it is largely a commentary. All I can do at this stage is to list both in the section on Further Reading, and, in this brief note, draw the reader's attention to their importance, not only in the sociological theory of witchcraft, but also as contributions to the more general theory of tension and conflict.

An entry in the subject index, 'Unanswered questions about witchcraft', directs the reader to two passages, one by Wilson (pp. 262–3) and one by Macfarlane (p. 304). Both are concerned with the problem of specifying the conditions under which accusations of, and beliefs in, witchcraft decline, are absent or become transformed into other kinds of 'scapegoating'. Swartz's paper, founded firmly though not uncritically on Mitchell's contribution, takes this intriguing question further; and the solution that his and Mitchell's papers offer is all the more convincing because of its convergence with some general theoretical points made by Coser (1956) in his reformulation of Simmel's theory of conflict, dating from the early years of this century (Simmel, 1955).

Swartz (1969, p. 27) points out that, while the evidence is

1. I am grateful to my colleague, Otto Newman of the University of Stirling, for some helpful discussions on general theoretical points relating to this postscript.

inconclusive, it seems probable that there are fewer accusations of witchcraft among urban Africans than one would expect from the prevailing hypothesis that links the frequency of accusations with the tenseness of social relations, which has almost certainly increased with urbanization and related social changes. In a careful analysis, which contains references to his own research among the Bena of southern Tanzania, Swartz in general confirms Mitchell's explanation for the fact that the increased tensions attendant upon urbanization are not necessarily expressed in the idiom of witchcraft. Mitchell's view (1965, p. 201) is that, in the towns, a preponderance of strangers not linked intimately or emotionally makes it possible for hostility and opposition to be expressed openly rather than supernaturally, and that, where tension between intimate associates arises, the typically urban solution of social separation is available as an alternative to mystical projection.

In the towns, social relations are more often segmental than total, i.e. they have specific goals and involve limited roles or facets of personality rather than all aspects of the lives of the persons concerned. According to both Swartz and Mitchell, townsmen, being less often involved in total cooperative relations than are rural kinsmen and neighbours, find legitimate expression for social tensions in segmented, competitive relations. Moreover, even such closer, total relations as they may have can be terminated, if they become insupportable, by the simple process of separation, which the large-scale, anonymous character of the town facilitates; and they need not be blasted away by so drastic a measure as an accusation of witchcraft. This urban situation contrasts with its rural counterpart in which, as Swartz puts it (1969, p. 29), 'competition for some particular end occurs between kinsmen and others who are united in a broad scope of other shared ends and activities' in such a way 'that hostility arising from the tension of competition cannot be expressed in any direct or open way without harming one's own interests and commitments in other respects and contexts'. Summing up Mitchell's view, Swartz writes (1969, p. 30), '... his position is that, despite the looser rules governing this competition, less witchcraft accusation occurs in the cities because the relations between the competitors are so often without the crucial ties between them which cross-cut their competition and complicate their separation'.

The point on which Swartz extends Mitchell's analysis has to do with the urban African's explanation of failure in competitive pursuits such as retaining employment. Mitchell argues (1965, pp. 201–2) that, while those townsmen who are involved in co-operative enterprises in work groups or as rival brewers in a neighbourhood may in the first instance offer witchcraft as an explanation for their misfortunes, they are prevented by urban judicial processes from sustaining this contention and from taking action appropriate to it; and they ultimately fall back on an alternative explanation, such as one in terms of the actions of an angered ancestor-spirit. Swartz offers the alternative solution (1969, p. 31), 'that the witchcraft of the competitor is an unsatisfactory explanation because the relations with the competitor are not of the sort that produces witchcraft and that, in fact, the competitor has the status of a part of a natural disaster, not that of a malign, personal antagonist'. This minor divergence of view may well be the result of exposure to different ethnographic data, the Shona, in whose country these of Mitchell's observations are set, being well known for their having preserved their traditional spirit cults.

This, then, is the Mitchell–Swartz explanation for the decline in preoccupation with witch-beliefs that accompanies urbanization and differentiation. Their hypothesis would seem to be applicable also to places and periods other than modern Africa. Its cogency increases when it is compared with the following Coser–Simmel statement of the contrast in tension management between intimate and more diffuse social groups:

... the closer the group, the more intense the conflict. Where members participate with their total personality, and conflicts are suppressed, the conflict, if it breaks out nevertheless, is likely to threaten the very root of the relationship.

In groups comprising individuals who participate only segmentally, conflict is less likely to be disruptive. Such groups are likely to experience a multiplicity of conflicts. This in itself tends to constitute a check against the breakdown of consensus: the energies of the group members are mobilized in many directions and hence will not concentrate on one conflict cutting through the group (Coser, 1956, p. 206).

February 1970

Postscript

References

COSER, L. A. (1956), *The Functions of Social Conflict*, Free Press,
   pp. 151–6. (The page reference in the text is to the extract reprinted
   in L. A. Coser and B. Rosenberg (eds.), *Sociological Theory*,
   Collier-Macmillan, 1964.)

MITCHELL, J. C. (1965), 'The meaning in misfortune for urban
   Africans', in M. Fortes and G. Dieterlen (eds.), *African Systems of
   Thought*, Oxford U.P. for International African Institute.

SIMMEL, G. (1955), *Conflict*, translated by K. H. Wolff, Free Press.

SWARTZ, M. J. (1969), 'Interpersonal tensions, modern conditions,
   and changes in the frequency of witchcraft/sorcery accusations',
   African Urban Notes, vol. 4, pp. 25–33.

Further Reading

Several of the Readings in this volume are abridgements of, or excerpts from, longer books or articles which should be consulted. Details of the longer versions will be found at the beginnings of the relevant Readings, i.e. nos. 4 (Macfarlane, 1970), 6 and 9 (Baroja, 1964), 12 (Trevor-Roper, 1967), 15 (Marwick, 1950), 16 (Willis, 1968), 18 (Parsons, 1927), 19 (Malinowski, 1925), 20 (Kluckhohn, 1944), 26 (Crawford, 1967) and 29 (Horton, 1967).

Of the items listed below, about a quarter have to do with European (including New England) witchcraft; and all the remaining ones, except two or three in general works, with witchcraft and/or sorcery in non-literate societies. They have not been classified, since in most instances their titles are reasonably good guides to their contents. Where necessary, chapter or page references have been given.

G. L. Burr, *Narratives of the Witchcraft Cases 1648–1706*, Scribners, 1914.

R. Cavendish, 'Magic: a revolt of the soul', *Observer Magazine*, 1 December 1968, pp. 20–23.

R. Cavendish (ed.), *Man, Myth and Magic*, Purnell, 1970.

C. Cross, 'The witches ride again', *Observer Magazine*, 1 December 1968, pp. 12–18.

E. E. Evans-Pritchard, *Witchcraft, Oracles and Magic among the Azande*, Clarendon Press, 1937.

C. L. Ewen, *Witch Hunting and Witch Trials*, Kegan Paul, Trench, Trubner, 1929.

C. L. Ewen, *Witchcraft and Demonianism*, Heath Cranton, 1933.

A. H. Gayton, 'Yokuts – Mono chiefs and shamans', *University of California Publications in American Archaeology and Ethnology*, vol. 24, 1930, pp. 361–421, especially pp. 408ff.

M. Gluckman, 'Social beliefs and individual thinking in primitive society', *Memoirs of the Proceedings of the Manchester Literary and Philosophical Society*, Session 1949/50, pp. 1–26.

M. Gluckman, *Custom and Conflict in Africa*, Blackwell, 1956, ch. 4.

M. Gluckman and E. Devons, 'Conclusions', especially pp. 240 ff., in M. Gluckman (ed.), *Closed Systems and Open Minds*, Oliver & Boyd, 1964.

H. I. Hogbin, 'Sorcery and administration', *Oceania*, vol. 6, 1935, pp. 1–32.

M. Hopkins, *The Discovery of Witches*, 1647, M. Summers (ed.), Cayme Press, 1928.

M. Hunter [now Wilson], *Reaction to Conquest*, Oxford U.P. for International Institute of African Languages and Cultures, 1936, ch. 6.

G. L. Kittredge, *Witchcraft in Old and New England*, Harvard U.P., 1929.

E. J. Krige and J. D. Krige, *The Realm of a Rain Queen*, Oxford U P. for International Institute of African Languages and Cultures, 1943, ch. 14.

H. Kuper, *An African Aristocracy*, Oxford U.P. for International African Institute, 1947, pp. 172 ff.

P. Lawrence, 'Sorcery among the Garia', *South Pacific*, vol. 6, 1952, pp. 340–43.

G. Lienhardt, 'Some notions of witchcraft among the Dinka', *Africa*, vol. 21, 1951, pp. 303–18.

L. Mair, *Witchcraft*, Weidenfeld & Nicolson (World University Library), 1969.

M. G. Marwick, 'The social context of Cewa witch-beliefs', *Africa*, vol. 22, 1952, pp. 120–35, 215–33.

M. G. Marwick, *Sorcery in its Social Setting*, Manchester U.P., 1965.

M. G. Marwick, 'The study of witchcraft', in A. L. Epstein (ed.), *The Craft of Social Anthropology*, Tavistock Publications, 1967.

J. Middleton, *Lugbara Religion*, Oxford U.P. for International African Institute, 1960.

J. Middleton and E. H. Winter (eds.), *Witchcraft and Sorcery in East Africa*, Routledge & Kegan Paul, 1963.

J. Middleton (ed.), *Magic, Witchcraft and Curing*, Natural History Press (American Museum Sourcebooks in Anthropology), 1967.

A. Miller, *The Crucible*, Viking Press, 1952.

J. C. Mitchell, *The Yao Village*, Manchester U.P., 1956, ch. 6.

J. C. Mitchell, 'The meaning in misfortune for urban Africans', in M. Fortes and G. Dieterlen (eds.), *African Systems of Thought*, Oxford U.P. for International African Institute, 1965.

W. Notestein, *A History of Witchcraft in England from 1558 to 1718*, American Historical Association, 1911.

G. K. Park, 'Divination in its social contexts', *Journal of the Royal Anthropological Institute*, vol. 93, 1963, pp. 195–209.

G. Parrinder, *Witchcraft*, Penguin Books, 1958.

B. Reynolds, *Magic, Divination and Witchcraft among the Barotse of Northern Rhodesia*, Chatto & Windus, 1963.

R. H. Robbins, *Encyclopedia of Witchcraft and Demonology*, Crown, 1959.

E. E. Rose, *A Razor for a Goat*, University of Toronto Press, 1962.

R. Scot, *The Discoverie of Witchcraft*, 1584; reprinted with a Preface by H. R. Williamson, Centaur Press, 1964.

B. Simon and D. Cripps, 'Double, double, toil and trouble . . .', *Observer Magazine*, 1 December 1968, pp. 24–5.

M. L. Starkey, *The Devil in Massachusetts*, Knopf, 1950; Dolphin, 1961.

M. J. Swartz, 'Interpersonal tensions, modern conditions, and changes in the frequency of witchcraft/sorcery accusations', *African Urban Notes*, vol. 4, 1969, pp. 25–33.

D. Tait, 'A sorcery hunt in Dagomba', *Africa*, vol. 33, 1963, pp. 136–47.

V. W. Turner, *Schism and Continuity in an African Society*, Manchester U.P., 1957, chs. 4, 5, *et passim*.

V. W. Turner, *Ndembu Divination: Its Symbolism and Techniques*, Manchester U.P. (Rhodes-Livingstone Paper no. 31), 1961.

V. W. Turner, 'Witchcraft and sorcery: taxonomy versus dynamics', *Africa*, vol. 34, 1964, pp. 319–24.

V. W. Turner, 'Sorcery in its social setting', *African Social Research*, no. 2, December 1966.

B. B. Whiting, *Paiute Sorcery*, Viking Fund, 1950.

M. Wilson *et al.*, *Keiskammahoek Rural Survey*, vol. 3, *Social Structure*, Shuter & Shooter, 1952.

Acknowledgements

Permission to reprint the Readings in this volume is acknowledged from the following sources:

Reading 1	International African Institute
Reading 2	*Sudan Notes and Records*
Reading 3	Thomas Nelson & Sons Ltd
Reading 4	Routledge & Kegan Paul Ltd
Reading 5	Philip Mayer
Reading 6	Weidenfeld & Nicolson Ltd and University of Chicago Press
Reading 7	A. P. Watt & Son and Collins-Knowlton-Wing Inc.
Reading 8	A. P. Watt & Son and Collins-Knowlton-Wing Inc.
Reading 9	Weidenfeld & Nicolson Ltd and University of Chicago Press
Reading 10	Routledge & Kegan Paul Ltd and E. P. Dutton & Co. Inc.
Reading 11	The Royal African Society
Reading 12	Macmillan & Co. Ltd and Harper & Row
Reading 13	Joyce Bednarski
Reading 14	International African Institute
Reading 15	International African Institute
Reading 16	International African Institute
Reading 17	A. D. J. Macfarlane
Reading 18	Royal Anthropological Institute of Great Britain and Ireland
Reading 19	Society for Promoting Christian Knowledge
Reading 20	Peabody Museum of Archaeology and Ethnology
Reading 21	*Theoria*, University of Natal
Reading 22	University of Chicago Press
Reading 23	American Anthropological Association
Reading 24	*Australian Journal of Science*
Reading 25	Routledge & Kegan Paul Ltd
Reading 26	Oxford University Press
Reading 27	Institute for Social Research, University of Zambia
Reading 28	Routledge & Kegan Paul and University of Chicago Press
Reading 29	International African Institute
Reading 30	A. Rebecca Cardozo

Acknowledgements

The Editor wishes to add his personal thanks to those authors who generously allowed him to use their unpublished material, Miss Joyce Bednarski, Miss A. Rebecca Cardozo and Dr A. D. J. Macfarlane, and to those who kindly consented to his abridging their articles, Professor E. E. Evans-Pritchard, Professor Max Gluckman, Professor Robin Horton, Professor H. R. Trevor-Roper, Dr R. G. Willis and Dr Florence R. Kluckhohn (Executrix to the Clyde Kluckhohn Estate). Despite many attempts, he was unable to contact the literary executor of the late Dr. Elsie Clews Parsons and will be glad to receive any information that will enable him to regularize his having abridged her important paper and to make due acknowledgement in a subsequent edition.

He would also like to record his gratitude for invaluable help received, in assembling the materials from which the Readings in this volume have been selected, from Miss Anne Edmonds, Librarian of Mount Holyoke College, and her staff; and from Mr John Stirling, Librarian of the University of Stirling, and his staff, especially Miss Carolyn Jamie, who obligingly and expeditiously borrowed books and journals on Library Interloan and produced photocopies. He owes his secretary, Mrs D. J. Kent, special thanks for the extra work she has been involved in as a result of his preoccupation with assembling and editing the materials.

Finally he would like to thank the Trustees of Mount Holyoke College in Massachusetts for having honoured him with the award of the Florence Purington Lectureship, and the Council of Monash University in Australia, whose generous leave provisions made it possible for him to accept it. The lectureship, with its light teaching load and its complete freedom from administrative chores, gave him the time for assembling materials and the opportunity of exploring them in the company of a senior undergraduate seminar, whose gifted, enthusiastic and charming members became known as 'Mr Marwick's witches'. A fitting secondary dedication of this volume would be 'to the Enchantresses of Mount Holyoke'.

Author Index

Author Index

391

Conceptual Index

Conceptual Index

This index aims at bringing out similarities and contrasts in the material presented in the thirty Readings. Its scheme of classification reflects the principles that have been set out in the general introduction and in the introductions to the four parts. It was compiled by collecting references under headings of tribe, region and historical period or episode and then distributing them to categories that may be regarded as aspects of, or approaches to, witchcraft and sorcery and the events of everyday life that are related to them.

The geographical or historical identities of the items thus collected and distributed have, however, been preserved and are shown by labels that appear within the conceptual categories or their subdivisions wherever this is appropriate. Some of these have been abbreviated as shown on the list below. Page numbers not preceded by labels are general references. In addition, the index has independent main entries for the various tribes, peoples or periods, and these will enable the reader to find the connected accounts of them quickly. In the section on 'Theories of Witchcraft', the names of authors associated with particular viewpoints have been used in the same way as the ethnographic or historical labels.

In keeping with the usage in the Introduction (see p. 13) and in most of the Readings except the one from Crawford's book, the words 'witch' and 'witchcraft', unless followed by the word 'proper', are used as generic terms to include 'sorcerer (sorceress)' and 'sorcery' respectively.

Abbreviations

Bwanali	: Bwanali-Mpulumutsi movement
Eng. (T & S)	: Tudor and Stuart England
Eur. (c.w.)	: Europe, classical world
Eur. (G & S)	: German and Slavonic Europe
Eur. w.cr.	: European witch-craze
med.	: medieval
Nyanja-spkrs	: Nyanja-speaking peoples